Macworld Guide To Microsoft

QUICK REFEREN

MW01222332

Works shortcuts

To do this...	Press...
Cancel operation	Command-period
Click default button	Return/Enter
Close window	Command-W
Copy	Command-C
Copy ruler settings	Command-K
Cut	Command-X
Delete or remove	Backspace/Delete
Draw on/off	Command-J
Find	Command-F
Go down a window	Page Down key
Go to document end	End key
Go to document start	Start key
Help	Command-?
Hide/Show tools	Command-T
New	Command-N
Open	Command-O
Paste	Command-V
Print	Command-P
Quit	Command-Q
Save	Command-S
Select All	Command-A
Undo	Command-Z

Word Processor shortcuts

To do this...	Press...
Copy ruler settings	Command-K
Hide/ show ruler	Command-R
Insert footnote	Command-E
Insert page break	Shift-Enter
Merge fields	Command-M
Spelling	Command-L
Thesaurus	Command-D

Draw shortcuts

To do this...	Press...
Auto close shape	N while drawing
Bring to front	Command-F
Clear object or text	Backspace/Delete
Duplicate	Command-D
Go to page...	Command-K
Group	Command-G
Move one pixel	Arrow keys
Perfect shape/line	Shift key, draw
Select multi objects	Shift key, click
Send to back	Command-B
Ungroup	Command-U

Formatting shortcuts

To do this...	Press...
Bold	Command-B
Decrease font size	Command-[
Increase font size	Command-]
Italic	Command-I
Underline	Command-I

Other shortcuts

To do this...	Press...
Calculate now (ss)	Command-equal
Duplicate/previous (db)	Command-D/E
Fill Down/right (ss)	Command-D/R
Insert record (db)	Command-I
List view (db)	Command-L
Match records (db)	Command-M
Move (db & ss)	Arrow keys
Open/close connect (com)	Command-K
Show info (com)	Command-I
Start timer (com)	Command-T

Macworld Guide To Microsoft Works 3 By Barrie Sosinsky

IDG BOOKS

QUICK REFERENCE CARD

Working with text and windows

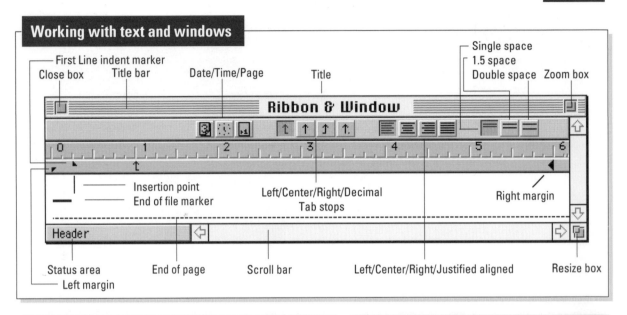

First Line indent marker
Close box
Title bar
Date/Time/Page
Title
Single space
1.5 space
Double space
Zoom box

Insertion point
End of file marker
Left/Center/Right/Decimal Tab stops
Right margin

Status area
Left margin
End of page
Scroll bar
Left/Center/Right/Justified aligned
Resize box

Working with the Communications Tool palette

Working with the Draw Tool palette

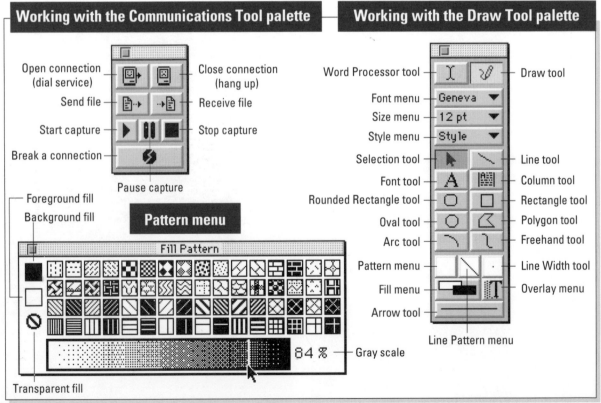

Open connection (dial service)
Close connection (hang up)
Send file
Receive file
Start capture
Stop capture
Break a connection
Pause capture

Foreground fill
Background fill

Pattern menu

Fill Pattern

84 %
Gray scale

Transparent fill

Word Processor tool
Draw tool
Font menu — Geneva
Size menu — 12 pt
Style menu — Style
Selection tool
Line tool
Font tool
Column tool
Rounded Rectangle tool
Rectangle tool
Oval tool
Polygon tool
Arc tool
Freehand tool
Pattern menu
Line Width tool
Fill menu
Overlay menu
Arrow tool
Line Pattern menu

About *Guide To* Books

Guide To Microsoft Works 3 is part of the *Macworld Guide To* series of books, brought to you by IDG, the leading publisher of computer information worldwide. This *Guide To* is a new kind of book designed to meet your growing need to quickly find what you want to do and learn how to do it.

These books work the way you do: They focus on accomplishing specific tasks — not learning random functions. *Guide To* books are not long-winded tomes, manuals, or even quick reference guides, but feature the best elements of these three types of publications. *Guide To* books have the easy-to-follow step-by-step sections of a manual, the comprehensive coverage you'd expect to find in a long tome, and the brevity you need from a quick reference guide.

This book is designed so that you can find what you want to do without having to read the book from cover to cover. To this end, chapters are called Topics. Topics are stand-alone sections that teach you what you want to learn — when you want to learn it.

The designers of the *Guide To* series use the following visual elements to make it easy to find the information you need:

Overview sections provide a summary of the topic's subject and are meant to be read when you want help accomplishing your goals without having to work through the tutorials. These sections serve as good learning tools for the intermediate user who does not need — or want — any hand-holding.

Step-by-Step sections demonstrate the concepts given in the Overview sections with easy-to-follow instructions. If you're a beginner, these Step-by-Step sections will go a long way toward getting you up to speed on unfamiliar topics.

Quick Tips sections include tips and insights contained on the material in each Topic. The Quick Tips enable you to get the most out of your application or operating system — no matter what level of user you are.

The authors of the *Guide To* books are leading *Macworld* columnists, technology champions, and Mac gurus. Each author is uniquely qualified to provide you with expert advice and insightful tips and techniques not found anywhere else. We're sure you'll agree that the *Guide To* approach is the best.

— David Solomon
Publishing Director, IDG Books

MACWORLD

GUIDE TO MICROSOFT
WORKS 3

MACWORLD

GUIDE TO MICROSOFT
WORKS 3

By Barrie Sosinsky, Ph.D.
Apple-certified developer

IDG
BOOKS

IDG Books Worldwide, Inc.
An International Data Group Company
San Mateo, California 94402

Macworld Guide To Microsoft Works 3

Published by
IDG Books Worldwide, Inc.
An International Data Group Company
155 Bovet Road, Suite 610
San Mateo, CA 94402
(415) 312-0650

Library of Congress Catalog Card No.: 91-72345

ISBN 1-878058-42-8

Printed in the United States of America

10 9 8 7 6 5 4 3 2 1

Distributed in the United States by IDG Books Worldwide, Inc.

Distributed in Canada by Macmillan of Canada, a Division of Canada Publishing Cor-poration; by Woodslane Pty. Ltd. in Australia; and by Computer Bookshops in the U.K.

For information on translations and availability in other countries, contact Marc Jeffrey Mikulich, Foreign Rights Manager, at IDG Books Worldwide. Fax: (415) 312-1260.

For sales inquiries and special prices for bulk quantities, write to the address above or call IDG Books Worldwide at (415) 358-0650.

Dedication

This book is dedicated to Alexandra Zoie Sosinsky, whose birth at 9:03 a.m. on June 20, 1992 has changed my life.

Acknowledgments

Many people contributed to this book. I'd especially like to thank the following individuals:

My literary agent, Matt Wagner, at Waterside Productions, who introduced me to Terrie Solomon, Acquisitions Editor at IDG Books

Mike McCarthy, formerly of IDG Books

Jeremy Judson, the editor for the project, who kept me focused and in good humor throughout.

David Drucker and Lisa Spangenberg, who served as technical editors for the project

IDG Books Worldwide is a group of dynamic folks, real go-getters. John Kilcullen, IDG's publisher, has collected some of the best minds in the computer book trade. It's been fun working with them, and I think they will be a force to be reckoned with.

Thanks also to the vendors who provided information on Works-related topics; their templates are discussed in Topic 14. Most particularly, I would like to thank Ray Heizer for his help.

The Macintosh community has long awaited Microsoft Works 3, and to Katie Jordan and the other team members at Microsoft, I offer my best wishes for a successful product run for Microsoft Works 3.

My wife, Carol Westheimer, did her best to motivate me as the project drew to a close. Even as the delivery date for our first child approached, she refused to pack a bag until I finished the last Topic. The tactic didn't work, however. Our lovely daughter Alexandra Zoie was born one week before the completion of the project.

(The publisher would like to give special thanks to Patrick J. McGovern, without whom this book would not have been possible.)

About IDG Books Worldwide

Welcome to the world of IDG Books Worldwide.

IDG Books Worldwide, Inc., is a publication of International Data Group (IDG), the world's leading publisher of computer-related information and the leading global provider of information services on information technology. IDG publishes over 181 computer publications in 58 countries. Thirty million people read one or more IDG publications each month.

If you use personal computers, IDG Books is committed to publishing quality books that meet your needs. We rely on our extensive network of publications, including such leading periodicals as *Macworld, InfoWorld, PC World, Computerworld, Lotus, Publish, Network World,* and *SunWorld,* to help us make informed and timely decisions in creating useful computer books that meet your needs.

Every IDG book strives to bring extra value and skill-building instruction to the reader. Our books are written by experts, with the backing of IDG periodicals, and with careful thought devoted to issues such as audience, interior design, use of icons, and illustrations. Our editorial staff is a careful mix of high-tech journalists and experienced book people. Our close contact with the makers of computer products helps ensure accuracy and thorough coverage. Our heavy use of personal computers at every step in production means we can deliver books in the most timely manner.

We are delivering books of high quality at competitive prices on topics customers want. At IDG, we believe in quality, and we have been delivering quality for 25 years. You'll find no better book on a subject than an IDG book.

John Kilcullen
President and Publisher
IDG Books Worldwide, Inc.

IDG Books Worldwide, Inc. is a subsidiary of International Data Group. The officers are Patrick J. McGovern, Founder and Board Chairman; Walter Boyd, President; Robert A. Farmer, Vice Chairman. International Data Group's publications include: **ARGENTINA'S** Computerworld Argentina, InfoWorld Argentina; **ASIA'S** Computerworld Hong Kong, PC World Hong Kong, Computerworld Southeast Asia, PC World Singapore, Computerworld Malaysia, PC World Malaysia; **AUSTRALIA'S** Computerworld Australia, Australian PC World, Australian Macworld, Profit, Information Decisions, Reseller; **AUSTRIA'S** Computerwelt Oesterreich; **BRAZIL'S** DataNews, PC Mundo, Mundo IBM, Mundo Unix, Publish; **BULGARIA'S** Computerworld Bulgaria, Ediworld, PC World Express; **CANADA'S** ComputerData, Direct Access, Graduate Computerworld, InfoCanada, Network World Canada; **CHILE'S** Computerworld, Informatica; **COLUMBIA'S** Computerworld Columbia; **CZECHOSLOVAKIA'S** Computerworld Czechoslovakia, PC World Czechoslovakia; **DENMARK'S** CAD/CAM WORLD, Communications World, Computerworld Danmark, Computerworld Focus, Computerworld Uddannelse, LAN World, Lotus World, Macintosh Produktkatalog, Macworld Danmark, PC World Danmark, PC World Produktguide, Windows World; **EQUADOR'S** PC World; **EGYPT'S** PC World Middle East; **FINLAND'S** Mikro PC, Tietoviikko, Tietoverkko; **FRANCE'S** Computer Direct, Distributique, GOLDEN MAC, InfoPC, Languages & Systems, Le Guide du Monde Informatique, Le Monde Informatique, Telecoms & Reseaux International; **GERMANY'S** Computerwoche, Computerwoche Focus, Computerwoche Extra, Computerwoche Karriere, edv aspekte, Information Management, Lotus Welt, Macwelt, Netzwelt, PC Welt, PC Woche, Publish, Unit, Unix Welt; **GREECE'S** Infoworld, PC Games, PC World Greece; **HUNGARY'S** Computerworld SZT, Mikrovilag Magazin, PC World; **INDIA'S** Computers & Communications; **ISRAEL'S** Computerworld Israel, PC World Israel; **ITALY'S** Computerworld Italia, Macworld Italia, Networking Italia, PC World Italia; **JAPAN'S** Computerworld Japan, Macworld Japan, SunWorld Japan; **KOREA'S** Computerworld Korea, Macworld Korea, PC World Korea; **MEXICO'S** Compu Edicion, Compu Manufactura, Computacion/Punto de Venta, Computerworld Mexico, MacWorld, Mundo Unix, PC World, Windows; **THE NETHERLANDS'** Computer! Totaal, Computerworld Netherlands, LAN Magazine, MacWorld Magazine; **NEW ZEALAND'S** Computer Listings, Computerworld New Zealand, New Zealand PC World; **NIGERIA'S** PC World Africa; **NORWAY'S** Computerworld Norge, C/world, Lotusworld Norge, Macworld Norge, Networld, PC World Norge, PC Worlds Product Guide, Publish World, Computerworld, Student Guiden, Unix World, Windowsworld, IDG Direct Response; **PERU'S** PC World; **PEOPLES REPUBLIC OF CHINA'S** China Computerworld, PC World China, Electronics International; **IDG HIGH TECH** Newproductworld, Consumer Electronics New Product World; **PHILLIPPINES'** Computerworld, PC World; **POLAND'S** Computerworld Poland, Komputer; **ROMANIA'S** InfoClub Magazine; **RUSSIA'S** Computerworld-Moscow, Networks, PC World; **SPAIN'S** Amiga World, Autoedicion, CIM World, Communicaciones World, Computerworld Espana, Macworld Espana, PC World Espana, Publish; **SWEDEN'S** Affarsekonomi Management, Attack, CAD/CAM World, ComputerSweden, Corporate Computing, Digital Varlden, Lokala Natverk/LAN, Lotus World, MAC&PC, Macworld, Mikrodatorn, PC World, Publishing & Design (CAP), Unix/Oppna system, Datalngenjoren, Maxi Data, Windows; **SWITZERLAND'S** Computerworld Schweiz, Macworld Schweiz, PC & Workstation; **TAIWAN'S** Computerworld Taiwan, PC World Taiwan; **THAILAND'S** Thai Computerworld; **TURKEY'S** Computerworld Monitor, Macworld Turkiye, PC World Turkiye; **UNITED KINGDOM'S** Lotus Magazine, Macworld; **UNITED STATES'** AmigaWorld, Cable in the Classroom, CIO, Computer Buying World, Computerworld, Digital News, DOS Resource Guide, Electronic News, Federal Computer Week, GamePro, inCider/A+, IDG Books, InfoWorld, Lotus, Macworld, MPC World, Network World, NeXTWORLD, PC Games, PC World, PC Letter, Publish, RUN, SunWorld, SWATPro; **VENEZUELA'S** Computerworld Venezuela, MicroComputerworld Venezuela; **YUGOSLAVIA'S** Moj Mikro.

 The text in this book is printed on recycled paper.

About the Author

Barrie Sosinsky started working with personal computers in 1987 when he bought a Macintosh II to start a business and to design an environmental testing kit. Through the design project, he began to learn more about his Mac and to write articles for the Boston Computer Society Macintosh user group's publication, *The Active Window.* Today, computers are his business.

The first product Sosinsky used on his Macintosh was Microsoft Works. A published article on Works led to his first book contract. The *Macworld Guide To Microsoft Works 3* is his sixth computer book.

Sosinsky has published articles on personal computers — both Macintosh and IBM PC — for many magazines. He is also a contributing writer for BCS Up*date* (the chief publication of the Boston Computer Society) and a contributing editor for the *Mindcraft Journals* and the *Desktop Publishing Journal.*

Sosinsky serves as a consultant to businesses in the area of personal computers, specializing in business applications, databases, desktop publishing, and graphics.

Sosinsky holds a Ph.D. in Inorganic Chemistry from Bristol University and has held postdoctoral fellowships at Cornell and UCLA. He taught at Rice University before taking positions in the chemicals and microelectronics industry. Before starting his own business, he was a research scientist and engineer in microcircuit fabrication, specializing in plasma etching and chemical vapor deposition.

Sosinsky lives in an electronic cottage in Newton, Massachusetts, with his wife, Carol Westheimer, and his daughter, Alexandra Zoie Sosinsky. He likes to ski in the winter, and jog and backpack in the summer. He enjoys the Celtics and ignores the Red Sox, thus preserving his sanity.

Credits

President and Publisher
John J. Kilcullen

Publishing Director
David Solomon

Project Editor
Jeremy Judson

Production Director
Lana J. Olson

Acquisitions Editor
Terrie Lynn Solomon

Copy Editors
Heidi Beeler
Mark Glaser
Charles A. Hutchinson

Technical Reviewers
David Drucker
Lisa Spangenberg

Text Preparation and Proofreading
Shirley E. Coe
Dana Sadoff
Mary Ann Cordova

Indexer
Anne Leach

Editorial Department Assistant
Megg Bonar

Book Design and Production
Peppy White
Francette M. Ytsma
(University Graphics, Palo Alto, California)

Contents at a Glance

Table of Contents

Topic 3: Works Basics 55

Part II: Using Works' Tools 89

Topic 4: Processing Your Words 91

Topic 6: Using Works' Databases 153

Part IV: Advanced Features 349

Topic 13: Using Works on Your Portable 351

Topic 14: Using Works in Business 367

Introduction

About This Book

Most *normal* people do not like to read computer manuals. Life is too short, and our work is too long to allow many such luxuries. There can be only one reason for buying this book. That reason is that it will save you time. Not just a little time, mind you, but lots of time. That is the author's promise to you, and it is his working definition of a good computer book. In the pages that follow you will find techniques, resources, and other tools that will help you learn Microsoft Works and use the program productively on whatever Mac you have at your disposal.

This author eschews obfuscation! You will find simple explanations and concise language here, and never see the words eschews and obfuscation again. Brevity is a blessing. Too many computer books suffer from technobabble, leaving the reader to wonder if they are being initiated into some sort of a cult, or learning to use a tool that will make their life easier. Although I can't entirely shield you from terminology, I will do my best to minimize the confusion, and clearly explain the concepts you must know.

Make no mistake about it — this book is different. For example, this book doesn't have chapters, it has Topics. This topic structure allows you to jump around in the book without getting lost, because each Topic stands on its own. *Macworld Guide To Microsoft Works 3* is not a replacement for Works' manual. There is inevitably some overlap that occurs as parts of Works are introduced in the Overview section in each Topic. Perhaps some of you will find another approach and explanation useful and enlightening. Some subjects are expanded upon in this book that are only alluded to in the manual, others that are discussed in depth in the manual are glossed over here. The second section found in a Topic, called Quick Tips, offers advanced insights into tasks you might attempt using Works; even experts can learn from these discussions.

Unlike the Works manual which must completely explain the product, this book focuses on getting projects accomplished. You can look at the larger picture, and find out what you like and dislike about the program. And you will. You can also go beyond the program to learn about third-party products that you might find useful, other worthwhile books or articles, using Works on an Apple PowerBook computer, and many other specialized topics that you simply won't find elsewhere. It's that larger and unbiased view that makes computer books so popular.

The *Macworld Guide To* . . . series uses several different stylistic elements to help you learn about Microsoft Works. *Macworld Guide To Microsoft Works 3* uses many visual examples to guide you: icons, Topic markers, figures, and so on. There are many ways to learn a concept. The Overview section is modeled after quick reference guides, the Step-by-Step sections allow you to work through a task in tutorial fashion in the manner of a users' manual, while the Quick Tips section distills the wisdom found in bibles and encyclopedias. All of these approaches have been integrated and condensed into a book of reasonable length that I hope you will find easily readable and readily accessible.

Whom This Book Is For

Studies show that most users of Microsoft Works are Mac beginners. Works is often the first application purchased with a Mac, and many dealers offer the program as part of a purchased bundle with that first computer. Works can go a long way towards satisfying most users' computer needs. You may even find that it is powerful enough for you to use over the years, so that you may never need to upgrade to a program with more powerful capabilities.

This book is written with the beginner in mind, and makes no assumptions about a reader's competence with the Macintosh. I attempt to be clear, without being condescending. If you are an absolute Mac beginner, then reading the book cover to cover will be educational. In particular, two of the introductory Topics — Topic 2 "Macintosh Basics," and Topic 3 "Works Basics" — should be most helpful to help you get up and running. Since our main focus is learning Works, these Topics also refer you to other resources that will aid you, and give you more thorough explanations of basic concepts than is possible here.

The *Macworld Guide To Microsoft Works 3* contains useful information for the more experienced user. Perhaps you are a current user of a previous version of Works and are in the process of upgrading to the new version. You will find all of the new features in version 3.0 covered in this book. Works 3 contains many refinements that users have requested and the program is much more attractive than previous versions. Version 3.0 is not radically different than previous versions, so users that are upgrading to 3.0 should have a relatively easy time learning to use this new version. If you are a user in the process of upgrading, you may want to glance through Topic 3 paying particular attention to the section "What's New in Works 3," and begin by installing the program, which is the subject of Appendix A.

If you are an intermediate computer user, and are familiar with Works, this book still has much to offer you. Many sections of the book are conceptual. For example, you may know how to use the spreadsheet and understand how functions work. Still, it's likely that you can find value in the section that explains the principles of good spreadsheet construction. Information like that is always hard to find, and of great value.

It has long been conventional wisdom among the cognoscenti (know-it-alls) that Microsoft Works was only for beginners, but that may no longer be the case. Expert users with specialized needs may find Works to be just the ticket. They may be found using Works on their PowerBook at 30,000 feet over the Grand Canyon. Few other programs offer so much functionality with so little memory requirement. "Using Works on Your Portable" is the subject of Topic 13.

All users will benefit from Topic 14, "Using Works in Business", which describes how to set up Works for a variety of common business needs. Topic 14 also compiles and describes many useful additions to Microsoft Works. There are a host of solutions for small businesses, tax preparation, document templates, and many other functions that will enrich your experience using the program, and make you more productive. In keeping with Microsoft Works itself, most add-ons are of modest cost.

How This Book Is Organized

As I mentioned, Topics in *Macworld Guide To Microsoft Works 3* have a unique construction. You won't find chapters in this book; there are stand-alone Topics that are divided into two sections: the Overview and Quick Tips sections. This construction lets you find and get into a topic quickly, cutting through the wall of words that you find in most computer books. These sections and their icons are as follows:

Overview provides a summary of the Topic's subject. This is the section to read when you want the big picture of how to accomplish a certain job.

Quick Tips provides tips related to the Topic's subject. Look here for the littler insights that will help you wring the most out of Works.

In addition to the above sections, there are other icons to help streamline the learning process. These include the following:

Step-by-Step elaborates on the information in the Overview section by providing succinct, step-by-step instructions that walk you through the task at hand.

Works 3 Feature identifies the new features contained in Works 3.0. Look for these to find out all the new things you can do with the latest release of Works.

Power User takes you beyond the basics of Works, and lets you in on shortcuts and secrets that are left out of the manuals.

Caution alerts you to areas that you should read before proceeding with the task at hand. Use these to avert the hidden traps that sometimes occur while using a program.

You will find at the very beginning of the book a tear-out quick reference card for Microsoft Works. *After* you buy this book, pull the card out and put it by your Macintosh to reference Works' commands and features.

Macworld Guide To Microsoft Works 3 contains wide margins. They are there for a purpose, not just to occupy space. As you read this book and learn about the program, you can use these margins to make notes about your experiences. We urge you to do so, and to use this book as a reference in your future work. Then when a subject comes up, those notes will remind you about your experiences.

This book is organized into four parts and 14 Topics:

+ **Part I, "Introducing Works,"** discusses basic concepts. There are three Topics in this part.

Topic 1, "What Can Works Do?" describes integrated software, and gives you some examples of projects that can be done in Works. If you are thinking about buying Works, reading this Topic would be useful.

Learning new software is a big undertaking, and I want you to be excited about the prospect. The best way to do that is to show you some of the cool things Works can do for you, right from the start.

Topic 2, "Macintosh Basics," discusses important techniques you must know in order to use your Mac, and is meant as an introductory Topic for beginners. This Topic serves as a review, and it's here for your reference in case you forget an important concept. More advanced users can safely skip ahead to Topic 3.

Topic 3, "Works Basics," contains introductory information specific to Microsoft Works. Think of this Topic as containing information and instruction that is common to all the parts of Works together. Rather than repeat that information in several places, you will find it all here.

Readers with previous experience in Microsoft Works can skim this Topic, but are advised to pay particular attention to the sections "What's New in Works 3" and "Works Help System."

✦ **Part II, "Using Works' Tools,"** is the largest part of the book. It explains the functionality contained in each of Works' modules in great detail.

Topic 4, "Processing Your Words," is a complete description of Works' writing module. Creating and formatting text, checking your spelling, and formatting pages are among the subjects discussed in this Topic. Studies show that most people use a word processor more than any other tool on a computer, and Works has a very functional word processor.

Topic 5, "Using the Draw Module," discusses how to create figures in Works. Draw can be invoked in its own document, or used to overlay and enhance a word processor, spreadsheet, or chart document by creating figures that overlay the text on a page. This arrangement allows for some very sophisticated effects. A full description of the drawing toolbox is contained in this Topic.

Using Draw you can also manipulate text on a page. It may surprise you to learn that Works is capable of some nice basic desktop publishing projects.

Topic 6, "Using Works' Databases," explains the use of Works to organize information into logical groupings. A database lets you find and select information based on criteria you specify. Do you have a record collection that you need to organize, or a recipe file? A database is just the place to do it.

Using a database you can create powerful selected mailings, print letters to clients, study the results of your business sales, and do numerous other projects of great benefit to yourself.

Topic 7, "Using Works' Spreadsheets," introduces a powerful tool for doing calculations. Spreadsheets take the concept of an electronic calculator and expand on it to allow you to create relationships that let you explore possible outcomes and play "what-if" games.

More than any other application, spreadsheets have been responsible for the explosion in the use of the personal computer. You can create sales projections, manage a business balance sheet, explore a business model, or do complex mathematics using a spreadsheet. A spreadsheet is to a calculator what an automobile is to a bicycle.

Topic 8, "Using Works' Charts," explains how spreadsheet data can be displayed in graphical form so that it is meaningful. Numbers are only useful when they can be visualized, and a spreadsheet chart can let you quickly grasp the outcome of a spreadsheet calculation.

Topic 9, "Using Works' Communications," opens up a whole new world of information and companionship with other computer users. Works' communication module lets you connect to another person, another computer, or an electronic service.

All of the needed terminology and set-up information is described in this Topic in easily understandable and concise language.

✦ **Part III, "Integrating Works' Tools,"** focuses on making you more productive with Works.

Topic 10, "The Macro Recorder," describes Works' automation tool. Macros are sequences of actions that can be saved and replayed, and macros are available throughout Works' modules. They are a great timesaver. Topic 10 explains how to create and manage macros within each of Works' tools, and describes some useful macros that you may want to use with your work.

Topic 11, "Spreadsheet and Database Functions," is a description of the available functions in the database and spreadsheet modules. Examples of their use are also included.

Topic 12, "Exchanging Information," tells you how to move data to and from Works and another program. The Topic also explains a method for saving a setup of Works files for a particular project so that it can automatically be used when needed.

✦ **Part IV, "Advanced Features,"** covers the subject of laptops, using Works in business and third-party products.

Topic 13, "Using Works on Your Portable," contains information on how to configure Works in a limited memory and storage environment; why you should use Works on a laptop in place of other software; useful hardware and software add-ons; and how to create a working laptop environment.

Topic 14, "Using Works in Business," describes some commercial offerings that extend Works' performance.

In addition there are four appendixes to aid you in your work:

✦ **Appendix A, "Installing Works,"** applies to all users. It shows you how to configure Works on your Mac and describes Works' requirements.

If you are a new user, first read Topics 1-3 before installing Works. If you are an experienced user, visit Appendix A first to install the program, then go read "What's New in Works 3" in Topic 3, before continuing on to Topic 4.

✦ **Appendix B, "Keyboard Shortcuts,"** is a compilation of all keystroke combinations in the program for all of Works' modules. Using keystrokes in place of mouse strokes can be a great time saver, and a productivity enhancer. This section is here to help you learn them all.

✦ **Appendix C, "Glossary,"** is a compilation of all of the important terminology you need to know. Think of it as distilled technobabble. Although each new term is defined in this book in its first occurrence, this is the place to look when you need a definition.

✦ **Appendix D, "Task Index,"** is a convention unique to this book series. It lists all of the Step-by-Step instructions that appear in the Topics.

How To Use This Book

Novice users should read this book in sequence covering Part I and all of the tools in Part II and Part III that are of interest. Experienced users who are new to Microsoft Works should begin with Topic 3. If you are a user upgrading to the new version of Works, start by reading "What's New in Works 3" and "The Works' Help System" in Topic 3. All readers should read Appendix A to install the program correctly.

It isn't necessary that you read this book sequentially, or in its entirety. The book is arranged in the order of importance that Topics will have for an average reader. Your needs may be different, and you may have no use for some of Works' tools. You can always learn about those additional features later, when they become necessary.

There are several ways of finding information quickly in this book. Use the Table of Contents to locate the general title that describes a particular subject. Turn to that section in the book, and what you'll find may encompass one or more sets of instructions. For more detailed information with only a single task detailed, turn to the Task Index (Appendix D) for its description and location. The Task Index breaks down complex multipart tasks into components. Lastly, for general information on a Works feature, or the location of the description of some terminology, look in the general index at the back of the book. For the explanation of a term, check also the Glossary (Appendix C).

For the Beginner

Unfortunately, there isn't room in this book for a complete explanation of all beginning concepts on operating a Macintosh. You should know: how to turn your Macintosh on; what a mouse is; how to use a keyboard; how to work with disks; how to choose menu commands; and how to select and manipulate items the screen by pointing and clicking. The discussion found in Topic 2 amplifies this basic knowledge and is really a review of many of these concepts.

If this is your first time using a Mac, you can't find a better place to start than by reading the Apple manual that came with your computer. These manuals are highly regarded throughout the computer industry for their clarity and style. Look at that manual first, and then return here *soon* to get started. Don't be overwhelmed, there was a first time for each of us. Little children learn to use Macs, so do the elderly, and the seriously handicapped. You will too, in your own time, and at your own pace.

Other Titles To Enhance Your Mac Knowledge

As you travel in the Mac world, be sure to check out our other Mac books that are written by the experts on the topics you want to know.

Macworld Complete Mac Handbook, by Jim Heid, is the ultimate Mac reference that includes hardware and software from soup to nuts and powerful tips and shortcuts.

Macworld Guide To System 7, by Lon Poole, is loaded with valuable undocumented tips and secrets on the new Mac operation system — all you need to know about manipulating your hardware and software.

Macworld Read Me First book, edited by Jerry Borrell, gives you no-nonsense advice from the experts you trust on the hardware and software you need.

Macworld Guide To Word 5, by Jim Heid, is a task-oriented guide to all the new features of Word 5, including helpful tutorials and valuable tips.

Macworld Guide To Excel, by David Maguiness, is a task-oriented guide to all the new features of Excel 4, including helpful tutorials and valuable tips.

Macworld Music & Sound Bible, by Christopher Yavelow, is the definitive guide to multimedia, music and sound. Over 1400 pages of the latest hardware, software and techniques.

Macworld Networking Handbook, by David Kosiur, Ph.D., is the only practical, hands-on guide that explains Macintosh networking from the ground up.

Macs For Dummies, by David Pogue, is a light-hearted approach to learning the Macintosh that teaches you all you need to know to get up and running on your Mac. It is the Mac reference guide for the rest of us.

The Works Companion

At the back of this book, you will find an offer form for *The Works Companion,* a set of disks that will help you with your use of the program. Contained on those disks is an electronic version of this book that you can refer to as you use Microsoft Works.

Several other worthwhile products may be found on the disk set. There is a library of document templates for you to use, a listing of third-party products, and offers from other manufacturers mentioned in this book for discounts on their products. You can print out a keyboard template, find a zip code, and use one of the several useful databases included on the disk. Many of the examples used in this book — corporate balance sheets, purchase orders, and card files — are on this disk. There is also a file of handy macros that you may wish to use.

Part I:
Introducing Works

Topic 1
Is Works Right for You?

Overview

Works is different from other programs you might buy for the Macintosh in that it is multipurposed and multifunctional. With Works, you use the same program to handle several types of data — text, numbers, graphics, and communications. There are entire small businesses run on Microsoft Works. The common command set and wide functionality allow beginning users to get up and running quickly without much training or support. It's also easier to get complex projects accomplished in Works than in many other programs.

In this Topic I cover what Works can do, why you might want to buy the program, and how it is different from more individually capable and complex stand-alone software programs. Do you really need several programs, each with their own manner of working, or can Works do the job for you? Look over the following examples of what Works can do, and you will know the answer.

Understanding integrated software

Microsoft Works is an example of a class of software called *integrated* software. Whereas programs like Microsoft Word, Microsoft Excel, Claris MacDraw, Claris FileMaker, Aldus PageMaker, and Software Ventures' Microphone II are highly capable programs meant for a single endeavor, Microsoft Works incorporates elements of all of these programs into a single package. You can think of all of the aforementioned packages as being narrow and deep; Works is broad and shallow. For many years, Microsoft has advertised Works as being the "Swiss army knife" of Macintosh software. This is an apt analogy.

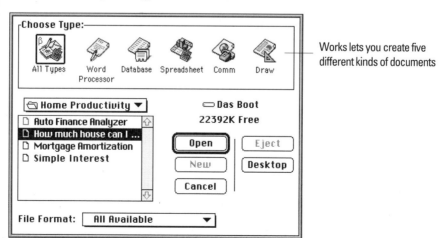

Works lets you create five different kinds of documents

Works contains a word processor, database, spreadsheet, drawing, charting, and communications module, as well as a macro recorder, spell checker, thesaurus, and more — all in the same program. Throughout this book I will be referring to each of the major functions in Works as a *module*. The first six aforementioned parts of Works are modules each of which can open a specific document window. The draw module can also open as a layer in each of the other five documents. That's an amazing amount of functionality, and it is easy to see why complex projects can be attempted in Works.

Obviously, in order to keep the size and memory requirements of Works down to something reasonable, only a subset of the more important features of each of the major functions are included in Works. Microsoft has taken the most commonly used parts of programs like Word to make Works. You might ask how Microsoft knows which features to use. The company makes heavy use of focus groups, reads comments on registration cards, and uses other techniques. Works has undergone several iterations and is very refined software. A lot of user input has contributed to this product. Just in case you're wondering what you're missing, at the end of each of the Topics describing aspects of Works, I'll tell you what you get when you move up to a single-function program and what the best choices are in upgrade software.

Integrated software is more than just a collection of disparate capabilities. It is also a system for interconnecting files with a proprietary file structure. Works' interface lets you use the Macintosh file system to find and open these different document types. That used to mean a whole lot more than it does today. In System 6 and earlier, in which you could only run programs in the Finder, Works let you open different documents and application types without having to switch between programs. There was no waiting while programs closed and launched to use these different applications. System 5 and 6's MultiFinder, and System 7, make an integrated file system unnecessary. Now you can open many programs and quickly switch between them in memory, a process called context switching. However, Works still is the champ in low-memory situations.

Integrated software is very much a compromise. You give up special features in order to get a more broadly capable program at a good price. If you bought all of the individual software programs, you might spend over $3,000 for that software, whereas purchasing Microsoft Works 3 would cost you less than $200 (street price). So if price is a consideration, Works gets you up and running cheaply.

This concept of the "all-in-one" computer program has proved very popular on all personal computers. The first of the integrated programs to appear on a personal computer was AppleWorks for the Apple II. Shortly thereafter, Microsoft introduced Works version 1.0. From the date of its introduction nearly 63 months (to June 1992) ago, Works has been near the top of the best-seller list for Macintosh software. Version 2.0 of the program was introduced in Fall/Winter 1989. The latest version

— 3.0 — appeared in late summer 1992. Many hundreds of thousands of copies of Works have been sold — it is perhaps the second or third most successful software product ever sold for the Mac. It is estimated that the word processor in Works is the second most commonly used on the Mac, behind only Microsoft Word.

The start-up
screen for
Microsoft Works

Several other companies have introduced integrated software packages over the years. Some, such as Lotus Jazz, have come and gone. Works has had the integrated software market to itself for several years until just recently. Now there's ClarisWorks, BeagleWorks, GreatWorks, PublicWorks, BurgerWorks, and a host of imitators. Today, Microsoft Works remains the entrenched leader in this product category because the program is well designed and thought out, stable, and a good value. In its new incarnation, it is also really attractive.

That compatibility thing

Many experts deride Works, advising purchasers of a new computer system to buy "full-featured" packages instead. Often that is not very good advice. Few users require many of the special features found in major packages, and there is a distinct advantage in having all the pieces together in the same software. It's that compatibility thing. You don't have to worry about making software work together, moving data from one program to another, or having multiple programs running in memory. Having all of these functions under the same roof also simplifies the process of using these tools together. Compatibility issues rarely, if ever, come up.

Works uses the 80/20 rule: 80 percent of the features for 20 percent of the hassle. So, do you want to impress your friends with the mind-blowing software with many features you will rarely, if ever, use, or do you want to get some work done?

Interestingly, integrated software was a creation from the days in which personal computers were very limited in the amount of memory and storage they had. Today, users of Macs with 1MB RAM, who are using System 6's Finder, will still be well served by Works 3. In System 7, Works runs in the 2MB minimum RAM required. Works is also valuable for Apple PowerBook laptop computers, another (generally) low-memory application that is the subject of Topic 13.

There is a school of thought in the computer industry that software has become too bloated and difficult to learn — a phenomenon referred to as *creeping featuritis*. If a word processor has 50 features, then one with 100 features (one that wakes you up in the morning *and* makes coffee and breakfast) is even better. No wonder people are always reaching for computer manuals. Future computer system software that allows much smaller pieces of software to work together in a modular form is now being developed. In a way, Works presages these industry trends. The design principles found in integrated software are becoming popular again, with future versions of the system software playing the role of the integration. While other people wait for that day, you can have that modular functionality now available in Works.

Works is also popular because it provides a logical upgrade path to Microsoft's larger and more capable products. Many of Works' modules are designed similarly to their big brothers; they share common commands and construction principles. So generally, if you have learned to use Works, you can learn to use these other programs quickly. Also, the files you create in Works can be easily exported and used in other programs, particularly Microsoft's. This is one way in which going with an industry leader helps you out.

Works makes sense for users with compatibility problems, users without abundant financial or hardware resources, and for new users who don't need professional software. Macintosh owners of smaller Macs with limited RAM or with PowerBooks fall into this category. Reducing the number of software packages running also makes your Macintosh more stable. Users of Microsoft Works often mentioned peace of mind as a reason they continued to use Works, even after outgrowing some of its capabilities.

Evaluating the tools

Works' word processor is highly functional and comes complete with the most commonly used special writing tools. There is a complete set of document, paragraph, and character formatting tools in the word processor, available either from menu commands or from a floating Tool palette. Works is suitable for any business correspondence you might want to produce, and it uses the power of Macintosh graphics to create high-quality output that is indistinguishable from anything that you can create in another word processor. The word processor is the subject of Topic 4.

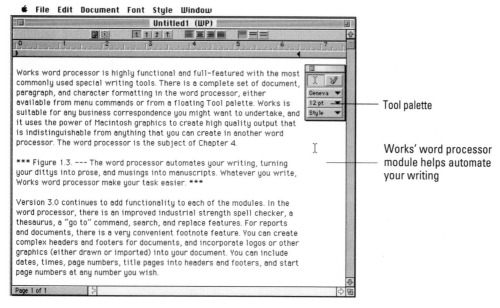

Tool palette

Works' word processor module helps automate your writing

Version 3.0 continues to add functionality to each of the modules. In the word processor, there is an improved industrial-strength spell checker, a thesaurus, a Go To... command, and search and replace features. For reports and documents, there is a very convenient footnote feature. You can create complex headers and footers for your document and incorporate logos or other graphics (either drawn or imported) into your document. You can include dates, times, page numbers, title pages into headers and footers, and start page numbers at any number you wish.

The improved Tool palette (found in every Works module) provides instant access to a drawing layer that appears above the word processor. You can see the Tool palette in the text mode of the word processor shown in the previous figure. What you see displayed in the following figure is the combination of the word processor and draw layers. Notably, Works supports drawn text objects and linked text columns where text autoflows from one column in a sequence to the next — a feature that allows you to do complex page layout. With Works you can quickly and easily produce a newsletter that your readers will think was created with PageMaker or QuarkXPress.

Works' draw module supports gray scale and color

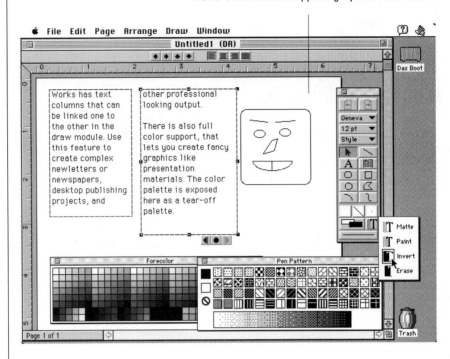

The Draw feature was available in version 2.0 of Works, but many beginning users had trouble finding the menu command to turn Draw on. Version 3.0 puts the improved Tool palette right there on your screen and expands the number of tools on the palette to give you click-and-drag control of many more features. In addition to having a draw layer in the word processor, database, spreadsheet, and communications (header and footers only) documents, Works now supports special draw documents with no underlying module. You can also use draw in the charting feature found in the spreadsheet module.

New to Works 3 is the ability to use gray scale and color. There's color on the screen, color output, and a well-designed color palette that is part of the Tool palette. Both background and foreground colors are supported; Works' draw tool is a complete object-oriented drawing tool with MacDraw II power. There are many special effects: different text overlay qualities (opaque, transparent, and inverted, among others), attaching text to a line or arc, rotations, flips, shadows, three-dimensional effects, and more. (The draw module is discussed in Topic 5.) Draw lets you do some amazing things in your projects, and when used in combination with other modules, it provides a capability not found in high-end products. This is one of the advantages of integrated software: The total is more than the sum of the parts.

The database module in Works is a flat file system with no relational features. A database lets you organize information in logical groupings, search and sort data, and create reports that analyze your data in new ways. In version 3.0, the database has been substantially improved to make it more graphical so that it can print multiple forms per file. Data entry can be automated using calculated fields containing equations built from over 50 operators, and relationships can be built in Works to make automated forms possible. For example, when you enter the pay rate and hours worked into two fields, Works calculates the pay in another field and formats it into pounds, liras, shekels, farthings, or into what we use in the U.S., federal reserve units (dollars).

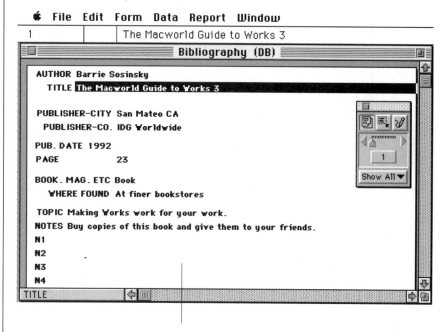

Works' database module can organize your research project, letting you find information quickly, and examine your data in new ways

Using the database module you can automate a business, run a research project, keep your address book, and do many other things that are invaluable. When coupled with a word processor, Works' database can do mail merges allowing you to create form letters and manage repetitive output tasks. Unlike other programs, Works' database makes this easy for average users to do.

The spreadsheet module is a tool that lets you build values and relationships into a matrix of cells called a worksheet. Because the relationship of each cell found at the intersection of a row and column can be unique, spreadsheets are special tools that let you perform complex data and numerical analysis. They are commonly used to perform "what-if" analyses. Spreadsheets are the subject of Topic 7.

You can think of spreadsheets as the next generation of the calculator. Define the structure using any of 64 functions, and Works does the calculations. There are arithmetic, mathematical, time and date, logic, location, statistical, and financial functions available for your use; most are common to both the spreadsheet and database modules. Functions, and examples of their uses, are the subject of Topic 11.

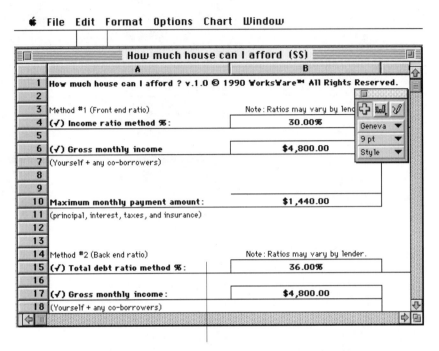

This spreadsheet template from WorksWare analyzes your income, debt, and the cost of a house to find out if you can afford the mortgage

Numbers are pretty meaningless when there are a lot of them to understand. In order to help you make sense of your spreadsheet data, there is a charting feature in Works. Line, bar, pie, stack, combination, and hi-lo-close charts are only a couple of mouse clicks and drags away. Works automates charting to such an extent that you will be amazed how fast the feature is. Nearly every time, Works gives you a useful graphic that you can leave in your spreadsheet linked dynamically to the data that produced it, or paste into another module like a word processor. Charting is covered in Topic 8.

I know what you're thinking. Did I tell you about six modules or only five? Well, in all my excitement, I forgot to mention that Works has a communication module that lets you connect and talk with real computers everywhere — and sometimes with the people who are working with them. The communication module has been substantially improved to provide many new services: connection settings, auto-mated log-on, time and cost tracking, and others. This module is probably the most improved part of version 3.0. For information on the communication module and its use, see Topic 9.

You might buy Works for the other stuff in the program but if you are like most computer users, communicating with people in distant places, finding and retriev-ing useful information, buying things and services, checking the weather and news, and getting the latest public domain software will be great fun. There's CompuServe, Delphi, GEnie, and thousands of other bulletin boards maintained for special purposes. On your local user group's bulletin board, you can make new friends and share common interests. Talk to other users on-line and save your conversation to a disk file. Do your work at home, on the road, or (better yet) at the beach, and send it to your office by phone. You will find that the Works com-munication module will serve you well and open up a new world to you.

Just to top it off, there is a macro feature in all of Works' modules that records and saves repetitive tasks. Whenever you want to run that macro again, it is just a key-stroke away. We could go on describing the neat features in Works but that is what the Topics are for. Besides, features are for cereal boxes; what real users want are benefits. What can you do with the program? Let's take a look at some samples of Works in action, and peek at what's ahead in the Topics that follow.

Looking at sample projects

You can get a good idea of what Works is capable of by simply cracking open its box, installing it, and looking at the examples that Microsoft has provided for you. Works ships with many canned files, called templates, that you can duplicate and modify. A template can be saved as a stationery file; stationery opens an untitled copy for your use, leaving the original document always unchanged. Why struggle to create something fresh when you can use something that has been created already?

You can see the power of an integrated software product when you use its mod-ules together to accomplish a task. In the following figure, a mail merge is shown using the word processor and a database file. In an accounts receivable database, you can age your receivables and find all the people who are past due on their payments. Then you can set up a word processor form letter and print out special letters to all those deadbeats, requesting that they cross your palms with some cash. It's easy, and it's fast. Something you wouldn't dream of doing with so many people involved suddenly becomes simple with a few menu commands. You find where those people live, and your letter hunts them down.

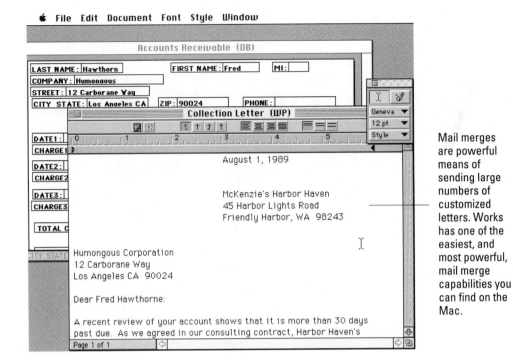

Mail merges are powerful means of sending large numbers of customized letters. Works has one of the easiest, and most powerful, mail merge capabilities you can find on the Mac.

With Works you can also produce sophisticated publishing projects using the draw module. In the word processor you can create and work with text, then either switch to the draw layer to put the text in columns or use a separate draw document. The following figure shows the result of a desktop publishing project, a newsletter of a large corporation announcing a new product's availability. Draw also lets you create fancy forms in a database, (called database publishing); forms in a spreadsheet, (called spreadsheet publishing); fancy headers and footers with flying corporate logos; and also embellish your charts and database reports. There are so many difficult things that Works makes easy that you will be reaching for your printed page from Works while your friends, who are using other programs, will be reaching for some aspirin.

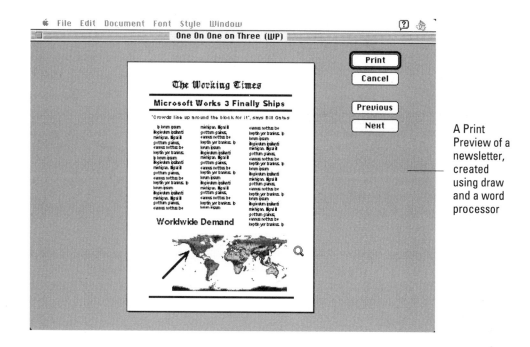

A Print
Preview of a
newsletter,
created
using draw
and a word
processor

So what do you have to lose with Works? Even if you upgrade to other products later, there will always be something special you can use Works for long into the future. Buy the book (buy several); try the software. You'll like it.

Summary

✔ Integrated software takes several different kinds of applications and combines them into a common file structure with a single program that launches them all.

✔ Works has a word processor, database, spreadsheet, drawing, and communication module.

✔ The draw module can also be opened as a layer above the other four modules, so you can include drawn graphics in your documents.

✔ Each module supports its own specific menus and opens a slightly different document window.

✔ Works offers specialized tools, such as a spell checker and thesaurus for the word processor, reports for databases, charts for spreadsheets, a macro recorder for all modules, and many other tools to help speed your work and make it more professional.

✔ Integrated software works well in computers with low available memory (RAM) and in system software where only a single application can run at a time.

✔ Works imports and exports data from a variety of sources and eases the task of making data compatible between many different programs and data types.

✔ Integrated software presages a trend in the computer industry to make smaller modular programs work together flexibly.

Topic 2
Macintosh Basics

Overview

Before jumping into Microsoft Works (or any other application), it's important to have a basic understanding of the hardware and software you'll be using to make the program function properly. For the beginning Mac user, this Topic covers what you need to know to get Works up and running on your system. If you're a more advanced Mac user, this Topic serves as a valuable refresher. Of course, you're free to skip ahead if you want to get right to the task at hand.

The Macintosh is a computer with a personality. It uses pictures and concepts from everyday life to help you accomplish tasks. For example, a picture (called an icon) of a floppy disk appears on your computer monitor whenever you insert a floppy disk. Whenever you turn your computer on, you'll find an icon of a trash barrel and a list of options called a *menu bar* across the top of your screen. These pictures present computer commands in the form of a metaphor taken from everyday life, so that you have a good idea of what to do without learning a complicated computer language. This kind of computer display is called a *graphical user interface* (GUI, pronounced *gooey* — a term only a computer nerd could have coined). The Macintosh made computer history by being the first popular personal computer with this type of display. Studies show that GUIs cut down learning time substantially and aid in the retention of concepts.

Trash

The empty
Trash can
icon

Trash

The Trash
can icon
with
something
in it

Understanding how to use a Mac boils down to knowing how to manipulate the elements on your screen and understanding what the appearance of those elements means. For example, the Trash icon is used to remove information, in the form of files, from your computer. When the Trash icon is empty, it has the normal appearance. However, when there are file(s) in the Trash, it bulges. You discard items on your screen by clicking on the item and holding the mouse button down while dragging the item to the Trash. Select Empty Trash from the Special menu, and the Trash becomes sleek and thin again. The trash can does exactly what its name suggests, that is, it trashes any file you no longer want. If you accidentally drag an item into the trash that you want to keep, don't despair; you can save the item by immediately dragging it out of the trash before executing another command or restarting your computer.

Understanding your Mac's roots

The first Macintosh computer was introduced in 1985. Several types of Macs are now in existence. The original Macs, now called Classic Macs, have a small, 9-inch built-in monitor. The Mac Classic and Classic II are the current generation of this type manufactured by Apple Computer. Previous versions of Classic Macs, in order of introduction and increasing power, are the Mac 128, Mac 512, Mac Plus, Mac SE, and Mac SE/30. You can use the Mac Plus, Mac SE, and Mac SE/30 with Works 3. The Mac 512 works only with previous versions of Works.

You can tell what kind of Macintosh you have by reading the name on the front of the case or by checking your Macintosh manual. Another way to tell is described in the section called "Finding out what System you have," at the end of this Topic.

If you have a Mac 128 or 512, you're using an obsolete computer that should be replaced. You can find upgrade kits that convert the 128 and 512 to a Mac Plus, but it's really not worth the bother. There are good deals out there to be had on more powerful used or new equipment.

The next level in the Macintosh computer line is the Macintosh LC, or its replacement, the LC II. This computer is named LC because it is Apple Computer's first low-cost color entry to the PC market. The LC, which is stylishly flat like a pizza box, allows you to stack components onto one another. The LC is a good choice as an entry level machine for an individual or a small business.

The Macintosh II series is the next level of Macintosh computers. Current models include the IIsi, IIci, and IIfx. These are good, powerful, business computers that will serve you for many years, and in many tasks. The most powerful line on the market is the Macintosh Quadra — the 700, 900, and 950.

Each Macintosh has a power-on switch, usually at the back of the machine. With some Mac models, you can use the power key (with a small triangle on it) found on some keyboards to turn on your Mac. Additionally, most Macs come with a hard drive that contains information needed to start your computer. If the hard drive is inside your Mac (internal), it is powered on when you turn on your Mac. If your hard drive is external, it appears on the screen as a smaller case icon connected to your Macintosh. The external hard drive must be turned on before you turn the Macintosh on because it contains the instructions necessary to make your computer run.

A power-on switch is located in the back of some Macs

The power key on certain keyboards can be used to start some Macs

Starting up your Macintosh:

1. **If you have an external hard drive, turn it on.**

2. **Press the power key on your keyboard, if you have one.**

— or —

2. **Turn on your Macintosh using the power switch at the back of the machine.**

3. **If a flashing disk with a question mark appears, this means that the computer cannot access information it needs to run. Repeat steps 1 and 2, as your hard drive may not be on. If the hard drive is on, turn everything off,**

check the connection between your hard drive and your Mac, and repeat steps 1 and 2.

4. **If a flashing disk with an X through it appears, there's a problem with
your hard drive or disk.** Perhaps there's no system file on that disk, or
there's a malfunction.

5. **If you hear a three-toned "boing!" sound and a sad-faced Mac icon appears, you have a fatal hardware error that needs repair.**

If all is well your Macintosh will go through the start-up procedure by first showing a
Macintosh icon, then the "Welcome to Macintosh" start-up screen, then a series of
extension or INIT icons at the bottom of the screen, and finally, the Macintosh Desktop. Now you're ready to start.

Getting back to computer basics

A Macintosh, like nearly all modern computers, is a digital device. The computer
operates by breaking all information down to the binary numbers, 1 or 0, and each
single number is called a *bit*. A set of bits is called a *byte*. Numbers, as you may
know, can be represented as binary figures. For example, the number 39 is binary
100111. Text is represented similarly in a scheme of eight bits under a standard
called the American Standard Code for Information Interchange or *ASCII* (pronounced
askey). Even images can be broken down into binary notation, like a mosaic of tiles
with black represented by 0 and white represented by 1.

A computer runs using a set of programmed instructions. Those instructions are found
partly in a permanent memory chip on the motherboard of your computer, in *read-
only memory* (or *ROM*), and partly in a software program called *System Software*
supplied by Apple Computer, Inc. System Software is normally loaded onto your computer at the factory, or it can be found on your hard drive. Sometimes, especially in
older machines, you run the system software from a floppy disk. Generally, you can
expect to turn on and run your Macintosh right out of the box (although you may
have to attach a hard drive to it).

The computer chip that orchestrates the flow of information in your Macintosh is
called the *microprocessor* or *central processing unit* (CPU). Macs use 68000 series
chips from the Motorola Corporation. The 68000 chips are used in the Mac Classic
and PowerBook 100. The 68020 is used in the Mac LC; the 68030 in the Mac LC II,
the PowerBook 140 and 170, and the II series; and the 68040 in the Quadra series.
The higher number chips have some additional functions such as advanced
memory management and the internal clock in the CPU that times the execution of
instructions run at higher speeds. However, you should be able to run most Macintosh software with any of these microprocessors.

In addition to ROM (the permanent memory), your computer contains volatile
memory, called *random access memory* or *RAM*. You can think of RAM as an electronic scratch pad that holds all of your running software (including System Software)
and information while you're working on the computer. The more RAM you have, the

more programs you can run and information you can store. You can buy additional RAM for your Mac as it is needed. RAM is erased when you turn off your machine, so to keep information permanently you must store the information on floppy disks or hard drives.

Storing information on disks and drives

Obviously, it takes a lot of bytes to convey any useful information. A group of a thousand bytes is called a *kilobyte*, abbreviated as K. A group of a million bytes is called a *megabyte*, abbreviated as MB. Because computers use binary numbers, the closest representation of 1,000 is the binary number 1,024, and of 1,000,000 is 1,048,576. These are the precise numbers of bytes in a kilobyte and a megabyte, respectively.

That's all well and good, but how much space does a kilobyte or a megabyte represent in the real world? Computers use disks for storing and retrieving information. The Macintosh uses 3½-inch floppy disks — one was included with your computer. Current Macs use high-density double-sided disks, which are identified by the two holes or small windows at the top edge and hold up to 1.4MB of information. These kinds of disks are used by the Macintosh SuperDrive (the name of the current floppy disk drive in a newer series Macintosh). You can store about 1,000 pages of typewritten text on a disk that size, or about three times the amount of the text in this book. Other kinds of data may have different requirements. A single 8½ × 11-inch black-and-white photographic (gray scale) image, for example, would use the entire 1.4MB disk storage space.

In order to use a disk of any type, the disk must be prepared first. The process is called *formatting* a disk, and the first time you format a disk you are *initializing* it. Most people use the terms format and initialize interchangeably. Your Macintosh's floppy disk drive will prompt you automatically when a disk requires formatting; you only need to indicate the type of disk and the name you wish to call it. When you format a disk, you erase all data from that disk and replace it with 0's. Be careful and only erase disks that don't have data on them that you require. Formatting also magnetically marks the metallic surface of a floppy disk with concentric rings called *tracks* and cuts each of those tracks into parts called *sectors*. Finally, a table of contents is written on the disk that allows your Macintosh to find data written in each sector.

INSIDE A DISK

Sliding shield

Plastic case

Protective liner

Sector

Track

Floppy disk

Write-protect hole

Plastic case

Opening a disk's case reveals the floppy disk it protects. What you can't see is how the disk is divided into concentric rings, or tracks, containing sectors that store your data and programs.

Older Macintoshes have floppy disk drives that use normal double-sized disks that hold 800K of information. A SuperDrive can read and write onto an 800K disk but cannot format an 800K disk to a higher density. An older floppy disk drive cannot format or read a 1.4MB disk at all. SuperDrive recognizes older disks by the virtue of their having only one notch. You put floppy disks into a disk drive with the metal piece first and the label side up. Inserting it any other way jams the disk into the drive.

A hard drive or hard disk is a much larger version of a floppy disk with a much faster speed in accessing data. Common sizes of hard drives are 40MB, 80MB, 105MB, 170MB, 210MB, and 300MB. An 80MB hard drive contains the same information as 57 1.4MB floppy disks. The use of a hard drive is strongly recommended — it's nearly impossible to get by without one these days. Don't get a hard drive with less than 80MB — you'll fill it up too quickly. Give yourself room to grow for the future. I use a 170MB hard drive on my own system.

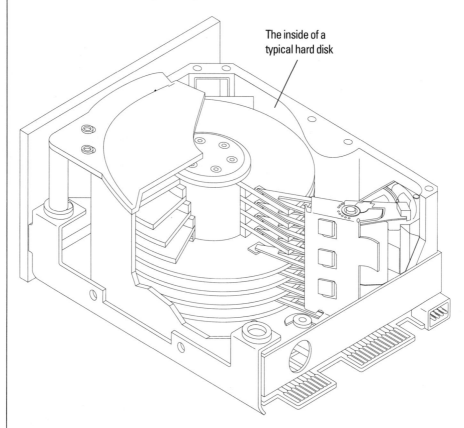

The inside of a typical hard disk

Hard disks require formatting too, but that's normally done using special software at the factory. Very rarely you may need to reformat when the hard drive is misbehaving. Unlike a floppy disk, hard disks can be reformatted without the data being erased. Tracks and sectors are recreated and data is moved appropriately. Never format a hard drive unless you're sure you know what you're doing. Always and frequently make backup copies of your data to protect yourself against malfunctions or accidental erasures.

There are many other advanced features of hard drives available that you can learn about and several worthwhile utilities that you should own. Two valuable packages are Norton Utilities and Symantec Utilities for the Macintosh (SUM). These programs let you perform tune-ups, copy your data to a backup, and repair your disk in emergencies. One of the leading programs for reformatting or initializing a hard drive is La Cie's SilverLining. Reformatting a disk is an advanced topic, and if you're a beginner, you should seek assistance the first time you do it.

Booting up your Mac

Your Mac needs startup instructions on how to configure itself. When you turn on the power switch or press the power-up key on your keyboard, your Mac performs some simple hardware tests to see that there are no malfunctions. All of the installed RAM is polled to see if it's properly installed and how much is available. A happy Macintosh then appears on your screen if the computer is functioning properly.

Next, your Macintosh looks for a hard drive or floppy disk containing the needed instructions or operating system. When the Mac finds the hard drive or floppy disk with the information, it gives you a "Welcome to Macintosh" message, perhaps displays some icons at the bottom of the screen, and finally displays the Macintosh desktop. Just which icons appear during start-up depends on what additional software you've installed on the hard drive. The whole start-up process is called *booting up* a computer, and the expression comes from the idea that a computer is pulling itself up by its bootstraps.

Any Macintosh coming from the factory, or any hard drive coming from a third-party manufacturer, normally has the operating system needed to boot up a Macintosh already installed on it. Normally, you turn on the power switch and the start-up process begins automatically. If, instead of displaying the "Welcome to Macintosh" screen, your Mac shows a flashing disk with a question mark on it, make sure your hard drive is turned on. If your hard drive is not connected, first turn off your Macintosh, connect your hard drive, and turn them both on. Never connect anything to your Macintosh without first turning everything off, as you can short out your computer's electronics.

You can also boot up your Macintosh using a floppy disk with an operating system stored on it. One should have been supplied with your computer. You should always keep that disk handy, or have someone make you one for emergencies. Whatever disk you use to start up your Macintosh is called the *start-up disk,* whether it's a hard disk or a floppy, and its icon appears in the upper-right corner of the Macintosh Desktop.

System

System Folder
icon

Understanding the operating system

An operating system is a set of software programs that manages your computer. Typical tasks managed by an operating system include disk input and output (I/O), memory access, and how other software packages interact with one another. The analogy is often made that system software acts like an orchestra conductor at a symphony. Most of the important parts of the Macintosh system software are found in two large files called the *System* and the *Finder,* which are inside the System Folder on your start-up disk. Icons for these two files, and all system files, are mini Macintosh computers.

The System file and Finder are located in the System Folder

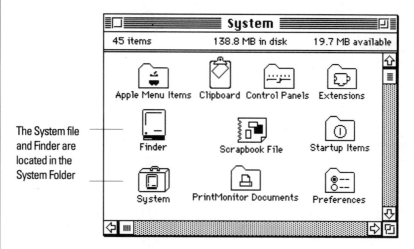

System software, like all other computer software, is constantly being improved. When a program is released, it's given a version number. The latest Macintosh System file in use is version 7.0.1.

The different system software versions look and act differently from one another. Most of the screen shots (pictures of images displayed on your screen) in this book are taken from System 7. If your screen doesn't look exactly like the figures in this book, it is probably because you are using Sytem 6.x.

Just as there can only be one conductor per orchestra, there should only be one set of System and Finder files on your start-up disk. Delete any additional systems you find (see "Finding your way around the Macintosh desktop") on the start-up disk, saving only the latest one for use. If you experience flaky behavior from your Mac or if it crashes, it may be because you have more than one system folder on a disk. Don't confuse your Macintosh!

Finding your way around the Macintosh desktop

The computer's desktop is the first screen you see after booting your Macintosh. The program responsible for the appearance of the desktop is the Finder. Most people think of the desktop as the essence of the Macintosh, but it's really only the face of the Macintosh — the System is its soul. What you see on your desktop is determined by the version of the system you use, but there are many important similarities throughout all versions.

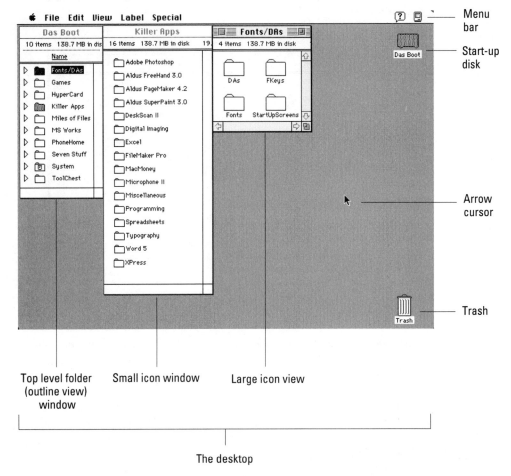

The desktop

The desktop is a metaphor for your office desk. Your desktop can have desk accessories (like a calculator or a note page), files with data, and folders or disks that can contain files. *Documents* are files of any type created by programs called *applications*. Icons for documents often look like pieces of paper, sometimes with a dog-eared corner, or may bear a special icon determined by the creator application. Applications themselves are contained in files because all applications are created by other applications. Many of the Quick Tips later in this Topic can make you more productive by helping you to organize your files.

The desktop is displayed when the Finder is the active application — that is, the program that is currently running. Depending on the version of the system software you use, you may or may not have to leave the Finder to work with your other software. With versions prior to System 6, you start a program, that program changes your screen, and you only return to the Finder when you quit that application. System 5 introduced an option in the system software called *MultiFinder,* available only if your computer had enough RAM. The System 5 MultiFinder lets you hold the Finder and other program(s) in memory so that you can rapidly switch between them. System 7 merged Finder and MultiFinder together, standardizing this time-saving option but making additional installed memory necessary.

Across the top of the desktop in System 7 is, from left to right, a menu bar indicating your menu choices: the Apple symbol, File, Edit, View, Label, and Special. System 7 also has two icons at the right of the menu bar — a screen with a question mark that represents the Help menu, and the Mac icon that represents the Application menu. You can always tell you're in the Finder when you see the Special menu.

System 6 has a somewhat different arrangement. From left to right are the Apple symbol, File, Edit, View, and Special. When you've accessed MultiFinder in System 6, a small Macintosh icon appears at the right of the menu bar. That Mac icon is missing when System 6 isn't using MultiFinder. Finder uses only one program in memory (RAM) at a time.

Changing your desktop

Just as you can rearrange the accessories on your desk at work, you can place the icons on your desktop anywhere you'd like. To do this you use the mouse to select and move items. Try moving your mouse across your desk, rolling the ball inside the mouse's plastic casing. You'll notice that the small arrow on the screen, called the *pointer* or *arrow cursor,* moves in the same direction. The tip of the arrow, called the pointer's *hot spot,* is the portion of the pointer used to select items. The cursor can take on different appearances in different computer applications, but all cursors have a hot spot at a single location.

When you pick up the mouse, the arrow cursor stops moving. Only when you roll the ball inside the mouse is there cursor motion on your screen. Place the arrow cursor over an icon on your Desktop, such as the Trash, and press or *click* the mouse button. Notice that this action darkens the icon — this is known as *selecting* or *highlighting* an item. (You'll find more information on selecting under "Commanding your Macintosh," later in this chapter.) Now click on the icon again and continue to hold the mouse button down while moving the mouse so that it moves, or *drags,* the icon around the screen. Releasing the mouse button sets or *drops* the icon in place. Pressing and releasing the mouse button is called *clicking,* whereas holding the mouse button down is referred to as *pressing* it.

The cursor can change appearance and give you information about the mode your Macintosh is in. For example, a watch cursor indicates you must wait while your Mac is busy performing a task, an I-beam or text cursor points out the position where text will be edited, a hand cursor allows you to move objects, and so on. Throughout this book, you'll read about the appearance of the cursor and what it means in the current operation.

Commanding your Macintosh

There are two ways to run a command on your Mac: using the mouse and using the keyboard. To select a command with your mouse, place the arrow cursor over any of the words or symbols in the menu bar and press the mouse button to make the hidden menus pop down. These menus are often called *pull-down menus,* but pop-down is a better description. Notice when you release the button, the menu pops back up into the menu bar.

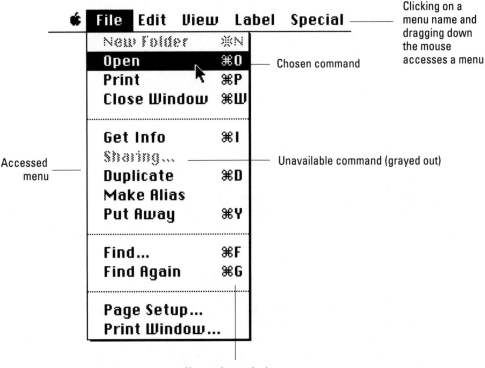

Clicking on a menu name and dragging down the mouse accesses a menu

— Chosen command

Accessed menu

Unavailable command (grayed out)

Keystroke equivalents

To run a command with the mouse, place the arrow cursor over a menu title and drag down through the command names. The selected command is highlighted (in reverse text). Any command in black can be run; commands in gray aren't currently available for use. Releasing the mouse button while highlighting a command runs the command. The menu flashes the command name before executing it.

Many commands have a set of three dots (…) next to them, called an *ellipsis*. The ellipsis indicates that the command offers additional choices. When you select the command, a dialog box opens, offering you these additional choices. The interactive nature of a dialog box is part of the Macintosh operating system, although dialog boxes can vary from application to application. To make choices in a dialog box, select an item and click the appropriate response buttons and type in any information needed. See "Using alert and dialog boxes" later in this Topic.

Some menu commands have arrows that point sideways to the edge of the menu. This symbol indicates that moving the mouse in that direction allows you to access another submenu. Menus stacked within menus are called *hierarchical menus*. You'll find hierarchical menus much more common in applications than in the Finder. However, many Finder add-ons (called *extensions* in System 7 and *INITs* in System 6 and lower) add hierarchical menus to increase access to additional commands and features. See "Using third-party file managers" at the end of this Topic.

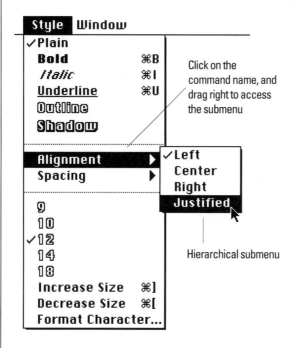

When you access a menu, notice that there's sometimes a key combination given next to the command name. Most of these key combinations show the cloverleaf symbol on the left, next to a letter. The cloverleaf symbol represents the Command key, and the two symbols together indicate that you press the two keys at once, called a *keystroke*. The best way to do this is to is to hold down the Command key while pressing the other alphabetic key. If you select commands with a keystroke, your Mac executes them without you accessing the menu. That's faster than mousing around, but you need to remember the key combination.

Keys on the keyboard that change the behavior of other keys (like the Command key) are called *modifier keys*. There are four main modifier keys on your keyboard: the Command, Shift, Control, and Option keys. To use a modifier key, you hold the modifier key down while pressing the key that it modifies. You can also combine modifier keys to make additional keystrokes, so some applications might use Command-Shift-1, Command-Option-B, or even Command-Control-Option-Shift-A. Some programs even allow you to remap a keyboard and assign keystrokes to commands yourself. These programs are discussed in Topic 10.

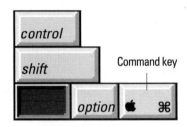

To run a command, you often have to indicate what items you want the command to work on. You do this by *selecting* the object. Clicking on a floppy disk to select it makes that disk icon darkened or highlighted.

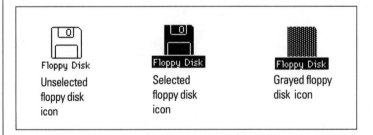

Similarly, you click on any document or file to select it. If you want to select several items at once, you can hold Shift and click on the items in turn. Also, you can press the mouse button and drag a *selection marquee* (a border that looks like marching ants) around a group of items. To deselect an object, press Shift and click on that object again. You can deselect the entire group by clicking elsewhere on the desktop. The instructions for selecting items follow.

Selecting an item:

1. Determine the item you want selected.

2. Click on the icon or filename. Selected items are highlighted or darkened. To deselect an item, click anywhere else on the desktop.

Selecting a group of items:

1. Determine the items you want selected.

2. Press and hold down the Shift key while clicking on each item you want to select. To deselect an item in a selected group, press and hold down the Shift key and click again on that item.

Selecting a range of adjacent items:

1. Determine the items you want selected.

2. Click on the desktop and drag a selection marquee (indicated by a moving border) around those items, and release the mouse button. You can also combine the selection methods, using the selection marquee and holding down the Shift key to add to the range of objects selected.

Dragging the selection marquee across several items selects all items within the marquee

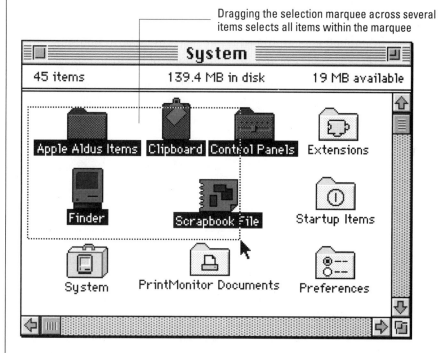

Manipulating disks and folders

You can also open items on the desktop. To open a disk or folder to examine its contents, position the arrow cursor over the item's icon and quickly press and release the mouse button twice, or double-click on it. Doing so opens a rectangular area called a *window* in which other files or folders may be found. As an alternative to this procedure, you can click once on the disk or file to select it and then press Command-O. This keystroke executes the Open command from the File menu and displays the item's window. There are often several ways of accomplishing the same results on a Macintosh — use the one you find most convenient.

To remove, or *delete,* a file or a folder from a disk, use the Trash icon at the lower-right corner of the desktop. Drag the file or folder icon into the Trash. To clear the item from the Trash, select Empty Trash from the Special menu. In Systems 5 and 6, the Trash is emptied automatically whenever the computer needs the RAM the deleted items occupy, whereas in System 7 you need to explicitly execute Empty Trash. The computer deletes the files by removing them from a disk's table of contents, and the space that the files took on the disk becomes available to be overwritten as needed.

When you drag a disk icon to the Trash, the disk is ejected, it disappears from the desktop and spits out of your computer. If that disk is the System disk, then a dimmed icon of the disk remains, indicating that it's still in use. It's a little counter-intuitive to drag a disk you want to keep to the Trash but rest assured that no data is erased and your disk remains in the same condition.

Some other basic operations you can perform on disks and folders include the following:

Opening a disk or folder:

1. **Determine the disk or folder you want to open.**

2. ***Double-click* (twice in rapid succession) on it.** The disk or folder will open presenting you with a window that may or may not have files contained in it.

Creating a new folder:

1. **Select New Folder from the File menu or press Command-N.**

2. **Name the new folder by typing in a name.** The folder is called "Untitled Folder" until you rename it. In System 7, the name is highlighted when first created, letting you immediately type the new name.

Renaming a disk or folder:

1. **Click on the name of the disk or folder to highlight it.**

2. **Select all or part of the name by clicking and dragging the I-beam cursor over that text.**

3. **Type the new name (the selected portion disappears).** If you make a mistake typing, either use the Backspace or Delete keys to remove text, or reselect the text you want to replace and start typing.

I-beam
cursor

Clicking on a folder selects it and allows you to edit or change its name. Typing a new name will replace the old name already in the box ("untitled folder").

Moving an item:

1. Determine what item you want to move.

2. Drag the item you want to move to the spot you want it. To move an icon into a folder, a disk, or the Trash, simply drag the item icon over the item and release the mouse button.

Copying an item:

1. Determine what item you want to copy.

2. Select the item you want to copy by clicking on it and choose Duplicate (Command-D) from the File menu.

3. Rename the item.

Copying an item to a specific location:

1. Determine what item you want to copy to another location.

2. Select the item.

3. While pressing Option, drag the item over the target folder or disk and release the mouse button.

The Finder posts an alert box to show you the progress of the copy and move operations. You can also move and copy multiple items. In order to do that, you need to select a group of items (see "Selecting a group of items," earlier in this Topic). You can even copy and move items in the Finder in the background while you work in another application in the foreground. See "Switching between applications" later in this Topic.

Working with windows

Opening a disk or folder reveals a Macintosh window. The window is a set of standard interface elements created and managed by the System file. The Finder uses these elements to organize files and folders. Each Macintosh application modifies the Macintosh window slightly. In this section, you'll learn about the features of a Finder window as they display many elements common to all windows. Special features of Works windows are described in many of the subsequent Topics, where appropriate.

To view an item's window, double-click on its icon, or select it and choose Open from the File menu. When a folder or disk has a window opened, its icon appears gray on the desktop. Experiment with opening windows and try double-clicking on the Trash can to view its contents. If it contains any items, you can retrieve them by dragging them onto your desktop and releasing the mouse button.

Note: Selected items are black and open items are grayed. When you have more than one window open, double-clicking on a grayed icon brings its window to the front, and makes it the *active window,* or the window on which your keystrokes are performed. You can also make any window active by clicking on it.

Like folders and disks, the files within them can be opened into windows. When you double-click on a file, you launch the program opening that file in a window. Double-clicking on the program icon creates a new untitled document in most cases. For Works, because there are several document types, you must select the document first from an Open dialog box.

Launching Microsoft Works:

1. **Open the folder containing the Works icon.** (Installing the program is covered in Appendix A.)

2. **Double-click on the Works program icon.** The program launches automatically.

— or —

2. **Select the Works icon and choose Open from the File menu (Command-O) to launch the program.**

— or —

2. **Double-click on any document created in Works.**

In System 7, you can launch Works and open the selected document by dragging an existing Works document (file) icon onto the Works program icon.

Microsoft Works 3.0

All Macintosh windows contain a central area and a set of specialized borders in addition to other elements. These elements are described below and appear in the following figure.

✦ *Title Bar.* Centered along the top border of the window, the title bar shows the name of the item, folder, or disk that is open. Document windows in applications such as Works are untitled until saved, then the title shows the name of the document. The title bar also indicates which window is active on your screen. Only one window on the desktop at a time can be active — the window in which files and folders can be selected and manipulated. Click anywhere on a window to make it active. The active window is indicated by the appearance of six horizontal lines in the title bar while inactive windows show the title with no lines. You also use the title bar to move a window by clicking and dragging the bar. When you wish to move an inactive window without making it active, press the Command key and click and drag that window.

◆ *Window header.* Below the title bar is an informational area that tells you how many items are in the window, the size of the disk or folder, and how much storage in the disk remains. You can change the display of the header using the View menu. There are also different views of a window's contents you can display on the desktop. Using the View menu, you can also display the window's contents by name, creation date, size, kind, icon, and label.

◆ *Close box.* The *close box* is the white square located at the upper-left corner of a window in the title bar. When you click the close box, the window closes and returns its data to the file or folder that holds that information (which stays selected). This is a shortcut for choosing Close Window from the File menu or pressing Command-W. Pressing the Option key and clicking the close box closes all windows on the desktop. (There are many other shortcuts like this one to learn about.)

◆ *Zoom box.* Clicking the *zoom box* — the double square at the upper-right corner of a window in the title bar — toggles the window between a selected size and the full screen in System 6, or between a selected size and a size large enough to contain all items in the window in System 7.

◆ *Resize box (or size box).* The *resize box* — the overlapping squares at the bottom-right corner of a window — lets you adjust the size of the window manually. Click and drag that box to resize the window.

◆ *Scroll bars. Scroll bars* are used to move the contents of a window into view. These are located along the bottom and right borders of the window.

All windows have both a vertical and horizontal scroll bar and a set of directional arrows within the scroll bars. When there are additional items or information not visible beyond the borders of a window, then the scroll bar appears gray with a white *scroll box* in it. Clicking an arrow moves the window incrementally in the arrow's direction. To shift the screen one entire window's worth, click on a gray area of a scroll bar in the direction you want to move. Or you can click and drag the scroll bar to move the window's contents as desired. A white scroll bar indicates that the contents in that direction (horizontally or vertically) are already displayed. System 7 has *active scrolling*. That is, if you click in the window to drag a document or other icon, and drag in any direction, the window scrolls as it follows where you are dragging.

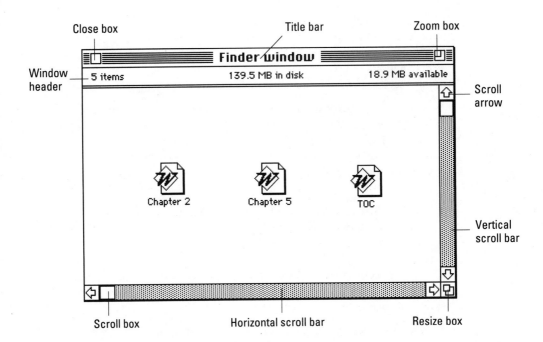

Close box Title bar Zoom box

Window header

Scroll arrow

Vertical scroll bar

Scroll box Horizontal scroll bar Resize box

MultiFinder allows you to run several applications at once so that you can switch rapidly between them. By activating a window, you are making the program that created the window active in memory.

Switching between applications:

1. Determine what application you want to switch to.

2. Click on an open window of the application to make it active.

— or —

2. In System 7 you can choose the name of the program from the Application menu located in the upper-right hand corner of your desktop.

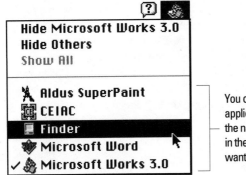

You can switch between applications by choosing the name of the application in the Application menu you want to switch to

— or —

2. In System 6, you can select the application icon at the right side of the menu bar, or choose the name of the program from the bottom of the Apple menu.

— or—

2. If you can see the program icon, double-click on it.

The current application in use is called the active or *foreground application,* while all other applications are called *background applications.* Your Macintosh operating system supports some application processes (like copying and moving, telecommunication, printing, and so on) in the background. Don't be confused if an application disappears — unless you quit that application, it's still available in the background and only needs to be reselected.

You can also use the Hide commands from the Application menu to leave an application's windows in memory. This removes them from the screen but allows you to retrieve them instantly by choosing Show from the Application menu. Hide and Show are on a toggle switch.

Using alert and dialog boxes

Your Macintosh has several specialized kinds of windows that inform you either about the condition of your Mac, some action that is about to take place, or a variety of choices you can make in executing a command. These windows have elements in them that are different from the windows discussed in the previous section. Windows that provide information are called *alert boxes;* those that offer you choices are called *dialog boxes.*

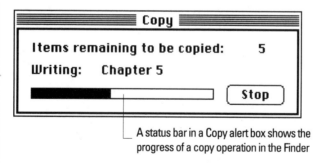

A status bar in a Copy alert box shows the
progress of a copy operation in the Finder

One of the programming parameters defined by Apple requires that you be allowed a graceful exit from any action. An alert box is posted when you execute a command that has far-reaching and serious consequences. For example, when you choose Quit from the File menu, an alert box appears on your screen and asks if you want to save any changed data. Without that alert box, quitting would destroy any unsaved work. If you remove data from a window with the Cut command, no alert box is posted because you can restore that information with the Undo command in the Edit menu. Alert boxes are also posted to give you general information or messages. When you copy files in the Finder, a progress alert box is posted.

Dialog boxes appear when there are choices to be made. Many program commands (those with an ellipsis after them) have dialog boxes, and the convention is to give the dialog box the name of the command. Thus, the dialog box that appears when you choose the Page Setup command from the File menu is called the Page Setup dialog box. The elements of a dialog box are listed below:

◆ *Text boxes.* Text boxes allow you to type in either a number or text. Text boxes tend to support the Edit menu commands: Cut, Copy, Paste, and Clear.

◆ *Check boxes.* Check boxes are selected by clicking on them. When the choice is active, the box has an X in it. Check boxes are *nonexclusive*, which means that any number of boxes in a set may be selected.

◆ *Radio buttons.* Radio buttons are circles that you can select by clicking on them. A black circle appears in them when they've been activated. Radio buttons are *exclusive;* only one radio button in a set may be selected.

◆ *Push buttons.* Push buttons are large, generally oval buttons that determine what happens to your selections in the dialog box. Clicking OK executes the command with your choices. Clicking Cancel dismisses the dialog box without executing the command and returns you to your original screen. Other push buttons, such as Option, Preview, and Help, may take you to a second dialog box with more choices.

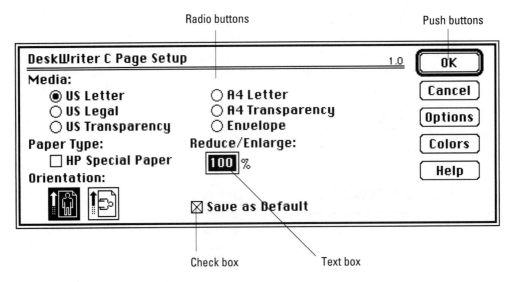

A double-outlined button represents the default choice. Press Return or Enter to effect it. Normally, the default choice is the OK button, but not always. The Cancel button is often activated by pressing Command-period (for stop). You'll see many examples of dialog and alert boxes in the Topics ahead.

Filing with your Macintosh

The files on every disk are organized in an inverted tree structure. This system is called the *hierarchical file system* (HFS). At the very top level of the file system in System 7 is the *Desktop folder*. When you double-click on that folder, its top level or folder is shown. This first level is also called the *root directory*. The Desktop folder was introduced in System 7. In prior system software, the top level of the HFS was considered to be each disk's top level. Opening each folder's window within the root directory reveals another lower level in the file system.

The Macintosh system software contains two standard dialog boxes that let you open and save a file in the HFS. Sometimes called the *Standard File Get box* and the *Standard File Put box,* respectively, these dialog boxes let you jump to any level in the file structure. Every Macintosh application uses these Open and Save boxes to work with files.

Works' Save dialog box lets you save a file at any level in the hierarchical file structure (HFS)

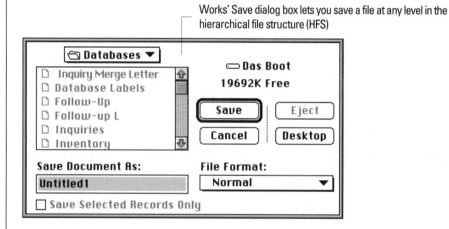

Files that can be opened by the program in use will appear in the scrolling window. If you can't find a file in an Open or Save dialog box, it's probably because it's the wrong file type. Nothing causes beginning users more panic than this peculiarity of the Macintosh file system.

To open a folder from an Open dialog box, use one of the methods described in the following instructions:

✦ Find and highlight the name of the file you want to retrieve in the scroll box. Double-click on it, or select the file and click the Open button.

✦ If you're opening a file from within an application and the file is in a folder higher in the file system, click on the current folder name above the scrolling list and hold the mouse key to reveal the path of folders. Then drag the cursor down to highlight the folder you want to open and release the mouse.

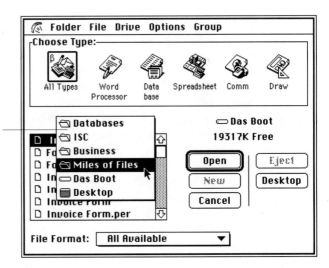

Using the drop-down folder allows you to open a folder from the Open dialog box

+ If the folder is on another disk, in System 7, go to the Desktop folder level to change disks or select the Desktop button; in System 6, select the Drive button.

+ When you find the file you want, double-click on its name, or highlight it and select Open.

Finding a file in the Finder:

1. **Choose Find File from the File menu, or press Command-F.** The Find dialog box appears.

2. **Enter all or part of the filename into the Find text box.**

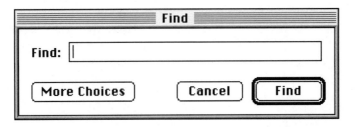

3. **Select Find.** Your Macintosh locates the first matching file and opens its folder on the desktop.

4. **To continue finding other matching files, choose Find Again from the File menu, or press Command-G.**

By selecting More Choices in the Find dialog box you can narrow the search but also make it more comprehensive in scope. Also, the Find command can be used in the background while you work in another application like Microsoft Works.

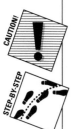

New work you do exists in volatile memory (RAM) only. When you save a file, that data is written to disk and preserved. You don't own what's on your screen — only what's on your disk. So save your work often.

Saving a file within an application:

1. **Choose Save from the File menu, or press Command-S. The standard File Save dialog box appears.** If you want to save the file in a new folder, you must create and name the folder first before using the Save command.

2. **Open the target folder by double-clicking on its name, or select the folder and click the Open button.**

3. **If the target folder is held in a folder higher in the file system, you can click on the current folder name above the scrolling list and press the mouse key to reveal the path of folders. Then drag the cursor down to highlight the folder you want to open and release the mouse.**

4. **If the target folder is on another disk, in System 7, go to the Desktop folder level to change disks or choose the Desktop button; in System 6, select the Drive button.**

5. **Press Tab to activate the Name text box, or click in the text box to place an insertion cursor in it.**

6. **Type the name of your file.**

7. **Select Save.**

Using the Macintosh Clipboard and Scrapbook

The Macintosh operating system reserves a part of the volatile computer memory called the *Clipboard* to move information between documents and applications. Only one item can be held in the Clipboard at a time. Nevertheless, the Clipboard is very versatile. The Clipboard can contain text, spreadsheet or database data, graphics, sounds, and even video. Only information (not entire files) can be moved to the Clipboard.

Every Macintosh application supports the Clipboard, and most applications have a command that lets you view the Clipboard. In the Finder that command is the Show Clipboard command in the Edit menu. The commands used to move information on and off the Clipboard are found in the Edit menu. The following list summarizes the Edit commands.

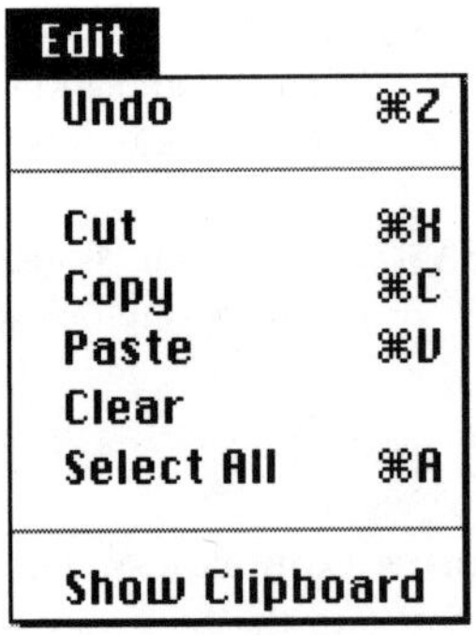

```
 Edit
 Undo        ⌘Z

 Cut         ⌘H
 Copy        ⌘C
 Paste       ⌘U
 Clear
 Select All  ⌘A

 Show Clipboard
```

✦ *Cut command* (Command-X). Removes a selected item and places it on the Clipboard.

✦ *Copy command* (Command-C). Duplicates the selected item and places the copy on the Clipboard, leaving the original selection in place.

✦ *Paste command* (Command-V). Puts a copy on the Clipboard and puts it where the cursor is currently located.

✦ *Clear command*. Removes the selection, but doesn't place it on the Clipboard. A similar result is achieved by g the Backspace or Delete key.

✦ *Undo command* (Command-Z). This restores your condition before the last action.

Whenever you place an item on the Clipboard, it replaces whatever was there before it. Also when you restart your Mac, the Clipboard contents are erased. If there's something on the Clipboard you wish to save, you can use the Scrapbook as a permanent repository. To do this, open the Scrapbook by choosing it from the Apple menu. Choose Paste from the Edit menu, and the contents of the Clipboard are placed onto their own page in the Scrapbook. Close the Scrapbook by clicking its close box. Whenever you need to retrieve a copy of an item, open the Scrapbook, turn to the page with those contents by clicking in the scroll bar, and choose Copy from the Edit menu to place that information onto the Clipboard.

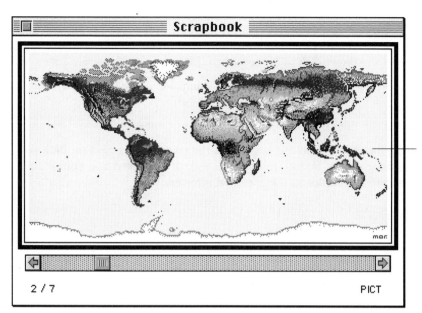

The Scrapbook holds information or graphics you want to save from the Clipboard permanently

Scrapbook

2 / 7   PICT

The Scrapbook is saved to the disk as a file — therefore, it's permanent. The file resides at the top level in your System Folder in System 6, and within the Apple Menu Items folder within the System Folder in System 7.

Making backups

Backups are like insurance. You may only need them once, but when you need them, you really need them. Expect and plan for disaster, back up your work often.

Making a duplicate of an entire disk:

1. **Insert the source disk with the files to be copied.**

2. **Choose Eject Disk from the Special menu, or press Command-Shift-1.** The disk is ejected though its icon is left dimmed on the desktop.

3. **Insert the target disk where the information will be copied to, initializing it if needed.**

4. **Click and drag the dimmed icon of the source disk over the target disk and release the mouse button.** Insert each disk as requested, and your Macintosh makes an exact copy of the entire source disk.

Copying files between disks with a single floppy disk drive:

1. **Insert the source disk with the files to be copied.**

2. **Double-click the source disk to open its window.**

3. **Choose Eject Disk from the Special menu, or press Command-Shift-1.**
   The disk is ejected, and the icon is left dimmed on the desktop.

4. **Insert the target disk to be copied to, initializing it if needed.**

5. **Choose Eject Disk from the Special menu, or press Command-Shift-1.**
   The disk is ejected, and the icon is left dimmed on the Desktop.

6. **Select the file(s) to be copied.**

7. **Drag those files onto the target disk they are to be copied to; then release the mouse button. Insert each disk as requested and your Mac makes exact copies of the files you selected.**

Quitting Works

When you are ready to stop work and leave the program, use the Quit command or press Command-Q to remove Works and and all its files from memory. You may wish to create a Works Wordspace file first using the Save Workspace command in the File menu. The Workspace will open all your current files for a project. Workspaces are discussed in the section "Creating a Workspace" in Topic 12.

Shutting down your Mac

To turn your computer off, you simply choose Shut Down from the Special menu. It's good practice to leave your computer on most of the time — turning a computer on and off ages it much more than leaving it on. I turn off my computer when leaving for extended periods, such as weekends or vacation, or during a storm when an electrical surge might damage it. For those times when you do want to turn off your Mac, the steps below show you how to do so.

Turning off your Macintosh safely:

1. **In the Finder, choose Shut Down from the Special menu.** Your Macintosh will quit each application in turn, asking you if you wish to save any unsaved work.

2. **Turn off the power switches to your computer and hard drive.**

If there's a problem with your computer, sometimes restarting your computer can correct the problem. Using the Restart command in the Special menu allows you to reboot your computer directly without shutting it down first.

Restarting your computer

Choosing the Restart command from the Special menu will restart your computer. There is, of course, another way: Pressing the programmer's restart switch (if it has been installed) also restarts your computer.

Quick Tips

In this section, you'll learn how to access on-line help from the Finder; find out what system you have; set up your hard disk; name files; and use third-party file managers.

Getting help

You can get help in the Finder in a couple of different ways. One method is to display the Balloon Help system. To do this, choose Show Balloons from the Help menu. Then whenever you move the cursor over an item or highlight a command for which a Balloon Help entry exists, information is displayed in a cartoon-like balloon. Turn off Balloon Help by choosing Hide Balloon from the Help menu.

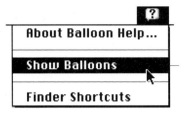

Choosing Show Balloons in the Help menu of System 7 activates Balloon Help

Balloon Help is fun, but it's only really useful when you're first learning a program, as the explanations can be terse. Balloon Help only exists in System 7 and in newer applications that take advantage of System 7 features.

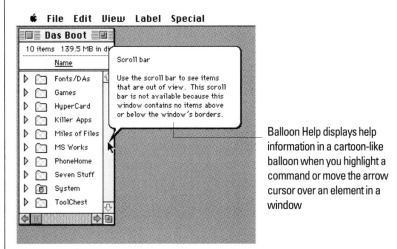

Balloon Help displays help information in a cartoon-like balloon when you highlight a command or move the arrow cursor over an element in a window

Another source of on-screen help in System 7 is the Finder Shortcuts command in the Help menu. This command displays five screens of useful information, indexing keystroke equivalents (also called keyboard equivalents) for commands and various operations.

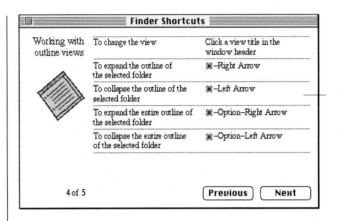

The Finder Shortcuts window is another source of help in System 7

Works offers both Balloon Help and Finder Shortcuts in its Help menu. They work in an entirely analogous fashion to the Finder's system. Additionally, Works offers a separate Microsoft Works Help system that is the subject of Topic 3, "Works Basics."

The best sources of help for learning to use the Macintosh, though, are some of the fine books available. Beyond the Apple manuals provided with your computer, which should be your first stop, try reading the following IDG books:

> *Macworld Complete Mac Handbook,* by Jim Heid, 1991, IDG Books, San Mateo, CA. The best detailed overview of the Macintosh technology and a good reference.

> *Read Me First Book,* edited by Jerry Borrell, 1991, IDG Books, San Mateo, CA.

> *Mac For Dummies,* by David Pogue, 1992, IDG Books, San Mateo, CA.

Another good source of help for beginners is a local Macintosh user group. Many user groups offer get-togethers, newsletters, help lines, and training sessions to help you get started. Users range from beginners to experts, and undoubtedly you'll find people with problems similar to your own.

Finding out what System you have

You can easily determine what Macintosh you're working on, your current System and Finder, how much memory has been used by what applications, and how much memory is available. That information is available in the About This Macintosh dialog box, accessed by choosing About This Macintosh from the Apple menu.

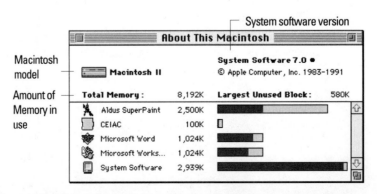

Setting up your hard disk

There are nearly as many schemes for organizing a hard disk as there are people using Macintoshes. The bottom line is that it's your disk and you should use the method with which you feel most comfortable.

One good scheme is to separate each application into a separate folder. Since applications rarely change, you only need to create backup copies of the application folder every so often. Your data files can then be placed into other folders. Consider organizing these files functionally by project, or by type. When organizing by project, you'll likely have files of several types in that folder. Remember not to be confused if they aren't listed in Open dialog boxes. You can also organize files by subject and retrieve files from folders based on a topic.

Filename alias

Alias icon

Two features of System 7 are particularly useful in organizing your hard drive: aliases and labels. An *alias* is a pointer to an original file, so you can directly access an application or a folder without searching through the HFS. You create an alias by selecting a file or folder and choosing Make Alias from the File menu. The resulting icon or folder displays the title *Filename Alias* in italics. You can place that alias anywhere you want, and when you double-click on the alias, it launches the original file or opens the original folder. Dropping a file into the alias of a folder copies the file into the original folder. Aliases also show up in standard file dialog boxes.

A *label* is an attribute that you attach to a file or folder using the Label menu in the System 7 Finder. Labels have a name and a color that you can assign them. Labels help you recognize where a file belongs. You can search for labels using the More Choices option in the Find dialog box.

Aliases and labels have many other uses that I don't have space to discuss here, but they make project management in the Finder much easier. For more information, see Lon Poole's fine book, *The Macworld Guide To System 7,* published by IDG Books.

Whatever system you use, try not to have too many folders on any level. Folder clutter makes it hard for you to find the folder you want. Six or eight folders is a good, practical limit. If you do need more than eight folders or files in a folder, then make sure that folder's window in the Finder is viewed by name, date, kind, or size. These formats are more efficient than an icon view. The most powerful window view is the outline view offered by System 7, because it lets you look into more than one folder. You can get an entire view of your disk from outline view.

Naming your files

File naming conventions abound. The Macintosh Finder allows you to name a file using any combination of text and numbers. Up to 31 characters can appear in the name under the icon on the desktop. More characters in a name won't appear, although you can type many more characters in a Save dialog box.

Because Works creates several different kinds of files, you might want to name those files in a way that lets you easily identify the file type. Works has five file types: word processor, draw, database, spreadsheet, and communication documents. Typical schemes for naming files might include Filename.wp, Filename.db, Filename.ss, Filename.com; or Filename Letter, Filename Data, Filename Worksheet. You can see these file types in the Works standard file Open dialog boxes. If you select a particular file type, only that kind of file appears in the scroll box. Select the All Types files icon to see all Works files.

It normally isn't a good idea to date documents because a date is already assigned to a file when it's created and when it's modified. You can view those dates in the window of the Finder. To get more information about a file when you're in the Finder, choose Get Info from the File menu, or press Command-I. The Get Info dialog box opens, showing you all of that file's attributes.

Using third-party file managers

As great as the Macintosh Finder is, and it *is* a great system, there are third-party file managers available that improve it. Some of these programs add hierarchical menus to the Finder. Others add their own proprietary menus.

Highly recommended is the NOW Utilities package from NOW Software, a collection of extensions that improve the Macintosh interface. One part of this package, NOWMenus, adds hierarchical menus; another, SuperBoomerang, adds menus to the Open and Save dialog boxes, keeping the names of recently used or specially marked files and folders handy to let you move to them without searching through the HFS. The NOW package has several other features. Alternatively, the On Cue package is equally well regarded. If you think you'll be creating a large amount of files, you should seriously consider installing either of these two utilities.

Summary

✔ The Macintosh computer uses a graphical user interface to perform various system-wide functions.

✔ The Macintosh is an event-driven environment. You must first specify an object and then specify the action to be taken on that object.

✔ Start your Macintosh by turning on your external hard drive (if you have one), inserting a start-up floppy disk (if desired), and then turning on the Mac power switch or keyboard power key.

✔ Computers use binary codes to store and process information.

✔ An electronic scratch pad in memory, called RAM, is used to do calculations; data is stored to a disk as files.

✔ A computer's start-up sequence, called booting a computer, puts the operating system into memory. An operating system is software that controls computer actions; this software is partially in permanent memory (ROM) and in the System file.

✔ The Finder file is responsible for the look of the Macintosh desktop (Screen display). Little pictures called icons allow you to manipulate files, programs, and groups of objects.

✔ Run a command by choosing the command name from the menu (click on it with your mouse cursor or by typing its keystroke equivalent using your keyboard).

✔ Select objects by clicking on them to highlight them.

✔ Delete (remove) objects like files by clicking and dragging them into the Trash icon.

✔ A window provides a view into a file's contents. You can expand or reduce that view, or move the file around.

✔ Launch Works by double-clicking on the program icon, or any of its file icons. Quit Works by selecting the Quit command on the file menu. Save your work by selecting the Save command on the File Menu.

✔ You can use the Cut, Copy, and Paste commands to transfer data to the Clipboard.

✔ Shut down your Mac by first using the Shut Down command on the Special Menu, and then turning the power switch off.

Topic 3
Works Basics

Overview

If you want to know what's new in Works 3 and don't have much time, read this Topic. Here you'll learn about all of the new features you can use as soon as you install Works 3.

What's new in Works 3

Works 3 is much improved from previous versions; user feedback contributed greatly and coerced Microsoft into making beneficial changes. Long-time users will immediately notice how much more attractive the screens are. Nearly all of the menus have been reworked, including some that are new or consolidated. This section details the most important changes in the program and indicates where you can find information on them in this book.

Understanding changes to the overall program

The major changes that were made to the overall program and are active in all five Works modules are summarized below:

◆ *Installer program.* Works is now installed automatically with an Apple installer, unlike previous versions of the program that were simply copied from a disk. Installation details are given in Appendix A, "Installing Works." An Easy Install option installs all files; a custom installation allows a limited selection of files to be installed. The price of System 7 support is that Works now requires 1MB of memory and 2MB of RAM to run. That's nearly twice the memory (512K) of Works 2. A minimum of 2MB of disk storage space is also required in System 7. For System 6, minimum requirements are System 6.0.4, 1MB installed RAM, 2MB of disk storage, and access to a Macintosh SuperDrive (1.4MB disks).

◆ *System 7 Support.* Works 3 is System 7 *friendly* (to use Apple's jargon), but not System 7 *savvy,* meaning it can't take advantage of all the new system features. Missing are some notable features of System 7 including Publish and Subscribe, Apple events, and Interapplication Communications.

◆ *TrueType fonts.* This feature is discussed in "Working with fonts" later in this topic. The TrueType fonts feature lets you print and display characters perfectly at any size. These fonts are included with the Macintosh System 7 software.

+ *The Apple Communication Toolbox.* This is installed in System 7, but Works also installs it in System 6. The toolbox is used by the communication module, as discussed in Topic 9, "Using Works' Communications."

+ *Help Systems.* Balloon Help, Works 3 Shortcuts, and the Works 3 Help System are new. Works 3 is a proprietary on-line, context sensitive, hypertext system. See "Getting help in Works" later in this Topic.

+ *Enhanced draw.* Topic 5 is devoted to the draw mode, and it's also discussed in Topics 4, 6, 7, and 9. The draw mode now supports the creation of separate documents and improves the handling of graphics in the program. Draw also works as an overlayer in word processor, spreadsheet, database, and communication documents. Further changes to the draw mode are given below.

+ *Tool palettes.* All documents now open automatically and display a floating tool palette that puts a set of tools within easy reach. These palettes let you switch quickly into draw mode and back again to the original module when done. This feature makes the tools much easier to find than when they were hidden as options within menus.

+ *Headers and footers.* These now support automatic date and time stamping, page numbering, and multiline text or draw graphics.

Using System 6 vs. System 7

Works was originally created to provide a common interface in an environment that had only modest memory to allocate to the program. The sharing of common commands between applications lets the user switch between several types of data while keeping the program active. That was important prior to System 5's introduction, when all the Macintosh system software could handle was one program loaded in memory in place of the Finder.

With the advent of System 5 and System 6, MultiFinder was introduced, which increased RAM, allowing several programs to be loaded in memory at the same time. Adding MultiFinder to the package allowed users to switch between programs running in memory to activate the program they wanted — called *context switching.* A program that's currently running and active is called the *foreground application;* but in System 6, MultiFinder also allowed some limited background processing, notably printing and communications. System 7 merged Finder and MultiFinder making them one program.

You can always tell when you're in System 7 by the appearance of the Help and Application menus. There are some advantages to using Works in System 7 — aliases, labels, improved help facilities, and networked file sharing are some examples. Nearly all of the other functions in Works are identical in any Macintosh system software version.

Although the need for a common interface has subsided, the benefits of sharing a common command set and using the same program for several different data types have not. Works provides a system that lets the user learn the program quickly and not worry about the compatibility of data between programs.

◆ *Stationery documents*. Works comes with a set of personal, business, or educational stationery documents; or you can create your own stationery. You can also now preview stationery through the New dialog box. See "Creating a new document" and "Streamlining with stationery documents" later in this Topic, and in Topic 14, "Accessing Works' stationery files."

◆ *Preference settings*. A new Preference command, found on the Edit menu, lets you make changes to your default settings. These changes can be specific to a particular Works mode or universal to all five. See the section titled "Works' default settings" in this Topic.

◆ *Incorporation of Microsoft Mail*. Send and receive mail directly from Works via Works menu commands. See "Using electronic mail" in Topic 14.

◆ *Better file conversion*. Works includes a number of Dataviz's (Trumbull, CT) MacLinkPlus translators. These translators provide better support for file conversion between Macintosh applications, and you can convert and open files from MS-DOS and Windows applications. See "Exchanging information" in Topic 12 for more details.

Understanding improvements to Works' word processor

The Works word processor, described in Topic 4, now ships with the following features:

◆ *Improved interface*. A floating palette for Draw also allows you to choose font characteristics for text. A 3-D ruler and ribbon, and time and date stamp icons are among the more significant changes.

◆ *Enhanced spelling checker*. Performance is better, and custom dictionaries are now an option.

◆ *Thesaurus*. Use the 190,000-word thesaurus to find synonyms and antonyms.

◆ *Footnotes*. Footnotes can now be placed at the bottom of each page or at the end of the document.

◆ *Better mail merge*. Print merge now supports fields taken from multiple database files. The option is available from the Print dialog box as a Print Merge option. See Topic 6 for the section titled, "Mail merging in Works."

Understanding improvements to Works' database

The Works database is the subject of Topic 6. Additions to the database module include the following features:

◆ *Multiple Forms view*. You can now have up to 16 forms that you design and print for each database file. See Topic 6 for the section titled "Using three database views."

◆ *Design view*. Create customized forms within the Design View option by resizing fields and using draw to create graphics. See Topic 6 for the section titled "Using graphics in a database."

◆ *Data view.* Data View displays the form how it will be printed and lets you enter data one record at a time. See Topic 6 for the section titled "Entering data."

◆ *Selection filters.* A *filter* is a set of up to 6 selection parameters. You can name and save up to 16 filters and recall them for your searches. See Topic 6 for the section titled "Finding or copying information."

◆ *Fill down.* In List View, information can now be copied in a field to any number of records. In Topic 6, See "Entering data" and "Finding or copying information."

◆ *Paste Function.* Works now has a Paste Function feature in the database, just as it does in the spreadsheet. A Paste Function dialog box contains a filter that lets you find a particular type of function more easily. A Sample box gives an example of that function's use. See Topic 6 for "Using fields" and "Creating fields," and Topic 11 for "Using functions." Topic 11 gives a complete explanation of functions and their use.

◆ *Format fields.* This new command and dialog box lets you enter formulas and values and choose the type for a field. See "Using fields" and "Creating fields" in Topic 6.

◆ *Mailing labels.* A database form can now print a mailing label without requiring a mail merge.

You will not be able to open and convert databases from version 2.0 correctly in version 3.0.

Understanding improvements to Works' spreadsheet

The spreadsheet module is the least changed of all of Works' modules. Topic 7 describes spreadsheets. See Topic 11 for information about using spreadsheet functions. The notable changes are summarized below:

◆ *Paste Function.* Works now has a Paste Function feature in the spreadsheet. The Paste Function dialog box contains a filter that lets you find a particular type of function more easily. A Sample box gives an example of that function's use. In Topic 7, See "Entering a Formula."

◆ *Time and Date Handling.* Different formats are now recognized automatically.

◆ *Charting Graphics.* Charts are more object oriented. You can change components of a graph and use Draw to touch it up. Charts are also now color supported. A new Hi-Lo-Close graph is now included for market transactions. See Topic 8, Using Works' "Charts," for further information.

Understanding improvements to Works' draw module

Draw is the most changed feature in Works. It is now a full-fledged Works module and can create and use its own documents. Improvements to the draw module are summarized below:

♦ Color palettes now have a series of pop-up color selectors that display 256 colors on screen. Colors can be assigned to characters, lines, shapes, borders, and patterns, both as background and foreground colors.

♦ Added special graphics effects now allow figure rotation (flips), 3-D imaging, smoothed polygons, and variable transparency of objects. Imported bitmapped pictures can now be cropped to size.

♦ Improved text column features offer better column linkage and both horizontal and vertical rulers. This makes it easier to create page layouts and do desktop publishing.

Understanding improvements to Works' communication module

The communication module has a few improvements, as discussed in Topic 9. Additions to the communication module are summarized below:

♦ *Improved interface.* A floating palette lets you connect, transfer files, capture text, and hang up with a click of the mouse. A clock gives you time and connection time, and tracks cost. See "The communication window" and "Keeping track of time and cost" in Topic 9 for more details.

♦ *Apple communications toolbox support.* There are now built-in routines that improve modem, AppleTalk, and serial device communication at a system level.

♦ *Automated sign-On.* You can create automated scripts to log onto on-line services and bulletin boards. See "Automating log-On" in Topic 9 for more details.

♦ *More terminal emulation.* The VT102, VT220, VT320, and TTY standards are supported and improved. These terminal emulations let you call up and talk with VAX and UNIX computers. See "Surveying the communication features" in Topic 9 for more details.

Communication documents created in previous versions of Works aren't compatible with this new version and new setting files will need to be established.

All Works modules support the use of a macro recorder, which is the subject of Topic 10. A macro recorder records your keystrokes and saves them to a macro file. It functions similarly to a part of System 6 that disappeared in System 7. The soon-to-be-released AppleScript will provide additional functionality.

Getting to know Works' document types

Works has five different types of documents that it can create, one for each of the major modules: word processor, database, spreadsheet, draw, and communication. Each of these files shows a different document icon when displayed in the Finder, so that you can tell the file type by looking at it.

Word Processor Data base Spreadsheet Comm Draw Macros

Each kind of file contains a different type of information formatted in a different way. The file types aren't directly compatible with one another — that is, you can only open a file in its own type of window. Works takes care of the details for you since it knows what file type it's working with at the moment. Should you need to transfer the information, you can cut, copy, and paste data using the Clipboard.

It helps to think of Works as a collection of five separate programs sharing a common file system. This visualization isn't quite accurate, because some functions, like macros and the draw features, are common throughout all the modules. However, it helps you understand why the different modules can't directly use one another's data. When you create a draw document, for example, though draw is used in all of the other modules, you still have to use the Clipboard to move graphics from that draw document to another document type.

Charting, a common spreadsheet feature, doesn't produce a separate file type. Charts are associated with a worksheet, and they're saved along with that worksheet. Open a spreadsheet file, and all of the charts associated with that file will appear. You can, however, copy a chart to any other kind of Works document as a graphic, but the copy loses its dynamic link to the data used to create it back in the worksheet.

Macro files, a sixth file type, can also be created. A *macro* is a file that contains an often-used series of keystrokes which can be executed with the touch of a few buttons. Macro files can be opened within any of the other five kinds of documents. When you open a macro file, no information is displayed, but the capability of those keystrokes is made available to that document. When no other document is open and you open a macro file, the macros are available for your use, but no document window or data appears. As a conceptual example, think of a custom dictionary in spelling checkers. Custom dictionaries have unique icons and enhance your spelling checker, but they don't have their own document window or display data.

Working with document windows

Works has five different document windows for each of its five data types. Document windows use most of the elements of the Finder window, described in Topic 2, in the section titled "Working with windows." All five documents have scroll bars, close boxes, windows, and other standard features. Each kind of document window in Works has many specialized features described in each of the topics on Works modules.

After using Works for a short time, you'll instantly be able to tell the document type from the appearance of the window — they're that different from one another. Additionally, to ensure that there is no confusion distinguishing between file types, the designers of Works included the file type in the title. You'll see the abbreviations *WP* for word processor documents, *DB* for database documents, *SS* for spreadsheet documents, *DR* for draw documents, and *CM* for communication documents. These abbreviations are shown in the window title bar after the filename.

Choosing output devices

The page you see on your screen and the finished copy you obtain from your output device are determined by the output device you choose. Each printer has different requirements that limit the type of page it can print. For example, due to the mechanical assembly that moves a page through a LaserWriter, a blank ½-inch margin on all sides is required for that printer. Other printers and output devices, such as fax machines and modems, have other requirements. It's important that you select the output device *before* you begin your work on a new document. Since you probably use the same output device most of the time, it's easy to forget this rule. When changing output devices, you should reselect your output device before you create the document. If you don't, you may have to reformat an entire document.

A printer is a piece of hardware controlled by software in your computer. This software, called a *printer driver,* interprets what your computer applications send to the printer. You change output devices by selecting them from the Chooser desk accessory found in the Apple menu. Chooser devices are called *RDEVs,* an abbreviation for resource devices. RDEVs can be printers, faxes, network devices, or other devices. You can choose serial devices attached to your computer's modem or printer ports, or AppleTalk devices attached by the AppleTalk connection.

When you install system software on your Mac, several printer drivers are often installed at the same time. If you chose the Easy Install option for System 7, you probably have all of Apple's printer drivers in your Extension folder: the LaserWriter, Personal LW LS, Personal LaserWriter SC, AppleTalk ImageWriter, LQ AppleTalk ImageWriter, ImageWriter, LQ ImageWriter, and StyleWriter. In System 6, these files appear in the top level of your System Folder. You can also choose the Custom Install option and copy only the printer drivers you need. Whenever you use a non-Apple printer, you need to get the printer driver from the manufacturer for that printer. For example, the popular Hewlett-Packard DeskWriter printers come with software that lets you connect printers as serial devices, or connect to an AppleTalk network.

To select a printer, open the Chooser desk accessory by selecting it from the Apple menu.

The Chooser desk accessory, found in the Apple menu, allows you to choose the printer or other output device you wish to use

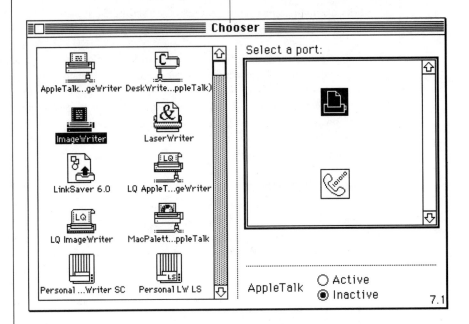

In the scrolling window on the left hand side, select the icon for the printer you desire to use. In the right hand box, select the serial port you wish to send output to — either the Printer or Modem port. Both these ports function identically. You could hook a printer to the modem port, if you chose, and a modem to the printer port. Turn the AppleTalk setting on or off, depending on the type of device you're using. StyleWriters and ImageWriters are serial devices; they hook to either the printer or modem ports. LaserWriters are parallel devices that hook to your AppleTalk port. The plugs used for serial printer and AppleTalk printers aren't interchangeable so you can't mistake them.

When you change to a device that requires AppleTalk, Works posts the following alert box:

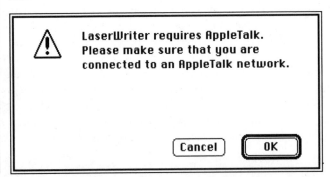

Also, when you change to another printer, Works posts the following warning to remind you to change your Page Setup settings in open documents:

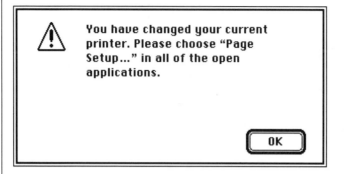

⚠ **You have changed your current printer. Please choose "Page Setup..." in all of the open applications.**

[OK]

The following instructions will show you how to choose a printer.

Choosing a printer:

1. **Select the Chooser desk accessory from the Apple menu.**

2. **Select the icon for the appropriate printer from the window on the left side of the Chooser. Scroll through the box if necessary.**

3. **Select the name of the port that the printer is attached to — either modem or printer port.**

4. **If this is a serial printer, turn off the AppleTalk option by selecting the Inactive radio button.**

5. **If this is an AppleTalk or LaserWriter printer, choose its name from the list in the right-hand side of the window.** You may need to first select the zone for that printer in order to find the printer name you want to select. Also, for an AppleTalk printer, click the Active radio button to make sure that AppleTalk is turned on.

6. **With your printer selected, choose Close to dismiss the Chooser and update your changes.**

Determining the look of your output

The device you've selected in the Chooser determines the printing options you have available to you. You control what your printed output looks like in two separate places: the Page Setup and Print dialog boxes. The Page Setup command in the File menu allows you to choose the page size or type, orientation of the page, and any other features that your printer allows. The Print dialog box lets you determine the number of copies, the specific pages printed, the quality of the print job, and other options. Which options appear in these dialog boxes depends on the particular printer chosen as both are controlled by the printer driver. Thus, installing a StyleWriter generates one set of dialog boxes, while installing a LaserWriter gives you another, different set of dialog boxes.

The following figure shows the Page Setup dialog boxes for the three most popular Apple printers: the StyleWriter, ImageWriter, and LaserWriter. To get a complete feel for their capabilities, compare them with their counterpart Print dialog boxes in the figure in the section titled "Sending a document to the printer" later in this Topic.

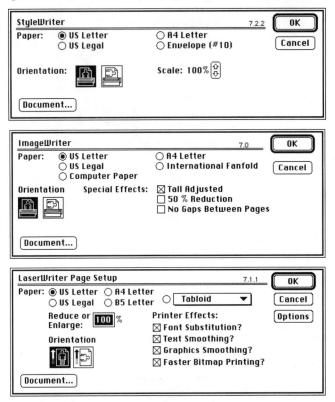

A summary of the options found in the Page Setup dialog box follows:

◆ *Paper sizes.* US Letter size (8½ × 11-inches) is the default option. To change the size, select any of the other radio buttons: Legal (8½ × 14-inches), Tabloid (17 × 11-inches), A4 Letter (8½ ×11⅔-inches), B5 Letter (7 × 10-inches), Envelope (#10 size — 9½×4¼-inches), Computer Paper (continuous feed), and International Fanfold.

◆ *Scale ratio, Reduce, or Enlarge.* Resizes the output by the percentage you enter. Fifty percent reduction makes the image half-sized.

◆ *Tall Adjusted.* An effect that adjusts the screen image resolution to a printed bitmap by reducing the printed image by 4 percent. This feature has the same effect as Precision Bitmap Alignment in the LaserWriter Options dialog box.

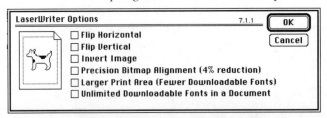

♦ *No Gaps Between Pages.* Meant for labels or computer paper, this option prints one page right after another.

♦ *Orientation.* This option allows you to select either portrait orientation (man standing up) or landscape (man on his side) printing. Use landscape for wide printing, particularly spreadsheets and databases.

♦ *Document button.* Pressing this button opens a dialog box allowing you to set margins and distance between pages.

LaserWriters also have some special options. The Printer Effects in the LaserWriter Page Setup dialog box has the following additional options available:

♦ *Font substitution.* Automatically substitutes Times for New York, Helvetica for Geneva, and Courier for Monaco for better print results.

♦ *Text Smoothing.* A set of routines to eliminate ragged edges, particularly on bitmapped fonts.

♦ *Graphics Smoothing.* A set of routines that smoothes rough edges on graphics.

♦ *Faster Bitmap Printing.* Improves printing speed for bitmapped graphics and text.

The following instructions will show you how to select the page setup options before you print.

Selecting Page Setup options:

1. **Choose Page Setup from the File menu to open the Page Setup dialog box.**

2. **Choose all appropriate options in the Page Setup dialog box, including paper type, orientation of image, scaling, and other special effects.** For an explanation of these options, see "Determining the look of your output" earlier in this Topic.

3. **Click the Document button to open up the dialog box and set page margins and (when using continuous feed paper) the space between forms. Type in the values you want, and click the OK button to accept these values.**

4. **Choose OK or press Return to enter your settings and close the Page Setup dialog box.**

— or —

4. **Alternatively, choose Cancel or press Command-Period to close the dialog box without altering your previous Page Setup settings.**

You can change Page Setup anytime you wish, even after a document is complete. However, if you do so, be careful that your document is formatted correctly. Your line endings and page breaks may change. If you know that your document is correctly set up, and you don't wish to see either the Page Setup or Print dialog boxes, choose the Print One command from the File menu. Works bypasses both dialog boxes and prints a single document to your current printer.

Making your printer work with special LaserWriter features

Some documents won't print with the LaserWriter Faster Bitmap printing option on. If you have a problem printing, go into the Page Setup dialog box and try turning this option off.

The special LaserWriter effects are turned on by default. When you choose Options from the LaserWriter Page Setup dialog box, an Options dialog box appears (see previous figure). Claris the Dogcow (Is he a dog or a cow? No one knows.) shows you the result of your choices. The options that refer to fonts determine the amount of memory allocated to working with the page's printed image. For more detailed information regarding these options, check your printer's manual.

Once you've set the Page Setup options you desire, set your document's margins. To do this, select the Document button and fill in the Document dialog box as appropriate.

Set the Left, Right, Top and Bottom margins here

Set any gaps you want between pages here

Creating and opening documents

When you first create a new document, you're asked to specify the file type. That document is given a temporary name, "Untitled 1," or "Untitled 2," for instance, depending on how many documents you've created during a particular work session. Everything you type or create in a document is held in RAM, or temporary memory, until you save the document. When you save a document, RAM writes the document's data to a disk file making it a permanent record. Any subsequent changes you make to a file once you've saved it exist only in memory, until the file is saved again. For this reason, when working on a document in Works or most other programs on the Macintosh (there are some exceptions), you should save your work often. You can only lose what you don't save.

Creating new files in Works

There are several ways to create a new file in Works. The different methods are summarized below:

✦ *The New command.* Choosing New from the File menu (Command-N) opens a dialog box that lets you choose the kind of file you want and allows you to work with stationery documents.

✦ *The Open command.* Choosing Open from the File menu (Command-O) lets you choose the kind of file you wish to create, but does not specifically show you stationery documents or their previews. Choose Stationery Preview from the New dialog box to accomplish that.

✦ *The Save As command.* You can use one document to create another by opening the existing document and choosing Save As from the File menu. The Save As command creates another document under a new name. The original document serves as a template which you can then modify without losing your original.

✦ *Stationery documents.* Stationery documents are locked documents of a specific file. When you open a stationery document, an identical duplicate is opened in an untitled window as a new document which you can then modify. Stationery documents can be opened from the New file dialog box by choosing Show Stationery. When this check box is selected, a dialog box opens and shows you stationery documents and their previews. You can also open a stationery document from the Open file dialog box.

The specific instructions for these approaches are covered below.

Creating a new document:

1. **With Works running, choose New from the File menu, or press Command-N.** The New file dialog box appears.

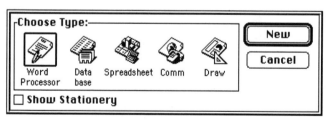

2. **Select the icon of the file type you wish to create and then choose New.**

— or —

2. **Alternatively, double-click the icon to create a new untitled document.**

You can also create documents using the Open command from the File menu. To do this, choose Open from the File menu then double-click on an icon in the

Open file dialog box to create a new document of the desired type. Alternatively, you can open an existing document, choose Save As from the File menu, and type the new name in the resulting Save dialog box.

The following instructions show you how to create a new document from an existing document.

Creating a new document from an existing document:

1. **Choose Open from the File menu.**

2. **Find the file you wish to work with and open it (see "Opening existing documents" for instructions, later in this Topic.)**

3. **Choose Save As from the File menu.**

4. **Type the name of the new document in the resulting Save dialog box.**

5. **Choose Save or press Return to execute the command.**

Streamlining with stationery documents

Stationery files are a great tool for automating your work. Works 3 ships with a number of useful stationery documents for personal, business, and educational uses. You can pick up additional stationery files from Heizer Software (see "Finding other Works resources" later in this Topic). Some programs refer to stationery files as templates, but a stationery file is actually a Macintosh file specification. A stationery file is a locked file whose contents are automatically opened into an untitled document without alerting you that the file is locked.

Stationery files are recognizable in the Finder as simplified versions of the Works document icons. Compare these stationery document icons with those in the first figure in this topic.

Word Processor   Database   Spreadsheet   Draw   Communications

Take advantage of this great timesaver by creating stationery files for all your commonly used documents, such as letters, envelopes, reports, forms — anything that's repetitive in nature. The following instructions tell you how. To create your own stationery file, use the instructions above, and save the new file as a stationery file.

The following instructions show you how to access Works' stationery files.

Accessing Works' stationery files:

1. **Choose New from the File menu to open the New file dialog box.**

2. **Choose Show Stationery, and the Show Stationery preview dialog box will open up.**

3. **Choose the stationery document you wish to view in the Preview window.** Only Works stationery can be viewed here.

4. **Choose Open and Works will create an untitled duplicate of the stationery in a new window.**

Opening existing documents

Once you have documents saved on your Mac, there are three basic ways to open them.

✦ *Choose Open from the File menu.* This command (Command-O) posts the Open file dialog box. Navigate the standard file system to find the file you want and then open it. This is the most common method of opening a file.

✦ *Double-click on an icon.* In the Finder, double-click on the file you want to open.

✦ *Drag a file to Works.* In System 7, when you drag the icon of a file onto the Microsoft Works icon, the file is opened. Works automatically launches before it opens a file, if necessary.

When you start Works, the Open file dialog box is displayed and the current position in the file system is shown. If you select a file from another program, that folder is shown first in Works. Use the Desktop button to switch between disks to find the file you want. Works has a set of translation filters so what you see in the Open file dialog box depends on what you choose in the File Format pop-down menu. This is discussed in more detail in Topic 12.

The following Step-by-Step instructions give details for opening an existing file.

Opening an existing file:

1. **With Works running, choose Open from the File menu or press Command-O.**

2. **Navigate the file system to find the file you wish to open.** If you're having trouble finding the file in the HFS (hierarchical file structure), refer to "Filing with your Macintosh" in Topic 2.

3. **To see only files of one document type in the scrolling list, select the icon for that file type.**

4. **Highlight the desired filename and choose Open. Alternatively, double-click the filename to open the file directly.**

Works can open files created by other programs. Which files will appear in the open scrolling file list depends on what you've chosen in the pop-up File Format menu. If Works can translate your document from another program it posts an alert box requesting permission to do so. Your document opens in a window with the document type shown in the title bar.

You can also open Works files from the Finder. To do this, locate the document icon in the Finder and double-click on it. Alternatively, highlight the document's icon and choose the Finder's Open command from its File menu, or press Command-O. As mentioned earlier, in System 7, you can drag the document icon over the Works application icon and then release it. This action launches Works if it isn't already running and opens your document into its own window.

Moving around in a dialog box

Let's look briefly at how to move around in the standard file dialog box; this discussion applies to both the Open and Save dialog boxes. Clicking the icon for a file type either shows or saves that type of file in the dialog box.

The following figure shows an Open file dialog box:

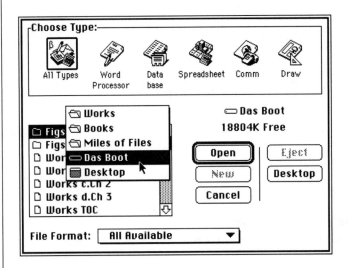

To move down the file structure, double-click a folder name, or click once and press the Open button. If an alias folder appears in the scrolling list, opening it moves you to wherever that folder is in the file structure. You can move up the scrolling list by pressing the up arrow and move down the scrolling list by pressing the down arrow. The Command-up arrow keystroke moves you up one folder in the file structure, the Command-down arrow keystroke moves you down into the selected folder. To move up the file structure along the path of open folders, click the current folder name and drag down to the level you wish to go. Select the Desktop button to jump to the top of the file system. If you type the first letters of a file or folder, that file or folder will be selected in the scrolling file box. Some of these features, including aliases, the Desktop folder, or typing letters to select a file or folder, will not work in System 6.

Works' default settings

In Works 3 you now have the capability to change some of the default characteristics of Works' files. The changes you can make are fairly limited; some changes are common to all types of Works files while others are specific to each module. To set default preferences, open a document window on your monitor, and choose Preference from the Edit menu. In the resulting dialog box, select the icon for the type of document you wish to set preferences for. A square outline will appear around the icon you've selected, and the preference choices become available.

This dialog box allows you to select default preferences that apply to all of the Works document types

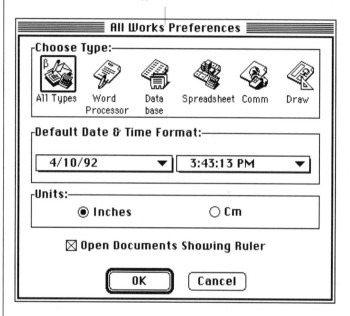

Universal changes you can make to all file types when you choose Preferences from the Edit menu are summarized below:

✦ *Default date and time format.* Click on the pop-up menu on the left to reveal the list of possible date formats. Drag to highlight your choice and release the mouse button. To change the time format, click and drag the pop-up menu on the right and select a new format.

✦ *Units.* Select the Inches or Cm radio buttons to define option measurements in inches or centimeters. These measurements appear in the windows' rulers, in dialog boxes, and in other places too.

✦ *Open documents showing ruler.* With this option checked, the ruler automatically appears in open documents. If the option is not checked, the ruler must be activated to appear.

These choices are the only universal preferences available. The other modules offer additional preferences individually:

- *Word processor preferences.* Sets default font type and size, footnote separator lines, and print locations.

- *Database preferences.* Sets default font type and size, and field type (text, number, date, and time).

- *Spreadsheet preferences.* These are for font type and size, and chart type.

- *Draw preferences.* Sets the default font type and size, and offers a snap-to-grid effect or a Vertex Snap effect for new drawings.

- *Communications preferences.* Sets the size of the overflow area for text that appears on your communication screen, lets Works capture text, and has Works notify you before breaking connections.

Entering text in Works' windows

Once a new window is opened, you can start typing text into it. You can enter text in all of Works' windows, and most of its dialog boxes. To do so, use the following instructions.

Entering text:

1. **Move the cursor over the window or text box that you want to enter text in.** The cursor turns into an I-beam.

2. **Click an insertion point where you would like to begin typing.** This action turns the cursor into a flashing vertical insertion bar at that position and leaves the I-beam cursor on your screen to be moved.

3. **Type the characters you wish.**

Working with fonts

Any font you've installed on your Mac shows up in all of Works' Font menus. A font is a family of characters in a particular style. There are several different categories of fonts available, they generally fall into two categories — bitmapped fonts or outline fonts. You can tell a bitmapped font by its city name (such as New York, Chicago, Geneva, Los Angeles, San Francisco, Venice). Outline fonts use traditional typesetting names (Helvetica, Times, Gothic).

Some fonts require two descriptions — one to display properly on your computer, called *screen fonts,* and another to print properly, called *printer fonts.* This is the case for PostScript outline fonts. TrueType fonts, which ship with System 7, require only one description. Bitmapped fonts are designed for a specific size and resolution only, and except at certain ratios of their intended size, scale poorly. Bitmapped fonts generally only require a single font description. Outline fonts come with software called a *font rasterizer,* which scales the characters so that they look good at any size and resolution. For TrueType, the rasterizer is built into the system software. For PostScript fonts, the rasterizer is the Adobe Type Manager, which is scheduled for inclusion with the next interim release of a System 7 upgrade.

In System 7, fonts (like other resources, such as sounds) can be installed by simply dragging an icon into the System file icon in the Finder. This method works for individual font files, but not *suitcases,* which are collections of fonts. If you have a font suitcase, simply double-click on it to open the suitcase and remove individual fonts. If a font has two file descriptions install the screen font in the System file and the printer font in the System Folder.

In System 6, fonts are installed in the System file through the use of the Font/DA Mover. Make sure you use version 4.2 or later of this utility to handle TrueType fonts. Printer fonts are copied to the System Folder.

The disadvantage to installing fonts into the System file is your System file gets to be very large. That can be a drawback when you keep an emergency start-up disk. A better system of font management is a resource manager like Fifth Generation Systems' Suitcase 2.0 or ALSoftware's MasterJuggler. These products let you access fonts, as well as desk accessories, FKeys, and sounds from inside a suitcase file and place those suitcase files anywhere you wish. (For systems prior to 7.0, this was the only way to work around the limit of using 15 desk accessories at a time.) This resource management system also makes sense in System 7, because it lets you manage a set of fonts for special purposes.

One of the best ways to manage fonts is with a resource manager like Suitcase 2.0

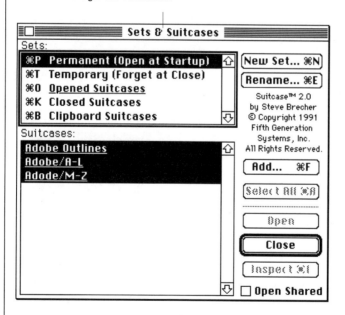

There are several methods used to find a character in a specific font. The Key Caps desk accessory in the Apple menu shows you a virtual keyboard. Press keystrokes to see the characters they produce. What appears in the text box can be copied and pasted into your document. A better system is Günther Blaschek's shareware classic PopChar (see following figure). Click in the upper-right corner of your screen, and the entire set of characters for your current font appears. Choose the one you want; when you release the mouse button, the character is copied to your document.

PopChar is a helpful shareware program that allows you to access all characters in a font set

Fonts, their properties, uses, and handling are a large subject that I don't have space to fully describe here. For more information, read Erfert Fenton's book, *The Macintosh Font Book,* 2nd Ed., 1991, Peachpit Press, Berkeley, CA.

Manipulating text in Works

There are many things you can do to make your document look professional. In this section you will learn how to edit, move, and copy text within a document.

Editing text

If you make a mistake, the following steps allow you to correct them easily without retyping your entire document:

✦ Press Backspace or Delete to remove unwanted characters to the left of the insertion point.

✦ To insert characters into existing text, move the I-beam cursor to the desired position and click to make an insertion bar. Then type the characters you desire.

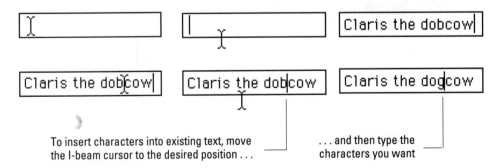

To insert characters into existing text, move the I-beam cursor to the desired position . . .

. . . and then type the characters you want

◆ To remove a word, double-click on that word and just continue typing to replace the highlighted word.

◆ To remove a selection, click at the beginning of that selection, drag the cursor to the end of the selection to highlight it, and release the mouse button. Type the characters you desire and they will replace the highlighted text.

The following instructions show you how to move text around in your document.

Moving text in your document:

1. **Highlight the text you wish to move using any selection method you wish.**

2. **Choose Cut from the Edit menu, or press Command-X.** Works removes the selection and places it on the Clipboard.

3. **Click an insertion point where you wish to place the selection.**

4. **Choose Paste from the Edit menu, or press Command-V, to place the selection at the insertion point.** (Remember, a copy of the text is still held on the Clipboard until you replace it.)

When you copy a selection to another location, you make a copy of a selected passage and move the copy but leave the original in place. The details are summarized below.

Copying text in your document:

1. **Highlight the text you wish to move using any selection method.**

2. **Choose Copy from the Edit menu, or press Command-C.** Works removes the selection and places it on the Clipboard.

3. **Click an insertion point where you wish to place the selection.**

4. **Choose Paste from the Edit menu, or press Command-V, to put a copy of the selection at the insertion point.**

The Undo command provides a graceful recovery from errors or mistakes. Works can undo your last action and will remove entered text or restore replaced text. Always use the Undo command immediately after you discover a mistake, or Works might not be able to recover it for you.

The following instructions show you how to undo mistakes that you have introduced into your document.

Undoing major disasters:

1. **To undo the last action, choose Undo from the Edit menu, or press Command-Z.** Works remembers your typing, up until the point you either execute a menu command or move the insertion point.

2. **If you require a greater level of undo, you can always return to the last saved version of your document. To do this, close your document by choosing Close from the File menu, or press Command-W.**

3. **Works asks you if you wish to save changes. Choose No.**

4. **Choose Open from the File menu, or press Command-O.**

5. **Find your file in the file structure, and open it.** Your file appears as it was last saved.

Saving your work

There really is only one way to save a document, and that's to choose Save from the File menu (Command-S). When you save a document for the first time, the Save file dialog box is posted, you are prompted to name the document (up to 31 characters) and position that file within the hierarchical file structure (HFS).

The steps involved in saving a file are summarized below.

Saving a file:

1. **Choose Save from the File menu, or press Command-S.**

— or —

1. **Alternatively, you can choose Close from the File menu, press Command-W, or click the window's close box.** Works prompts you to save changes:

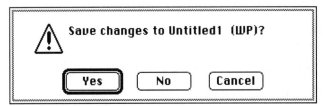

Click the Yes button.

Works saves your changes. If you click the No button, the window closes and your changes aren't saved. Cancel takes you back to your document window.

2. **Locate the position in the file structure you wish the file to be stored to.** If this is the first time the file's been saved, a Save file dialog box appears after you choose Save.

3. **Type the new filename in the text box.** You can press Tab to highlight the text in that box; any text you type will replace what's there.

If the document is untitled, the Save As command (in the File menu) behaves the same way as the Save command. With a previously saved document, the Save As command posts the Save file dialog box and allows you to create a new file. The name of the creator file is suggested for the new name and appears highlighted. Type in the name you wish to give the new document and the highlighted name is replaced. If you try to save the document using the name of the original document, Works posts an alert box, asking you if you wish to replace that document.

For details on creating a new document with a different name than the current document see "Creating a new document from an existing document" earlier in this Topic.

To save a file as a stationery file, choose the Stationery option in the File Format pop-up menu. For more information on working with stationery documents, see "Streamlining with stationery documents" earlier in this Topic.

Allocating memory to Works

Microsoft Works allows you to have as many windows open on the desktop as your memory will allow. You have some control over this limitation; you can change the size of the documents you open and the amount of memory you allocate to Works.

If files grow too large to work with easily, you can simply break them apart into logical pieces and place them in several documents. For example, a word processing file containing a book can be broken into topics, or a database of sales can be separated into years, months, or weekly periods. Doing so is simply good computer practice — smaller files not only require less memory, they also perform faster.

Sometimes it's simply not practical to improve your computer's performance by reorganizing your files. You can improve Works' ability to fit more information into memory, however. Depending on the amount of RAM you have installed on your Macintosh, you can change the memory allocated to Works. The following Step-by-Step section shows you how.

Increasing memory available to Works:

1. **Go to the Finder's window.**

2. **Open the window containing Microsoft Works 3.**

3. **Select the application icon by clicking on it.** The icon becomes highlighted (darkened).

4. **Choose Get Info from the Apple menu.** The Get Info dialog box appears.

```
▤□▤  Microsoft Works 3.0 Info  ▤▤▤

       Microsoft Works 3.0

   Kind: application program
   Size: 1 MB on disk (1,141,248 bytes
         used)
  Where: Das Boot: MS Works:


 Created: Tue, Feb 4, 1992, 7:07 PM
Modified: Thu, Mar 12, 1992, 2:53 AM
 Version: 3.00, Copyright © 1986-1991
          Microsoft Corporation
Comments:



┌─────────────────────────────┐
│                             │
│                             │
└─────────────────────────────┘

             ┌─Memory──────────────
             │ Suggested size: 1,024  K
 ☐ Locked    │ Current size:  1024   K
             └──────────────────────
```

The Works application Get Info box allows you to allocate RAM as needed

5. The dialog box suggests a memory size. Change the number in the Current Size text box, increasing it as required.

6. Close the Get Info dialog box.

Now when you launch Works, it accepts the additional memory allocation. Graphics files are particularly large and allow you fewer opened files at any one time.

You can also decrease the amount of memory allocated to Works if you're using a Mac with limited installed RAM, or if you want to work with other applications that require a large amount of RAM. The Suggested Size (1,024K or 1MB) the Get Info dialog box offers is just that, suggested. If you reduce the Current Size below the Suggested Size, Works continues to function, but you may experience flaky behavior or malfunctions. The lower you set the Current Size below the recommendation, the more problems you experience.

Once you've got more than one window open on your screen, you need to know how to jump between them. Windows are views of a file. Switching between files in the same program leaves that program still active in memory. Switching between windows of files in different programs changes the program that is active in memory. Instructions for two different methods of switching among documents are summarized below.

The following instructions show you how to switch between Works documents.

Switching between Works documents:

1. **If you can see the document's window that you want to switch to on the desktop, click on it to activate it.**

— or —

1. **You can also use the Window menu to select the name of that document and bring it to the front.**

2. **In the Finder, locate the open file's icon and double-click on it to bring it to the front and activate it.**

The following instructions show you how to relate documents in a Workspace.

Relating documents in a Workspace:

1. **Open all the files you wish to use simultaneously.**

2. **Position their windows on your screen as desired.**

3. **Choose Make Workspace from the File menu.** Works posts a Save file dialog box.

4. **Navigate the file structure to save the Workspace file in the desired menu.**

5. **Type the name of your Workspace in the text box.**

6. **Choose OK to save the Workspace file.** Works saves the file and places a Workspace icon in the Finder.

Works'
Workspace icon

Locking a file

You can protect an important file and give it to read-only status by choosing the Locked check box in the Get Info dialog box. When you lock a file, you're able to open that file, view it if it's a document, or use it if it's an application; but no changes can be saved to that file. You can tell that a file is locked because you can't change the name of that file. Click on the name in System 7, and nothing happens. In System 6, you can't drag select any part of the icon's name. Works also alerts you that a file is locked — when you double-click on it, it posts an alert box:

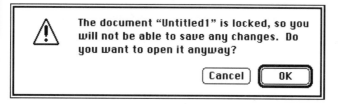

While you can't change a locked file, you can choose Save As from the File menu to create a copy of that file under a new name. When you do that, the read-only status is removed from the new file and you can make any changes you wish.

Locking a file or application provides some modest protection against virus infections, protects your work from changes, prevents accidental deletion in the Trash, and lets you use that document to create other copies. However, it's much more convenient to create template documents as stationery. Stationery doesn't require you to dismiss a dialog box, and it can be previewed inside the New file dialog box. You can save any file as stationery within Works, but you can also create stationery from the Finder. To do so, select the icon for that file from the desktop, choose Get Info, and click the Stationery Pad check box, as shown in the following figure.

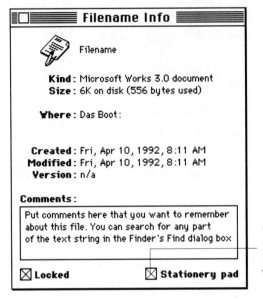

Checking the Stationery pad check box in the Filename Info box creates a stationery file of a word processor document

The Get Info dialog box also has a Comments text box to help you remember information about the file. Anything you type in that text box can be searched for by selecting the Finder's Find command from the More Options section. Although a promised enhancement of System 7 was that Get Info comments would be saved with a document, at this point whenever you rebuild the Desktop, those comments are erased.

Previewing a document

What you see on your screen can look somewhat different from what prints on your page. The accuracy of your screen display depends on the module you're working in and the view you use in that module. To see what a document will look like when it's printed, choose Page Preview from the File menu to examine your pages. When you choose Page Preview, the full page appears reduced in a window. In this window you can use the magnifier cursor to enlarge an area by clicking on the magnifier icon and then clicking on the area you want enlarged. Use the hand cursor to drag your view through the pages, and the Next and Previous buttons to see other pages in your document. The following figure shows you a sample of a document in a Page Preview window.

The Print Preview window allows you to view your document as it will appear when printed

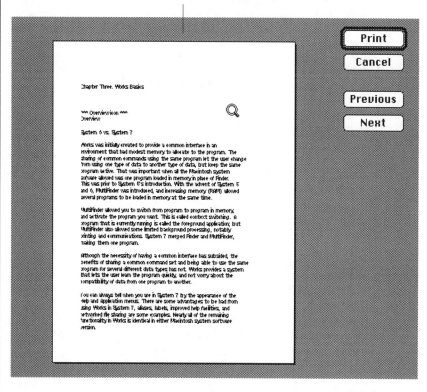

The following instructions show you how to display a preview of your document.

Displaying a preview of your document:

1. **Choose Print Preview from the File menu.** The Print Preview dialog box (see previous figure) appears.

2. **Choose either Previous or Next, as appropriate, to display each page.**

3. **Use the magnifying glass cursor to enlarge the page by clicking where you wish to enlarge.**

4. **Drag the hand cursor about to see other parts of the page.**

5. **Double-click on the page to return to reduced view.**

6. **Click the Print button to execute the Print command directly from the Page Preview mode.** More on printing your document follows in the next section.

— or —

6. **If you don't wish to print, simply close Page Preview by clicking the window's close box.**

Sending a document to the printer

When you choose Print, Works posts a dialog box, and like the Page Setup dialog box, the contents depend on the printer selected. The following figure shows the Print dialog boxes for the StyleWriter, ImageWriter, and LaserWriter printers.

The important printing features offered by these printers are summarized as follows:

✦ *Print Quality.* Changes the manner in which the print mechanism operates, so that quality is diminished when speed is increased. For LaserWriter print, quality is 300 dots per inch (dpi). ImageWriters print at 144 dpi when Best is selected, 78 dpi at the Faster setting, and use the built-in fonts for high speed in draft mode. StyleWriters print at 340 dpi at high resolution and 260 dpi at Faster.

✦ *Copies.* Sets the number of copies of the pages you want printed.

✦ *All, From, To.* Sets the range of the pages in a document to be printed.

✦ *Sheet Feeder, Automatic,* or *Paper Cassette.* Uses mechanical feeder to print cut sheets (loose sheets found in a ream, as opposed to a roll of paper used in a tractor feed mechanism) in StyleWriter or ImageWriter, or lets you print continuous feed paper in the ImageWriter. Uses the paper tray with the LaserWriter.

✦ *Manual, Hand Feed,* or *Manual Feed.* Uses a single sheet of paper and waits for you to insert the next cut sheet.

♦ *Print Merged Fields.* Uses data placeholders in word processor documents, and inserts data from databases to print form letters. See Topic 6 for the section titled "Mail Merging in Works."

♦ *Cover Page.* A LaserWriter option that prints the name of the document, who printed it, and when.

♦ *Black & White* or *Color/Grayscale.* A LaserWriter option that lets you print in black-and-white to a monochrome PostScript printer. Color printing outputs color to a color PostScript printer, while grayscale printing prints graytones for more natural photographic images. Black-and-white printing is much faster than color or grayscale.

♦ *Destination.* Allows you to choose the printer or a PostScript file. Checking printer prints your document, but creating a PostScript file gives you a disk file. PostScript files can be sent to high resolution printers (like Imagesetters) at professional printer services.

When you print a document, a temporary file is created that Works uses to print with. You will be unable to continue working in the program until that print job is sent to the printer, unless you have a system for background printing. Apple system software ships with software for background printing, and you can buy commercial products for this task. These products, called *print spoolers,* queue and manage print jobs. You'll find more information on them later in this Topic. Detailed instructions for printing your document follow below.

Printing your document:

1. **Make sure your printer is turned on and connected, and that it has paper loaded in it.** Your Mac alerts you if it can't find the printer (usually because it's turned off or disconnected), or if it's out of paper.

2. **Choose Print from the File menu to open the Print dialog box.**

3. **Choose the print options you desire: number of copies, pages to print, special effects, and others.**

4. **Click OK to send your print job, or click the Cancel button to dismiss the dialog box without creating a print job.**

Using a print spooler

Tying up your Mac when you're printing files is a major inconvenience. Some printers, like StyleWriters, ImageWriters, DeskWriters, and others, use your Mac to drive the print engine. They also use the Mac's language to form graphic images to create their printed page. These printers don't have a CPU to process data, and they don't often come with much memory to store processed images. By comparison, LaserWriters have between 2MB and 8MB of RAM, and they ship with 68020 or 68030 processors. In other words, LaserWriters are computers in their own right, and your Macintosh can off-load printing jobs to a LaserWriter without performance suffering.

When you have multiple print jobs and you're using a LaserWriter, your Mac can write some temporary print files and let special system software take care of sending them to the printer. This is called *background printing,* because it happens in the background as you continue working in the foreground. This software is called Backgrounder in System 6, and it communicates with a program called the Print Monitor, which manages a queue of print jobs. A print queue manager is referred to as a *print spooler,* and the temporary files it operates on are called *spool files.* In System 7, Backgrounder and Print Monitor were merged into a single program.

When you spool a print job on your Mac, the disk file is created quickly because it doesn't have to wait for the printer, and your Mac is returned to you for further work. You turn background printing on as an option in the Page Setup dialog box. If you want to change the order of jobs in the print queue, you can choose Print Monitor from the Application menu to either cancel a print job or move it around in the queue.

I've found the Print Monitor to be fairly buggy software with limited utility. The other major problem is that Apple's print spooler only operates on LaserWriters. One very valuable piece of application software is Fifth Generations' SuperLaserSpool, just recently updated for System 7. With SuperLaserSpool, you can print to any Macintosh-compatible printer, manage the print queue, and preview the print job — even on a Mac with only 1MB of RAM. If you print often to a dedicated printer, you should have this software.

You can monitor and preview your print job using SuperLaser Spool's Laser Queue print spool manager

Quick Tips

The following tips show you how to get help from the three help systems available in Works, as well as additional third-party resources available for learning Works.

Getting help in Works

Works has three different systems installed for on-line help: Balloon Help, Works 3 Shortcuts, and the Works 3 Help System. The first two kinds of help were discussed in Topic 2, and they operate the same way in Works as they do in the Finder. The third is discussed here in this section.

The Works Help System is a special facility that contains hypertextual features, meaning that words are linked to their definitions and to other related topics. The Works Help System is also contextual, that is, what you see in the window on your display depends on what you've selected in Works. For each separate tool you use in Works, you see an individual set of topics in the table of contents. Switch to another tool and a different set of topics appears.

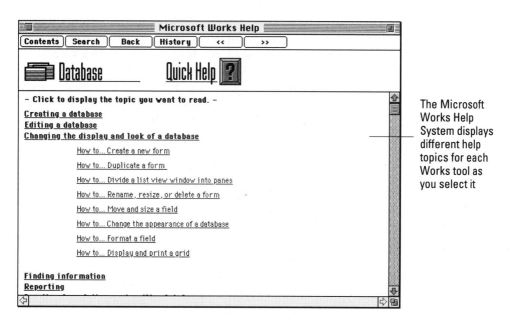

The Microsoft Works Help System displays different help topics for each Works tool as you select it

The important features of the Microsoft Works Help System are summarized below:

♦ *Contents button.* Press this button to display the index for the Help information available for the currently selected tool.

♦ *Search button.* This button opens a dialog box that lets you enter a text string you wish to find. Enter all or part of the word(s) of interest.

♦ *Back button.* Sends you back sequentially through your previously viewed screens.

♦ *History button.* Lets you return to previously viewed pages.

- *Double Arrow buttons.* Left-facing double arrows (called *chevrons*) sends you back one information page in the Help System. Right-facing double arrows advance you forward one page in the Help System.

- *Tool icon.* Click a tool icon to return to the table of contents for that tool.

- *More... button.* Click this button to show additional information on a subject.

- *Underlined text.* Topics that are underlined in the explanation move you to a linked topic when you click on them. This text is green on a color monitor.

- *Dotted Underlined text.* This indicates the term is a defined term. Select it to display its definition. This text is green on a color monitor.

Works' Help System uses a fully constructed window. In System 7, you open the Help System on your screen by choosing the Works 3 Help command from the Help menu. In System 6, you choose Open from the File menu (Command-O) to open the Help file. The Help file is found inside the Tools folder in Works.

Close the Help System by clicking the window's close box. The window scrolls and resizes, just like any other Works window. If you're just learning the program, it can be convenient to leave the Help System window open on your screen. When you change tools, activate the Help System window as it's updated with new information. You can activate the window by either choosing it from the Window menu, choosing the Microsoft Works 3 Help command, or clicking on the Microsoft Works Help window on your display. This kind of help is found only in Microsoft products, and Works is the first program to have it. Plans to incorporate this system into other Microsoft products over time are in the proverbial works.

The Works help options that are supported by System 7 are summarized below:

- To show Balloon Help, choose Show Balloons from the Help menu. Move the cursor over different window elements and commands to display the information available.

- To turn off Balloon Help, choose Hide Balloons from the Help menu.

- To see Works 3 Shortcuts, choose Works 3 Shortcuts from the Help menu.

- Close Works 3 Shortcuts by clicking the window's Close box.

- To access the Works Help System, choose Works 3 Help System from the Help menu.

Works also has an on-line interactive tutorial system. The "Take a few lessons" section in the *Getting Started* brochure that comes with the Works package documentation describes this tutorial fully.

Finding other Works resources

There are several other sources for information on Works training and information that might be of interest to you. You can get a set of on-line tutorials on Works from Heizer Software in Pleasant Hill, CA (800-888-7667 or 510-943-7667). Heizer puts out publications such as *Guided Tour of Works* ($15) for new users, *Word Processing Tour* ($9), *Database Tutorial* ($12), *Financial Function Tutorial* ($12), and *Integrating Works* ($10).

The Heizer catalog also offers the 12-page, monthly newsletter *Inside Microsoft Works* ($39), written by the highly regarded Cobb Group. These newsletters give tips, tricks, and techniques, letting you improve your mastery of the program.

If you want to listen to a Works tutorial on cassette tape, you might check out *Personal Training for Works*, four cassette packages at $99 each. Personal Training System in San Jose, CA, can be reached at 800-832-2499 or 408-286-1635. The MacAcademy Video Training Series Microsoft Works tape ($49) is a two-hour training session, available from MacAcademy in Ormond Beach, FL, at 904-677-1918.

Summary

- Works 3 comes with an installer program, System 7 support, enhanced draw and communication modules, a help system, a better interface, and numerous other improvements.
- You can use Works 3 equally well on System 6 or System 7.
- Works produces five different document types that each have characteristic windows. The document types are the word processor, database, spreadsheet, draw, and communication documents.
- Print by selecting the desired printer in the Chooser desk accessory. Make selections in the Page Setup dialog box, followed by selections in the Print dialog box.
- Create new files using the New command from the File menu; open previously saved files using the Open command, and others from the File menu.
- Stationery are files or documents that open as a new, duplicate untitled copy.
- To improve Works' performance, change the amount of memory (RAM) allocated to it.
- Use the Print Preview command to see what a print job will look like, then use the Print command (both are on the File menu) to print your file.
- A print spooler can queue up print jobs and free your computer for other work.
- Use the Works Help System available from the Help menu to get information or instructions on a topic.
- The Keyboard Shortcuts command displays a dialog box with keystroke equivalents of commands and actions.

Part II:
Using Works' Tools

Topic 4
Processing Your Words

Overview

Word processors are the most heavily used computer application today, and for good reason. A word processor frees you from the drudgery of having to retype a document if you make an error and it lets you think about your writing in new ways. You can organize your document beforehand, use powerful automated tools to correct and enhance your writing, and then change your writing as you work — all almost effortlessly.

Writing with a word processor fulfills the promise of the personal computer, and if you do any kind of writing at all, that's enough reason to justify the purchase of your own personal computer. How odd to think that the first word processors written for computers were viewed as wasteful extravagances for programmers. But then, there was a time when experts thought that the world would need only six computers, and look how many there are now.

When you sit down to use Works' Word Processor module, you're using the better elements of Microsoft's powerhouse word processing program, Word. Over the years, Microsoft has distilled the most widely used and appreciated parts of Word into Works. Early versions of Works' word processor were, in fact, precursors to Microsoft Word.

Today it's believed that the word processor in Works may be the second most commonly used word processor on the Apple Macintosh. The interface of this module is clean, highly functional, logical, and much improved over the 2.0 version. Works' word processor may well be the only one you'll ever need.

Using the word processor window

A word processor window contains most of the features of the Finder window which was discussed in Topic 2. When you open a word processor document, you see a window like the one shown in the following figure. If the document has been previously saved, then the filename appears with (WP) following it in the title bar. New, unsaved documents are assigned the name "Untitled1 (WP)," with the number in the title indicating the number of previously untitled documents opened in a session.

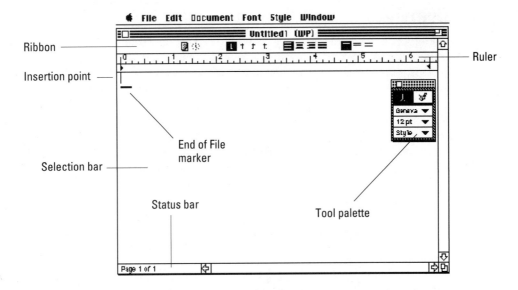

Most noticeable in the word processor window is a ribbon, a ruler, a floating tool palette, a selection bar, a status bar, an insertion point, and an end-of-file marker. The functions these elements perform are summarized below:

✦ *Ribbon.* This strip includes a set of icons that can change the setup of your document. Three-dimensional looking buttons let you enter data for the current day or time, set four different kinds of tabs, and choose from four kinds of line justification and three kinds of line spacing. Current tab, justification, and line spacing settings are indicated by highlighting the appropriate button. Remember, the format of the date and time — entered by clicking the ribbon icons — is determined by your settings in the Alarm Clock desk accessory or the General Controls control panel time section.

✦ *Ruler.* The Ruler lets you manually set margins, change indents, and set tabs. You can dismiss the ruler to see more of the word processor window by choosing Hide Ruler from the Window menu, or by pressing Command-R. To return the Ruler to the screen, choose Show Ruler from the Window menu, or press Command-R again.

◆ *Selection bar.* You can't see the selection bar, per se, but you can tell where it is by moving the cursor to the left side of the window. When you're in the selection bar, the cursor changes from an I-beam to an arrow. The selection bar lets you select entire lines and paragraphs quickly by clicking and dragging.

◆ *Insertion Point.* The flashing horizontal insertion point marks the place where text is entered when you type. It automatically appears at the beginning of the file when you create a new document. As you type, characters are entered to the left of the insertion point. Move the insertion point by moving the I-beam cursor to the desired location and clicking. The insertion point jumps to the new location. What you type then appears to the left of that location. Using the insertion point is discussed in Topic 3 in the section "Editing text."

◆ *Status bar.* This bar tells you the current position of the insertion point, the number of pages in your document, and the page number you're currently working on.

◆ *End of File Marker.* This horizontal bar indicates the position of the last character in your document. As you type, this bar moves down, always appearing at the bottom left-hand edge near the margin.

◆ *Tool Palette.* The Tool Palette lets you switch between text and draw modes when you select the Text Layer tool (an I-beam cursor icon) or Draw Layer tool (a pencil icon), respectively. Three pop-up menus appear in the palette which duplicate menus found at the top of the screen.

Note: Works considers the Ribbon and the Ruler to be one entity. When you hide the ruler, the ribbon also disappears. They both reappear when you show the ruler.

Adjusting the insertion point

You can adjust the speed at which the insertion point flashes. To do this, choose Control Panel from the Apple menu and look for the Rate of Insertion Point Blinking option. When you select a speed, a sample insertion point demonstrates what your selection looks like. Closing the Control Panel window enters your choice.

You have some control over the appearance of the word processor window. Using the Preference command in the Edit menu, you can change the default font and font size, and the format of footnotes when you select the word processor icon. For further information about footnotes, see "Working with footnotes," later in this Topic. As discussed in Topic 3, you can choose to have your windows open up with or without the ruler showing and choose either inches or centimeters by setting defaults in the All Types (every module) mode. You can also set the format of the date and time in the All Types dialog box.

The Word Processor Preferences dialog box allows you
to choose default settings for font style and size, and
footnote formatting in your word processing documents

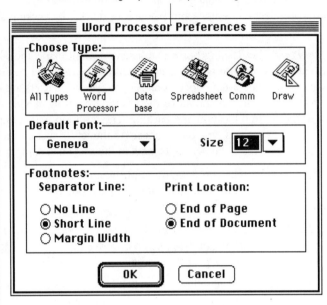

Font, Size, and Style menus are accessed from the Tool palette. The latter two pop-up menus are consolidated at the top of your screen in the Style menu. Click on these palette menus and select your choice by dragging and releasing. Any text selected in the window changes as does your subsequently typed text.

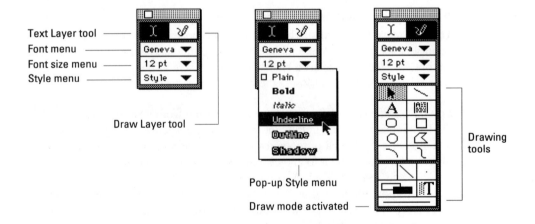

You can remove the Tool palette from the screen by selecting Hide Tools or by pressing Command-T. You can also close the Tool palette by clicking the close box in the title bar. With the Tool palette hidden, Command-T changes to Show Tools on the menu. You can bring the palette back by choosing Show Tools or by pressing Command-T again.

Note: Although there's no title in the palette, you click and drag the title bar to move it, just as you would any other window.

The word processor window has two, separate layers on your screen — what you see is actually a combination of both layers. The Text layer is active when you first open the window and any time the Text Layer tool is selected. Only text can be typed or pasted into the Text layer. Floating above the Text layer is the Draw layer. To activate the Draw layer, choose the Draw Layer tool from the Tool palette, or choose Draw On (Command-J) from the Windows menu. When you do that, the Tool palette changes to show the drawing tools available. You can't change the Text layer at this point. One drawing tool in the Draw palette, though, is a Text tool (the letter A icon), so it's possible to enter either graphics or simple text into the Draw layer.

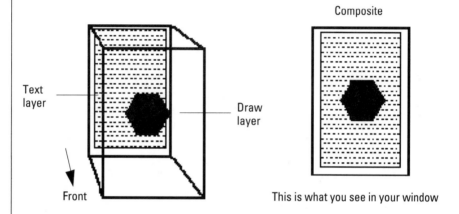

Composite

Text layer

Draw layer

Front

This is what you see in your window

In Works version 2.0, you specifically had to turn on the Draw module in your word processor by choosing Draw On from the Edit menu (Command-J). Few people could find that feature there, so in version 3.0 the Draw palette appears on your screen automatically. When you paste graphics into word processor documents, Works activates the Draw layer for you and places the graphic there. For now, though, don't be confused by Draw. When you find an expanded Tool palette on your screen and you just want to use the word processor, turn off Draw by either choosing the Text Layer tool, choosing Draw Off from the Windows menu, or by pressing Command-J. If you quit Works with the Tools palette hidden, Works opens subsequent documents with the Tool palette hidden from your screen. Choose Show Tools or press Command-T to put the palette back.

I'll have much more to say about the Draw tools in the next Topic. The uses of each tool are defined, and you learn how to use Draw with your word processor to do complex tasks, such as page layout and desktop publishing. Because Draw now supports its own document type, you might want to use a draw document in place of a word processor document if you know that you won't use the Text layer and only use graphics. Not only is this less confusing, but Draw also has some additional interface features, such as a vertical ruler, that helps you align objects. A notable feature in Draw is linked text columns. You can create text columns in the Draw layer above a word processor or in a Draw document, with no difference in function.

Entering text

When you create a word processor document, Works opens an empty window. Typing enters text to the left of the insertion point. By moving the insertion point to another location, you can enter text at that position again, to the left of the insertion point. Move the I-beam to the location you desire and place an insertion point there by clicking. Your cursor disappears as you enter text. Don't worry — this is a standard Macintosh feature that makes it easier to see what you are doing. When you move the mouse slightly, your cursor returns.

When you get to the end of a line, just continue to type. Works *wordwraps,* or drops any word that doesn't fit on that line down to the next line. This feature allows you to change the margins of a document without going through a document line by line to move or delete the end-of-line carriage returns when editing. This might seem odd to you if you've previously typed on a typewriter. Word processors use the Return key only to mark the end of a paragraph, and you should press Return twice after a paragraph to create a blank line between paragraphs. Another difference between a word processor and a typewriter is that it's common practice in word processing to type only one space after a sentence period.

It's important to understand that every character you enter from the keyboard is written to your disk file when you save a document. This includes the alphanumerical characters that you see printed out as well as many special invisible characters or codes that give your computer information about the way the document should look. For example, the space characters and the end-of-paragraph characters that are entered when you press the spacebar and the Enter or Return keys, respectively, are there, even though you can't see them on the screen.

Works has no feature to show you these hidden characters, which is too bad. Once you understand them, they help you to visualize the construction of your document and figure out what's wrong if your document looks odd. Unfortunately, these codes are considered to be an advanced feature and distracting to beginners, so they are left out. You can make these codes visible in other word processor applications, such as Word, MacWrite, and WordPerfect.

Searching for text

One of the great benefits of using a word processor is its ability to search for and find characters and strings of text of any length. This feature can help you organize your document and correct mistakes quickly. To find characters or a string of text, Choose Find from the Edit menu (Command-F) which opens the Find dialog box.

Type the characters you wish to search for the Find What text box. When you use Find during a work session, Works remembers the characters you last searched for so that you can find their next occurrence quickly. Simply open the Find dialog box and select Find Next. Or to bypass this dialog box, choose Find Again directly from the Edit menu, or press Command-G, and your computer finds the next occurrence.

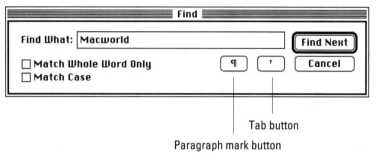

Tab button

Paragraph mark button

The important elements of the Find dialog box are summarized below:

◆ *Find What text box.* Enter the text string you want your computer to find here.

◆ *Paragraph mark button.* Select this button to enter a paragraph mark (¶) into the text box as a search symbol for this hidden character.

◆ *Tab mark button.* Select this button to enter a tab mark into the text box as a search symbol for this hidden character.

◆ *Match Whole Word Only check box.* This option searches for your text string with a space character before and after it.

◆ *Match Case check box.* Normally, Works searches for characters without paying attention to capitalization. This option narrows your search to exact upper- or lowercase character matches.

◆ *Find Next button.* Press this button, or press Return or Enter, to jump to the next match.

◆ *Cancel button.* Press this button or Command-period to dismiss the dialog box. Works leaves your insertion point or current selection where it was before you selected Find.

When Works finds a character match, that text is highlighted on your screen. If there are no matches in the document, an alert box is posted informing you of this. In searching for text strings, Works starts from the position of the insertion point and runs through to the end of your document. If during a search you reach the end of the document, Works displays a dialog box giving you the option to search from the beginning. The following section gives you details on how to use your computer to search for text in a word processor document.

Finding and replacing text:

1. **Choose Find from the Edit menu, or press Command-F.**

2. **Enter the character string you want to find in the Find What text box in the Find dialog box (see previous figure).**

3. **Click the Tab or Paragraph buttons to include those characters in your search string.**

4. **Click check boxes for Match Whole Words Only or Match case if appropriate.** The more precise your search parameters, the faster and more accurate your search will be.

5. **Click Find Next to initiate the search.**

6. **To repeat a search without opening the Find dialog box, choose Find Again from the Edit menu, or press Command-F.**

Selecting text in Works

Selecting text allows you to change aspects of your document quickly and easily. Selected text can be moved, formatted, resized, or deleted all at once. Learn a few simple tricks to select text and you can save yourself many hours of frustrating work.

Advanced techniques for selecting text:

1. **Click at the beginning of the text you want to select.**

2. **Press and hold down the Shift key.**

3. **Click at the end of the text you want to select.**

4. **Release the Shift key.**

5. **If you want to extend or reduce a selected range of text, press Shift.**

6. **Click at the new beginning or end of the range of text you desire and release the Shift key.** Works expands or reduces the selection to include all of the text in between.

You can also select the entire document quickly and easily by choosing Select All from the Edit menu, or by pressing Command-A. Selections are, of course, highlighted on your screen with the color you've chosen from the Color Control Panel. To deselect a block of text, click anywhere in your document.

Works offers some shortcuts for selecting text in a word processor. The following section summarizes them:

✦ To select a single word, double-click on that word. Works selects the word and the space in front of that word.

✦ To select a line, move the I-beam cursor to the left of that line into the selection bar until it becomes an arrow cursor. Then click once to select the line.

- ◆ To select several lines, move the arrow cursor into the selection bar and drag the pointer up or down to select the lines you want.

- ◆ To select a paragraph, use the arrow cursor in the selection bar, and double-click anywhere next to that paragraph.

The following section details steps for quickly replacing a selection.

Replacing a selection:

1. Select the text you want to replace.

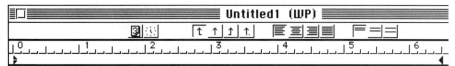

2.   To select a line: move the I-Beam cursor to the left of that line into the Selection bar, until it becomes an Arrow cursor. Then click once to select that line.

3.   To select several lines: use the Arrow cursor in the Selection bar, then drag the pointer up or down to select the lines you want.

Moving the mouse cursor to the far left of a document allows you to select whole sections of text at a time

2. Type the new text. Your selection disappears with your first keystroke, replaced by the newly entered text. This is much more convenient than re-peatedly using Backspace or Delete.

3. Alternatively, choose Paste from the Edit menu (Command-V) to replace your selection with whatever is on the Clipboard.

Replacing a text string automatically

Often, you not only want to find a text string, but also replace it with another string. You might want to eliminate a frequently made misspelling or change a figure that appears throughout a document, for example. Works provides a shortcut for making repetitive finds and substitutions in the Replace command, found in the Edit menu (Command-R). The Replace dialog box, shown in the following figure, is similar to a Find dialog box, but with the additional features summarized below:

- ◆ *Replace With text box.* Type in your replacement text, just as you would in the Find What text box. The paragraph and tab buttons are used to enter appropriate codes here as they are in the Find dialog box.

- ◆ *Replace button.* Once a text string has been found, select Replace to replace the current highlighted match with your replacement text. Use this button in combination with the Find Next button to examine each match before replacing it.

✦ *Replace All button*. Select this button to automatically replace every match with its substitution. Upon completion, Works alerts you to the number of substitutions that have been made.

The Replace dialog box allows you to search for one text
string and replace it with another throughout your document

Replace		
Find What: MacUser		Find Next
Replace With: Macworld		Replace
☐ Match Whole Word Only	¶ '	Replace All
☐ Match Case		Cancel

Be careful when searching and replacing text. Computers are stupid — they can only do exactly what you tell them to and can't infer what you meant to tell them. If you type in *real* as a search criterion, Works replaces not only the word *real* with your replacement text, but also the words *realty, surrealistic,* and any other *real* string. You could replace *real* with *unreal* and get unexpected results.

Formatting text

Formatting includes any attributes you apply to the contents of your document. There are two main types of formatting: character and page formatting. Character formatting includes any changes you can make to *individual* characters like fonts, font size, style. Paragraph formatting applies to all characters in a paragraph and includes alignment, line spacing, margin and tab settings. Only one set of paragraph formats can be applied. A paragraph is defined as all the characters between two Return characters.

Works stores all formatting information for a paragraph within the end-of-paragraph mark that you type when you press Return. Settings for overall font, size, style, alignment, or line spacing are all stored in that paragraph mark. If the paragraph has a different font, size, or style, then the beginning and end characters for that exception are also stored in the end mark.

Use the Font or Style menus to format text. Or use the shortcuts for their menu commands in the Tool palette, the Ribbon, or the Ruler. Any font available within your Macintosh system appears as an option in these menus. (For more information about fonts, see "Working with fonts" in the previous Topic.)

Font sizes installed on your computer appear as outlined numbers in the Style menu. To make menu choices for fonts, you can either open the Font menu or the top pop-up menu on the Tool palette. The current font selection appears check-marked in the Font and Style menu, and has a dot next to it in the top pop-up menu of the Tool palette. There are a wide range of font styles you can choose from, including Plain, Bold (Command-B), Underline (Command-U), Italics (Command-I), Outline, and Shadow.

Any text formatting you do affects all of the subsequent text you enter until you manually change the insertion point location or make new formatting choices. If you've highlighted text, then your formatting is applied to that text only.

The following instructions summarize methods for changing the font:

+ Choose a font and font size from the Font menu.

+ Choose the font from the top pop-up menu on the Tool palette.

+ Select Format Character from the Format menu. Then make a selection within the dialog box on the pop-up Font menu.

While you can only apply one color or size to text and make text either normal, super- or subscripted, you can apply multiple character styles. A character can be bold, italic, outlined, underlined, and shadowed. (That character would be truly ugly, but you could create it if you wanted to.) To remove all character styles at once, highlight the appropriate text and choose Plain. If you want to remove styles one attribute at a time, highlight the appropriate text and select that style again individually.

The various methods for applying a style to a font are summarized below:

+ Choose style options from the Style menu. You can make as many style selections as you wish.

+ Make selection(s) from the bottom pop-up menu on the Tool palette.

+ Choose Format Character from the Format menu then make your selection within the dialog box on the pop-up Font menu.

+ Remove styles one at a time by selecting them again (they act like a toggle switch) or by choosing the Plain style.

Note: The Format Character dialog box is the only method available for applying color to text, or creating super- or subscripts.

Topic 4
Processing Your Words

```
┌─────────────────────────┐
│ Style                   │
├─────────────────────────┤
│ ✓Plain                  │
│  Bold              ⌘B   │
│  Italic            ⌘I   │
│  Underline         ⌘U   │
│  Outline                │
│  Shadow                 │
│ ┄┄┄┄┄┄┄┄┄┄┄┄┄┄┄┄┄┄┄┄┄┄ │
│  Alignment          ▶   │
│  Spacing            ▶   │
│ ┄┄┄┄┄┄┄┄┄┄┄┄┄┄┄┄┄┄┄┄┄┄ │
│  9                      │
│  10                     │
│ ✓12                     │
│  14                     │
│  18                     │
│  Increase Size     ⌘]   │
│  Decrease Size     ⌘[   │
│  Format Character...    │
└─────────────────────────┘
```

The Style menu for a word processor document displays font styles and sizes available on your Macintosh

Font sizes and styles are chosen from the Style menu or from the middle and bottom pop-up menus on the Tool palette, respectively. Current selections are check-marked to the left of their commands and have a dot next to them on the pop-up menus. To increase the font size by one installed increment, you can choose Increase Font Size from the Style menu, or press Command-]. Choose Decrease Font Size or press Command-[to decrease your selection by one installed font size. Remember these keystrokes by thinking of them as the equivalents of the greater-than and less-than symbols they resemble, with the greater-than bracket increasing the selection and the less-than bracket decreasing it. The various methods for changing a font size are summarized below:

◆ Choose a size from the Style menu.

◆ Choose a size from the middle pop-up menu on the Tool palette.

◆ Choose Format Character from the Format menu then make your selection within the dialog box on the pop-up Font menu or enter the size in the Text box.

◆ Increase the size of the font by choosing Increase Font from the Style menu, or by pressing Command-].

◆ Decrease the size of the font by choosing Decrease Font from the Style menu, or by pressing Command-[.

Works offers a command that allows you to set multiple text formatting characteristics all at once. Choose Format Characters from the Style menu to open the Format Characters dialog box for this purpose. (Unfortunately, there's no keystroke for this menu command — you might want to create one using a third-party macro program. The Works macro recorder doesn't let you assign keystrokes to menu commands, only to sequences of actions, so it's not appropriate for this purpose.)

The Format Character dialog box is the ideal place to change several text attributes at once, and it's the only place to change the text color or create super- or subscripts. When these attributes are selected in the Format Character dialog box, the choices are also check-marked on the Style menu.

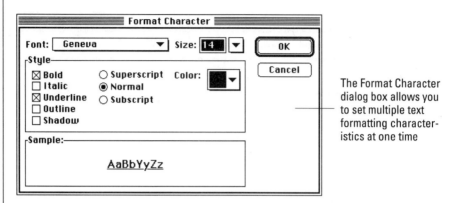

The Format Character dialog box allows you to set multiple text formatting character-istics at one time

The elements of the Format Characters dialog box are summarized below:

◆ *Font menu.* Choose the font you want from the pop-up menu.

◆ *Size menu.* Choose the font size you want from the pop-up menu, or type the size into the text box.

◆ *Style check boxes.* Choose as many of the style choices as you desire.

◆ *Case radio button.* Choose either normal, subscript, or superscript.

◆ *Color pop-up menu.* The color palette you're offered depends on the number of colors you can display on your monitor. Change this number in the Monitor Control Panel.

◆ *Sample box.* The text displayed in this box shows the effect your formatting choices have on text.

Formatting paragraphs

Just like characters, each paragraph has a set of formatting attributes. Format attributes associated with paragraphs include tab settings, line justification, line spacing, and right, left, and first-line indents. The default settings for paragraphs are left-aligned tabs, left-aligned justification (called *ragged right*), and single-spaced text. You can assign each paragraph its own individual settings. For character-based formatting, such as fonts and sizes, you have to highlight the paragraph to change its formatting. For paragraph-based formatting, such as alignment or line spacing, select any part of that paragraph, including a simple insertion point.

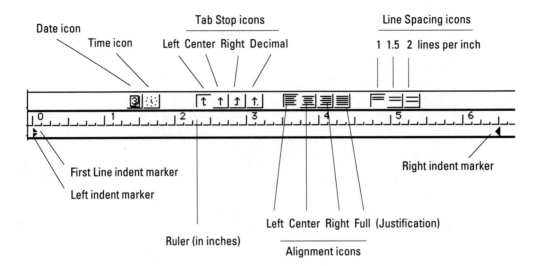

Date icon
Time icon
Tab Stop icons
Left Center Right Decimal
Line Spacing icons
1 1.5 2 lines per inch
First Line indent marker
Left indent marker
Right indent marker
Left Center Right Full (Justification)
Ruler (in inches)
Alignment icons

Setting tabs

Documents are created with preset tab settings. If you set no stops of your own, every time you press Tab, your text moves a half-inch if your ruler uses inches, or one centimeter if the ruler measures in centimeters. When you set a tab stop, it overrides the default tab setting, every default tab stop to the left of your new tab setting disappears, and only default tab stops to the right of your setting remain.

There are four types of tab stops: left, right, center, and decimal aligned. Each of these kinds of tab stops is shown in the following figure. Left tabs align text so that the first character after the tab appears to the left of the tab setting. Right tabs align text so that the last character of a text string appears to the left of the setting. Center tabs center the text after a tab character.

Note: With a decimal tab stop until you type a decimal point, any text you type center aligns around the tab stop.

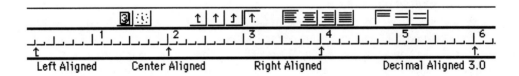

Left Aligned   Center Aligned   Right Aligned   Decimal Aligned 3.0

To place tab settings in a paragraph, you select the kind of tab you want by clicking on the tab icon in the ruler, then clicking on the location on the ruler you want the tab stop to appear. Tabs can be set with as little as 1/16 inch or 2 millimeters between them. There are no menu commands for working with tab settings. To set a tab stop, drag a tab to a new location on the ruler. Tabs are removed by dragging them off the ruler, and tabs are changed from one type to another by clicking on the tab stop until the desired type appears. The tabs you set in a paragraph are retained in all subsequent paragraphs you create, until you change them. Tab settings are the best and most convenient way of working with tables. See "Working with tables" later in this Topic.

Selecting line spacing options

You can change a document's line spacing either by choosing one of the four commands from the Spacing submenu on the Style menu, or by selecting the corresponding icon from the ruler. There are menu choices for single spacing, one-and-one-half spacing, double spacing, and six-lines-per-inch spacing. Icons for the first three of these choices appear on the ruler. Use single space for normal correspondence and text. One-and-one-half and double spacing are commonly used to leave space for editing text or for a looser appearance to text. The six-lines-per-inch setting is a special setting that lets you insert text on forms created for typewriters. It looks the same as single spacing on your screen, but prints at the typewriter size. The following section summarizes how to change your line spacing:

Changing the line spacing:

1. **Select the paragraphs you wish to respace.**

2. **Choose Spacing from the Style menu and choose the desired spacing.**
   The six lines per inch spacing used with commercial forms can only be chosen from the Spacing submenu.

— or —

2. **Choose one of the spacing icons from the ruler.**

<u>Single line spacing</u>
Changing line spacing can be accomplished either by choosing one of the four commands on the Spacing submenu on the Style menu, or by clicking the corresponding icon on the ruler. There are menu choices for single, 1 1/2, double, and six-lines-per-inch spacing.

<u>1 1/2 line spacing</u>

Changing line spacing can be accomplished either by choosing one of the four commands on the Spacing

submenu on the Style menu, or by clicking the corresponding icon on the ruler. There are menu choices

for single, 1 1/2, double, and six-lines per-inch spacing.

<u>Double line spacing</u>

Changing line spacing can be accomplished either by choosing one of the four commands on the Spacing

submenu on the Style menu, or by clicking the corresponding icon on the ruler. There are menu choices

for single, 1 1/2, double, and six-lines-per-inch spacing.

<u>6 Lines per inch spacing</u>
Changing line spacing can be accomplished either by choosing one of the four commands on the Spacing submenu on the Style menu, or by clicking the corresponding icon on the ruler. There are menu choices for single, 1 1/2, double, and six-lines-per-inch spacing.

Selecting text alignment

You can choose the alignment of text in paragraphs, commonly referred to as *justification*. Works offers you the options of left, right, center, and fully justified text alignment. Left justified text is also called *ragged right,* while right justified text is called *ragged left.* (The term *ragged* refers to the variable line endings on the indicated side of the paragraph.) Center-justified text has both ragged left and right line endings. Fully justified paragraphs are aligned along both the right and left sides, using variable spacing between words.

Left aligned
You can align text in a paragraph, commonly referred to as justification. Works offers: left, right, center, and fully justified text alignment. Left justified is also called ragged right, while right justified is called ragged left. This indicates the variable line endings on that side of the paragraph.

Center aligned
You can align text in a paragraph, commonly referred to as justification. Work offers: left, right, center, and fully justified text alignment. Left justified is also called ragged right, while right justified is called ragged left. This indicates the variable line endings on that side of the paragraph.

Right aligned
You can align text in a paragraph, commonly referred to as justification. Works offers: left, right, center, and fully justified text alignment. Left justified is also called ragged right, while right justified is called ragged left. This indicates the variable line endings on that side of the paragraph.

Fully aligned
You can align text in a paragraph, commonly refered to as justification. Works offers: left, right, center, and fully justified text alignment. Left justified is also called ragged right, while right justified is called ragged left. This indicates the variable line endings on that side of the paragraph.

When using fully justified text, certain words may have an unusually large amount of space between them. You can eliminate extra spacing in fully justified text by typing a Return character — Works uses the default spacing to separate words. There's no right or wrong use of justification. It's a stylistic decision you make depending on how you want your document to look. You can choose the alignment settings from the Alignment submenu of the Style menu, or you can choose the appropriate icon from the ruler.

Aligning paragraphs:

1. Select the paragraphs you wish to align.

2. Choose the desired alignment — left, right, center, or fully justified — from the Alignment submenu of the Style menu.

— or —

2. Choose one of the alignment icons from the ruler.

Placing indent markers

Even though your document can have only one set of margins, your paragraphs can vary in width and in where they start and end. You change these paragraph formats using the *indent markers* on the ruler. An indent is measured as the distance between a margin to the text; Works allows you three different kinds of indent settings: a left, right, and first-line indent. You move the indent markers by dragging the appropriate icon to the desired spot on the ruler. As you move an indent marker, a vertical line appears and moves with the indent marker, and the status bar at the bottom left-hand corner of the window indicates the indent position along the ruler. This measurement helps you align text and place the indents exactly where you want them. Using indents is a great way to add emphasis and flair to your documents, and when coupled with tab settings, make many special effects possible.

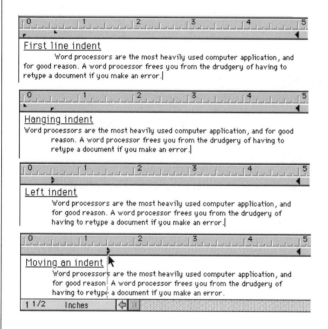

The instructions for indenting paragraph(s) are detailed in the following section.

Indenting paragraphs:

1. **Highlight the paragraph(s) you want to indent.**

2. **To indent the first line only, drag the first-line-indent marker (the upper triangle on the left side of the ruler) to the desired location.** As you move an indent marker, a horizontal line appears, and the status bar shows the measurement for the current position.

— or —

2. **To indent all lines, drag the left or right indent marker to the position you desire.**

— or —

2. To create a *hanging indent* — a paragraph with the second and subsequent lines indented further than the first — press Shift and drag the left indent marker to the desired location without moving the first-line indent marker.

3. To remove indents, drag the markers back to the margins. Press Shift and hold while dragging the left indent.

Copying format settings

Complex paragraph formatting is tedious, especially when you need to apply formatting repetitively in several different places in a document. Once you've formatted a paragraph the way you want it, choose Copy Ruler Settings from the Document menu, or press Command-K, to apply those settings elsewhere. Then select the paragraph(s) to be changed and choose Paste Ruler Settings, or press Command-Y, to change the highlighted paragraphs.

A paragraph's ruler settings can be copied to another paragraph. The instructions are detailed in the following section.

Copying paragraph settings:

1. Select the paragraph with the desired formatting.

2. Choose Copy Ruler Settings from the Document menu, or press Command-K.

3. Select the paragraph(s) you want to reformat.

4. Choose Paste Ruler Settings from the Document menu, or press Command-Y.

Note: The Copy Ruler Settings command doesn't replace what appears on the Clipboard and won't work between word processor documents.

Formatting a document

The formatting options that apply to an entire document are found in several different places. The size and orientation of a page is set within the Page Setup dialog box. Page margins are changed within the Document dialog box. You'll remember from Topic 3 that choosing Document in the Page Setup dialog box opens the Document dialog box.

On your screen the size of your document is defined by the margin settings. The ruler provides a visual clue as to the relative size of your page margins but not their absolute placement. If you set a 2-inch left margin, then the ruler's zero setting refers to the location on the page 2 inches from the left edge. A right margin indicator appears as a dotted vertical line in the ruler, but it's hidden by the right indent marker (a left-facing triangle) until the marker is moved by dragging it.

As your document grows, Works automatically places page break markers to show you where a new page begins. The process of measuring text and assigning it page numbers is called *automatic pagination,* and it's a feature found in any word processor application. Pagination occurs whenever you stop typing for a few seconds, but you force pagination whenever you save or print preview your document. An automatic page break appears across your page as a dense dotted line. The status bar in the lower left-hand corner of your document gives the current page number that the insertion point is on.

If you want to force a page break in a more convenient location, choose Insert Page Break from the Document menu, or press Shift-Enter. Your document repaginates and a manual page break appears as a dotted line across the page. The remainder of your document automatically paginates from the manual page break forward. To remove a manual page break, simply position the insertion point after the dotted line, and press Backspace or Delete to remove it, as you would any other character. Less conveniently, you can choose Remove Page Break from the Document menu. Only manual page breaks can be deleted.

Working with headers and footers

The areas at the top and bottom of your page where you place information to label your document are called the *header* and the *footer,* respectively. You can use these areas for topic names, page numbers, dates, your name, and whatever other information you deem appropriate to your document. Works places the header below the top margin in the first line of the printable area, and the footer above the bottom margin in the last line of the printable area. The procedures for creating and using headers and footers are the same for the Works Word Processor, Database, Spreadsheet, Draw, and Communication modules.

A sample header window includes the same elements as a regular document window. Note how the dotted line and position measurement appear in the status bar as the tab is moved

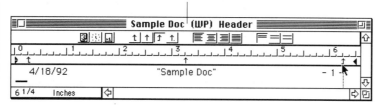

Choosing Show Header or Show Footer from the Window menu presents you with a Header or Footer window. All of the formatting options available to you in a regular document are also available in a header or footer window. You can enter text in the text layer or draw graphics in the draw layer to add to your headers and footers. This is a great place to put logos. Add dates, time, and page numbers to documents by selecting the appropriate buttons on the ruler.

Creating a header or footer:

1. **Choose Show Header or Show Footer from the Window menu to open a Header or Footer window.**

2. **Choose the appropriate justification for your text, and set any appropriate tab stops.**

3. **Enter your header or footer text.**

Document	
Copy Ruler Settings	⌘K
Paste Ruler Settings	⌘V
Insert Current Date	
Insert Current Time	
Insert Page Number	
Insert Document Title	

The Document menu for a header or footer allows you to insert the Current Date, Current Page Number, and Document Title with the click of a button

You can adjust the Current Date, Current Time, or Page Number button icons on the ruler as you would with any other document window. You can also choose Insert Current Date, Insert Current Time, Insert Page Number, or Insert Document from the Document menu to enter that information quickly and accurately. To delete page numbers or other information from a header or footer, open the Footnote or Header window from the Window menu and edit out the information.

Note: The page number button in the ruler appears only in header and footer windows. You can add information using the Insert Current Date, Insert Current Time, Insert Page Number, and Insert Document Title commands that appear above the document window when a header or footer is opened.

The size allotted to a header or footer is limited by the size of your page margin. If the text you enter into one of these windows doesn't fit, it appears dimmed in the window and won't appear when you print. Graphics that are too large are cropped at the dotted line that indicates the limit of the header or footer. To fit larger headers and footers into a document, increase either the width or height of the margins, as appropriate. If you recall, margins are changed within the Document dialog box which is opened from the Page Setup dialog box.

Formatting a Footer or Header window:

1. **Format your text as you would in any other word processor window.**

2. **To use graphics, choose Draw On from the Window menu, or press Command-J.**

— or —

2. **Click the Draw Layer tool on the Tool palette.** Draw your graphics. When done, switch back to the text layer, if desired.

— or —

2. **Paste a graphic into a header or footer.** This automatically selects Draw On in your header or footer window.

3. **Close the window by clicking in the close box, or choose Close from the File menu (Command-W).**

Title pages don't normally carry headers or footers. To turn off first page headers and footers and change page numbers, follow the steps detailed below:

Using headers and footers with title pages:

1. **Choose Page Setup from the File menu, and then click the Document button.**

2. **Choose the Title Page check box.** With the Title Page option selected, headers and footers start on the second page, numbered from page 2 on.

3. **Enter the number your pagination should start with if it's different from the default case.** If you're using a title page, enter 0 to have the second page start as page 1 (or subtract one from the number you desire to start with). If your document has no title page, enter the exact number.

4. **Click OK to close the Document dialog box, and click OK in the Page Setup dialog box to enter your change.**

5. **Use Print Preview to view your headers and footers.**

Using the spelling checker

Nothing lowers the opinion of a reader more quickly than incorrectly spelled words. Business and professional writing particularly demands perfect spelling. With Works' spelling checker, you can make sure that most errors are corrected quickly. Every document you create should be spell-checked as a last step in the writing process before anyone else looks at it and followed by a final proofreading.

A spelling checker looks for incorrectly spelled and repeated words by matching each word in your document, or some other selected part of your document, to an index of words in its dictionary. A correctly spelled word is matched and disregarded. Unmatched words are flagged and matched with closely related words through a series of language algorithms. An unknown or unmatched word might be spelled correctly even though the spell checker flags it, giving you the choice to accept the suggested spelling.

The Spelling dialog box flags words not matched in the Works
dictionary and allows you to correct all occurrences of the misspelling

```
=============================== Spelling ===============================
Not in Dictionary: ardvarks

Change To:     [aardvarks          ]     ( Ignore )   ( Ignore All )

Suggestions:   [aardvarks       ⬆]      (  Change  )  ( Change All )
                earmarks
                earmark
                radars                   (  Add  )     (  Cancel  )
                awarders
               [                ⬇]       ( Suggest )   ( Options... )

Add Words To:    Custom Dictionary 1
```

To perform a spelling check, highlight the part of the document you want to
check. When nothing is highlighted, the entire document is searched. Choose
Spelling from the Document menu, or press Command-L to begin the operation.
Works goes to the first questionable text string and posts the Spelling dialog box
shown in the above figure. This dialog box indicates some possible correct spellings and waits for you to tell it what to do. Options you choose from are
summarized below:

✦ *Change To text box*. Spelling suggestions appear below for your use. Type in
the correct string if it is different from the Not in Dictionary listing.

✦ *Suggestions scroll box*. A list of possible correct spellings are presented in a
scroll box. If you see the correct spelling, you can double-click on that word
to make the change and proceed to the next flagged spelling.

✦ *Ignore button*. Choosing this option leaves this one instance of the word unchanged and proceeds to the next questioned word, even if that word is the
same as the one you just left unchanged.

✦ *Ignore All button*. Leaves the word unchanged and doesn't question the word
again.

✦ *Change button*. Enters the change suggested in the Change To text box for
this one instance of the word.

✦ *Change All button*. Changes a given word throughout the document to the
suggested word.

✦ *Delete button*. Removes this instance of a word from your document.

✦ *Delete All button*. Removes all instances of a word from your document.

✦ *Add button*. Enters the word given in the Change To text box into your
custom dictionary.

✦ *Suggest button*. Displays the list of possible spellings in the Suggestion scroll
box. This button is useful when the Always Suggest check box is checked in
the Spelling Options dialog box (see the following figure).

◆ *Options button.* This button opens a dialog box that lets you create and edit your custom dictionaries.

Checking the spelling:

1. **Select the passage you want to check for misspellings, or simply leave an insertion point to check the entire document.**

2. **Choose Spelling from the Document menu, or press Command-L.**

3. **If the flagged word is misspelled, type the correct spelling in the Change To text box.**

— or —

3. **Double-click on the correct spelling in the Suggestions close box.**

4. **Press the button that's appropriate to the action.**

5. **Continue checking your spelling until you reach the end of the selection.**

6. **Click OK to accept your changes.**

The Spelling Options dialog box offers you additional options to streamline your search

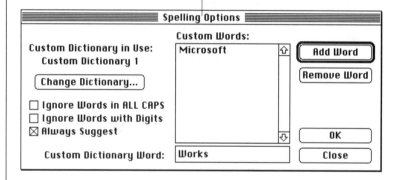

When you choose Spelling Options from the Document menu or select Options from the Spelling dialog box, you're presented with another dialog box (see figure above) offering the following additional choices:

◆ *Ignore Words in ALL CAPS check box.* Doesn't question words with all capital letters. This is useful for bypassing acronyms.

◆ *Ignore Words with Digits check box.* Bypasses text strings that contain numbers.

◆ *Always Suggest check box.* Choose this option, and Works always suggests the list of similar words. Leaving it unchecked speeds up the initial spell-check process, but may be inconvenient if you usually make use of the Suggestions scroll box.

Remember, Works defines a word as a text string with a space character on either side of it. Works adds a list of words to your file that were questioned by your spelling check and left unchanged. This list appears at the end of your file, but is hidden so that you can't see it.

Although the Works dictionary is large, it's not all-inclusive. Many words you might use, such as proper names or some pronouns, aren't included. Works lets you add these words, along with any other text strings you like, into your own custom dictionary, or into several specialized custom dictionaries. One company, Working Software (located in Santa Cruz, CA; 408-423-5696), the makers of Spellswell, sells custom dictionaries for use with Works.

To create your own custom dictionary, use the following steps.

Creating custom dictionaries:

1. **Choose Spelling Options from the Document menu, or choose Options from the Spelling dialog box.**

2. **Click the Change Dictionary button.** To change to another dictionary that already exists, select the name of the dictionary. To create a new dictionary, enter a name and select New.

3. **To remove a word from the dictionary, choose that word from the Custom Words scroll box. Then click Remove Word.** Alternatively, you can type that word into the Custom Word Dictionary Word text box, and click Remove Word.

4. **To add a word to the dictionary, type that word in the Custom Words scroll box, and then click Remove Word.**

5. **Click OK to execute your choices.**

Using Works' thesaurus

It's common to find yourself searching for that exact, right word, when the one you're using isn't quite right. Also, it's more interesting to the reader if you vary your vocabulary in a document, rather than repeating the same words. Rather than rack your brains to come up with substitute expressions, use the Works thesaurus to help you find that right word. The Works thesaurus is a dictionary that tells you which words are related to, have the same meaning as, or are opposite in meaning from the word you select. Similar words are called synonyms, and opposites are called antonyms. The thesaurus also offers synonyms for simple phrases.

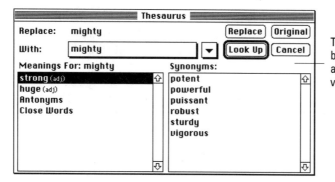

The Thesaurus dialog box suggests synonyms and antonyms for a wide variety of words

To use the thesaurus, first highlight the word or phrase you want to find alternatives for and choose Thesaurus (Command-D) from the Document menu. The Thesaurus dialog box shown in the previous figure then appear and offers the following features:

✦ *Replace.* Displays the word or phrase you selected.

✦ *With text box.* This box is where the replacement word is entered. The pop-up list shows you previous words you have looked up.

✦ *Meanings For scroll box.* Displays synonyms, related words, and antonyms for the original word.

✦ *Synonyms scroll box.* Lists the synonyms for the word you highlight in the Meanings For scroll box. This can be a synonym of your synonym, antonym, or related word or phrase. Also see the Look Up button, below.

✦ *Replace button.* Click to replace the selected word with the contents of the With text box.

✦ *Original button.* Click to display the search results of the original word or phrase.

✦ *Look Up button.* Finds synonyms for any word you highlight in either scroll box and places them in the Synonyms scroll box.

✦ *Cancel button.* Returns you to your document without making any changes.

Works lists many more synonyms than antonyms or related words. Not every word is in the thesaurus, so if Works doesn't find your word or phrase, similarly spelled words are displayed in the Meanings For scroll box. If any of those words are appropriate, you can highlight that word and search for meanings.

Working with footnotes

Footnotes are just one advanced word processing feature that Works supports. Footnotes are often requested by writers and required in documents, and Works has some good automated tools to make using them easy. Depending on what you've chosen in the word processor Preferences dialog box (see the second figure in this Topic), your embedded notes will appear either at the bottom of the page as footnotes or at the end of the document as endnotes. Functionally, they are exactly the same critter. You can place up to 255 footnotes in each Works document.

To insert a footnote, position the insertion point where the number should go and choose Insert Footnote from the Document menu. The Footnote window opens, and you can enter the text of your footnote. Works automatically numbers footnotes in the text and inserts them into the document window where they belong. The Footnote window contains a ruler like any regular document window and the text you type can be fully formatted. Click the close box to close the Footnote window. Choose Show Footnotes from the Document menu to open the window again for viewing or editing.

Creating a footnote:

1. **Choose Insert Footnote from the Document menu to open the word processor Preferences dialog box.**

2. **Choose your preferences for footnotes and headers from the word processor Preference dialog box and click OK to enter them.**

3. **Position the insertion point where the reference number should go. Then choose Insert Footnote from the Document menu.**

4. **Type the footnote text in the Footnote window and format it as desired.**

— or —

4. **Type the footnote text directly into the text of the main document at the place where you want the number to appear. Then choose Insert As Footnote from the Document menu.**

5. **Close the Footnote window by clicking Close, or by clicking on the close box.**

Window

Help...	⌘?
Draw On	⌘J
Show Tools	⌘T
Hide Ruler	⌘R
Show Clipboard	
Show Header	
Show Footer	
Show Footnotes	
Macro	▶
✓Untitled1 (WP)	

The Window menu for a word processor includes commands for creating footnotes

Footnotes are stored as text with an embedded hidden code. As an alternative to creating footnotes in a separate Footnote window, you can type footnote text in your document. Highlight that text, and choose Insert As Footnote from the Document menu to move that text into a Footnote window. Only 30 lines can be highlighted at a time. A reference number is placed at the original location of the text in the document. This won't work if you have a footnote reference number embedded in the text you're placing in the footnote. Works will give you an error message if you attempt this.

You can delete a footnote by deleting its reference number, or you can cut, copy, or paste that footnote to another location again by altering the reference number accordingly. If necessary, Works renumbers your footnotes for you so that they're correct. When you move text containing a footnote, the footnotes are also renumbered if needed, and the text in the Footnote window is rearranged.

When you select your word processor preferences, you can specify whether your notes are footnotes or endnotes and specify the length of the mark that separates text from footnotes. You can select no mark, a short line, or a line from margin to margin.

If you try to print several footnotes with references to the same line of text in your document there may not be enough room at the bottom of the page. Works alerts you to this when you attempt to print your document. This problem is also obvious if you use Page Preview first. To correct this problem, move some of the reference numbers to a line that prints on the next page or, if you can, delete some of the reference numbers.

You can manipulate footnotes in the following fashion:

✦ To see your footnotes, choose Show Footnotes from the Window menu. You can edit footnotes in this window. Or, less conveniently, use Print Preview or Print your document to view your footnotes.

✦ To delete a footnote, delete the reference number by pressing Backspace or Delete, or choose Clear from the Edit menu.

✦ To move a footnote, select the reference number. Choose Cut from the Edit menu to remove the footnote, and reposition the insertion point at desired location. Then choose Paste from the Edit menu.

✦ To copy a footnote, highlight the reference number. Choose Copy from the Edit menu to place the footnote on the Clipboard. Then reposition the insertion point as desired, and choose Paste.

Note: When you delete, move, or copy a footnote(s), Works renumbers your footnote, and repositions the footnote text automatically.

Footnotes can appear at the bottom of pages or at the end of your document depending on the preferences you set. You can only see footnotes in Print Preview, in your printed document, or in the Show Footnote window. Use the Show Footnote window to view and edit footnotes as you work.

Locating a footnote:

1. **Choose Show Footnote from the Window menu to open the Footnote window.** Take note of the footnote number.

2. **Choose Go To Footnote from the Edit menu.**

3. **Type the Footnote number into the text box.**

4. **Click OK. The footnote will appear at the top of the Footnotes window.**

5. **Close the footnote window when you are done.**

When you need to break a document into separate files — for example, to create topics for a book — you can start footnote numbering in a file at any number you choose. The procedure is summarized in the following section:

Resetting the footnote numbers:

1. **Choose Page Setup from the File menu.**

2. **Click the Document button to open the Document dialog box.**

3. **Enter the number you want the first footnote to have in the Number Footnotes From text box.**

4. **Click OK to dismiss the Document dialog box.**

5. **Click OK to dismiss the Page Setup dialog box and enter your choice.**

Remembering to save

What you type on your screen only exists when you save it to disk. Save your work often. You don't own what you don't save. You might think that it's only a beginner's mistake not to save work, but even experienced users sometimes forget to save often enough. There's no recovery procedure for work you haven't saved.

You should save your work at short enough intervals so that you won't mind too much if you have to recreate material lost if you lose power or have a system crash. A good rule of thumb is to save either every 15 minutes of work or 500 entered characters for word processing. When you enter data in a spreadsheet or database, the need to save often increases dramatically. You may not be able to recreate lost numbers for a phone order to your business, for example.

Some programs come with an autosave feature built in. Works is *not* one of those programs. You can add Autosave to Works by using the NowSave control panel in the Now Utilities package. You can also program some macro applications, such as CE Software's QuicKeys2 or Infinity Microsystems' Tempo II Plus, to do timed save operations.

Lest you forget, remember also to back up your files regularly.

Moving quickly through your document

Works contains some powerful methods for moving you about your document, in addition to the standard Macintosh window scroll bar techniques. You can go directly to a specific page by choosing Go To Page from the Edit menu. In the resulting dialog box, type the page number, and then click the OK button to jump directly to that page.

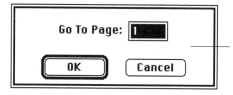

The Go To Page dialog box lets you jump directly to a specific page without your having to scroll through the document

To move around in your document you can use some handy keyboard shortcuts. Press the arrow keys to move in the corresponding direction — the left arrow to go left one character, the right arrow to go right one character, the up arrow to go up to the previous line, and the down arrow to go down to the next line. If you have an extended keyboard, you can also use the arrow keys on the numeric keypad as an alternate to the arrow keys on the main keyboard section. Other keys on the numeric keyboard are supported by Works 3. You can press Home to jump to the start of your document, End to jump to the end of the document, Page Up to scroll up one window, and Page Down to scroll down one window. If you forget these keystrokes, you can find them summarized in the Works Shortcut Keys dialog box, shown when you choose that command from the Help menu.

Measuring your document's size

Many documents must be a specific size to be appropriate for their intended use. A magazine article, a report, and a "lonely hearts" ad are all examples of documents in which size is important. Just as Charles Dickens got paid by the word, you too may have to count your words to make them count. Works helps you out with a counting function that gives you the vital statistics.

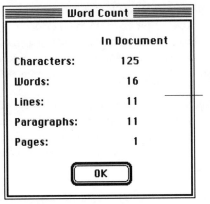

The Word Count dialog box gives you information about the size of a word processing document

To use this feature, first select the text you wish to measure, or simply leave an insertion point in your document to count the words in the entire document. Choose Word Count from the Document menu. No further action is required. Click OK to close this dialog box.

The Word Count dialog box shows you the following information:

+ Whether the entire document or just a selection was searched

+ The number of characters, including spaces in your document

+ The number of words, defined as any text string between two spaces

+ The number of lines

+ The number of paragraphs with text (it ignores the paragraph marks used to create blank lines between paragraphs)

+ The number of pages in your selection

Working with tables

A table is a columnar list of data. Whereas databases, spreadsheets, and even the Draw modules naturally support columns, a word processor requires you to format a set of paragraphs in order to align them into a table. Works has no special command that creates and manages tables for you, but fortunately, setting up tables isn't difficult. You simply create a paragraph with the correct tab stops and duplicate these tabs in subsequent paragraphs. Create a new paragraph and press Return or Enter immediately below the correctly formatted paragraph to transfer the tab stops to the next paragraph. Or choose Copy Ruler Settings from the Document menu (Command-K) to copy settings from your original paragraph then click OK to apply the Paste Ruler Settings to existing paragraphs.

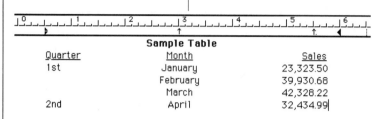

A table correctly set up in a word processor document

Quarter	Month	Sales
1st	January	23,323.50
	February	39,930.68
	March	42,328.22
2nd	April	32,434.99

Sample Table

To set the left and right edges of a table, set the left and right indent markers. Set tab stops to separate columns in a table. When importing data from a spreadsheet or database file, the information is inserted as tab-separated columns with each line separated by a paragraph mark. So, if you want to export your table to other Works modules, use this format for your word processor table to make exporting easier. To sort data in a word processor table, consider moving that data to a database if the lines of data need to be sorted as a unit, or to a spreadsheet if each column of data is to be sorted independently. Moving data about for use in tables is covered in Topic 12 in the section titled "More about tables."

If you want to spruce up a table with graphics, the best and most convenient way is to turn on the Draw module in your word processor. This makes drawing lines or boxes, adding shading, and other effects easy. For information about using draw, see Topic 5. Using draw to create lines is easier and more accurate than adding spaces with underlining, and it doesn't interfere with your table's data.

Quick Tips

The following tips offer advice about upgrading to a more powerful word processor.

Looking beyond Works' Word Processor module

If you do a lot of writing, eventually you may want to consider upgrading to a more powerful word processor package. There are several good choices to consider. The most natural upgrade is to Microsoft Word 5 as it has many of the same commands and keystroke equivalents as Works' word processor. Word also has many powerful features. Some of these additional features are summarized below:

◆ *Advanced formatting.* Word has features that allow you to create multiple columns, and create and position graphics, and offers other formatting options.

◆ *Integrated outline.* Word provides a document is available that lets you switch between a written outline and the full document. This view allows you to better plan and reorganize your writing.

♦ *Styles*. Automate paragraph formatting by creating paragraph styles with format settings preset by one selection. You can apply styles quickly to a paragraph, export styles to a page layout program, and quickly change the formatting of an entire document by changing a style's definition.

♦ *Indexing and table of contents*. With this feature, you can create index entries and have Word automatically collate them into an index. Word can also collect headings or marked phrases, and use them to create a table of contents.

♦ *Glossary*. Collect a set of commonly used data, such as addresses, phrases, paragraphs, dates, time, or page numbers, and insert them into your document.

♦ *Publish and subscribe*. Word can support automated linkage of data to and from other programs.

♦ *Grammar checker*. Uses language usage rules to check your document, and grades it according to reading level.

♦ *Tables*. Create and format tables easily.

♦ *Long document tools*. Word offers advanced automated hyphenation, line numbering, file searching, and so on.

Word gets great reviews, and the features listed above are just a partial list. Word isn't the only full-featured word processor that's highly regarded, however. You may also want to consider WordPerfect, which is similarly well endowed. Other good products include Claris' MacWrite, and T/Maker's WriteNow. WriteNow is a particularly good choice when your computer has memory limitations (it runs on the Mac 512 and later models); WriteNow is fast and well thought out.

Buying additional fonts

Keep in mind that you can purchase fonts in different weights and styles. For example, you can buy Helvetica Bold, a boldfaced version form of the Helvetica font. When you apply the style Bold to the Helvetica Bold font you obtain an even darker set of characters. Whether you use Helvetica Bold or bold the Helvetica font to get a similar effect depends on your application. Designed font styles always produce better printed results, although they require you to make an additional purchase.

Summary

✔ Word processors are powerful tools for writing. They improve your writing by changing the way you write. You can use a word processor to easily change the organization of your document, and apply powerful writing tools to strengthen your content.

✔ The word processor window contains a number of features for formatting and working with text. Use the ruler to format paragraphs, set tabs, and align text.

✔ A word processor document has two layers — a text layer and a draw layer. Choose Draw On from the Edit menu, or the Draw Layer tool from the Tool palette to switch to draw.

✔ The Text Layer tool, or Draw Off command, switches you back to the text layer. What you see in your window is a combination of what's in both layers.

✔ The Format and Style menus allow you to format text. You can also use the pop-up menus in the Tool palette for this purpose.

✔ A word processor records all characters, even the ones you can't see, (space characters and paragraph markers). Paragraph marks record all of the formatting for the characters that precede it up to the previous paragraph mark.

✔ Choose Find from the Edit menu to search for text, and Replace from the Edit menu to make substitutions.

✔ Character-based formatting choices include fonts, font sizes, and styles. To apply these choices, first select the text to be formatted.

✔ Paragraph formatting options include alignment, line spacing, tab settings, and indenting. You only need to place the insertion point in a paragraph to change paragraph formats.

✔ Works calculates where a page break should be, a process called automatic pagination. To place a page break where you want it, insert a manual page break by pressing Shift-Enter.

✔ Use headers and footers to separate information that appears at the top and bottom, respectively, of every page.

✔ A spell checker matches your words against a list of correctly spelled words and reports unknown words for you to change. A thesaurus matches a selected word or phrase against a dictionary of words with similar meanings.

✔ Use footnotes to reference or explain details of your text. They are created, automatically numbered, and managed by choosing Insert Footnote from the Window menu. You can also place endnotes at the end of a document for the same purpose.

✔ Save your work often. Changes you make only exist on your screen until you save them.

Topic 5
Using the Draw Module

Overview

A draw program allows you to create and manipulate graphics in your document. Microsoft Works' Draw module lets you work with graphics in two ways — you can create draw documents in which only drawn objects appear, or you can use Draw as an overlying layer in your word processor, database, and spreadsheet documents. Draw lets you undertake some very sophisticated projects that you couldn't normally tackle with an inexpensive software product. Using Draw, you can do desktop publishing, create forms, and make reports. You'll learn how in this Topic.

Draw is used for any type of graphic and for text that's used as a graphic. That may sound confusing now, but this Topic provides the necessary underlying foundation to get you started using Draw in your work. Draw has many tools, and if you've worked with other draw programs, such as Claris MacDraw, Aldus SuperPaint, or Deneba Canvas, then Works' drawing tools will seem familiar.

Of all of Works' tools, the Draw module has undergone the most extensive enhancement. In earlier versions of Works, the word processor was the first Macintosh application to sport an integrated draw program. Now that capability has been added to the Database and Spreadsheet modules, and you can also create separate graphics documents. Works 3 adds gray scale and color support, convenient tear-off tool palettes, many special effects, and numerous small enhancements. These new changes are detailed in Topic 3, if you want to review them. Draw is fun and livens up your work.

What is a drawing program?

A drawing program is an application that creates graphics, based on mathematical relationships. A circle may be described in terms of its origin, the size of its radius, the width or stroke of the line, and the color or pattern used to fill it in. Draw programs are used for technical illustrations, computer-aided design (CAD), and other graphics in which precision is desired.

Drawn graphics are called *vector graphics,* because they often use the mathematics of vector algebra in their description. They're also called *object-oriented graphics,* because each mathematical relationship describes an object.

The other type of graphics programs commonly found on computers are called *paint programs.* A paint program uses a fundamentally different method for creating pictures called a *bitmap.* A bitmap is a pattern of small dots, called *pixels,* that are used to create a larger picture. If you look at a newspaper photo, you can see the halftone spots used to print the image. Similarly, if you look at a filled scroll bar in a Macintosh window, you can see black dots, which are individual pixels on a Macintosh monitor.

Paint programs store a matrix of color data for each location or pixel, so these programs are also referred to as *bitmapped graphics.* Painted graphics are sometimes also called *raster graphics.* The word raster comes from the imaging technique used by a cathode ray tube, television, or computer display, in which the electron beam paints sequential lines by turning on and off appropriately at each location (or pixel) on your screen. To do this, any description of a graphic image is translated into a bitmap so that it can be displayed on a computer monitor.

Working on the draw layer

When you open a draw document, there's a single screen into which you can enter data. Works calls this screen the *draw layer,* although as you'll see, the word layer can also be correctly used in other modules. You know you're in a draw-only document from the appearance of the vertical ruler and the absence of the underlying word processor, database, or spreadsheet text, fields, cells, forms, or graphs.

Draw documents have a single tool layer and display a vertical ruler. You know the draw layer is active when you see a dedicated draw document open on your screen or when the draw tools appear in the Tool palette.

Vector vs. raster graphics

Although both types of graphics might look the same on your Macintosh display at 72 dots per inch (dpi), there's a fundamental difference between vector and raster graphics. Painted graphics have a fixed pixel size dictated by the resolution of their bitmaps. Drawn graphics are perfectly represented by mathematical formulas that can be scaled to any size and are only limited by the quality your output device offers. This perfect scaling is called *device independence,* and it can be an important advantage in many situations, such as high resolution printed output. A drawn picture looks nearly perfect at 2,450 dpi on an Imagesetter (a high resolution laser printer), while a painted graphic looks very jagged. It's one reason that the designers of Works chose to use a draw program instead of a paint program. Painted graphics do have their special uses and applications, though — for instance, they're particularly good for natural looking images.

Creating a separate draw document:

1. Select New from the File menu, or press Command-N.

— or —

1. Alternatively, select Open from the File menu (Command-O) to open a draw document or draw stationery.

When you open the Draw module within the Word Processor, Spreadsheet, or Database modules, you can still work with all of draw's many tools but what appears in the window is actually the combination of both layers. The methods for starting Draw from within a word processor, spreadsheet, and database document are detailed below.

✦ Select the Draw tool (the pencil icon) from the Tool palette.

✦ Alternatively, select Draw On from the Windows menu, or press Command-J.

Works switches you to the draw layer and opens the drawing tools on the Tool palette. The palette is shown even if you've elected to hide it previously.

Having two layers in a document can be confusing when text is being used. It's particularly problematic when you use Draw with the word processor, because there are fewer visual clues to distinguish between the modules. More than likely, there'll be times when you'll try to select text in one layer and find that the text is hiding in another.

Anything you create in Draw is considered to be an *object*. You need to select an object to change its properties or attributes, edit it, or resize it. Generally, after you've created an object, it's automatically selected, so you can format it immediately. A selected object is enclosed by a *bounding box* — the smallest rectangle that can contain that object. You can tell an object is selected when you see the object's handles (little black boxes) on your screen and the Selection tool is currently active in the Tool palette. Handles are found at the edges and the midpoint of the bounding box's line segments. You can have one object or many selected in the same draw document, and attributes you apply to one object are also applied to any subsequent objects you create.

Topic 5
Using the Draw Module

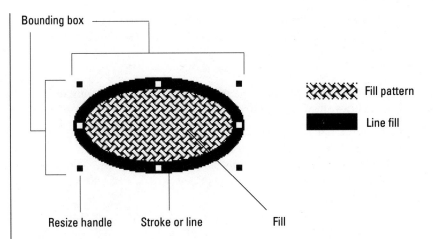

Bounding box

Fill pattern

Line fill

Resize handle   Stroke or line   Fill

Setting up your Draw window

There probably aren't many new features in a Draw window that you haven't seen before. The most noticeable feature is the vertical ruler that appears on your screen. This ruler appears in your Draw window whenever you select that preference from the Preferences dialog box (open this dialog box by selecting Preferences from the Edit menu). You can select either inches or centimeters as the unit of measurement in the ruler. Choose Hide Ruler or Show Ruler from the Window menu as appropriate, or press Command-R.

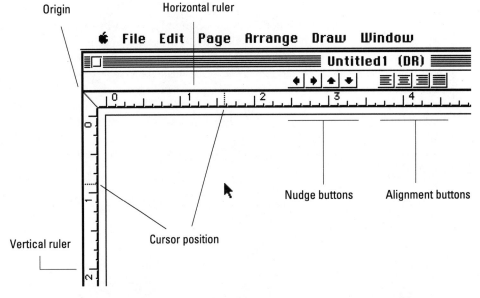

Origin   Horizontal ruler

Nudge buttons   Alignment buttons

Vertical ruler   Cursor position

The ribbon part of the ruler contains the same four text alignment buttons that were discussed in Topic 4 in the sections titled "Using the word processor window" and "Formatting paragraphs." Alignment in the draw layer applies to paragraphs in selected text objects. Four new *nudge buttons* appear on the ruler in the draw layer — click one of these buttons to move or nudge a selected object one pixel in the corresponding direction. The nudge buttons first appeared on the Tool palette in Works version 2.0.

Although you don't see it even when it's activated, you can set a *snap-to grid* in a Works window. A grid helps you to precisely place and align objects. As you select and move objects, they will align with the grid if you move them within a specified distance of a horizontal or vertical gridline. Choose the size of the gridline spacing by selecting Set Grid Spacing from the Arrange menu. Select the radio button for the spacing you desire. Selecting Snap To Grid from the Arrange menu turns the grid on and puts a check mark next to the command in the Arrange menu. Choose that command again to turn off the grid and remove the check mark. By selecting the Snap To Grid check box in the draw Preference dialog box, you make the grid appear in every new document.

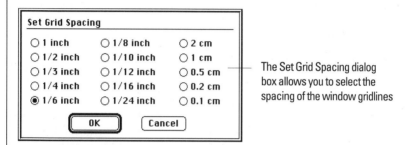

The Set Grid Spacing dialog box allows you to select the spacing of the window gridlines

The Draw window has many features that are similar to other Works windows. The Draw module supports the use of headers and footers. Headers and footers (explained in Topic 4 in the section titled "Working with headers and footers") function in the same manner in a draw document as in a word processing document. Select Page Setup from the File menu to change the size of a document page and to set page numbers in a draw document, just as you would in other documents. These subjects are fully described in Topic 2.

The Page menu, found in the draw document, offers you options for adding, deleting, and jumping between pages

Creating new pages:

1. **Select Add Pages from the Page menu.**

2. **In the Add Pages dialog box, enter the number of new pages required and the position they are to be placed into the appropriate text boxes.**

3. **Select Add or press Return or Enter.**

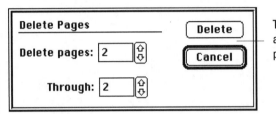

The Add Pages dialog box allows you to select the number and position of pages added

Deleting pages from your draw document:

1. **Select Delete Pages from the Page menu.**

2. **Enter the range of pages you wish to delete in the text box.**

3. **Select the Delete button.** Press Return or Enter to cancel the operation.

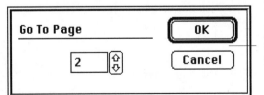

The Delete Pages dialog box asks you for the range of pages you wish to delete

Now that you know how to add or delete a page, you need to learn how to move around in a draw document. The following section summarizes different methods for moving around quickly in your draw document.

✦ Use the vertical or horizontal scroll bars. See the section titled "Working with windows" in Topic 2 for more information.

✦ Select the Page Forward or Page Back icon from the draw Tool palette (these appear as arrow icons).

✦ Alternatively, select Next Page (Command-equal) or Previous Page (Command-minus) to move through your document a page at a time.

✦ If you know the specific page you want to jump to, select Go To Page from the Page menu, or press Command-K. Then enter the page number in the Go To Page dialog box, and select OK.

```
Go To Page                    [    OK    ]

        [ 2 ]                 [  Cancel  ]
```

The Go To Page dialog box allows you to jump directly to a specfic page

Using the draw palette

Whether you open a draw document or switch to Draw in another module, an expanded palette of drawing tools appears — this is one of the ways you can tell that Draw is active. Also, the draw palette can only be hidden in a draw document if the draw layer is active. Most of the draw palette tools are also found on the Tool palette of the other Works modules, but there are some specialized tools that only appear on the Tool palette as appropriate to the kind of document you have open on your screen.

The methods of opening the draw Tool palette are summarized below.

Opening the draw Tool palette:

1. **Choose Show Tools from the Window menu, or press Command-T to display the palette.**

— or —

1. **Select the Draw On (Command-J) from the Window menu to place the Tool palette on your screen.**

2. **To move the palette about, click and drag the title bar at the top of the palette.**

3. **Choose Hide Tools or press Command-T again to remove the Tool palette from your screen.** You can also remove the palette by clicking its close box.

Note: When you hide the Tool palette in a module other than draw, you switch from draw into the original module. See "Setting up your Draw window," earlier in this Topic.

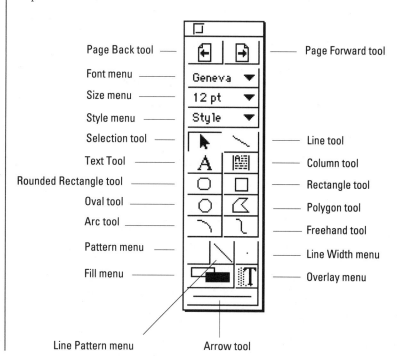

Page Back tool		Page Forward tool
Font menu		
Size menu		
Style menu		
Selection tool		Line tool
Text Tool		Column tool
Rounded Rectangle tool		Rectangle tool
Oval tool		Polygon tool
Arc tool		Freehand tool
Pattern menu		Line Width menu
Fill menu		Overlay menu
Line Pattern menu		Arrow tool

The elements of the Tool palette are summarized below:

◆ *Page tools*. Select the Left Arrow or the Page Back tool to move back, or the Right Arrow or Page Forward tool to move forward one page in a document. These icons are dimmed when there's no page in that direction. When a draw layer is open, these Page tools are replaced by tools that let you switch to other modules: an I-beam tool for the Word Processor module, Form and Design tools for the Database module, and a Cell Selection or Charting tool for the Spreadsheet module.

◆ *Font menu*. Click on the pop-up menu and select a font by dragging to the appropriate font name and releasing.

◆ *Size menu*. Select a font size here.

◆ *Style menu*. Use to apply any font styles you desire.

◆ *Selection tool*. This tool is the initial default. Generally, it's only used when you've finished using the other tools on the palette. It lets you select and manipulate objects.

◆ *Text tool*. Select to create text in the currently selected text area. When you select this tool in a text column, the text wordwraps in that column.

◆ *Rounded Rectangle tool*. Select to create a rounded rectangle. The cursor changes to a magnified plus sign called a crosshair. Click and drag to create the size of rectangle you desire. Press and hold down Shift and drag to create a square with rounded sides.

◆ *Oval tool*. This tool works similarly to the Rounded Rectangle tool. Press Shift and hold it down while dragging to create perfect circles.

◆ *Arc tool*. Click and drag the crosshair to make a 90-degree arc. Press Shift and hold it down to limit your arc to quadrant diameters of circles, and not ovular arcs.

◆ *Line tool*. Allows you to click and drag a straight line. Press Shift and hold it down to limit the lines drawn to 45-degree angles.

◆ *Column tool*. Click and drag text columns. The Column tool is used to place and constrain text on a page.

◆ *Rectangle tool*. Similar to the Rounded Rectangle tool, except it draws straight edges. Pressing Shift while dragging creates perfect squares.

◆ *Polygon tool*. Creates shapes with any number of straight lines, both closed and open. Click to place the first point, drag the mouse and click to place the next, and so on until you double-click on the last point to create an open shape. To close a shape, click on top of the first point. You can draw triangles, angles, and trapezoids with this tool.

◆ *Freehand tool*. This tool allows you to draw any shape on your screen with your mouse as if you were holding a pencil.

✦ *Pattern menu.* The Pattern menu is a pop-up, tear-off palette used to select the pattern and shades of gray for shapes (see the following figure). You can select any of 60 patterns and 100 shades of gray.

Background fill

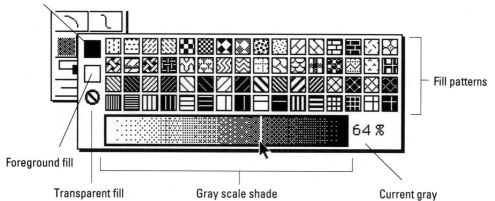

Fill patterns

64 %

Foreground fill

Transparent fill   Gray scale shade   Current gray

✦ *Line Pattern menu.* This menu is identical to the Fill menu, described later in this Topic, but it operates on a line or the stroke of a shape, rather than the space inside.

✦ *Line Width tool.* Select this tool to reveal the pop-up Pen Size menu. The default is a line width one pixel square. Drag the selection square to the right to increase the line's horizontal width and down to increase the line's vertical width. The menu tears off when you drag it off the Tool palette.

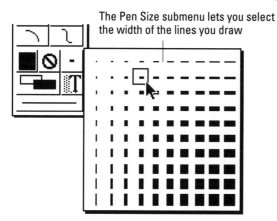

The Pen Size submenu lets you select the width of the lines you draw

✦ *Fill menu.* This tool opens two pop-up, tear-off menus. The back rectangle lets you select background color; while the front menu sets the foreground color. Click on either Color tool to switch between them. Selected colors appear in the Fill menu. See "Applying patterns and colors to a graphic" later in this Topic for more information. Shapes, lines, or text can have both foreground and background colors assigned to them. Text appears in the foreground color, above the bounding box in the background color surrounding it.

♦ *Overlay menu.* The Overlay menu allows you to choose the transparency of an object and how it interacts with objects behind it. Choices include *Matte* (opaque with a bounding box around the object); *Paint* (applies the selected color to the selected object, ignoring the underlying object); *Invert* (changes the color of the selected object to its opposite where it overlaps with the underlying object); and *Erase* (leaves the object white, ignoring the underlying object). The following figure illustrates these different choices.

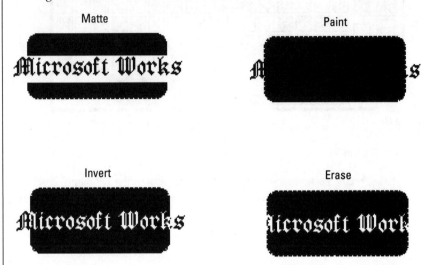

Matte   Paint

Invert   Erase

♦ *Arrow tool.* Allows you to change the angular position of a line on the screen. To use this tool, select the line and drag one of its handles. Or select Rotate from the Draw menu to flip an arrow horizontally.

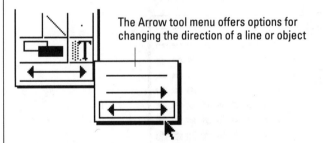

The Arrow tool menu offers options for changing the direction of a line or object

Each selection on the draw tool palette displays a pop-up menu that's also a *tear-off menu.* When you drag a tear-off menu to another position on the screen, the menu remains open in a small window for quick access to the options inside. If you find yourself frequently using a tool palette option on a particular project, you'll most likely want to tear off its menu. The downside, of course, is that open tear-off menus take up space on your screen. To close a menu you no longer need, click its close box.

The Font, Size, and Style pop-up menus on the palette duplicate choices found on the Font and Style menus. The choices you make in a draw document or in a draw layer of another kind of document can be applied to text objects drawn in that layer and to text created in another Works module.

In the Pen Size submenu, each choice for a line width is one pixel wider than the choice to the left or below it. Choosing a width of four pixels and height of two pixels has the effect of creating a square with the top and bottom sides two pixels wide, and the right and left sides four pixels wide.

Working with graphic objects

Once you have your document set up and understand the function of the tools in the Tool palette, you can begin working with objects.

Creating objects and shapes:

1. **Open a new Draw window.**

2. **Select default characteristics for any text you might type — including font, size, and style.** You may also want to select a background color.

3. **Select a pattern, fill, line width, overlay characteristic, and foreground color from the appropriate pop-up, tear-off menus on the palette.**

4. **Select the Text tool from the Tool palette, and place an insertion point on your screen to type your text.** If you click within a text column, your words will wordwrap.

5. **Select one of the shape tools from the Tool palette, and click and drag the crosshair cursor to draw your shape.** See "Using the Draw Palette" earlier in this Topic for more information. If you press Shift when dragging, you'll create a perfect shape — a circle, square, line constrained to 45-degree angles, and so on.

6. **To close a polygon or freely drawn object automatically, select Vertex Snap from the Arrange menu, or press N and hold it while you draw.** Then when you click within the current grid spacing, your shape closes. You can also click on your original point.

Click the first point

Double-click on a point to create an open polygon

Click on the original point to close the polygon

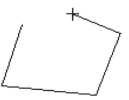

Drag and click the second point

Continue dragging and clicking points

A selected polygon is shown

When you create a shape, the Selection tool is activated and your shape or object is selected to let you manipulate it. To prevent the Selection tool from being automatically selected, and to continue working with your text or shape tool, hold Shift *before* clicking on that tool. Click on another tool to switch to that tool.

Pasting objects into the draw layer:

1. **Highlight the text or other data you want to insert into the draw layer from any other kind of document.**

2. **Select Copy from the Edit menu to place a copy of the data onto the Clipboard.**

3. **Activate the draw layer and select Paste from the Edit menu (Command-V).** Works opens Draw and places the data as a graphic in the center of your screen.

4. **To center one object on top of another, highlight the preplaced object and paste the new one.**

5. **To switch back to the main module, select the tool for that module from the left of the Pencil icon.** The icon for the Word Processor module is an I-beam cursor. The Database module uses either the Form or Design icon and the Spreadsheet module uses either the Charting or Selection (plus symbol) icon.

6. **You can turn Draw off by selecting Draw Off from the Windows menu, or by pressing Command-J.**

After pasting, anything you create in the draw layer of a document remains in view, even when the other layer of a document is active and the draw tools aren't displayed. To move an object, click and drag on any part of that object.

Moving an object:

1. **Select the object you wish to move.**

2. **Click and drag it.** Drag on the border of an unfilled shape, or any part of a filled shape.

Works shows you the outline of the new shape as you drag it. Pressing Shift as you drag moves the shape in a precisely horizontal, vertical, or diagonal direction.

Original shape

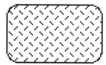

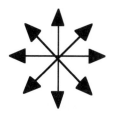

Moved position
(release mouse to move)

Hold down Shift key to limit
movement to these directions

Use an object's handles to resize it by clicking and dragging on the handles. As you drag, Works shows you an outline of the new size for comparison. When you drag a side handle, your shape is resized to appear proportionally wider or taller, depending on the direction you drag it. Dragging a corner handle resizes your shape by any amount in both directions. To resize your object proportionately, press Shift when dragging the handle.

Resizing an object:

1. **Select the object or grouped object you wish to resize.**

2. **Click and drag on one of the resize handles (the little black boxes along the bounding box).** Use an edge handle to drag in that direction only, or a corner handle to drag in either or both directions at once. Resizing a grouped object resizes all of the elements by the same amount.

3. **To maintain the object's original proportions as you resize, press Shift while you drag a handle.**

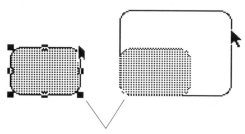

Resize an object by clicking and
dragging on one of its handles

There will be times when you might want to make a copy of a graphic, such as when you want to experiment on a graphic without affecting the original. You can create copies of a graphic object on your screen by following these steps.

Copying graphics:

1. Select the object you wish to copy.

2. Select Duplicate from the Edit menu, or press Command-D.

Works places the copy of your selection slightly offset to the right and below the original. You can then move or otherwise manipulate this object as you choose.

Deleting objects

If you make a mistake drawing an object, or you just want to get rid of extraneous objects, you'll want to learn how to delete objects.

You can delete objects in several different ways, as you can see from the following summary of deleting techniques.

◆ Select the object you wish to delete and press Backspace or Delete.

◆ Select Clear from the Edit menu. You can also press the Clear key on the numeric keypad for the same purpose. Clear deletes your selection.

◆ Select Cut from the Edit menu (Command-X) to remove the selection and move it to the Clipboard.

◆ Select Undo from the Edit menu (Command-Z) to return your deletion to its previous state. If it was the last action, select it again to delete it.

There'll come a time when plain shapes and angles just won't do. To make things interesting, turn your objects on their ear using the Rotate command as summarized in the following section.

Rotating an object:

1. Select the object you wish to rotate.

2. Select Rotate from the Draw menu. This opens the Rotate dialog box.

3. Enter the angle of the rotation desired in the Clockwise Angle text box, or select the Horizontal Flip or Vertical Flip check box for those rotations.

Works uses the center of a shape to determine its axis of rotation. Most shapes rotate *reversibly*, meaning the basic object remains the same. By selecting Undo, you can restore the object to its last position. An oval, however, can be transformed into a curve upon rotation, and once transformed, can't be restored by the undo operation. Text objects and bitmaps you've pasted into Draw cannot be rotated at all.

Once a shape has been created, you can still change its attributes. The following section gives you the details.

Reformatting an existing object:

1. **Activate the Selection tool in the Tool palette, if necessary.**

2. **Select the shape you wish to change.** A bounding box with handles appears around the shape.

3. **To select a range of objects, drag a marquee around them, or press Shift and click on the additional objects.**

4. **To deselect all objects, click anywhere in your document.** To deselect objects from a group, press Shift and click on the objects you wish to ungroup.

5. **To select text, click and drag the I-beam cursor over the desired text.**

6. **Select the attributes you desire from the appropriate pop-up menu, and they will be applied to the highlighted objects.**

The attributes you choose are applied to the selected objects, as well as to any text or shapes you subsequently create.

Smoothing an object:

1. **Before pasting or drawing the object, select Smooth from the Draw menu.** When Smooth is active, a check mark appears next to the command in that menu.

2. **To change a smooth object back to one with straight line sides, select Smooth again to delete the check mark.**

Original shape

With smoothing

Smoothed objects can have many more handles than you may want or need. This is particularly the case for objects drawn freehand. To change the number of handles an object has, use the following section.

Removing and adding handles:

1. **Select the object you wish to change.**

2. **To remove every other handle in an object, select Remove Handles from the Draw menu.**

3. **To add a handle between each existing handle, select Add Handles from the Draw menu.**

When you remove handles, your shape smoothes out. Reshaping becomes less precise, but you can manipulate your shape easier and faster.

Working with text objects

Text objects are groups of text created in a draw layer. Although these groups print the same as text in any other Works layer, many wonderful special effects are available to text objects that aren't available in the other modules. You typically use text objects when you want precise control over the placement of text, or when you want to apply any draw tools to text objects. Think of text objects as just another form of graphic. You can apply fill, pattern, line width, color, and other attributes to them. You can also scale or resize them, move them freely about the screen, and apply special effects to them. Use the text formatting options you learned about in Topic 4 — changing font, size, style, and alignment — for any character within a text object. To align text objects, select the appropriate button from the Ruler, or make selections from the Alignment submenu on the Arrange menu.

Given their versatility, text objects are almost too good to be true, and you may wonder why anyone uses a word processor at all. Actually, when you define text as a graphic, you do lose some of the features available in a word processing document. For one, only text formatting is available to text objects in layers other than draw. Word processors handle text faster and have special text preparation tools such as Find, Replace, Spelling, and Thesaurus. If you're creating a draw document with a lot of text, you may want to use a word processor to take advantage of its tools, and then cut or copy and paste the text into draw when you're satisfied.

Now is the time for all good men to come to the aid of their party. Party on, dude!

Now is the time for all good men to come to the aid of their party. Party on, dude!

Selected text object   Selected column

Creating text objects

Text objects are created using the Text tool. Select this tool from the palette, and click and drag a line of text. Don't worry about the size being correct or the text being correctly entered. You can resize the text box later using the resize handles and edit its content with standard editing techniques.

Working in columns

You can also create text objects using the Column tool. Text in columns can be edited and manipulated the same way text objects can. You can cut, copy, and paste to and from a column, and resize a column using its handles. You can also select

Show Column Borders or Hide Column Borders from the Arrange menu to display the window with or without its borders, respectively.

When you use columns, you can flow text from one column to the next on the page in the order you designate. A linked set of columns is called a *story*. Flowing stories across the page as you choose is the main purpose of the Text column feature. This arrangement allows you to create page layouts using templates you've either bought or created yourself.

Creating linked text columns:

1. **Select the Column tool from the Tool palette.** This tool has a small "A" with lines of text on it.

2. **Drag the crosshair cursor to the size and position of the column you desire.** For precision placement, use the rulers and set a grid to snap-to.

3. **Type the text you desire, or paste in text from another document using the Paste command from the Edit menu.** If you press the Option key while pasting, the text assumes the formatting that is active at the location of your insertion point.

4. **Select the Selection tool from the Tool palette and use it to select the first column in the sequence.** Notice that the column's Navigation tools below the column have grayed arrows indicating there is no linkage.

5. **Select the Linking tool — the center dot in the Navigation tools.**

6. **Select the next column in the sequence to link the two columns.**

7. **Continue selecting additional columns to add them to the sequence.**

8. **End the sequence and return to a Selection Arrow cursor by selecting the Linking tool.**

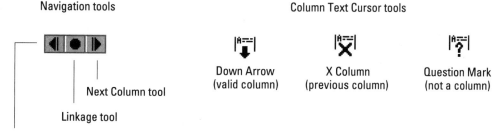

Navigation tools

Column Text Cursor tools

Next Column tool

Linkage tool

Previous Column tool

Down Arrow
(valid column)

X Column
(previous column)

Question Mark
(not a column)

When the columns are linked, Works flows additional text into any linked columns automatically. Works indicates the condition of a column and its suitability for linkage by changing its cursor shape. Columns that are valid for linkage display a Down Arrow text cursor. Columns that have been previously linked display an X text cursor, and any area not defined as a column displays a Question Mark text cursor. Clicking in a noncolumn area cancels the linkage attempt.

You can move the insertion point to a linked column quickly by selecting the Next or Previous Column tools from the Navigation tools.

Editing the column sequence:

1. **To break the link between columns, select the column you want to disassociate, and then select the Linking tool.**

2. **Select the column again, and it becomes the last column in the sequence; the Forward Column tool is dimmed.** Text in previously linked columns remains in those columns and doesn't flow beyond them.

3. **To change the position of a column in the sequence, repeat Step 1. Then, select the next column in the story.** Works empties the text that was in the first column and reflows text into the new column.

You can create sophisticated desktop publishing projects using these features — whether they're stories, newsletters, or even more complicated, multipage projects. For a general introduction to desktop publishing, read *Beyond the Desktop* by Barrie Sosinsky, 1991, Bantam Computer Publishing, New York, NY.

Working with groups and layers

There's another fundamental difference between vector (draw) and raster (paint) graphics. Drawn graphics describe an object as one, separate mathematical description — each drawn graphic may be comprised of many objects, each in its own layer. Raster graphics, on the other hand, use one bitmap to describe a single object — a bitmap that describes all the bits used to generate the complete graphic in a single plane. This makes drawn graphics far more versatile to manipulate and is another reason Works uses them. Because a drawn graphic is a collection of objects, each in its own layer, you can apply different options to each layer and even remove layers without disturbing the rest of the graphic.

What you see on your screen when you're working on a graphic depends on the ordering of the objects and the various properties assigned to them. Using the Overlay menu in the Tool palette, you can choose to make an object opaque or transparent. An opaque object hides any object or part of an object behind it. Transparent objects let the objects in layers behind them show through. You can reorder the layer an object appears in by selecting Bring To Front (Command-F) or Send To Back (Command-B) from the Arrange menu as appropriate. Unfortunately, Works has no commands for moving objects a single layer at a time, which is very inconvenient for drawing a graphic with many objects. Most full-featured draw programs include bring forward or send backward commands for this purpose.

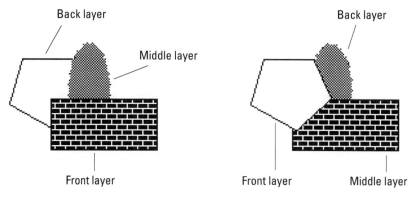

Back layer

Middle layer

Front layer

Back layer

Front layer   Middle layer

♦ To move an object in front of or in back of another object, highlight the object and select Bring to Front or Send to Back from the Arrange menu (Command-B).

♦ To manipulate a set of objects at one time, highlight the objects you wish to group and select Group from the Arrange menu (Command-G).

♦ Selecting Ungroup from the Arrange menu (Command-U) separates the objects.

If you want to manipulate a group of objects at one time, select them jointly before selecting an option. However, there will be times when you can't make that multiple selection due to an awkward ordering of layers or when it would be inconvenient to do so repeatedly. The Group command was included to create a set of objects that can be handled as a single object. When you select Group from the Arrange menu (Command-G), your set of objects lose their individual identities and respond to commands as a single object. A bounding box with a single set of handles for resizing or reshaping appears around a grouped set. To remove groupings so you can work on objects individually again, select the group and choose Ungroup from the Arrange menu (Command-U).

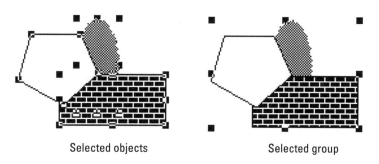

Selected objects   Selected group

You can also break shapes apart between different layers or combine them into one layer. The following section summarizes the commands available for this purpose.

Integrating and dividing shapes:

1. **Select the object or objects you wish to alter.**

2. **Choose Break Up from the Draw menu to break a shape wherever the lines intersect into separate line segments.**

3. **Select Join from the Draw menu to create shapes containing all of the lines of the separate objects.** The lines that intersect at endpoints become polygons.

Note: The Join command differs from the Group command in that it creates new objects. Group simply manipulates a set of objects as though it was one object.

Arrange	
Bring To Front	⌘F
Send To Back	⌘B
Group	⌘G
Ungroup	⌘U
Format Character...	
Alignment	▶
Hide Column Borders	
Vertex Snap	
Snap To Grid	
Grid Settings...	
Crop	
Spread Text	

The Arrange menu offers options for organizing and changing the appearance of objects

Once you have an object or object group in exactly the place or condition you want, you can freeze that object by selecting Lock Object from the Draw menu. You can lock one object of a drawn graphic at a time. Note, though, that there's no unlock command for a single object — you can only select Unlock All from the Draw menu for that purpose. Locking an object is particularly useful if you're doing precise work or working in an area with many objects. Unlock lets you manipulate objects nearby without changing your locked object in any way. You can tell that an object is locked, because if you try to select it, no handles appear. The following section details how to lock an object.

Locking an object's attributes:

1. **Highlight the object whose attributes you wish to lock.**

2. **Select Lock from the Draw menu.**

3. **Because locked objects cannot be selected, to unlock an object you must select Unlock All from the Draw menu and relock the other objects also affected.**

```
Draw
  Smooth

  Rotate...
  3-D Effect...
  Shadow

  Add Handles
  Remove Handles

  Break Up
  Join

  Lock Objects
  Unlock All
```

The Draw menu offers options for displaying special effects and locking off attributes of your objects

Applying patterns and colors to a graphic

Color is a wonderful enhancement to your documents, when displayed on your screen or printed on paper. Works color support was dramatically improved in version 3.0, so that any Macintosh with a color display can fully utilize its capabilities. The LC, LC II, IIsi, IIci, IIfx, and Quadra computers all support color — some as a built-in option, others with an added video board.

If your computer can display color or gray scale (intermediate shades of black and white), then you can select the number of colors you wish to use in the Monitor control panel. Choices for color display and output include black-and-white, or 4, 16, 256, or (if you're lucky) 16.8 million colors.

Objects have at least two colors associated with them that you select from the Fill menu of the Tool palette. The *foreground color* fills drawn objects and draws in the foreground pattern. The *background color* fills the space outside of objects and draws in the background pattern. The options offered in the Forecolor or Backcolor palette vary depending on the Macintosh you're using and how many colors you've chosen to display. You may be offered black-and-white, and 8, 16, or 256 colors or grays. Eight colors is the default choice for black-and-white display Macs that have access to color output devices. The color Fill menus display up to 256 different colors.

The Fill pattern applies whatever colors you select to create the effects you choose. For example, with 50 percent gray scale set, the color is interspersed with 50 percent white. A brick pattern uses the color to paint the bricks. You can get some truly cool effects if you play with the options, so have a good time with it. This is what you paid for when you bought a color machine.

If you want color output, your cheapest option is to buy four-color ribbons for an ImageWriter dot-matrix printer. The MacPalette ImageWriter driver improves the quality of your color output significantly. The next jump up in color provides significantly improved quality considering the moderate cost. The Hewlett-Packard DeskWriter C inkjet printer gives excellent results for about $800 in a printer that can be connected by AppleTalk. To produce better color images than this requires significantly more expensive thermal transfer or dye transfer printers, such as the Tektronix Phaser. In fact, these printers are a high enough quality and are often found in businesses or service bureaus. At the highest end are sublimation printers like the DuPont 4CAST or Iris inkjet printers. With these high-end printers, you can print color onto paper or onto film transparencies for overhead presentations.

When printing in color, be aware that printers use a color model different from that displayed in Works and based on printing inks called *CYMK* (cyan, yellow, magenta, and black). Your color files require separation into those colors to be printed by a commercial printer. Using two colors of ink and colored paper produces satisfactory results.

You can also separate layers by colors before printing. This separation is called *spot color* and can enhance your work. Any service bureau can use your Works files to do this separation. When you save your files to send to a third-party printer, be sure they're saved as PICT files, because most service bureaus don't use Microsoft Works. For more information on using color on your Mac, consult Michael Kieran's book *Desktop Publishing in Color*, 1991, Bantam Computer Books, New York, NY. Beach, Shepro, and Russon's *Getting It Printed*, 1986, Coast to Coast Books, Portland, OR, will help you learn about commercial printing.

Importing pictures and forms

The Macintosh Clipboard handles many kinds of objects — anything from simple text, to formatted text, to drawn graphics and bitmaps. Use your Scrapbook as a permanent repository for Clipboard data. You can paste any of these data types from other applications into the draw layer using either the Scrapbook or the Clipboard. As I've mentioned, graphics can be pasted *only* into the draw layer, and it's automatically turned on when they're pasted. Some of the graphics file formats supported by the Mac are PICT and its full-color descendent PICT2; TIFF; and PostScript files, normally in the form of Encapsulated PostScript (EPS). These are normally the best choices for working with graphics on the Macintosh. PICT and EPS use drawn graphics that also include text, and TIFF is a bitmap application. PICT can contain bitmapped graphics. Just to complicate things, TIFF can use either black-and-white, gray scale, or color. For further information on file formats of other graphics files and transferring or converting files, see *The File Format Handbook*, by Barrie Sosinsky, 1992, Peachpit Press, Berkeley, CA.

Your Mac and Works take care of the details required to paste these graphics into Draw, but there are different options you can use with different kinds of graphics. A bitmap graphic can be *cropped* — that is, you can make the graphic smaller so that it fits into an area. Cropping has the same effect as taking a photo and cutting it so that you create a vignette that fits into a picture frame. If you use drawn objects from PICT, and not a bitmap, then you can ungroup objects in the imported PICT file and work with them individually. The Crop command is found on the Arrange menu. When you use the Crop command, Works draws a dotted outline box around the graphic. You can resize the box to crop the graphic.

Finding outside sources of graphics

Few of us are artists, and those of us who are have little time to create graphics from scratch. You can drop a logo, a fancy border, or whatever into a document and customize it for your purposes. One way of incorporating quality graphics in Works is through the use of purchased artwork called *clip art*. Draw, EPS, PICT, and MacDraw files can be found, as well as TIFF bitmaps (normally in compressed formats). There are even computer data files for stock photographs in TIFF. Comstock in New York, NY, runs a pay-as-you-download library on an electronic bulletin board. You can purchase clip art on floppy disks or as complete collections on CD-ROM.

There's also a lot of public domain clip art available on on-line services and electronic bulletin boards, or through cheaply distributed shareware catalogs. Normally, these files are free for your use, but be careful to check the source if you plan to use them in a commercial venture. Commercial clip art offerings can be worth the expense — they have the best quality files, and they're sold to you with a license to use them freely in your work, although the license may vary depending on the source. Commercial clip art may be found in computer catalogs from many sources. For a definitive listing of clip art, with their samples printed out in miniature, see *Canned Art: Clip Art for the Macintosh*, by Erfert Fenton, 1990, Peachpit Press, Berkeley, CA.

Another simple way to get graphics into your work is to use the special fonts that print graphics as text characters. The best-known of these fonts is a collection of arrows, numbers, symbols, boxes, and other miscellaneous symbols called Zapf Dingbats. Other fonts in this category are the bitmapped fonts Cairo and Mobile. For special symbols used in maps, use Adobe's Carta font; music symbols are included in the Adobe Sonata font. The biggest advantage to using these font characters is that they work equally well in Draw and other Works layers, and they're small and easily processed.

Note: Symbol fonts place graphics into a word processor's text layer, as a way around using drawn graphics.

People, Humans

Font- Cairo

Using special effects with text

In addition to normal text attributes, you can also attach text to a path, a line, or an arc. You might want to do this to create a logo or a headline. The effect isolates each character in a text string and attaches it to the line.

Attaching text to a path, line, or arc:

1. **Select your text and the line or arc that it's to be attached to.**

2. **Choose Spread Text from the Arrange menu.** The following figure shows the effect. You can group your spread text to manipulate it further. Make sure that you make the line or arc large enough to spread the text without the characters overlapping. Works places the characters evenly over the entire line or arc. When you deselect Spread Text, the underlying arc or line disappears and the reshaped text remains.

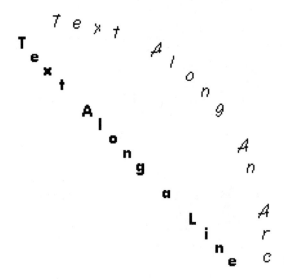

There are many special effects new to Works 3 that you can use on shapes, lines, and text. A 3-D effect is available that allows you to create a perspective, give depth to an object, and choose the angle of the effect. Use 3-D for splashy headlines, emphasis, and panache. Apply 3-D to text, lines, shapes, and PICT objects. (PICT is a Macintosh graphics file description.) You apply the 3-D to a selected object by choosing 3D Effect from the Draw menu. In the 3D Effect dialog box, enter the appropriate numbers for the depth and angle of the perspective you desire.

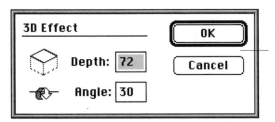

The 3-D Effect dialog box allows you to select measurements for the angle and depth of perspective

Be sure to work on a duplicate copy of your original object as you experiment — once a 3-D effect is added to an object, that object cannot be changed back to its original form using the Undo command.

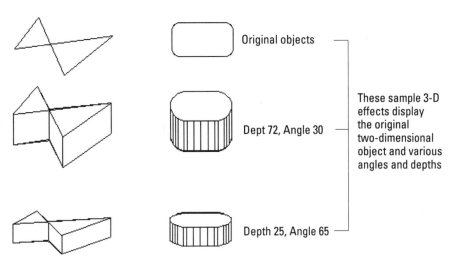

Original objects

Dept 72, Angle 30

Depth 25, Angle 65

These sample 3-D effects display the original two-dimensional object and various angles and depths

Another way to emphasize an object is to add a shadow. You do this by duplicating a shape, shading it, offsetting the filled shape at an angle, and sending it to the back of your original. Works automates this process with the Shadow command on the Draw menu. The shadow is selected, so if you don't like the effect, you can either move the shadow around or remove it by pressing Backspace or Delete.

Quick Tips

The following tips explain what you should look for in a draw program and the programs that are currently available.

Looking beyond Works' Draw module

There are many choices of products in the draw category, but no outstanding options from Microsoft. The two best overall products are Deneba Canvas and Aldus Super-Paint. Both of these products create drawn graphics in one layer, paint graphics in another, and print the combined results. They are so functional for the money that they'll allow you to complete almost any project. Less satisfactory is the upgrade to Claris MacDraw, the original draw package that came bundled with the Macintosh. It has fewer tools for the money.

In the area of technical illustration, Aldus FreeHand and Adobe Illustrator are the market leaders. Both create high quality PostScript graphics and are used by professional graphic artists in much of the commercial artwork you see around you. The Macintosh has many computer aided design products. MacDraft would be a low-priced choice, whereas Claris CAD would be the best choice for a mid-level, general purpose product. Ashlar Vellum is noted for many innovative features, and Autodesk, AutoCAD, and Computervisions' VersaCAD, the industry leaders, are available if you have a couple thousand dollars to spend on a high-end product.

Draw features to look for

You should expect to find the following additional features in the more complete packages:

- ✦ Additional tools and special effects.
- ✦ Outline tools with variable arcs like Bézier curves.
- ✦ Precision placement and alignment tools.
- ✦ High quality color support, separation, and output.
- ✦ Pattern creation and tiling effects.
- ✦ Object libraries, sometimes organized in databases.
- ✦ Autotracing, or raster-to-vector conversions.
- ✦ Advanced outline font handling.

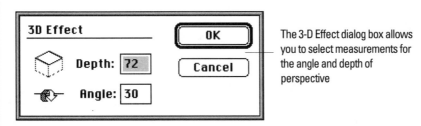

The 3-D Effect dialog box allows you to select measurements for the angle and depth of perspective

Be sure to work on a duplicate copy of your original object as you experiment — once a 3-D effect is added to an object, that object cannot be changed back to its original form using the Undo command.

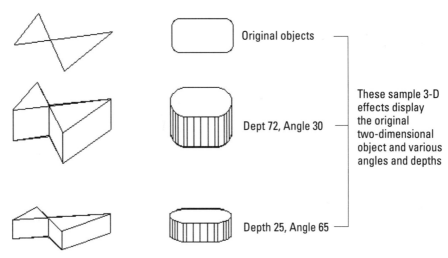

Original objects

Dept 72, Angle 30

Depth 25, Angle 65

These sample 3-D effects display the original two-dimensional object and various angles and depths

Another way to emphasize an object is to add a shadow. You do this by duplicating a shape, shading it, offsetting the filled shape at an angle, and sending it to the back of your original. Works automates this process with the Shadow command on the Draw menu. The shadow is selected, so if you don't like the effect, you can either move the shadow around or remove it by pressing Backspace or Delete.

Topic 5
Using the Draw Module

Quick Tips

The following tips explain what you should look for in a draw program and the programs that are currently available.

Looking beyond Works' Draw module

There are many choices of products in the draw category, but no outstanding options from Microsoft. The two best overall products are Deneba Canvas and Aldus Super-Paint. Both of these products create drawn graphics in one layer, paint graphics in another, and print the combined results. They are so functional for the money that they'll allow you to complete almost any project. Less satisfactory is the upgrade to Claris MacDraw, the original draw package that came bundled with the Macintosh. It has fewer tools for the money.

In the area of technical illustration, Aldus FreeHand and Adobe Illustrator are the market leaders. Both create high quality PostScript graphics and are used by professional graphic artists in much of the commercial artwork you see around you. The Macintosh has many computer aided design products. MacDraft would be a low-priced choice, whereas Claris CAD would be the best choice for a mid-level, general purpose product. Ashlar Vellum is noted for many innovative features, and Autodesk, AutoCAD, and Computervisions' VersaCAD, the industry leaders, are available if you have a couple thousand dollars to spend on a high-end product.

Draw features to look for

You should expect to find the following additional features in the more complete packages:

- ✦ Additional tools and special effects.

- ✦ Outline tools with variable arcs like Bézier curves.

- ✦ Precision placement and alignment tools.

- ✦ High quality color support, separation, and output.

- ✦ Pattern creation and tiling effects.

- ✦ Object libraries, sometimes organized in databases.

- ✦ Autotracing, or raster-to-vector conversions.

- ✦ Advanced outline font handling.

Summary

✔ Drawn graphics use mathematical relationships to create entities called objects. The Draw module creates this kind of graphic.

✔ The Draw module can be opened as a separate file or as a layer above a word processor, database, or spreadsheet file.

✔ What you see in a word processor, database, or spreadsheet window is a combination of the draw and underlying layer.

✔ Use the options on the expanded Draw Tool palette to create drawn objects.

✔ Objects have attributes or characteristics that affect their appearance, and those attributes can be changed at any time.

✔ Text can appear in the draw layer as an object or in columns, which can be linked so that text flows into them automatically.

✔ Objects appear in layers, one in front of another.

✔ Objects can be grouped and manipulated as if they were a single object.

✔ Color and patterns can be assigned to an object as an attribute, either as foreground or background color.

Topic 6
Using Works' Databases

Overview

A *database* is an electronic collection of detailed and interrelated information that can be automatically reorganized as you need it. The advantages to using a database are compelling. Using the organizational features of a database, you can easily accomplish many tasks central to your business and personal life. Any information you collect as a set of related facts can be electronically organized and stored in a file. A database can store large amounts of information in a small space and can be used for any number of tasks. You can create sales records, inventory your household goods, or put your address book on-line.

When you use a database, you won't have to rely on your memory to find something. Instead, search your database for information using criteria you specify to retrieve matches. Your searches can involve more than a simple find, and you can use several sets of selection criteria in your queries. You manipulate your data in new ways with the results of your search and examine information in a manner that lets you create valuable relationships you couldn't find any other way.

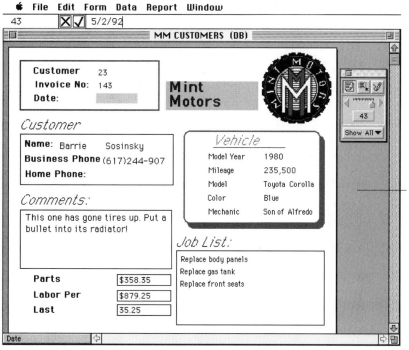

A database lets you create and print electronic forms, like this work order for a large number of entries

Works' database streamlines repetitive tasks by repeating a given operation for each entry in your section. You can take your data and print it on electronic forms that you create yourself, and you can add graphics or a logo to the form using the draw feature in the Database module. The database also prints mailing labels, performs mail merges (which permit personalized mass mailings), and creates and saves reports based on your queries. You can access canned databases stationery or template forms, and adapt them to your own use. You will learn to do all these things in this Topic.

What is a database?

A database is a filing system that organizes data into a collection. You probably work with a database many times during your week and don't realize it. When you use a bank's teller machine, you're accessing a database located on a large, remote computer. Your travel agent uses a database, such as the American Airlines SABRE system, to find available flights; you can do the same by dialing an on-line service and logging onto the SABRE system. On-line services, such as CompuServe, GEnie, America On-line, and BIX are examples of extended databases.

A phone book, Rolodex, *TV Guide,* dictionary, and other reference materials are also databases. Although they aren't thought of as electronic, you can find many of these reference works in electronic form in a computer store, or by browsing through a computer magazine or catalog. Reference databases are normally distributed on CD-ROM as read-only, or sometimes they can be found on floppy disks. Works lets you create your own databases that you can add to and alter as the need arises.

Database systems impose a standardized structure on information. An underlying unit, called a *record,* varies with your project and forms the basis for database organization. For example, people are the basis for records in an address book, words form records in a dictionary, and time periods form records in the *TV Guide.* If you ran a radio station and wanted to organize the song collection into a database, then the name of each CD or record album might be the basis for a database record, and each song name, recording artist, and song length would be included in that record. Databases use files to hold records, and each record holds its chunk of data in a container called a *field.* In Works, fields can hold text, numbers, dates, and times, and they can contain absolute values or the results of calculated formulas. Other Macintosh databases let you work with sounds, graphics, and any other information that can be represented by a computer's binary code.

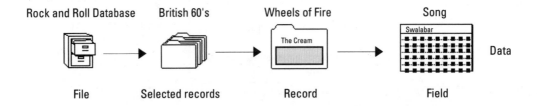

Rock and Roll Database	British 60's	Wheels of Fire	Song
File	Selected records	Record	Field

On the surface, databases appear to be similar to spreadsheets because both display data in a matrix arrangement. They both use many of the same functions for internal calculations that place values into either database fields or spreadsheet cells. The underlying concept of a record makes a database unique. Operations performed on fields in a database leave the records you enter intact, whereas it's possible to perform operations on a spreadsheet that scramble cells and rows. This difference is so critical and difficult to grasp at first that the entire section in Topic 7, "When to use a spreadsheet instead of a database," is devoted to it. Spreadsheets are the subject of the next Topic.

Understanding the principles of database design

Often, a filing cabinet analogy is used to describe a database. Imagine that all of your business records are placed in the cabinet, and each drawer contains different customer information. You might use a drawer for each year of sales and a divider for each client. Inside every divider might be folders for each important type of correspondence: purchase orders, invoices, and the like. Translated into database terminology, a drawer would be a file, a divider would be a record, a file folder would be a field, and each form inside the file folder would be data in that field. This design analogy is one of many possible ways to organize a database, although it's probably not the best design for an electronic database.

Consider how this scheme might limit you if you wanted to learn something fundamental about your business. For example, say you want to know your level of sales for a specific time period. That information is contained in your invoices, scattered throughout all of the folders. To find your answer, you'd have to search through every piece of paper in the drawer, or every record in the database, and then add all your sales totals. If the number of transactions are small, this might be fine, but a larger number would make this process tedious. It would be better to have a single file that held only invoices. This design would help you find your total sales for this project more quickly, but it removes the connection between invoices and related letters of correspondence to your customers. Designing a database is a series of compromises, and how you organize your database depends on the purpose that it's intended to fulfill.

Developing a database is something that takes planning, and practice. The important considerations are summarized below:

+ *Files*. What information is contained in the database?

+ *Records*. What is your organizing philosophy? What unit of information defines your project?

+ *Fields*. What are your data types, and how many of them are there? Fields are discussed in more detail in "Understanding fields" later in this Topic.

+ *Forms*. What do you want your data to look like on the screen and in printed form. Forms are also called *layouts*. Works lets you create up to 16 forms per file.

◆ *Reports.* What results do you wish to obtain from your database? What searches do you plan to conduct? Often, generating reports is the reason you constructed the database in the first place. If so, you need to work backwards to see that all of the data you need is contained in the file that generates the report.

Whatever you do, keep your database simple to begin with. This improves database performance and makes it easier to make changes as you learn. Consider the way you want your database to operate. If you're going to use names in a form, split the names up so you can work with the first and last names separately when using a letter salutation. Then your Dear John merge letters won't become Dear John Doe letters. The latter is so impersonal.

Test your database with some representative data. Flaws in your design become apparent early, and are more easily corrected before you've entered a hundred records. No one is ever satisfied completely with a database design, so don't be afraid to let your design change over time as you assess your needs.

Becoming familiar with the database window

Some common elements appear in all database windows. You can always tell that a database is on your screen by the (DB) that follows the filename in the title bar. The Form, Data, and Report menus are also specific to the Database module. Other elements, such as the entry box, cancel box, and entry bar, are found in the Spreadsheet module, as well as the database.

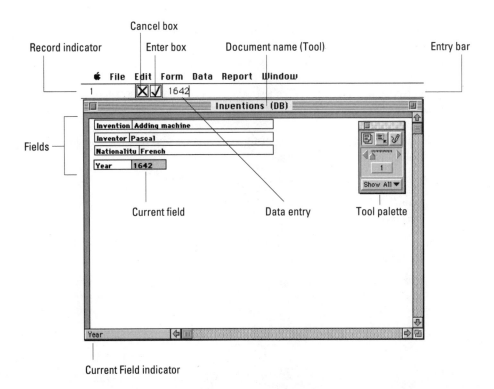

The functions of the database window elements are summarized below:

◆ *The entry bar.* Shows the contents of the current field. Click in this bar to enter the data into the current field, or select and edit data appearing there. If you type without clicking, your data replaces the previous contents of the field. The entry bar only appears in the two database views in which data can be entered, namely, the data and list views.

◆ *The enter box.* Select this box to replace a field's contents with the data that appears in the entry bar, or press Enter or Return for the same effect. If you type more than one line of data, the Enter box expands to display the entire contents, as shown in the following figure. You can type up to 255 characters in a field. The enter box doesn't appear until you've typed in some data.

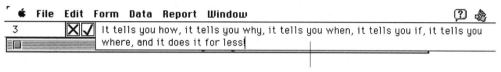

The entry bar expands to show more than one line of text when necessary

◆ *The cancel box.* Select to leave the field's contents as they were before you made a change. Like the enter box, the cancel box won't appear until you begin to type data.

◆ *The Record indicator.* Tells you the number of current records you're viewing. This indicator doesn't appear in the design view because no records appear in this view.

◆ *The Field Name indicator.* This information appears by default. To hide the field name in a separate box, uncheck the Show Field Names check box in either the Place Name or Field Names dialog boxes (from the Place Name and Field Names commands in the Form menu of the design view).

In the design view, the name of a field without a label appears within the field borders in an area called the *Field entry box*. That same field won't show the field name in the data view. Field names in the list and report views appear as a heading in the top row above the contents of that field.

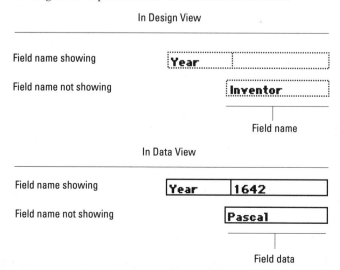

✦ *The Field entry box.* This area appears highlighted when the field is selected. Text entry is done in the entry bar only.

Learning the four views of Works' database

A database can appear on your screen in several different views. A *view* is a way of displaying data on your screen. Although the information in the database is the same, each view allows you to work with the information in different ways. Works has four views: the design view, data view, list view, and report view. You can see only a single record in the design and data views, whereas you can see any number of records (even one, if you like) in the list and report views.

Each view exists for a different purpose, as summarized below:

✦ *The design view.* You see this view when you first create a database. It allows you to create and delete fields, modify their position and appearance, and add graphics. No data can be entered in this view, so the entry bar doesn't appear.

✦ *The data view.* Use the data view to enter and find data. What appears in the data view is determined by how you set up the design view. Although the two views look similar, the data view has an entry bar, and data appears in a field's Field entry box.

✦ *The list view.* This view presents a tabular view of data in rows or columns. In this view, you can create fields; enter, sort, and find data; and view one, many, or all records at a time. Any formatting applied to the list view doesn't appear in the data or design views, but does carry over to the report view.

✦ *The report view.* This tabular view allows you to search, select, and sort records; perform calculations, such as sums; and print information. In this view, you can only display and not alter data, unlike the list view. To format data into a report, switch to the list view to make those changes.

You can have up to 16 forms per file. Create new ones by selecting New Form from the Form menu. You can modify the forms and switch between them using the Form menu. In the New Form dialog box, set a form size either as a standard or custom size. This dialog box is similar to a Page Setup dialog box. Form names are added to the Form menu as they're created. Each form is formatted using a design view that behaves independently of any other form. This lets you use the same data for many purposes.

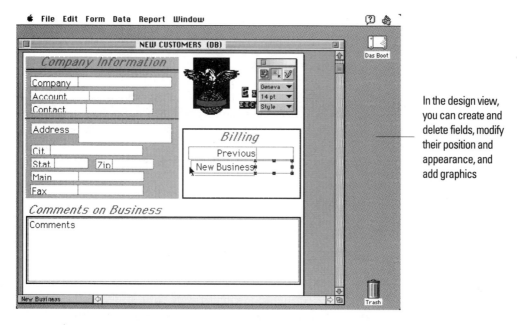

In the design view, you can create and delete fields, modify their position and appearance, and add graphics

Draw can be activated in the design view by selecting Draw On (Command-J) from the Windows menu, or by clicking the drawing tool from the floating Tool palette. You can use draw to add lines and boxes, import logos, and so on, using the skills you learned in Topic 5. To format a field, simply select it, and apply the appropriate commands. Any formatting done in the design view appears only in this view and in the data view, allowing you to create special output, such as forms.

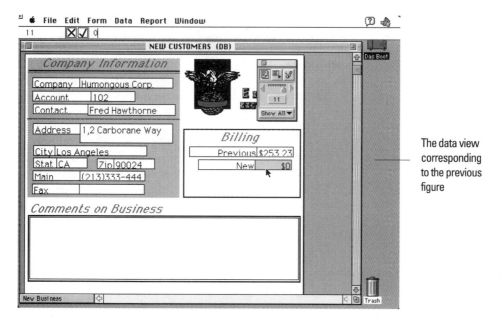

The data view corresponding to the previous figure

When you select Draw On from the Windows menu or select the Draw tool from the Tool palette to create graphics for your spreadsheet, you're switched to the draw layer associated with the design view.

The list view is meant to give you an overview of your database file. Only one list view exists in your database, but you can have many different forms and reports created in the design view and displayed in the data view. When you delete a field from the list view, it disappears from your database, along with all of its contents. However, adding fields while in list view won't change the display in the design or data views because these two views are meant for a specific purpose, such as producing a printed form.

Field name   Current record

Field entries (data)

🍎 File Edit Form Data Report Window

3   Sosinsky, Barrie

Bibliography (DB)

AUTHOR	TITLE	PUBLISHER-CITY	PUBLISHER-CO.	PUB. DA
Poole, Lon	Macworld Guide to System 7	San Mateo, CA	IDG Books Worldw	1991
Heid, Jim	Macworld Complete Mac Handbook	San Mateo, CA	IDG Books Worldw	1991
Sosinsky, Barrie	Macworld Guide to Microsoft Works 3	San Mateo, CA	IDG Books Worldw	1992
Heid, Jim	Macworld Guide to Microsoft Word 5	San Mateo, CA	IDG Books Worldw	1992

Current field

Record Selector box

3

Show All ▼
Geneva ▼
9 pt   ▼
Style   ▼

Several reports can be created and saved by name in your file. You can only see reports in the report view; you switch between reports by choosing their name from the Report menu. When you first create a report, all fields appear. Creating a report is discussed in more detail in the section titled "Creating reports" later in this Topic.

The list and report views look similar to a spreadsheet and can be confusing to new Works users. You cannot turn draw on in these two views, but you can format text, as well as move, resize, and delete fields in these views so that information prints properly. Remember that any formatting you apply won't appear in the design or data views.

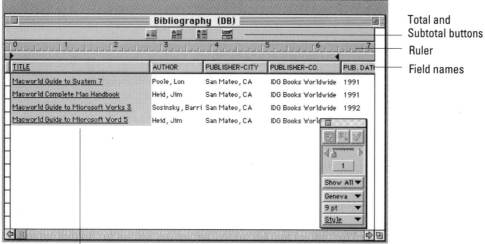

Total and
Subtotal buttons
Ruler
Field names

Current selected field

Both the design and data views can be rearranged so that what you see and print is appropriate to your purpose. Only fields within the printable area will print, so move and resize fields while you are in these two views.

Starting a database:

1. **Select New or Open from the File menu.**

2. **To create a new database in either dialog box, select the database icon, and then select the New button.**

— or —

2. **Double-click on the database icon to start a new database.**

4. **Create the fields you'd like to use (see "Creating fields" later in this Topic).**

5. **Save your database and give it a filename of up to 31 characters long.**

If you want to revise a database, you can open and change previously saved databases. Databases that are stationery documents will open as an untitled copy in a database window for you to work with.

Note: Stationery is a System 7 feature only.

Working with forms in the Database module:

1. **To create a form, select New Form from the Form menu.**

2. **If you wish to alter a form you've already created, select Setup Form from the Form menu.**

3. **Type a name of up to 31 characters in length in the Name text box.**

4. Select the Standard Size radio button, and then select the form size that is appropriate.

— or —

4. If you'd rather use an unusual size, select the Custom Size radio button and enter the appropriate numbers in the Height and Width text boxes. Forms can be no smaller than 0.5 × 0.5-inches or 0.5 × 0.5-centimeters, depending on your specified unit in the database Preference dialog box.

5. Select OK to create the form and have Works add its name to the Form menu.

The Field button lets you place fields on a form, using a Place dialog box. This feature is discussed later in the section titled "Adding, renaming, or deleting fields."

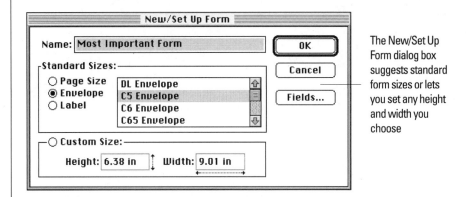

The New/Set Up Form dialog box suggests standard form sizes or lets you set any height and width you choose

Works adds your new form name to the Form menu. Select that name when you want to enter data into or print the new form. If you want to rename or resize a form, select Set Up Form from the Form menu to return to the New/Set Up Form dialog box.

Duplicating a form:

1. In the data or design views, go to the form you want to duplicate.

2. Select Duplicate Form from the Form menu.

3. Select OK.

Deleting a form:

1. Select the name of the form you wish to delete from the Form menu.

2. Select Delete Form from the Form menu.

3. Select the Delete button in the alert box to remove the form from your file.

4. If you change your mind, *immediately* **select Undo from the Edit menu** ▮
restore the deletion.

```
Form
   Data View
   List View            ⌘L
 ✓ Design View

   Place Field...
   Format Field...
   Field Name...
   Delete Field...
   Format Character...
 ✓ Show Field Border

   New Form...
   Set Up Form...
   Delete Form...
   Duplicate Form...

 ✓ Untitled Form 1
```

Switching views:

◆ To switch to the data, list, or design views using a menu command, choose the Data View, List View (Command-L), or Design View from the Form menu, respectively.

◆ To switch to the report view using menu commands, select Report View from the Report menu.

◆ To switch to the design or data views using the Tool palette, select the Design View tool or the Data View tool, respectively, from the Tool palette.

◆ Using the mouse, switch from the list view and return to your previous work by double-clicking on the Record Selector box, located to the left of any record. Whatever form was previously selected appears on your screen.

◆ Switch to the list view from either the data or design views by double-clicking on any white space in the form.

Data tool selected

Design tool selected

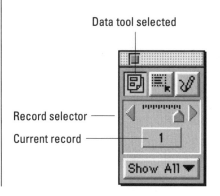

Record selector

Current record

lds can be thought of as containers that your database uses to hold the data you
ter. Each file can have up to 254 fields. You can control the names, formatting, and
ppearance of the fields. All fields appear in the list view, but only the fields you have
laced on a form using the design view appear in the list view for any specific form.
ach form you create in the design view can display a different combination of fields.

The method used to create and remove fields from a database depends on the current
active view. There are a few rules to remember as you go through this process, summarized below.

- ✦ When you create a field, it always appears in the list view, but it only appears on forms if you place that field there.

- ✦ If a form is active when the field is created, that field is automatically placed on the form.

- ✦ When you delete a field from the list view, that field and all of its data disappears entirely from your database.

- ✦ When you delete a field from a form, that field still exists in your database — the field still appears in the list view, and also on any other forms it was placed on other than the one you just deleted it from.

Fields must be defined to contain a certain type of data. By requiring you to format, or
define, a field's data, the database can greatly speed up its operation. Fields can have
default or constant values entered into them, or be the result of a calculation. Select
Format Field from the Form menu, or double-click in the list view on the field name to
open the Format Field dialog box. The field formats you can choose from are summarized below.

- ✦ *Text*. Any character you can type. Select text whenever you're unsure what will go in a field, or when you're performing a search for all characters in a field.

- ✦ *Numbers*. Only typed numbers, not text, are displayed. Using a number field allows you to globally format your data entry, control the number of places to the right of the decimal point, whether currency symbols are displayed, and so on. Negative numbers appear in parentheses on your screen. Use number fields whenever you know you'll be using numbers exclusively in that field.

- ✦ *Times*. A time field lets you enter time figures and have them automatically for-matted.

- ✦ *Dates*. Similarly, you can enter a date and have Works automatically display it in a format you specify.

Any field type may require that values be entered and that a specified default value appear on every record. All fields except text can be based on a calculation. When a field is based on an entered formula, Works automatically enters the result into the field, just as it does for a default value field. The result of a calculation is displayed on your screen, and Works doesn't allow you to enter a value into that field. Calculations greatly speed up your data entry and aid in eliminating errors. Topic 11 describes, in detail, operators used in calculations.

Always remember to divide your information into the smallest fields you'll use in your work. For example, create a field that contains a person's title for salutations (Mr., Mrs., Dr., and so on), and use one for the first name, and another for the last name. Break addresses into street, city, and zip code fields, adding a second street field if needed. Name your fields in a way that reminds you of their purpose, and try to name your fields consistently from one file to another.

The internal format for a field is different from the formatting that can be applied to a field's external appearance. By selecting a field, you can apply different fonts, font sizes, font styles, colors, and so on. You can set preferences for the character format of a field, default font, and font size in the database Preferences dialog box. In the design or list views, you can select a range of fields using selection methods you learned about in Topic 2. That is, you can drag a selection marquee around fields in the design view, or press Shift while selecting fields to add or subtract them from a selected range in either the design or list views. The methods of selecting fields are summarized below:

- ✦ *Select a field's data.* Click on the Data Entry portion of that field.

- ✦ *Select all entries of a field.* Click on the field's name. In the report view only one field can be selected at a time.

- ✦ *Select a range of entries.* Click and drag over the range of entries you wish to highlight.

- ✦ *Select a record.* In the list or report views, select the Record Selection box to the left of the record.

- ✦ *Select data in a field.* Select the appropriate text in the entry bar.

Current record

Current field

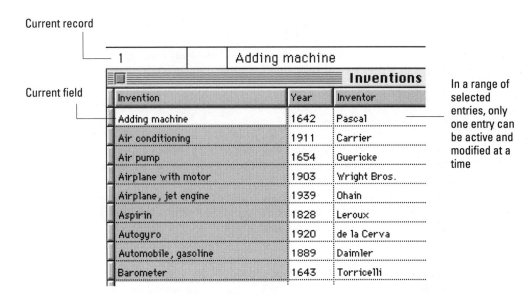

In a range of selected entries, only one entry can be active and modified at a time

Note: Although you can select a range for formatting, you can only have one active field entry to enter data into. That active field appears bordered in white.

Since the Database module supports Draw in a layer above all fields, you can also format drawn objects, including text objects, using methods you learned about in the previous Topic. All fields and graphics can be selected for formatting by selecting Select All from the Edit menu. Deselect your selection by clicking outside of the highlighted area.

Fields are moved on the screen by clicking and dragging them. Resize them in the design view by clicking and dragging on the field's reshaping or resizing handles. External formatting of a field is modified using methods identical to those you learned in the previous Topic. To display a field border, select the field, and select Show Field Border from the Form menu. Remove the border by choosing the check marked Show Field Border once again.

Data that you enter into fields can have only one set of character attributes applied to them. Select Character Formatting from the Form menu to make selections of fonts, sizes, styles, color, and so on.

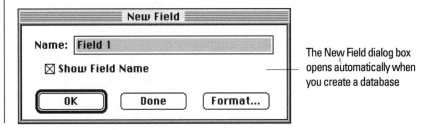

The New Field dialog box opens automatically when you create a database

Creating fields:

1. **Select New from the File menu.** When you create a database, Works automatically posts the New Field dialog box.

2. **Enter the field name into the Name text box.** Field names must begin with a letter, can be up to 63 characters long, and must not contain symbols that Works would interpret as being part of a mathematical expression, like asterisks, parentheses, hyphens, and periods.

3. **Select the Show Field Name check box if you wish your field name to appear on a label.** To hide your field name in the design field, select the Show Field Name check box again.

4. **Select the Format button to set the field's data type (text, number, time, or date) or to format the data in a special way on your screen.** The Format Field dialog box shown in the following figure is then posted. You can also get to this dialog box in the design view by selecting a field and choosing Format Field from the Form menu, or in the list view by double-clicking on the field name.

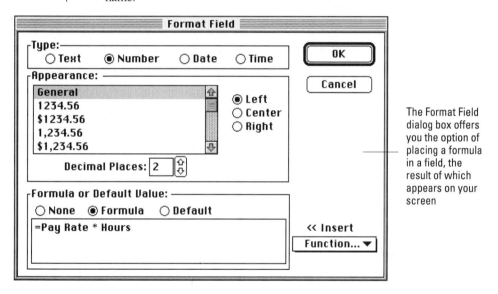

The Format Field dialog box offers you the option of placing a formula in a field, the result of which appears on your screen

5. **Select a function to enter into the Format calculation.** See the previous figure.

6. **Select OK or press Return or Enter to go back to the New Field Name dialog box. Then select the Done button to create the field.**

7. **Repeat to create additional fields, as desired.** Any new field assumes the formatting of the previous field, unless you change it.

```
┌─────────────────────────────────────────────┐
│  Paste Function                               │
│  ───────────────────────────────────────────│
│  ● Mathematical    │ Abs(n)        │ ⇧        │
│  ○ Statistical     │ Exp(n)        │ ▓        │
│  ○ Logical         │ Int(n)        │ ▓        │
│  ○ Trigonometric   │ Ln(n)         │          │
│  ○ Financial       │ Log10(n)      │          │
│  ○ Date & Time     │ Mod(n,d)      │          │
│  ○ Special         │ Rand()        │ ⇩        │
│  ┌Description:─────────────────────────┐     │
│  │ Calculates the absolute value of n.  │     │
│  │                                       │     │
│  │                                       │     │
│  └───────────────────────────────────────┘   │
│                                               │
│        Refer to User's Guide, Page 27         │
│                                               │
│      ┌────── OK ──────┐  ┌─── Cancel ───┐     │
└─────────────────────────────────────────────┘
```

The Function dialog box offers you a choice of preprogrammed calculations to enter into a field

Calculations can be entered in the text box at the bottom of the Field Formula dialog box. As a convenience, Works will auto-enter calculation operators for you if you click the Function pop-up menu and choose that option. See Topic 11 for more detailed information on calculations.

If you turn off the Show Field Name check box, then the name of the field only appears in the design view within the field's data entry portion and doesn't appear in the data view. In the design view, you can also drag a field name's left handle to the right towards the data entry portion of the field to hide its name. Field names always appear in the list and report views.

Once you've created a field, you can change its name or field label. The following section details how.

Changing a field name and label:

1. **Switch to the design view.**

2. **Select the field by clicking on any part of it.** Resize handles appear around that field to indicate that it's been selected and that its name is highlighted.

3. **Select Field Name from the Form menu.**

4. **The New Field dialog box is displayed. Edit the field name as desired.**

Be aware that when you change a field's format or calculation, what you see on your screen changes. You may lose some data, and Works posts an alert box before this happens. To return to your previous data, select Undo (Command-Z) from the Edit menu *immediately* after changing the data type, or that information will be permanently lost.

To add new fields to an existing database, do the following.

Adding new fields to an existing database:

1. **In the design view, select Place Field to open the Place Field dialog box.**

2. **Select the New button to take you to the New Field dialog box.**

3. **Follow the appropriate steps for creating a new field (outlined previously in this Topic).**

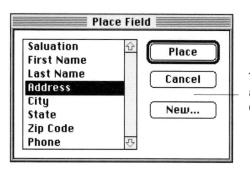

The Place Field dialog box allows you to add fields to existing databases

The Place Field command is also capable of adding a previously defined field to a form. To do that, use the instructions in the following section.

Adding a predefined field:

1. **Choose the form name you want to alter from the Form menu.**

2. **Switch to the design view, if necessary.**

3. **Select Place Field from the Form menu.** You can also open the Place Field dialog box by selecting the Fields button in the New/Setup Forms dialog box.

4. **Highlight the field name you wish to add and press the Place button. Or simply double-click on a field name.**

5. **To place a range of fields, press Shift as you select field names, or drag over the appropriate names.** Any selected field on a form has a check mark next to its name in the Place dialog box.

6. **To add a field without adding it to a form, switch to the list view.**

7. **Open the New Field dialog box, enter the name of the field you are adding, and then select the Create button.**

You can also add a field by turning on the Draw module, selecting the Text tool, and dragging to create a rectangle of the size you desire. The Place Field dialog box appears, and when you make your selection, that field is automatically placed into the rectangle.

Renaming a field:

1. Select the field to be renamed in the design or list views.

2. Select Rename Field from the Form menu.

3. Enter the new name in the Name text box.

4. Select the Rename button.

Deleting a field:

1. Select the field you wish to delete by clicking on its field name.

2. Select Delete Field from the Form menu.

— or —

2. Press Backspace or Delete on your keyboard.

Depending on your current view, deleting a field can either remove it from your current form, and leave its definition and data in the database (design view), or remove it entirely (list view).

Moving a field

There are different ways to move a field depending on the view you are in. The following instructions summarize how to move a field in design view and report view.

Moving fields in the design view:

1. **Drag the field to the spot you prefer.** Press Shift while dragging to move the field perfectly horizontally or vertically. To align a field when moving it, use a drawn line as a guide and drag the field to that line.

Moving fields in the list or report views:

1. **Highlight the field name.**

2. **Drag the field name to the right or left, using the Hand cursor.** As you move the selected field past other fields, they will be highlighted to show the path of movement.

3. **Release the mouse, and the fields will be rearranged.**

Note: You cannot either resize or move a field in the data view.

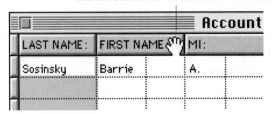

To move a field in the list of report views, drag the field name to the new location with the hand cursor

Resizing a field:

In the design view:

1. **Click on the field to highlight it and display its resizing handles.**

2. **Drag a handle until the field is the appropriate length.**

3. **Release the mouse when the field is the right size.**

In list or report view:

1. **Move the pointer to the right border of the field name.** The cursor becomes a cross with a double-headed arrow pointing right and left.

2. **Click and drag the field name to the right or left with this cursor.** A dotted line appears to indicate the new size of your field.

3. **Release the mouse when the field is the right size.**

LAST NAME:	FIRST NAME↔	MI:
Sosinsky	Barrie	A.

Note: Although a field's data box can be resized in any direction, the field name can only be lengthened horizontally.

Entering data:

1. **In the data or list views, click on a field to select it.** The field's data entry portion becomes highlighted. Any data contained in that field for that particular record appears in the entry bar.

2. **Select and edit text as desired, using standard text editing techniques.**

— or —

2. **Type replacement text without selecting any portion of the previous data.** Up to 250 characters can be entered into a field. The entry box expands and wordwraps.

3. **Select the entry box to place your new data into the field, or press Enter.**

4. **Select the cancel box to leave the data as it was before you altered it.**

Entering a date or time into a field:

1. **Select one of the following formats when you type in dates: 8/27/52; 27 Aug, 1952; 27, Aug; Wed, Aug 27, 1952; Wed 27 Aug, 1952; 27 August, 1952; August 27, 1952; Wednesday, August 27, 1952; or Wednesday, 27 August 1952. Any date valid for the Macintosh may be entered.** The range of dates available includes January 1, 1904, through February 6, 2040.

2. **Use one of the following formats when you type in times: 5:53:40 PM; 5:53 PM; 17:53:40; 17:53; 5:5 PM; or 17:5.**

You enter a lot of information into a database, often in a very short amount of time. Much of this information is nearly impossible to remember or re-create. Even a few keystrokes of numbers or text can be tough to remember, so remember to save often and keep multiple backups of your files.

Moving around in a database

+ If you see a field, you can click on it to select it. Otherwise, scroll around the database until it comes into view and select it.

+ To select a record in the list of report views, click on the record's Record Selection box to the left of the first field.

+ Select Next Record (Command-equal) or Previous Record (Command-minus) from the Data menu to move to another record.

The Next Record and Previous Record commands are most useful when working with forms, when only a single record is displayed at any one time.

You can use shortcuts to select fields for data entry so that you don't have to click on each field in turn. These shortcuts are summarized below:

+ *The Enter key.* Use this key to leave a field selected after entering data into it.

+ *The Return key.* From the data view, press this key to move to the next field down in the record in the data view. When you press Return in the last field in the record, Works moves you to the first field of the next record. In the list view, press the Return key to move the cursor down from the same field to the next record.

+ *The Shift-Return keystroke.* In the data view, use this keystroke to move the cursor up to the previous field in a record. When you press Shift-Return in the first field of a record, Works moves the cursor to the last field of the previous record. In the list view, this keystroke moves the cursor up to the same field in the previous record.

+ *The Tab key.* From either the data or list views, press the Tab key to select the next field to the right in a record.

+ *The Shift-Tab keystroke.* Selects the previous field to the left in the same record in either the data or list views.

+ *The left arrow key.* Press this key to move left one field and select it. In the list view, if the first field in a record is selected, press the left arrow key to move to the last field in the previous record.

+ *The right arrow key.* Press this key to move right one field and select the field. In the list view, if the last field in a record is selected, press the right arrow key to move to the next record.

+ *The up arrow key.* Press this key to move up one field and select it. In the list or report views, press the up arrow key to select the previous record's entry.

◆ *The down arrow key.* Press this key to move down a field and select the field. In the list or report views, press the down arrow key to select the next record's entry.

To move quickly through a database's records, use the Navigation tool on the Tool palette. The following section tells you how.

Using the Navigation tool:

1. **Select the Navigation tool from the Tool palette.**

2. **Click on the Forward Arrow tool to move to the next record while remaining in the same field.**

3. **Click on the Backward Arrow tool to move to the previous record while remaining in the same field.**

4. **Drag on the Slider tool until the number of the records you desire to move past shows in the Current Record text box.**

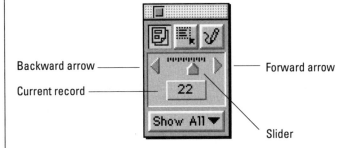

Adding new records:

1. **Advance to the last field of the last record.**

2. **Press the right arrow key or Tab key to advance to the next row in the data or list views.**

3. **Enter data for that first field.** Works automatically creates the new record.

You can insert a record anywhere in the database by following these steps:

◆ Making the record that follows the new record the current record. Either click on the record to place an insertion point in one of its fields, and move to the record by using the arrow keys, or use the Go To command to move to the record using its address name.

◆ Choose Insert Record from the Data menu, or press Command-I.

In the list view, the new record appears in the row above your previously selected record. In the data view, the new record appears on your screen.

Removing a record:

1. **Select the record you wish to remove.**

2. **Choose Delete Record from the Data menu.**

3. **In the list view, highlight those records to be removed and select Cut from the Edit menu, or press Command-X.**

Selecting Clear from the Edit menu leaves the selected records in your database but empties the field's data.

Using graphics in a database

Graphics are a great way to spruce up your database forms. Add logos, lines, boxes, and other graphics to add emphasis.

Draw appears in a layer above your database, so what you see on your screen is the combination of the two layers. Draw was covered in detail in the previous Topic. The following sections review some of the basics.

Turning draw on:

1. **Select Draw On from the Window menu or press Command-J.**

— or —

1. **Select the Draw tool (pencil icon) from the Tool palette.**

2. **Paste a graphic object onto the draw layer from the Clipboard.**

Turning draw off:

You can turn off draw using any of the following techniques:

✦ Select Draw Off from the Window menu, or press Command-J.

✦ Select the Data View or Design View tools from the Tool palette.

✦ Select one of the database view commands from the Form or Report menus.

Calculating with your database

A field can contain any value, whether it's a calculated value or a *default* (or constant) value, as you saw in the section titled "Creating fields" earlier in this Topic. To place formulas in your fields, use the Format Field dialog box. Once you've selected the appropriate data type radio button, set the appearance or format of the data, and set the alignment of the text using the Alignment radio buttons, then enter a calculation formula in the Formula or Default Value text box.

Any field name, value, or function that Works supports can be used to create a field calculation. That's why Works restricts field names to those that won't be confused with a calculation expression. There are 57 preprogrammed database functions available; Topic 11 contains a complete listing of them. Many functions are used identically in both spreadsheets and databases. There are only seven spreadsheet functions that can't be used by a database. Classes of functions include mathematical, statistical, logical, trigonometric, financial, date & time, and some other special functions.

Calculation formulas can use up to 238 characters, including field names, operators, functions, and number values. Use the following symbols for these common mathematical functions:

+ Adds the values on either side of the symbol.

- Subtracts the values on either side of the symbol or negates an operand.

* Multiplies the operators on either side.

/ Divides operator on the left by the operator on the right.

( ) Parentheses group an operation so that it's calculated in the formula before operations not in parentheses.

∧ Raises the operator found on the left to the power or exponential found on the right (for example, 2∧3 = 8).

An example of a calculation you could place into a field would be Pay = Hours * Pay Rate * % Not Withheld. This would return the value $640 in a record when the fields are Hours = 40, Pay Rate $20, and % Not Withheld = 80.

Calculated fields greatly enhance the value of a database, increase entry speed, improve accuracy, and reduce the frustration of repetitive entry. Whenever possible, let your Mac do the work for you. For the steps in creating a calculation field, see "Creating fields" earlier in this Topic.

A calculated field always displays the result of the calculation on your screen in the field's data box. The underlying calculation appears in the entry bar to remind you of the basis for that number. The only way you can change a calculation formula is to return to the Format Field dialog box. To reach this dialog box, select Format Field from the Form menu.

Copying information in your database

When you place database information onto the Clipboard, you store the information as a set of fields with field labels and highlighted data. Whenever you paste this information back into a database file, the data appears as a selected range. You can examine the Clipboard's contents by selecting Show Clipboard from the Window menu. The following figure shows a selected range and how that information appears placed on the Clipboard.

Selected range of data

Invention	Year	Inventor	Nationality
Adding machine	1642	Pascal	French
Air conditioning	1911	Carrier	U.S.
Air pump	1654	Guericke	German
Airplane with motor	1903	Wright Bros.	U.S.
Airplane, jet engine	1939	Ohain	German

Inventions (DB)

Resulting Clipboard

Clipboard

Invention	Year	Inventor	Nationality	
Adding machine	1642	Pascal	French	
Air conditioning	1911	Carrier	U.S.	
Air pump	1654	Guericke	German	
Airplane with motor	1903	Wright Bros.	U.S.	

Copying selected data:

1. **Highlight the entries you want to copy in the data or list views.**

2. **Select Copy from the Edit menu, or press Command-C.**

3. **Select the field(s) you want to accept the new data.**

4. **Select Paste from the Edit menu, or press Command-V.**

If there are more entries on the Clipboard than records to paste them into, Works truncates the remainder. Make sure you paste data into fields of the appropriate data format.

Other menu commands perform the various editing functions summarized below:

✦ *Cut command.* Removes data and places that information on the Clipboard. Cut enters the contents of a field or field entry, but removes selected records closing up the database.

✦ *Clear command.* Select this command from the Edit menu (or press Clear on the numeric keypad). This command empties a field, field entry, or record. It by-passes the Clipboard and leaves a blank formatted field behind.

✦ *Delete Record command.* This command, found on the Data menu, removes the record from the file and pushes all subsequent records back to fill in the space.

Copying a record in the list view:

1. **Select the record you wish to copy by clicking on the Record Selector box to highlight it.** The Record Selector box is the blank box to the left of each record's line in a list view.

2. **Choose Copy from the Edit menu.**

3. **Select the record you want the data to be pasted into.**

4. **Select Paste from the Edit menu, or press Command-V.**

If there's data in any of the fields that you paste data into, Works will overwrite it and the information is lost. If the record is blank or hasn't been created yet, Works fills in the space or creates the record as needed.

Duplicating an entry:

1. **In the list view, highlight the entry you wish to copy.**

2. **Select Duplicate Previous from the Edit menu, or press Command-E.**

3. **The duplicate entry is placed immediately below the original in the list view and appears on the next form in the data view.**

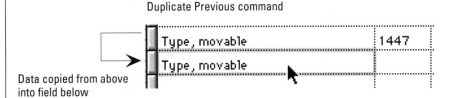

Duplicate Previous command

Data copied from above into field below

Copying information into adjacent records:

1. **In the list view, select the range of fields that you wish to copy into other records.** Make sure the first record has data in it.

2. **Select Fill Down from the Edit menu.**

Your selected range of records should include the top record in the range that has the data in it, with the blank records to be filled in beneath it. Works copies data from the first record into the records you selected beneath it. For information on copying selections between Works tools, see Topic 12.

Before Fill Down command

Type, movable	1447	Gutenberg	German

After Fill Down command

Type, movable	1447	Gutenberg	German
Type, movable	1447	Gutenberg	German
Type, movable	1447	Gutenberg	German
Type, movable	1447	Gutenberg	German

Sorting data using your database

Sorting data can be used for a variety of purposes: finding the oldest outstanding invoices, creating mailing labels for a sorted mailing, organizing your information, and so on. You can use Works to sort in any view other than the design view. Works sorts data in fields using ASCII code. A sort can either be *ascending*—with letters sorted from A to Z, followed by numbers sorted from 0 to 9 — or *descending* — with letters sorted from Z to A, followed by numbers sorted from 9 to 0.

Sorting data with Works is not very sophisticated and there are only a few options available to you. The following section details those sorting options that are available.

Sorting data with Works:

1. **Select Sort from the Data menu.**

2. **In the Sort dialog box, shown in the following figure, select the field you wish the sort to be based on from the Sort On Field pop-up menu.**

3. **Select the Descending check box if you want a descending sort.** For an ascending sort, leave the box unchecked.

4. **Select the Sort button, or press Return or Enter.**

All the records are sorted based on the key field you've selected. If you save the database after a sort, then the new order becomes permanent.

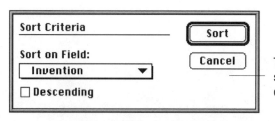

The Sort dialog box allows you to sort records in ascending or descending order

You can also sort on more than one field at a time to further organize your data. This is called a *multilevel sort*. To perform a multilevel sort, you simply sort each field in the sort order you desire, one sort at a time. That is, for a three-level sort, sort three times. When performing a multilevel sort, you should always sort based on the least important field first. When you sort by the least important field first, that sort order is retained only within the more important sorts that you do later. The most important sort would be accomplished last; this allows your data to be organized by the most significant information first.

Finding data in a database file

The most important feature a database gives you is the ability to organize your data in a logical manner, that is, the manner that best suits your purpose. If you can't find information in your database, then your computer is no better than a desk covered in mounds of paper, or a library filled with books placed on the shelf in no particular order. The find capability of a database lets you cut through the confusion and locate what you need. Finding information is one of the most important functions of a database program.

Select Find from the Edit menu (Command-F) to locate data with a text string, which you enter one field at a time. This command opens the Find dialog box. The only special option provided in this dialog box is the Search Text Fields Only check box. Executing Find takes you to each occurrence of the character string in turn and returns you to the beginning of the database to search when the last string is found.

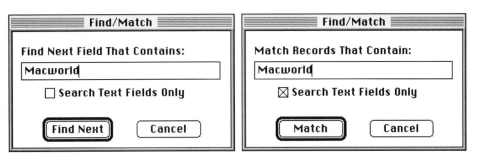

The Find/Match dialog boxes offer the option of searching
for your entered character string in text fields only

Select Match from the Data menu or press Command-M to find and highlight all the records with the specified character string at one time. You'll notice that the Find/Match dialog boxes are nearly identical, as shown in the previous figure. The best way to think of a Match operation is as an enhanced Find command. You can speed up your search for both finds and matches by entering more characters and searching only text fields, if that's appropriate. Once you've matched records, you can return to your entire database by selecting Match from the Data menu again to remove the check mark next to the command.

Finding and saving a database subset

To find a set of records that correspond to your specified criteria you must create *filters*, or record selection parameters. All of your original records and data entries are still contained in the database file when you create a filter, but you're shown only the subset of the database you wish to view. Works allows you to create up to 15 filters per file, in addition to a filter that returns all of your records to view, called the *Show All filter*. Each filter can be composed of up to six selection parameters. Each set of parameters uses comparisons based on English phrases, such as:

"Pay rate is greater than $15."

In this example, "Pay rate" is the name of a field, "is greater than" is the comparison, and "$15" is the comparison value. Other comparison phrases you can use to build filters include "equal," "not equal," "none," "greater than," "greater than or equal," "less than," "less than or equal," "contains," "does not contain," "ends with," "does not end with," "begins with," "does not begin with," "is blank," and "is not blank."

```
Data
    Next Record        ⌘=
    Previous Record    ⌘-
    Insert Record      ⌘I
    Delete Record
    ─────────────────
    Sort...
    Match Records...   ⌘M
    ─────────────────
    New Filter...
    Define Filter...   ⌘K
    Delete Filter...
    Duplicate Filter...
    ─────────────────
  ✓ Show All
    Camel Filter
```

The Data menu offers commands for controlling filters in your database

By using more than one set of selection parameters in combination in a filter, you can narrow selections to include or exclude only a specific range of data. Use filters in combination by selecting either the And or the Or operator to the left of the Field boxes in the New/Define filter dialog box. For example, by combining the filter above — using the And operator — with the filter "Pay Rate is less than $20," records in the intersecting range between $15 and $20 are found. Selecting the Or operator excludes records from the intersecting range, finding values of $15 and less, and of $20 or more. When you combine filters using both And and Or operators, the Or statements are performed first.

Using filters:

1. **To create a new filter, select New Filter from the Data menu.** The New/Define filter dialog box appears.

2. **Enter a name for the filter in the Filter Name text box.**

3. **Select field names from your database using the Field pop-up menu.**

4. **Select the comparison phrase you wish to use from the Comparison pop-up menu.**

5. **Enter the data to be used in the comparison in the Compare to text box.**

6. **If you want to combine selection parameters, select a connector (And or Or) from the pop-up list.**

7. **Select the OK button to initiate the search.**

Works then creates the filter and adds its name to the Data menu.

New/Define Filter			
Filter Name:	Camel Filters		☐ Invert Filter
	Field:	**Comparison:**	**Compare to:**
	Cigarettes ▼	equal ▼	Camel
And ▼	Cigarettes ▼	equal ▼	Filters
And ▼	Cigarettes ▼	does not contain ▼	Nicotine
Or ▼	Cigarettes ▼	ends with ▼	Death
And ▼	(none) ▼	equal ▼	
And ▼	(none) ▼	equal ▼	

OK   Cancel

The New/Define Filter dialog box allows you to define the selection parameters of a database filter

If you want to find the opposite values of your search criteria, select the Invert Filter check box. Select the Show All filter from the Tool palette to see all of your records again. By clicking on the Filter tool pop-up menu, you can select and use any filter you previously created. The Filter tool duplicates the action of selecting a filter from the Data menu. Selecting a filter brings up the New/Define Filter dialog box, where you can change the filter's name and selection criteria.

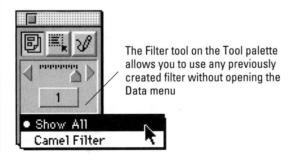

The Filter tool on the Tool palette allows you to use any previously created filter without opening the Data menu

Complex filters can be modified easily. Simply select Duplicate Filter from the Data menu and select the filter you wish to modify. In the And Name It text box, enter the new name and make any changes in the parameters you desire. Delete filters by selecting Delete Filter from the Data menu and selecting the filter you wish to eliminate.

Once you've selected a subset of your database using your filter(s), you can save those records as a separate file. There are many reasons why you might want to do this. You could be interested in saving and using only those records of interest, or archiving or deleting old records so that your database doesn't grow too large. Or you might want to back up only new records. The following section details saving a subset of your database file.

Saving a file subset:

1. **Switch to the list or data views.**

2. **Apply your filter(s), or select Match Records to select a subset of your records.**

3. **Select Save As from the File menu, and select the Save Selected Records Only check box in the Save dialog box.**

4. **Type a name in the File Name text box.**

5. **Select the Save button.**

The new file is created and stored, while the original file remains open for further use. If you use the Save command, Works asks you if you want to replace your original file.

Creating reports

A report allows you to set up and print a list view of your database in a meaningful and informative way. You can create and name up to 16 separate reports per database file. When you make formatting changes in the list view, such as font, font size, style, and data type, those changes are also reflected in the report view. For example, if you want grid lines to print in either view, choose Show Grid from the Form menu. Select this command again to remove the check mark if you don't want grid lines to print.

Unlike the design or data views — which show only one record at a time — the list and report views can show many records. This can make working with your data in different parts of the database difficult. Scrolling around the database can be very distracting and can make it difficult to choose the kinds of comparisons that allow you to work with your data. For this reason, the list and report view windows contain window devices — horizontal and vertical split bars in each of the two scroll bars — that let you split your window into panes. Using these split bars, you can separate your database into either two horizontal or vertical panes, or into a window with four window panes. This feature, which allows you to view different sections of your file simultaneously, also appears in spreadsheet windows.

Working with window panes:

1. **Move the pointer over either the horizontal or vertical split bars, which appear as dark black lines in the scroll bars.** The cursor changes to a double-headed arrow.

2. **Drag the split bar until the panes are the size you want, and then release the mouse button.**

3. **Each set of panes now has a corresponding set of scroll bars. Scroll in each pane until the data you want appears in view.** Your position in one pane doesn't affect your position in any other pane.

4. **Close a pane by dragging the horizontal split bar to the far left and dragging the vertical split bar to the upper edge of their respective scroll bars. Then release the mouse to close the pane.**

★ File Edit Form Data Report Window					

1   Black Classic Line

Inventory (DB)

Item Ordered	On Hand	Quantity	Ordered	Received	Vendor
Bottles	60		5/5/88	5/19/88	Olshen Bottle Supply
Bottles sulfide	165				
Bottles water	110				
Bubble Pack	35 ft		6/5/88	6/5/88	Waltham Paper
Foam Sets	150		5/30/88	5/11/88	Alpack, Inc.
Forceps	216		5/10/88	5/12/88	Fisher Scientific
Forceps	216		5/10/88	5/12/88	Fisher Scientific
Gloves	200	(2000)	5/10/88	5/12/88	Am Gloves & Safety Pro
Labels (bottles) Na2S	3900		5/5/88	6/7/88	Package Systems
Labels (bottles) H2O	4375		5/5/88	6/7/88	Package Systems
Labels (Paint Chip)	3705			5/16/88	Staples
Labels (TLD)	1040		4/22/88	5/19/88	Package Systems
Labels (TLPDK)	1094		5/5/88	5/25/88	Package Systems
Magnifiers	0		5/10/88	5/23/88	Pentapco

Pane cursor

Horizontal split bar

Vertical split bar

If you print a report that contains all records, all the fields that fit within the printable area — that is, between the margin markers — are printed. If your report is wide, consider printing the database in the landscape or horizontal print mode. Choose either of these print modes in the Page Setup dialog box. If you don't want a field to print, either extend the fields that do print to push that field beyond the margin markers, or drag that field outside of the printable area.

Matches, filtered searches, and sorts that reorder or provide a subset of your data in the list view change the report view as well. When you name and create a report, all the conditions that created it are saved with it. To return to that report later, you simply select its name from the Report menu. Once you are in a report view, you can apply filters, sorts, and matches to alter the data you see. Sorts you apply in the report view also affect the appearance of the data and list views.

Creating a new report:

1. **In the list view, apply all filters, matches, and sorts to order your database as you wish.**

2. **Switch to the report view.**

3. **Select New Report from the Report menu.**

4. **Type a name up to 31 characters long in the Name The Report text box.**

5. **Select the Create button.** Works adds the name of your report to the Report menu.

6. **Save your database file to save changes made to your report.**

You can continue to apply filters, matches, sorts, and to resize and move fields in the report view, as needed.

Renaming a report:

1. **Select the name of the report from the Report menu.**

2. **Choose the Report Name command in the Report menu.**

3. **Type the new name into the Rename The Report text box.**

4. **Select the OK button, or press Return or Enter.**

Duplicating a report:

1. **Select the name of the report you wish to duplicate from the Report menu.**

2. **Select Duplicate Report from the Report menu.**

3. **Type the name of the duplicate in the And Name It box.**

4. **Select the OK button.**

Duplicating a report is useful for creating similar versions of a report quickly, so that you don't have to create a report from scratch.

Deleting a report:

1. **Select the name of the report you wish to delete from the Report menu.**

2. **Select Delete Report from the Report menu.**

3. **Dismiss the alert box and execute the command by selecting the OK button.** Works deletes the current report and removes it from your screen.

To select a report in any view, choose its name from the Report menu.

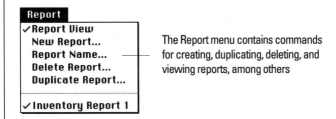

Report
- ✓ Report View
- New Report...
- Report Name...
- Delete Report...
- Duplicate Report...

- ✓ Inventory Report 1

The Report menu contains commands for creating, duplicating, deleting, and viewing reports, among others

You can enhance reports by adding calculated totals and subtotals of numeric fields. You can total your accounts receivable, your net worth, and so on, to obtain valuable information. Subtotals require that you define the range you want subtotaled. In order to see totals, rather than formulas, in a report, you must either select Print Preview from the File menu or print the report. You can also copy your report to the Clipboard, and your totals and subtotals will appear when you select Show Clipboard from the Window menu.

The subtotal of a field varies with the contents of the *key field,* or the field that defines the report. For example, if you sort by a customer name, you can define a subtotal for the amount of money the customer spent with your company. If you then selected only the records for 1993 in your report, your subtotal would contain only the sales to that customer for that year.

You can also have a subtotal appear whenever a letter in a field changes. In a situation in which you had an inventory part that was different for each record, it would be useless to have a subtotal for each change in the key field. However, if you named each inventory part with a starting letter to indicate the type of inventory it was, a sort and a subtotal would let you see the value of each class of inventory.

The following is an example of a report subtotaled by key field entry:

Name	Amount Spent
Franklin, Benjamin	$32.50
Franklin, Benjamin	$43.20
Subtotal	$75.70
Jefferson, Thomas	$120.25
Jefferson, Thomas	$25.50
Jefferson, Thomas	$56.29
Subtotal	$202.04
Washington, George	$15.32
Washington, George	$45.88
Washington, George	$99.63
Washington, George	$18.95
Subtotal	$179.78

Here is a report subtotaled by the first character:

Name	Amount Spent
Aardvark, Arnold A.	$32.50
Antelope, Andrew	$14.35
Subtotal	$46.85
Elephant, Edward	$52.50
Subtotal	$52.50
Lamb, Lisa	$88.35
Leopard, Liz	$18.55
Lion, Leo	$35.88
Subtotal	$142.78

Totaling a field:

1. **In the report view, select the field you want to total by clicking on its field name.** Works adds the name of that field at the top of the Totals menu, in dim view, to remind you of your selection.

2. **Select Sum This Field from the Totals menu, or select the Sum this Field icon from the Ruler bar.** Your total appears at the bottom of the report.

```
┌─ Totals ──────────────────────────────┐
│  Price Paid                            │
│ ──────────────────────────────────────│
│ +▦ Sum this Field         ─────────── │
│ ──────────────────────────────────────│
│ ▤▦ Subtotal when Contents Change       │
│ ▤▦ Subtotal when 1st Char Changes      │
│ ──────────────────────────────────────│
│ ▦ New Page after Subtotal              │
└────────────────────────────────────────┘
```

The Totals menu offers options for creating subtotals in reports

Subtotaling a key field when data entry changes:

1. **In the report view, select the field you want to total by clicking on its field name.** Works adds the name of that field at the top of the Totals menu, in dim view, to remind you of your selection.

2. **Select Sum this Field from the Totals menu, or select the Sum This Field icon from the Ruler bar.** Your total appears at the bottom of the report.

3. **Select the key field to be used for the subtotal.**

4. **Select Subtotal when Contents Change from the Totals menu, or select the Subtotal when Contents Change button from the Ruler.**

5. **Sort your database using the key field.**

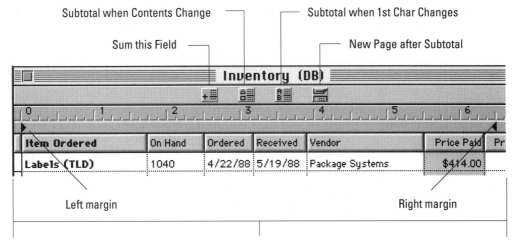

Subtotal when Contents Change

Sum this Field

Subtotal when 1st Char Changes

New Page after Subtotal

Left margin

Right margin

Printable area

Subtotaling a key field when the first character changes:

1. **In the report view, select the field you want to total by clicking on its field name.** Works adds the name of that field at the top of the Totals menu, in dim view, to remind you of your selection.

2. **Select Sum this Field from the Totals menu, or select the Sum this Field icon from the Ruler bar.** Your total will appear at the bottom of the report.

3. **Select the key field to be used for the subtotal.**

4. **Select Subtotal when 1st Char Changes from the Totals menu, or select that button from the Ruler bar.**

Note: Remember to sort your database first — subtotals only work properly after a sort.

You can also have Works print separate pages after each subtotal in a report. To do so, select New Page after Subtotal from the Totals menu, or select the appropriate button from the Ruler bar.

Printing your database

Printing in a database is somewhat unique in Microsoft Works. In other modules, what you see is what you print. In a database, there are several different ways to present your data so that it can be used for different purposes. The database view you use determines the manner in which that data is printed. You can print your data compactly in a list view, which hides the purpose of a database, but gives you an overall view of the data. A report view gives you a more selected view of part of your data, and shows you the data that fulfills the specifications of the report parameters you set.

You can print your data in a form view that lets you use single records for a special purpose: an invoice, statement, ticket, or other single use situation. You can even print from the design view, and let Works create blank forms that others can fill in. Many different types of printing capabilities are what really make a database a very useful device.

Printing each view of a database gives you different results. These results are summarized below:

+ *The design view.* Gives you a single copy of the form, with all fields showing their names and data entry boxes.

+ *The data view.* This prints the page with as many whole forms as possible. No partial forms print on a page. Only records that you select are printed out.

+ *The list or report views.* These views print whole pages of selected records.

Adjust the margins and the amount of space between forms if you want to change the number of forms that print per page. You do this by adjusting the margin and the space between forms settings in the Document dialog box, or by changing the size of the printed form in the Page Setup dialog box. See "Working with labels and envelopes" later in this Topic for details.

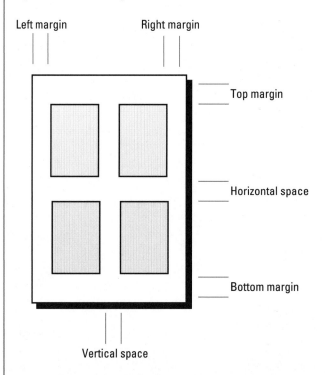

Left margin   Right margin

Top margin

Horizontal space

Bottom margin

Vertical space

The Database module supports headers and footers, as do all other Works modules. Headers and footers are particularly convenient and important for list and report printouts, in which document titles, date, time, and page numbers can help you organize a printout. For more information, headers and footers are covered in Topic 4. Remember, you can only see headers and footers in the Print Preview dialog box or on your printed output.

You can execute the Print One command to print a job without going through the Print dialog box. Works uses your previous settings when you execute this command. Also, you can cancel a print job by pressing Command-period.

Before you print, remember to set the page size, orientation, and margins by selecting the Page Setup command. Forms usually use a preset paper size, but databases in the list or report views can be large and wide and require a different setting. You can often fit more information on a page by changing from portrait (tall) to landscape (wide) orientation. Other methods you can use to fit more on a page include reducing the font sizes used and scaling down the print output using the % scaling boxes found in the Print dialog box.

You can print a report from the Finder. To do so, quit Works from the report view and leave the report you want to print active. Then select the file icon from the Finder, and select Print from the File menu. Works then prints your report.

Working with labels and envelopes

Unlike version 2.0, Works 3 allows you to create mailing labels and envelopes within the Database module. You may find the template you need for your label or envelope preset in the Works package, but it's also easy to create your own templates. An envelope or label is just another form that you create in the design view. The steps for doing so are detailed below.

Creating a label or envelope template:

1. **Select New Form from the Form menu, and then name that form.**

2. **Set the page size and select OK.**

3. **Select the Fields button to open the Auto Place Fields dialog box.**

4. **Select the field(s) to be printed and select the Place button.** Placed fields have a check mark next to them.

5. **Remove a placed field by selecting it, and then clicking the Don't Place button.**

6. **Exit the Auto Place dialog box by selecting OK or by pressing Return or Enter.**

7. **Move, format, change, and resize fields as required.** Remember to create a text object in Draw for the return address portion of a mailing label.

8. **With the form active, open the Page Setup dialog box and set the size of the form.**

9. **Select the Document button to open its dialog box. Enter sizes for margins and for spacing between forms.** You can set spacings between forms only when the form size is smaller than the page sizes.

10. **Choose the New/Setup Form dialog box and double-check that the correct options are set. Dismiss the dialog box by selecting OK.**

11. **You may want to preview your forms before you print them.**

Works 3 has two new options that allow you to print labels properly. Both are found in the Format Fields dialog box. When you click on the Slide On check box for a field, that field will close up blank space to the left for a field at the same vertical position on a form. If you have a blank field preceding a field for which the Slide On option is set, then the field overwrites the position where the blank field would be found. Another printing feature useful in mailing labels is the Comma Preceding Field option. When this check box is selected in the Format Fields dialog box, a comma will always appear to the right of your field in printed output. Both options can really enhance the appearance of your mailing labels, and you can also use them with form letters (merges), or with other database output to improve your results.

Doing mail merges in Works

A mail merge enables you to create many different versions of a standardized letter. It's one of the tasks that requires you to use both a database and a word processor. Since the task is largely a database project, I discuss it in this Topic. You can use a mail merge to print individualized letters, envelopes, mailing labels, and other personalized printed output. Since you can print mailing labels and envelopes as forms within the database alone, it only pays to do mail merges when you need to use your word processor for careful text placement or other special word processor features. Print simple forms from within the database only.

A form letter is set up to perform a mail merge by adding information from a database into the word processor document. You use in the letter special placeholders that describe the database field used to fill the form, and each record prints a form that has data in the appropriate place in the form letter. You can have multiple occurrences of a field in a form letter, and as a new feature to version 3.0, you can have placeholders for more than one database in a form letter at the same time.

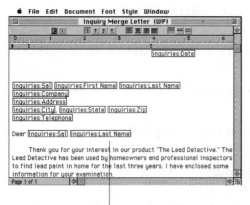

A word processor document with database field placeholders

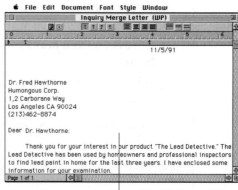

The same document as it would print with field data inserted from one record

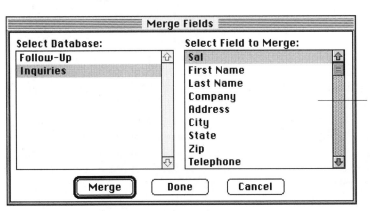# Creating a merge document:

1. **Open as much of the database as you want to use for merged information.**

2. **Open or create in the Word Processor module a word processor document that you wish to serve as the form letter.**

3. **In the form letter, position the insertion point in the location at which a merged field should print.** Works places the merge field boxes to the left of where your insertion point is. Works does not use merge markers as codes for the program to use but indicates the name of the file and the field to be merged inside the placeholder box.

4. **Select Merge Fields from the Document menu.** The Merge Fields dialog box appears.

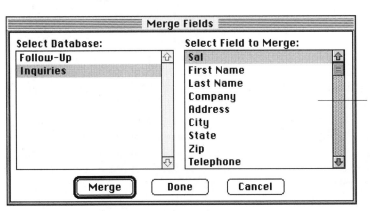

The Merge Fields dialog box allows you to create personalized form letters by in-serting data from the database module into a standardized letter in the Word Processor module

5. **Select the file from the Select Database scroll box, and then select the field name from the Select Field scroll box to merge the scroll boxes.**

6. **Select the Merge button, or after placing several fields, select the Done button to dismiss the dialog box.**

7. **To see field names, select Show Field Name (in the Word Processor module) from the Document menu. Or to see sample data, select Show Field Data in the Database module.**

8. **Preview the forms using the Print Preview command.** Select the Next and Previous buttons to view each form.

9. **Print your forms by using the Print command.**

It's more convenient to place several fields in your form letter at one time. That way you can move the insertion point in your document and still leave the Merged Fields dialog box on your screen. You can cut and paste the fields' placeholders to different locations in a document, and even to other form letters. Be careful when placing fields. Be sure to use correct punctuation and spaces. You can format placeholders as you would normal text.

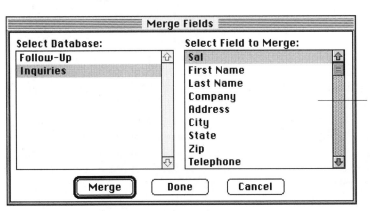

Note: If any of the databases you use for data aren't opened, Works displays the place-holders with the words "DB File Unavailable," and won't print the forms properly.

If you deselect the Print Merged Fields check box in the Print dialog box, you can print a single form with all of the placeholder boxes showing. This technique is useful for checking your work prior to printing a lot of letters. To cancel a merged print job in progress, press Command-period.

Quick Tips

The following tips explain other database options, including the more popular pro-grams. You will also learn the features to look for when shopping for a higher level database.

Looking beyond Works' Database module

Several more powerful databases are available for the Macintosh. Unfortunately, con-sidering compatibility issues, none of the best products are currently made by Micro-soft, although that situation should be changing shortly. Your database needs should be determined by how you plan to work with your data. If you can enter data in one place and don't require that the data be used in other files, then you can use what is called a *flat file database*. Perhaps the best flat file database, and the Macintosh market leader, is Claris FileMaker. This program is a database that strongly relies on graphics with good performance. It's networkable and has some security and relational data features. Panorama II is another good choice for a flat file database. Microsoft File is an older product that is scheduled for an update.

If your database requires that data entered in one place be used in several other places or that you construct reports based on data used from several files, then you need a *relational database*. The best of the Macintosh relational databases are Acius' 4th Dimension and Fox's (now Microsoft) FoxBase+/Mac. 4th Dimension is the more flex-ible of the two, whereas FoxBase+/Mac has the best performance. An update of FoxBase, called FoxBase Pro, is due to appear soon and will be faster still. Other rela-tional products worth considering are Odesta's Double Helix and Blyth Software's Omnis 5. 4th Dimension and FoxBase use a coded procedural programming language to create their structure. Double Helix and Omnis 5 use a more graphical, icon-based design approach.

High-end database features

When considering a higher level database, important extra features to look for are as follows:

♦ *Better performance.* Much faster sorts and searches. Also, the ability to handle large files with many records.

♦ *Automated data entry.* The program should enter serial numbers, dates, values, and so on, based on your design. Much more complex calculation and summa-tion fields can be created, some based on Boolean logic.

- ◆ *Data relations or lookups.* Based on data in one field, data in another field will be entered. For example, when you enter a name, the address is automatically entered.

- ◆ *Sophisticated reporting.* More control in distinguishing the nature of the data is available, and generating complex reports is possible.

- ◆ *Complex macros or scripts.* Automation features that let you create a file in a specific condition. For example, a more refined database product would let you create a macro that did finds, sorts, switched to a particular form, and then previewed the results, all in one command.

- ◆ *Network, multiuser capability.* This allows many users to work from the same file, locking records so that only one user at a time may make changes.

- ◆ *Privileges and access.* Passwords and access groups with different levels of ability can be created.

Summary

✔ A database is a collection of information organized into records. Every record in a file contains the same fields, which contain data of a specified type.

✔ Works allows up to 16 forms or printed output per file.

✔ You can define as many as 16 reports that let you output your data organized in new ways — such as sorted, matching specific selection criteria, with numerical fields totaled, and subtotaled.

✔ There are four database views: the design view, which lets you modify a printed form; the data view, which lets you see each record in your form output; the list view, a tabular view of all of your data; and the report view, a display of a specialized printout of some or all of your data.

✔ Fields can belong to one of four data types: text, number, date, and time. These types are referred to as character formatting. Fields can be default values, values you enter, or the result of a calculation.

✔ The database supports the draw layer and can format text and other objects in that mode or fields in the database layer.

✔ You can order your records based on the ASCII code by executing the Sort command.

✔ Execute the Find command to find data in a record. Find the same data in a set of records using the Match command.

✔ Filters let you look at a subset of your records based on a set of criteria you create. Works allows up to 15 filters per file with up to six selection criteria each. You can connect filters together.

✔ Selected and reordered records can be saved as a separate file.

✔ Use your database to print simple forms, but use a word processor document and database files together to do a mail merge to create complex form letters.

Part II
Using Works' Tools

Topic 7
Using Works' Spreadsheets

Overview

Perhaps no product category has had as much impact on the initial success of the personal computer as the spreadsheet. When word processors first appeared, they were pretty weak. You could still use a typewriter to write, and although you got productivity enhancement using a word processor, you could get by without one. Then, in 1979, along came VisiCalc (short for visible calculator) on the Apple II. This was the first electronic spreadsheet. In business, business calculations were done on a large piece of ruled paper called a spreadsheet, and rote calculations were tedious and error prone.

A spreadsheet analysis of an automobile loan

🍎 File Edit Format	Options Chart Window

C3 | 15000

Auto Finance Analyzer (SS)

	A	B	C	D	E	F
1			AUTO PURCHASE ANALYSIS			
2	Discount factor 10.00%		OPTION 1	OPTION 2	OPTION 3	OPTION 4
3	Enter gross sales price		$15000	$15000	$15000	$15000
4	Enter rebate/discount		$2000	$0	$2000	$2000
5	Net sales price		$13000	$15000	$13000	$13000
6	Enter loan amount		$0	$13000	$13000	$10000
7	Down Payment		$13000	$2000	$0	$3000
8	Loan as a % of value		0.00%	86.67%	86.67%	66.67%
9	Enter interest rate		0.00%	2.90%	9.00%	9.00%
10	Enter loan term (years):		4	4	4	4
11	Monthly payment		$0	$287	$324	$249
12	NET COST TO PURCHASE		$13,000	$13,323	$12,755	$12,812
13						
14	INSTRUCTIONS: This program allows you to compare various financing alternatives of					
15	purchasing an automobile. It takes into consideration any rebates or low interest loans that					
16	may be offered. It also allows you to enter your own discount factor (which can be the					
17	estimated inflation rate.) The column with the lowest Net Cost is the best buy.					
18						

The underlying formulas

🍎 File Edit Format	Options Chart Window

F3 | ☒✓ =E3

Auto Finance Analyzer (SS)

	A	B	C	D	E	F
1			AUTO PURCHASE ANALYSIS			
2	Discount factor .1		OPTION 1	OPTION 2	OPTION 3	OPTION 4
3	Enter gross sales price		15000	=C3	=D3	=E3
4	Enter rebate/discount		2000	0	2000	2000
5	Net sales price		=C3-C4	=D3-D4	=E3-E4	=F3-F4
6	Enter loan amount		0	13000	13000	10000
7	Down Payment		=C5-C6	=D5-D6	=E5-E6	=F5-F6
8	Loan as a % of value		=C6/C3	=D6/D3	=E6/E3	=F6/F3
9	Enter interest rate		0	2.9%	9%	9%
10	Enter loan term (years):		4	4	4	4
11	Monthly payment		••••••••••	••••••••••	••••••••••	••••••••••
12	NET COST TO PURCHASE		••••••••••	••••••••••	••••••••••	••••••••••
13						
14	INSTRUCTIONS: This program allows you to compare various financing alternatives of					
15	purchasing an automobile. It takes into consideration any rebates or low interest loans that					
16	may be offered. It also allows you to enter your own discount factor (which can be the					
17	estimated inflation rate.) The column with the lowest Net Cost is the best buy.					
18						

The spreadsheet was the next step up from the electronic calculator, and it made an electronic ledger possible. Suddenly, you could automate a company's balance sheet, do complex financial calculations, analyze net worth, project sales and cash flow, and play complex what-if games with numbers, mathematics, logic, statistics, and other functions. The only errors you could make were those of construction or logic, not calculation. Here was something unique, a new killer app (application) that defined a capability that wasn't possible before. VisiCalc sold over 100,000 copies and moved personal computers out of the stores. All of the powerful spreadsheets that came after it — Lotus 1-2-3, Microsoft Excel, Borland Quattro Pro, and many others, including the spreadsheet you will use in Works — are direct descendents of VisiCalc.

What is a spreadsheet?

Commonly, a single spreadsheet document is called a *worksheet*. A spreadsheet may be correctly defined as the calculating engine that displays the worksheet. However, the terms worksheet and spreadsheet are often used interchangeably.

A spreadsheet is a matrix of elements, called *cells*, which are defined by the intersection of rows and columns. Rows are lettered from left to right starting with A through Z, then AA through AZ, and so on to the last column labeled IV. Columns are numbered from 1 to 16,382. The largest spreadsheet you can define is 231 columns by 16,382 rows, or 3,784,242 cells. Cells are given an address or cell reference to identify them. A row's letter is used first, followed by a column's number, such as A1, B2, B12, and so on.

Although you can select many cells at once, and even the whole spreadsheet by clicking the Select All box or by click-dragging through a spreadsheet, only one cell can be the current cell. All selected cells can be formatted at once, but only the current cell can have its value or formula altered. An exception to this rule, the Fill commands, (Edit menu) let you enter the same data into any selected cells at once. You can tell which is the current cell by either looking for its highlighted border, or more conveniently, by checking the Current Cell indicator box at the right of the entry bar.

Most spreadsheets use only a small portion of the available worksheet area, but you can put many sets of calculations on a worksheet, if you so choose. Use the scroll bars to move about your document. It's a good idea to put related calculations in the same region of a spreadsheet so that you can see them all at once. Using the split bars, you can see up to four window panes or regions of the spreadsheet at any one time (see "Creating spreadsheet panes" later in this Topic).

Introducing the spreadsheet window

A spreadsheet window is similar in appearance to the list view of a database window. In the title bar, any spreadsheet will have (SS) to indicate that it is a spreadsheet; the other differences are that column headings appear as only letters, and the Current Cell indicator is at the right of the entry bar.

The elements of a spreadsheet window include:

✦ *Current cell.* The active cell, and the only one for which a label, value, or underlying formula can be modified. Click on a cell to make it the current one.

✦ *Current Cell indicator.* Shows the address of cell reference of the current cell.

✦ *Entry bar.* Enter labels, values, or formulas here for the active cell. Contains an Entry box (with a check) and a cancel box (with an X) to either enter or cancel the data in the entry bar. The entry bar was described fully in "Learning the four views of Works' database" in Topic 6.

♦ *Select All box.* Click on this box to select the entire spreadsheet for formatting.

♦ *Row and column headings.* Define the location of a cell in the worksheet and are used by Works to identify a cell's reference for a formula using that cell. Click on a heading to select that row or column.

♦ *Vertical and horizontal split bar.* Click and drag to create a set of window panes. Split bars were described in "Creating reports" in Topic 6.

♦ *Tool palette.* With Draw On, the Tool palette appears. There are three draw modes: Spreadsheet (Entry cursor or cross), Charting (Graph icon), and Draw Layer (Pencil icon). Use the Draw On command or Command-J keystroke on the Options menu to show the Tool palette.

Drawing was discussed in detail in Topic 5, "Using the Draw Module"; charting and graphs is the subject of Topic 8, "Using Works' Charts."

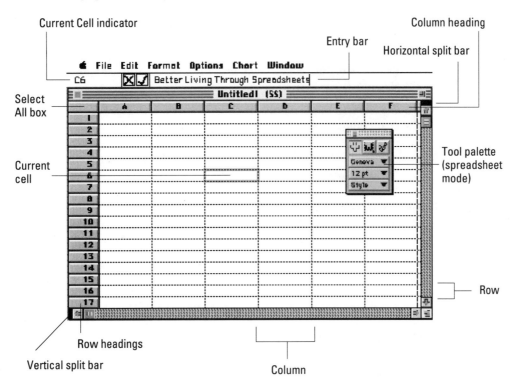

Opening a new spreadsheet:

1. **Choose the New command from the File menu, or press the Command-N keystroke.**

2. **In the New dialog box, double-click on the spreadsheet icon, or single-click to highlight the spreadsheet icon and then click the New button.**

— or —

3. **Choose the Open command from the File menu, or press the Command-O keystroke.**

4. **In the Open dialog box, double-click on the spreadsheet icon.** In either case, a new blank spreadsheet labeled "Untitled #" will open.

   You also start a new spreadsheet when you open a spreadsheet template from within the Open dialog box. A copy of that spreadsheet will appear with all of the values, formulas, and formatting intact, labeled as "Untitled #." Use the Preview feature within the Open dialog box to examine a spreadsheet before opening it.

5. **To open an existing spreadsheet, give the Open command and navigate the Macintosh File System to find the filename.**

6. **Double-click on the filename, or single-click on it to highlight it, then click the Open button.**

If you open a spreadsheet from a previous version of Works, the spreadsheet will be converted to the Works 3 format.

Manipulating spreadsheet windows:

1. **Choose the close box in the title bar or Close command on the File menu, or press the Command-W keystroke to close the spreadsheet.**

2. **Click on the zoom box in the title bar to expand the window to full screen or back to a reduced size.**

3. **Choose the Save command to save your work as you enter data.**

Creating a copy of a spreadsheet under a new name:

1. **Choose the Save As command on the File menu.**

2. **In the Save As dialog box, enter the new filename (up to 31 characters) and click the Save button.**

Finding and selecting data

Works has one active cell at any one time, but you can select any number of cells to format. Enter data into many selected cells by using the Fill Down or Fill Right commands. Two commands allow you to move about the spreadsheet: the Select Last Cell command, or more generally, the Find command. A Find is a simple search based on either the text string or contents, or a cell reference.

Selecting a cell:

1. **Make a cell active by clicking on it using the Data Entry cursor (the large plus symbol).**

2. **Use the arrow cursor keys to move one cell in that direction and make the cell active.**

3. **Choose the Last Cell command from the Select command submenu on the Edit menu, or press the Command-L keystroke to go to the last cell in the worksheet that has data in it.**

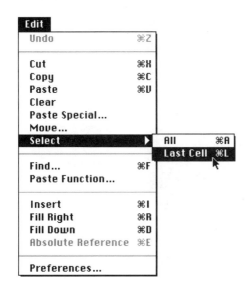

If you have an extended keyboard, follow these steps:

4. **Press the Home key to go to the beginning of the spreadsheet.**

5. **Press the End key to move to the end of the spreadsheet.**

6. **Press the Page Up key to move up a window and the Page Down key to move down a window in the spreadsheet.**

7. **Use the Find command on the Edit menu (Command-F) and enter a Cell Reference to go to any part of the spreadsheet.**

Although you can have only one active cell, you can select many cells. The following instructions show how to select a range of cells.

Selecting a range of cells:

1. **Click on the first cell in the range, and then drag to the last cell.**

— or —

2. **Highlight the first cell in the range, and then scroll to see the last cell in the range.**

3. **Hold down the Shift key and click on the last cell in the range.** For the first cell, B12, and the last cell, X24, a selected range is bounded by B12, B24, X24, and X12.

4. **If you press the Shift key and click on a cell within the selected range, the range is reduced, with that cell being the last cell. Or extend the range by clicking outside the selected area.**

5. **Click on a row or column heading to select that row or column.**

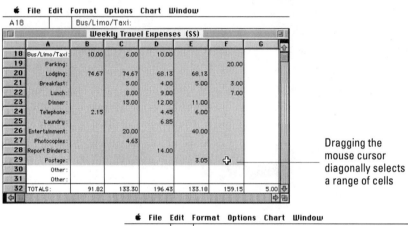

Dragging the mouse cursor diagonally selects a range of cells

Clicking on a column heading selects the entire column

Clicking on the Select All box selects the entire worksheet

6. **Click and drag on a range of row or column headings to select those rows or columns.**

7. **Select the entire worksheet by clicking on the Select All box.**

8. **Select the active area of the spreadsheet by choosing the Select command on the Edit menu and then dragging to the All command on the submenu. Or use the Command-A keystroke.**

The active area is contained between cell A1 and the last cell with data in it. If that cell is W26, the active area is bounded by A1, A26, W26, and W1.

Finding a cell:

1. **Choose the Find command from the Edit menu, or press the Command-F keystroke.**

2. **Enter either a value or cell reference in the Enter Text or Cell Reference to Find text box to find the cell.**

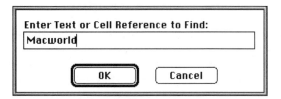

If cell B2 contains the value 3.14, you can search for that cell using either B2 or 3.14. If you search for 3.14 again, Works goes to the next cell address with that value in it.

3. **Click the OK button.**

A Find operation will locate stored information but not displayed information. If a cell has a value of 2.146 and displays 2.15, use 2.146 to find that cell.

Using labels vs. values

You can enter text, numbers, or formulas into cells. Many other spreadsheet programs refer to text as a *label*, and a number as a *value*. Works' spreadsheets refer to *any* constant as a value, thus lumping text and numbers together. A formula is an equation that calculates a value based on information you enter. Using a formula, you can specify what values, functions, and even cell references are used to calculate the value in that cell.

Works can show either values only or formulas only in its display. Choose the Show Values or Show Formulas commands in the Option menu to switch between the two views. A check mark appears next to the command of the current view. When you print a worksheet that is displayed in the formula mode, Works prints those formulas within the limits of the cell size.

```
Options
  Show Grid
✓ Show Values
  Show Formulas
  Show Note Indicator
  Open Cell Note...

  Manual Calculation
  Calculate Now      ⌘=

  Sort...
```

Entering data into a cell:

1. **Select the active cell to enter data into.** Use any of the methods mentioned previously.

2. **Type text, numbers, or a formula.** A formula requires an equal sign be typed as the first character. Works automatically enters what you type into the entry bar, replacing any entry that was there before you typed.

   You can enter up to 238 characters into any one cell. You can enter positive or negative numbers (precede them with a minus sign), numbers with or without decimal places, or a number in scientific notation. A negative number in a spreadsheet is displayed within a set of parentheses. Scientific notation has the format *#.##E##*, where the decimal number preceding the E is called the *mantissa* (it can have any number of decimal places), and the integer number after the E is called the *exponent* (range of ± 99). Works adjusts what is displayed to fit your data format (see "Formatting a cell" later in this Topic).

3. **If you make a mistake, edit the entry bar.** Use the Backspace or Delete key to remove characters. Or you can click the Cancel box in the entry bar. Also, to edit data already contained in a cell, use Text Edit techniques you have learned previously to replace text. You can use the Clear command on the Edit menu or the Clear key on the numeric keypad to delete both a cell's contents and its formatting.

4. **Click the Enter box, or press the Enter key to put your data into the cell.** Using the Enter key forces Works to update (recalculate) your spreadsheet. A worksheet is also recalculated whenever you save the file.

Use the Return or down arrow keys to place data into a cell and select the cell below, the Tab or right arrow keys to enter data and move to the cell on the right, the Shift-Tab keystroke or left arrow key to enter data and move to the cell on the left, and the

Shift-Return keystroke or the up arrow to enter data and move to the cell above. Whenever you use any of these keys or keystrokes, Works enters data without recalculating your worksheet and therefore speeds your data entry.

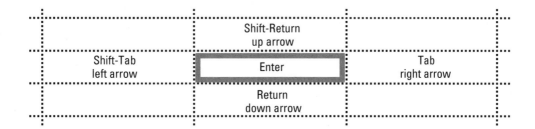

You may format a cell either before or after you enter data. Each cell can be a data type: text (default), numbers, dates, or times. See "Formatting a cell" later in this Topic. If a cell is formatted as a number, use a preceding quotation mark, like *"10th Month,"* to display that number as text. This technique lets you use number cells as titles or labels to help you and others understand your worksheet.

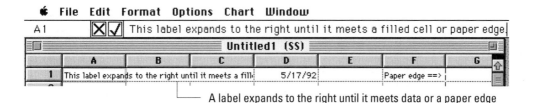

A label expands to the right until it meets data or a paper edge

Any cell that is too narrow to fit the data you have entered or the calculated result will show a set of # symbols. Widen the column to permit the actual value to show. See "Formatting a spreadsheet" for details on widening columns. If the data entered is text or numbers formatted as a label, Works expands the label into the blank cells to the right of the cell, until it meets either a filled cell or the edge of the paper. To stop the label flowing to the right, enter a space character in any cell to the right of the label.

Formatting a cell

Many of the same formatting options are available in a spreadsheet cell as in a database field. Database fields are internally formatted as a data type and have a display format. The situation is analogous for spreadsheets.

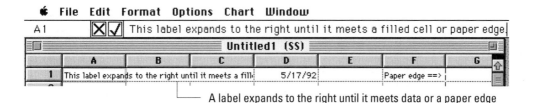

The Format Cells
command is accessed
from the Format menu

Format

Format Cells...
Column Width...

Protect Cell

Set Page Break
Remove Page Break

Freeze Titles Horizontal
Freeze Titles Vertical

Format Character...

Data in a cell must be specified to be a particular data type and only one data type. The default data type is text. To change the data type to number, date, and time, use the Format Cells command on the Format menu. Click on the radio buttons in the Type section of that dialog box. Works uses data formats to streamline operations and aid you in data entry. As a shortcut, double-click on a cell to open its Format Cells dialog box.

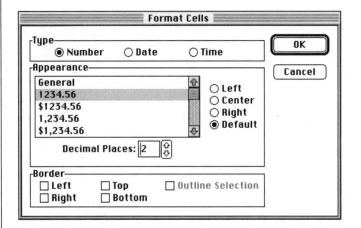

Depending on the data type, several Appearance formats are available in the scroll box. Choose a format that suits your needs or use the General format if you are uncertain. General format displays the number of decimal places you type. You can always change an Appearance later if you change your mind. For example, when you format a cell as a number and specify a dollar format with two decimal places, you need to enter only the numbers. Works will adjust what you see to fit your data format. Thus, when you enter *122*, you see $122.00 in that cell. Always use data formats to display data and enter simple numbers whenever possible.

You can type text into a field formatted as a number, but Works ignores those nonnumeric characters for calculations using that field. Some numbers have leading zeros, like postal codes. Normally, Works drops a leading zero in a number cell. To have Works display leading zeros and show the cell as text even though it is still a number, place opening quotation marks before the number, like this: "02168. You may consider formatting such a cell as a text entry.

Time and dates can be displayed in several formats. Works uses *serial date arithmetic* to calculate dates and times. Macintosh serial dates start on January 1, 1904, the first year of the century with a starting date on a Sunday (day 0); they end on December 31, 2039 (the day the Macintosh will die, day 49,673). Microsoft Works can use dates in the range from January 1, 1904 to February 6, 2040.

Time is normally shown in the 24-hour format (military time), but you can enter PM or AM, and Works will adjust the time accordingly. Works calculates time as a fraction of a serial date, so noon on January 1, 1993 is represented by the value 32508.5. Using this system, dates and times can be used in calculations or date arithmetic. Functions for this purpose are discussed in Topic 11, "Spreadsheet and Database Functions." Whatever date or time you enter, and in whatever format, is automatically converted to the format you chose in the Appearance scroll box in the Format Cells dialog box. For example, if you enter 8/27/52 and the Appearance is for Sun, May 17, 1992, your cell will show the value Wed, August 27, 1952.

Unlike a database, in a spreadsheet you can specify only a single set of attributes for each cell, although you can change the attributes for any number of selected cells at once. You can make a selection for the default font and font size from within the Preferences dialog box; choose the Preference command from the Edit menu. Alignment, font, font size, style, and colors are attributes you can change within the Format Character dialog box; you can find its command on the Format menu. One cell can have a single color or set of text attributes. You can also apply several formatting changes at once, including font, font size, styles, and font color. A sample is shown in the box at the lower part of the dialog box. Works adjusts the row sizes to accommodate your text.

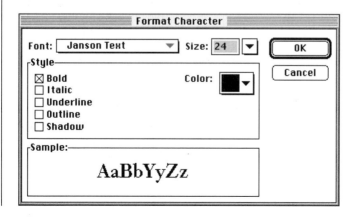

You can also apply text formatting changes one attribute at a time by using the Tool palette Font, Size, and Style submenus. Click on the pop-up menus and drag to select your choices. Works marks the current choice with a bullet.

Alignment and borders are added to a cell's format within the Format Cells dialog box from the command on the Format menu. You can right, center, or left-align characters in a cell, or in any number of selected cells at once. The default option is for numbers, dates, and times to be right-aligned, and for text to be left-aligned.

Use the Border check boxes at the bottom of the Format Cells dialog box to add borders to a cell. You can use these boxes to add lines to rows, columns, or any group of cells. When adding borders, the lines will always resize properly if the columns or text sizes are changed. Use cell borders when lines must border cells, but use drawn lines when the lines you need must be in a certain position or relationship to themselves.

Another formatting option for cells is the Protect Cell command. This command locks in the value or formula of a cell so that it can't be changed. See the section "Protecting your data or display from change."

Calculating with a spreadsheet

Calculations are at the heart of why people use spreadsheets. You can build calculations from values, cell references, operators, and functions. When you use a cell reference, Works uses the value in that named cell to calculate the result for the dependent cell. Works gives you 64 functions to build formulas from, including mathematical, statistical, financial, date and time, logical, trigonometric, and special functions. Operators and functions are detailed fully in Topic 11, "Spreadsheet and Database Functions."

Using cell references in place of values can make your spreadsheet perform different calculations. Whenever you want to analyze a situation (a "what-if" calculation), simply changing the value in a single cell can give you results in all cells that use that reference. If you enter a value in each of those cells, you must change that value in each occurrence to get the desired result. You can define a range of cells to be used in a calculation by using a colon between cell references: B12:D15 is all cells bordered by B12, B15, D12, and D15.

You can use two types of cell references: absolute and relative references. An *absolute* cell reference is one that always uses the address in the formula. A *relative* reference uses the relationship of the cell reference to the selected cell to build functions. For example, if you copy a formula with an absolute cell reference to another cell, that address stays the same. When you copy a relative reference of a cell two cells up and three cells over to another cell, that address changes to a cell the same direction and distance away. Absolute references are useful to point to values in other cells, whereas relative references are best used to retain relationships between cells.

Original relative reference

	A	**B**	**C**
1			
2			
3		=A1	
4			
5			=B3
6			
7			
8			
9	=$B$6		
10			
11			
12		=$B$6	

Copied
relative
reference

Original
absolute
reference

Copied absolute reference

To make a cell reference relative, use dollar signs in each component of the address. The reference $A$12 is absolute; A12 is relative. You can also have a mixed cell reference, either $A12 or A$12. When using relative references, be careful not to have a circular reference where one reference refers back to itself, or does so through another intermediate cell. A circular reference will give an alert box stating `Circular Reference(s) Found During Spreadsheet Recalculation. Cells XX to YY.` Click OK and correct the error, or it will stay in your spreadsheet.

To change an absolute reference to a relative reference, edit the formula of any dependent cells in the Edit menu to remove the dollar signs. You can also change an absolute reference to a relative one by selecting that reference in the entry bar and choosing the Absolute Reference command from the Edit menu, or using the Command-E keystroke. Using the Absolute Reference command on a relative reference changes it to an absolute one; this command reverses a mixed reference from $A12 to A$12.

Entering a formula:

1. **Select the cell in which you want to input the formula.**

2. **Type an equal sign (=), and then type the formula.** Works uses the equal sign to recognize a calculation. You can enter up to 238 characters into a calculation, which includes spaces, cell references (each character in a reference is counted), and so on.

3. **Type cell addresses, or as a shortcut, enter them by simply clicking on the cell in the worksheet.** Works fills in the cell reference into your building formula, entering a *relative cell reference.*

Part II
Using Works' Tools

4. Enter the operator between each operand (value or cell reference in your formula).

If you are doing simple cell arithmetic, click each cell you want to sum; Works automatically puts an addition sign between cell references. Or if you want to sum a range of cells, use the Sum function, and then click and drag the range of cells desired.

⌘ File   Edit   Format   Options   Chart   Window

D32 ☒ ☑ =Sum(D15:D31)

Weekly Travel Expenses (SS)

	A	B	C	D	E	F	
20	Lodging:	74.67	74.67	68.13	68.13		
21	Breakfast:		5.00	4.00	5.00	3.00	
22	Lunch:		8.00	9.00		7.00	
23	Dinner:		15.00	12.00	11.00		
24	Telephone:	2.15		4.45	6.00		
25	Laundry:			6.85			
26	Entertainment:		20.00		40.00		
27	Photocopies:		4.63				
28	Report Binders:			14.00			
29	Postage:				3.05		
30	Other:						
31	Other:						
32	TOTALS:	91.82	133.30	196.43	133.18	159.15	
33				Details on Entertainment Expenses			

Summing a range of cells using the Sum function is more convenient than summing each cell individually

5. Click the Enter box, or press the Return key to enter your formula.

Works normally recalculates your spreadsheet whenever a value is entered. If you have many complex formulas, the operation can be slow. To turn off recalculation until you command it, use the Manual Calculation command on the Options menu. When chosen, your worksheet will recalculate only when you use the Calculate Now command on the Options menu, or its Command-equal keystroke. Keep in mind that if you have not recalculated your worksheet, it may contain and display incorrect data on your screen. Choose the Manual Calculation command once again to remove its check mark and to resume automatic recalculation.

Some of the common operators you might want to use in a spreadsheet include the following: +, addition; –, subtraction; –, negation; *, multiplication; /, division; ^, exponentiation; =, equal to; <, less than; >, greater than; <=, less than or equal to; >, greater than; >=, greater than or equal to; and <>, not equal to. Arithmetic operators, like multiplication, yield a calculated result; comparison operators like the greater than operator will evaluate both operands and return a 1, for true, if the left operand is larger than the right, or a 0, for false, if not.

Certain operators are evaluated before other operators based on a hierarchy or order of preference. Exponentiation is evaluated first, negation second, multiplication and division third, addition and subtraction fourth, and all comparison operators are evaluated fifth. Works calculates a formula from left to right, evaluating the expression for each class of operator first. You can change the order of evaluation by enclosing inside parentheses parts of the expression you wish calculated first. For example, while 2*2^3=16, (2*2)^3=64.

You can also build calculations using *functions*, which are expressions that take values called *arguments*. Functions return results. When using a calculation, Works requires that you use the syntax required by the operator or function. Some functions, such as the Present Value function used to calculate equity in a house, require that data be entered as *PV(rate,nper,pmt,fv,type)*, where the function is operating on four different values. You will get anomalous results if you don't enter the function and data correctly. Similarly, entering a division with a divisor of zero will yield a cell value of *Error*, because this division gives infinity (a number beyond Works' range).

You can enter a function into a formula by typing it directly into the entry bar. However, in order to free you from remembering the syntax of a function and to reduce the number of data entry errors, Works offers you a shortcut. With the insertion point in the entry bar where you want the function to go, choose the Paste Function command from the Edit menu. In the Paste Function dialog box, click the radio button for the type of functions you wish to see, then click the function name to highlight it, and click the OK button. The function appears in the entry bar with any arguments that require values highlighted.

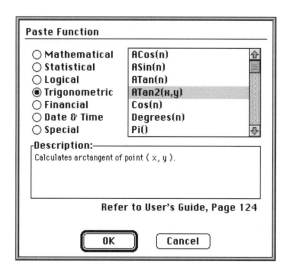

You can enter a date or time into a cell so that it is updated every time the spreadsheet is calculated. Use the formula =Now() in that cell. By formatting that cell as a date or time and setting its appearance, the actual date or time will be displayed in that format. Works uses the date and time used by your Mac. Use the Control Panel or the Alarm Clock desk accessory to adjust the time and date, if necessary.

Working with rows and columns

When you work with a spreadsheet, you will often find that you need an extra row or column within the spreadsheet. You can cut and paste areas of the spreadsheet to accommodate the blank row or column, but there is a better way to accomplish this task. The following instructions show you how to insert and remove rows and columns in a spreadsheet.

Inserting a row or column:

1. **Select a row or column by clicking the heading.**

2. **Choose the Insert command from the Edit menu, or press the Command-I keystroke.**

Edit	
Undo	⌘Z
Cut	⌘H
Copy	⌘C
Paste	⌘U
Clear	
Paste Special...	
Move...	
Select	▶
Find...	⌘F
Paste Function...	
Insert	⌘I
Fill Right	⌘R
Fill Down	⌘D
Absolute Reference	⌘E
Preferences...	

Works places a blank row above the selected row, or a blank column to the left of the selected column.

Removing a row or column:

1. **Select a row or column by clicking the heading.**

2. **Choose the Cut command from the Edit menu, or press the Command-X keystroke.** The Cut command places that row or column onto the Clipboard and closes up the spreadsheet. If you use the Clear command instead of the Cut command, the row remains with its formatting, but all values and formulas are removed.

When you insert or delete rows and columns, all rows below or columns to the right are renumbered, as are all relative cell references contained in any formulas. Cutting a row or column closes up the spreadsheet, thus removing any blank space.

Moving cell data:

1. Select the cells to be cut.

2. Choose the Cut command (Command-X) from the Edit menu to move those cells to the Clipboard.

3. Select the cell that will be the top leftmost cell in the pasted area.

4. Choose the Paste command from the Edit menu, or press the Command-V keystroke.

Works copies what is in the Clipboard to your spreadsheet. Paste copies values and formulas into your worksheet and overwrites any existing values and formulas in the target range. To use a paste that changes place values only, use the Paste Special command on the Edit menu and select the Values Only option. The results of the calculations are pasted, but the formulas are left behind.

You can repeat a paste to another location, if needed. Keep in mind that if you select the entire spreadsheet, cutting, copying, and pasting it will take a long time. Use only the cells you need.

A more powerful way of copying and pasting values and formulas to adjacent cells is to use the Fill Right (Command-R) and Fill Down commands (Command-D) from the Edit menu. If you select adjacent cells in a row and copy a cell on the left, choosing Fill Right will paste that cell's contents to the cells to the right. Similarly, selecting a set of cells in a column, copying a cell, and then choosing the Fill Down command will paste the cell's contents to the cells below. You get better performance in fill operations when you select only those cells to be filled.

Moving cell formulas:

1. Select the cells to be moved.

2. Choose the Move command from the Edit menu, or press the Command-M keystroke.

3. Enter the cell reference in the text box that will be the top leftmost cell in the area to be moved to.

4. Click the OK button.

Move Highlighted Cells to Location: D13

OK   Cancel

When you move a range of cells to a new location, Works adjusts any formulas in your worksheet so that the references still point to the moved cells. With the Move command, you can relocate formulas, not just data. As a shortcut, you can move a selected range of cells to a new location by holding down the Command and Option keys, and clicking on the top leftmost cell of the moved to range.

Changing rows to columns

In a Works spreadsheet, you can change rows to columns and columns to rows. You might want to do this if you have entered numbers horizontally into rows, but you want to sum those numbers vertically in columns, for example.

Transposing rows into columns:

1. **Select the range to be transposed.**

2. **Choose the Cut command (Command-X) from the Edit menu to remove the selection to the Clipboard.**

— or —

2. **Choose the Copy command (Command-C) from the Edit menu to copy the selection to the Clipboard.**

3. **Select the top leftmost cell in the range to be pasted to.**

4. **Choose the Paste Special command on the Edit menu.**

5. **Select the Values and Formulas radio button in the Paste Special dialog box if there are any formulas you wish to rearrange.**

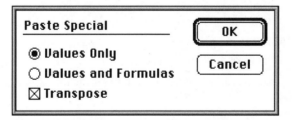

6. **Click the Transpose check box.**

7. **Click the OK button, or press the Return or Enter key.** Transposed rows become columns, and columns become rows. Any formulas in the cells have their relative cell references changed.

A range of cells before being transposed

	A	B	C	D	E	F
16	Airfare:			68.00		53.00
17	Rental Car:					71.15
18	Bus/Limo/Taxi:	10.00	6.00	10.00		
19	Parking:					20.00
20	Lodging:	74.67	74.67	68.13	68.13	
21	Breakfast:		5.00	4.00	5.00	3.00

The same range of cells after being transposed

	A	B	C	D	E	F
16	Airfare:	Rental Car:	Bus/Limo/T.	Parking:	Lodging:	Breakfast:
17			10.00		74.67	
18			6.00		74.67	5.00
19	68.00		10.00		68.13	4.00
20					68.13	5.00
21	53.00	71.15		20.00		3.00

Sorting and transposing data

Using the Sort command, you can organize your spreadsheet by the data it contains. Sorts are done on one to three specified columns, called *key columns,* and applied to any selected data. If you need to sort rows, use the Transpose command to turn row data into column data, and then sort and Transpose that column data into row data once again.

A sort allows you to organize a spreadsheet into a report, with subgroups that can be subtotaled. Sorts are done using the ASCII code — numbers sort before text, and blank cells sort last. As with any Works spreadsheet rearrangements — paste, transpose, and so on — absolute references are left unchanged.

Sorting data:

1. **Select the range of cells you want to sort or select entire columns, if desired.**

2. **Choose the Sort command from the Options menu.**

3. **Type the letter of the column you want to sort in the 1st Key Column text box.** Be sure to use capital letters for a correct sort.

4. **Click a radio button for the order of the sort.** The Ascending button sorts text first by A-Z, then numbers 0-9, and finally dates by chronological order. The Descending button sorts text by Z-A, then numbers 9-0, and finally dates in reverse chronological order.

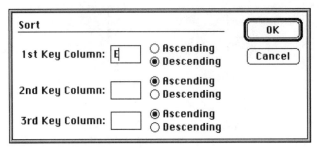

5. **Enter the letter for the second and third key columns for sorts, if desired, and choose the sort order.**

6. **Click the OK button, or press the Return or Enter button.** The sort changes the selection immediately, updating all references. If you make a mistake, immediately choose the Undo command from the Edit menu.

A	B	C	D	E	F
Student		**Inc**		**Avg**	
========================	=	====	=	=====:	= :
Simpson, Eric		0		63.8	
Biddle, Peggy		1		64.5	
Goggins, Paula		0		72.2	
Haberstro, Elizabeth		0		72.2	
Johnsen Alice		0		73.7	
Jones, Susan		0		75.0	
Lange, John		0		76.2	
Cummings, Jim		0		76.5	
Thompson, Richard		0		76.8	
Duval, Sam		0		80.5	
James, Brian		0		81.8	
Keller, Barbara		0		83.7	
Johnson, Max		0		89.0	
Novak, Carl		0		89.8	
Freeman, Dennis		0		90.2	
Peterson, Sally		0		91.3	

A range of cells before being sorted

A	B	C	D	E	F
Student		**Inc**		**Avg**	
========================	=	====	=	=====:	= :
Peterson, Sally		0		91.3	
Freeman, Dennis		0		90.2	
Novak, Carl		0		89.8	
Johnson, Max		0		89.0	
Keller, Barbara		0		83.7	
James, Brian		0		81.8	
Duval, Sam		0		80.5	
Thompson, Richard		0		76.8	
Cummings, Jim		0		76.5	
Lange, John		0		76.2	
Jones, Susan		0		75.0	
Johnsen Alice		0		73.7	
Goggins, Paula		0		72.2	
Haberstro, Elizabeth		0		72.2	
Biddle, Peggy		1		64.5	
Simpson, Eric		0		63.8	

The same range of cells after being sorted

Formatting a spreadsheet

As a default, a new spreadsheet opens with a set of dotted gridlines on it. The lines guide your eyes, making cells stand out. Gridlines will print and interfere with the use of spreadsheets to print forms and reports. You can turn gridlines off by choosing the Show Grid command from the Options menu to remove its check mark, or display the grid by choosing the Show Grid command once again. When the grid is not displayed, Works does not print it.

A spreadsheet with the grid turned off

A spreadsheet has an associated draw layer. Using drawn objects, you can give your document a professional look, as well as create forms, reports, tables, and many other kinds of output (see Topic 11, "Spreadsheet and Database Functions"). The capability of formatting cells with shades, colors, shapes, text and text columns, lines and arrows, and so on, greatly increases what you can achieve using cell formatting alone.

You can access the drawing tools in the Tool palette by using the Draw On command on the Options menu, or by pressing the Command-J keystroke. The Show tools or Hide tools command on the Option menu or the Command-T keystroke will show or remove the Tool palette from the screen. You can also hide the Tool palette by clicking the close box in the title bar. Clicking the Drawing tool on the Tool palette opens the Draw tools. (Draw was discussed fully in Topic 5.) The only new feature added to the draw layer of the Spreadsheet module is the Charting tool.

Charting tool

Spreadsheet tool ——— Draw tool

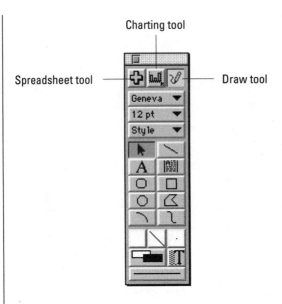

The standard cell width is ten characters, but can range from one to 40 characters. You can change the width of a column visually by moving the pointer to the left or right edge of the column heading. When the pointer turns into a double-headed arrow, click and drag to increase or decrease the column width.

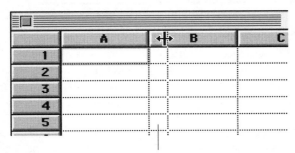

New column width

You can also change the width of one or more column(s) by selecting the columns you want to resize and then choosing the Column Width command from the Format menu. Enter the number of characters in the Column Width text box, and then click the OK button. Using this method, you can resize several columns to exactly the same size.

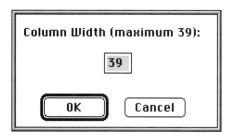

Column Width (maximum 39):

39

OK   Cancel

Spreadsheet documents can have headers and footers. You can use the header and footer area for titles, dates, times, page numbers, graphics or logos, or any information that will make your printed document more understandable. Headers fit in the first printable line below the top margin area; footers fit in the bottom margin ending on the last printable line. Headers and footers work as they do in any of Works' modules. They are described in detail in Topic 4, in the section "Working with headers and footers."

Use the Page Setup dialog box to adjust the margins in the spreadsheet document. When you print a spreadsheet, you will often get better results if you print the document wide, or *landscape*, instead of tall, or *portrait*. Spreadsheets are normally wider than they are tall, and using landscape printing lets you fit the spreadsheet on a page without having to print right-handed columns on additional pages. Use the Print icons within the Print dialog box to adjust these settings. If your printer supports it, you can also get more information to print on a page by scaling the page to some fraction of 100 percent. You can also print only a portion of your worksheet by selecting just those cells you want to print.

Works automatically creates page breaks where they belong. Many times you might prefer page breaks in a different place, such as when a group of numbers are summed to give a total or subtotal. You can place a manual page break where you like.

Setting a manual page break:

1. **Select the cell that will be in the upper-left corner of the next page.**

— or —

1. **Select a single row or column that will be below or to the right of the page break.**

2. **Choose the Set Page Break command from the Format menu.** Works places a set of dashed horizontal and vertical lines above and to the left of the selected cell and repaginates the document below and to the right. If a row or column was selected, then either a vertical page break (above) or a horizontal page break (to the left), respectively, is created.

3. **Remove a manual page break by repeating step 1 and then selecting the Remove Page Break command.**

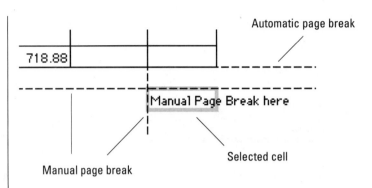

Automatic page break

718.88

Manual Page Break here

Selected cell

Manual page break

Automatic page breaks cannot be removed, only altered by the placement of manual page breaks before them. For multipage documents, Works prints pages in order from left to right and then down. You can use the Print Preview command to see what will be printed and in what order. If you are printing blank pages at the end of your spreadsheet, you may have blank formatted cells in your worksheet. Any cell with formatting is considered an active part of your worksheet. Use the Select Last Cell command to find that cell, and then cut any area up to the area with your data.

Quick Tips

The following tips show you when you should use a database and when you should use a spreadsheet; the elements of good spreadsheet design; how to use cell notes; how to create spreadsheet panes; and what features to look for in a high-end spreadsheet program.

When to use a database instead of a spreadsheet

On the surface, a database can appear to be very similar to a spreadsheet. This is particularly true when you compare the list view of a database to a spreadsheet. They use the same operators, functions, and only the terminology seems different. Spreadsheets use cells and rows; databases use fields and records. If they look the same and function the same, what is the difference? And when should you use a database instead of a spreadsheet?

The difference between a database and a spreadsheet is best understood through the concept of a database record. If you want to group data so that a group of data will always be associated with one another, then use a database. Whenever you want to use information in the most flexible way possible and it isn't necessary to have a column or row always be together, then use a spreadsheet.

In truth, many advanced spreadsheets blur the difference between a spreadsheet and a database even further. Using Microsoft Excel, for example, you can select an area of a spreadsheet and define it to be a database using a command. Rows become records, columns become fields, and many of the commands that were available for database products are then used on this database within a spreadsheet. Probably more databases have been created within Excel on the Macintosh than in any commercial database product. However, advanced databases offer more specialized features for handling database data than a spreadsheet. Works' spreadsheet does not offer the function of defining a database within a spreadsheet, and for good reason: Works already gives you a database you can use.

Elements of good spreadsheet design

Good spreadsheets are planned. Some people even chart them out on paper before committing them to electronic form. Try to use different areas of a worksheet for different purposes. Enter your formulas and values first, and format your spreadsheet only when you are done. It's a good idea to annotate your spreadsheet and place notes about its construction.

Put the name of the spreadsheet and its purpose at the top of the spreadsheet so that you, and others looking at the worksheet later on, know what it was trying to accomplish. You'd be surprised to learn how many spreadsheets end up being a mystery to all concerned because they weren't documented properly. Assume that someone viewing the worksheet will be trying to understand the logic of its construction; give them the assumptions and logic that will make reconstruction possible. That person may be you.

Two powerful concepts you might want to use are the ID Block and the P Block. An ID Block identifies your spreadsheet, creator, version and date, all variables, and assumptions. Put that block near the top of your spreadsheet and outside of the area of any data or calculations. The P, or Parameter Block, is the area that contains any variables you are going to use in formulas throughout the worksheet. By using a P Block, you can change a variable in one place only and have the worksheet change automatically wherever that variable is used. You might want to put borders around blocks in a spreadsheet so that they stand out, and protect their cells so that they cannot be changed.

Some spreadsheets, like Excel, allow you to link several worksheets together in a 3-D structure, so you can create complex interlocking calculations. Works uses a single worksheet and will not accept references from another spreadsheet. You can get around this limitation by using a patch spreadsheet design, where regions of a worksheet are grouped together as if they were a worksheet on their own. Bunching spreadsheet functionality into individual regions is good spreadsheet construction. You could use page breaks for this purpose.

It cannot be emphasized enough: When you are done constructing a spreadsheet, you should test it with sample data. Companies have lost many millions of dollars and some have gone bankrupt through spreadsheet errors. Most errors are errors of logic and user design. Occasionally, companies will find that spreadsheets themselves have programming errors, and some famous lawsuits have resulted.

Don't be lulled by all of those seemingly perfect calculations occurring in your spreadsheet. Computers can lie, or they can tell you what you want to hear!

Using cell notes

Although you can attach labels to your spreadsheet, either as values in cells or as drawn objects, data in a spreadsheet may require more detailed explanation. You can attach a cell note, which is a scrolling text field, to each cell. Cell notes are preferable to labels you attach as drawn objects because cell notes cut, paste, and move with the cell as data automatically. Notes are pasted only when you paste a cell's formulas as well as its values.

Works indicates that the cell has a note attached by putting a small black box, called a note indicator, in the upper-right hand corner of the cell. When you open the cell note, you can type in whatever information you want to remember about that cell. Use cell notes to provide a reminder about the underlying logic of the spreadsheet, an explanation of the data in that cell, or any information you choose.

Attaching a cell note:

1. **Select the cell to be noted.**

2. **Choose the Open Cell Note command from the Options menu.**

3. **Type the information you want into the cell note.** The window will scroll and zoom to show you more information.

4. **Close the Cell Note window by clicking the close box, or by choosing the Close Window command (Command-W) from the Edit menu.**

   Works puts a cell note indicator into the cell.

Cell Note indicator

	A	B	C	D	E
			Auto Finance Analyzer (SS)		
1			AUTO PURCHASE ANALYSIS		
2	Discount factor	10.00%	OPTION 1	OPTION 2	OPTION 3
3	Enter gross sales price		$15000	$15000	$15000
4	Enter rebate/discount		$2000	$0	$2000
5	Net sales price				
6	Enter loan amou				
7	Down Payment				
8	Loan as a % of v				
9	Enter interest r				
10	Enter loan term				

Auto Finance Analyzer (SS) Note C4

This rebate is only available throught December 31, 1992. It require a first time buyer.

Cell Note window

You can hide indicator marks so that they don't display or print by using the Show Note Indicator command on the Options menu. When that command is not check-marked, indicator marks disappear. This technique is useful when you don't want your printed output to show indicator marks.

View cell notes by highlighting the cell containing the note and choosing the Open Cell Note command from the Options menu. As a shortcut, hold the Command key and double-click on the cell. Cell notes are labeled by the spreadsheet name and cell reference "Filename (SS) Note B12."

Cell notes do not print on a spreadsheet, but they print after the spreadsheet if you choose the Print Cell Notes option from the Page Setup dialog box. Turn on the Print Cell Notes option by clicking the Document button in the Page Setup dialog box and then clicking the Print Cell Notes check box. Preview printed cell notes with the Print Preview command (File menu).

Creating spreadsheet panes

Using window split bars, you can divide each worksheet into either two or four window panes. Click in a pane to activate its scroll bar, and then move that pane around in the spreadsheet. This feature lets you look at one section of a spreadsheet while viewing a distant region somewhere else. Perhaps you want to look at labels in the row or column heading while scrolling to data that row or column contains. With spreadsheet panes you can do that. Window split bars are described in Topic 6, in the section "Creating reports." Window split bars function in a spreadsheet the same way that they do in the list view of a database. Draw is not available when window panes are on the screen.

Another feature found in the Spreadsheet module is the capability to lock row and column titles as you scroll in other panes. When you freeze rows and columns, they do not scroll, and you won't lose your place within the spreadsheet as you look around. The Freeze Vertical Titles command, found in the Format menu, freezes the horizontal split bar, removing the scroll bars from above the split bar on the right side of the screen. Similarly, the Freeze Horizontal Titles command will remove the scroll bars from the columns to the left of the horizontal split bar. These commands are toggle switches and display a check mark when active; reselecting them turns off the command.

Protecting your data or display from change

A spreadsheet is easy to change, and you can often make data entry mistakes that will be nearly impossible to find. Once a spreadsheet is set up, you may want to lock the contents of a cell so that the values or formulas it contains cannot be altered.

The Protect Cell command on the Format menu provides this function, essentially turning the cell into a "read-only" condition. You can always tell when a cell is protected because you will not see an insertion cursor in the edit bar when that cell is selected. To turn off cell protection, select the Protect Cell command again, removing the check mark from that command.

When you copy protected cells to a new location, those cells are protected too. It's a good idea to set protection upon completion of a spreadsheet so that protection doesn't interfere with the process of building the spreadsheet.

Beyond Works' Spreadsheet module

Works' spreadsheet is a scaled-down version of its big brother, Microsoft Excel. Excel is the market leader for Macintosh spreadsheets, with perhaps 75 percent of the market. Other powerful spreadsheets available include Lotus 1-2-3 Mac, Claris Resolve, Informix's Wingz, and Borland's Full Impact. All these spreadsheets are good choices, with Lotus 1-2-3 Mac being the best alternative to Excel.

Both Excel and Lotus 1-2-3 have an extensive library of templates and sophisticated macros that are available for many specialized tasks. They are favorites in the corporate market. Resolve has a clean and easily understandable interface. Wingz is noted for quality charts and graphs. Full Impact has a built-in word processor, but it is slow.

You get the following features in more powerful spreadsheet programs:

✦ *More functions*. Typically, high-end spreadsheet programs offer 150 to 200 functions, three times as many as in Works' spreadsheet.

✦ *More graphs and charts*. Data can be displayed in tens of different types of charts, covering nearly every graphing situation you can think of. Works' spreadsheets have only a basic set of charts or graphs (covered in the next Topic).

✦ *Macro language*. Complete scripting languages are part of upscale packages that automate most features and create complex calculations. Works has only a basic keystroke macro recorder function, described in Topic 10, "The Macro Recorder."

✦ *Outlining*. Just like word processors, some programs, such as Excel, let you examine your data organized by levels.

✦ *3-D worksheets*. These worksheets link to other worksheets and can cross reference them.

✦ *Sparse matrix management*. Only the cells used are saved in memory.

✦ *Minimal recalculation*. Only dependent cells are recalculated, not the entire spreadsheet.

✦ *Network support*. Multiuser spreadsheets provide support across networks.

✦ *Cross-platform compatibility*. Files can be shared across different computers using different versions of the same program.

Summary

✔ A spreadsheet is a matrix array of rows and columns that forms cells.

✔ Cells can have values or calculated formulas that return values.

✔ Format data in a cell as text, numbers, dates, and times in the Format Cells dialog box.

✔ Format cells so that font, font size, style, color, alignment, and borders can be added to them.

✔ You can select many cells, but only one cell can be current at one time. Generally, data can be entered into a current cell only.

✔ Cells are identified by their address or cell reference. You can use these references to build formulas or relationships.

✔ A relative cell reference like A12 defines a position in relation to a cell where its reference is used in a formula. An absolute cell reference like $A$12 always points to the same cell.

✔ Relative cell references are rearranged when copied, whereas absolute cell references are not.

✔ You can copy and paste to other locations a cell's values, formulas and values, or the results of formulas.

✔ Use the Find command to locate a cell by its contents or address. Use the Sort command to rearrange data within a spreadsheet.

✔ Build formulas from mathematical operators or functions. Sixty-four functions are available. Formulas are calculated from left to right based on the order of the operator.

✔ Enter formulas by first typing an equal sign and then the formula. You can click on a cell to place its cell reference in an equation; Works puts an addition sign between cell references when you don't type in an operator or function. To enter a range of cells, click and drag that range.

✔ Use a spreadsheet instead of a database whenever you want to treat each piece of information individually and not as part of any special group.

✔ Spend time designing and testing your spreadsheet. Label and annotate it carefully. Use a block of values that you can change in place of changing those values in formulas.

Part II
Using Works' Tools

Topic 8
Using Works' Charts

Overview

Numerical data can be hard to understand and analyze. Most people understand data better in the form of charts and graphs. A picture is worth a thousand words. Using data from a Works spreadsheet, you can create charts that you can use to interpret your data and present it to others.

Works gives you an easy way to generate six different kinds of charts directly from your data. It's as simple as selecting a range of cells and choosing a menu command. Works does all the work for you.

Understanding charts

A chart is not a separate Works document like the word processor, draw, database, spreadsheet, and communications documents. Charts are a specialized type of window found in a spreadsheet. They are created within a spreadsheet as a separate document, in the same way that cell notes can be attached to spreadsheet cells. You create charts using spreadsheet data, with numbers and values in the cells that you specify. Charts are linked to the data in the cells used to create them, and they change when you change that data. You can separate (unlink) a chart from the data (see "Unlinking a chart" later in this Topic), and when you do that, the chart will become a static set of drawn objects that you can use as a graphic in other documents or by itself.

The words *chart* and *graph* are used somewhat interchangeably. Some people consider charts to be strictly numerical representations, and graphs to be any kind of graphic that explains a concept. That is, charts are lists of things like *The New York Times* best-seller list, and graphs are pictures. A pictograph is a specialized kind of graph that uses pictures or icons to represent numbers and trends. A graph showing the population of countries in a region as men of different sizes, bank holdings as different-sized stacks of coins, or armies as different numbers of marching men are pictographs. Sometimes you will see the term *plots* used for graphs. Plots are where tomatoes are grown, where you build a house, get buried — or simple two-dimensional line representations. In this book, a chart is the same as a graph, and I use the term *plot* infrequently.

Knowing when to use a chart

Use a chart when you have too many numbers to make sense of them individually. If you are looking at a large collection of numbers of the same kind of thing, called a *series,* you can plot that series on a graph to determine things like minimum, median, and maximum values, trends, and variances. It's easier to see them graphically than it is to look at the numbers. Charts are also useful for comparison of one series to a value, or one series to another series.

Look at any popular business or news magazine. Nearly every story has some kind of chart in it. Charts demonstrate the main point of the story. If taxes are going up for the middle class vs. the rich and the poor, few people might read that in a story full of text. Some people refer to "the wall of text," meaning that reading it is hard. If you put a combination graph in the story that shows the average tax rate for different income levels as bars, and shows the trends by income class as lines, then the story becomes instantly obvious. You have conveyed several ideas to the reader at once and drawn them into the story at its most important point.

Introducing chart types

Works has six different chart types. Each has a different use and is most effective in situations that the others are not. These types include the following:

◆ *Bar chart.* A bar chart is a series of rectangles or bars that are of the same width, but whose height varies with the size of the number. Each number is a single bar. Bar charts work best when you need to compare numbers for a single category. Bar charts are best for getting a quick overall view of numbers' sizes.

◆ *Stack chart.* This chart is a variant of a bar chart. Stacks are two or more bars, one on top of another. A stack chart not only lets you compare values of a category, but lets you see the size of components that make up that category.

◆ *Line chart.* Each value in a line chart is marked by a point. Lines connect each point in a series of categories and have a point marker where the line crosses the horizontal axis. Line charts show trends most clearly.

◆ *Combination chart.* This chart has both a set of bars and lines. It shows both the overall sizes of values and the trend.

◆ *Pie chart.* This chart contains a circle with slices for each value in that category. Slices are sized relative to the percent of the total that value represents, and the percentage is displayed for each slice. Pie charts are the clearest method for showing the components of a multivalued category.

◆ *High-Lo-Close chart.* New to Works 3, this chart shows the variance of a number at a certain value and the number's final value. Most people are familiar with this kind of chart with stock market activity, where the value is the day, and the varying number is the stock market indexes (like the Dow Jones Index).

Bar chart
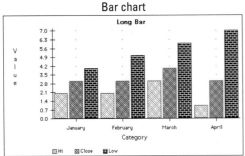

Stack chart
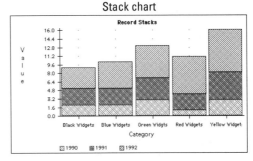

Line chart
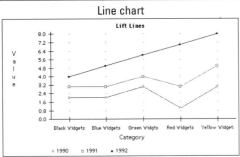

Combination chart
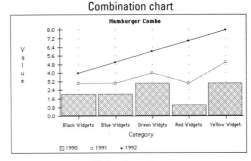

Pie chart
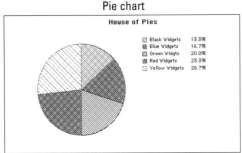

Hi-Lo-Close chart
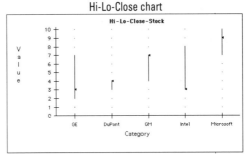

Of these chart types, the most common are the line, pie, and bar charts in that order. Line, bar, stacked bar, and combination graphs are called series graphs because they show variance of a series against another variable.

Charts and spreadsheets

Charts help you understand your data. Works makes it so easy to create a chart that the people who see the results will wonder where you got the time to do such a good job. The whole process is automated in the best sense of the Macintosh: it's just a point and click away, and the results are just seconds away. This feature is one of Works' best, giving you the time to experiment with several chart types until you get the one you want.

When you create a chart, you are creating a pictorial graphic that is attached to the Works spreadsheet. That picture is dynamically lined to the underlying data in the spreadsheet. However, you can cut and paste that chart to another module, and you can also unlink the chart from the spreadsheet data so that you get a static picture of your data at that time.

Creating a chart:

There are two ways to define a chart in Works:

1. **Select the cells in a spreadsheet you want to chart.**

   If you highlight text labels and numbers, Works uses that text as labels in the chart. You can select up to 400 data points, thus allowing you to chart a full year's worth of data.

2. **With the Tool palette showing, click on the Chart tool in the palette.** The Chart tool is represented by a chart icon.

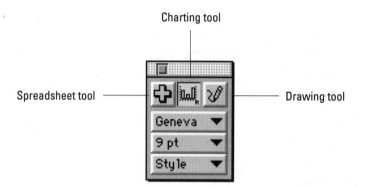

When you go into the chart mode, draw is active and you can use it to modify the chart. You can add lines, text labels, arrows, shadings, and so on to your chart. However, you must first remove any window panes in your worksheet before you can create a chart.

3. **Click and drag a chart box to the size you wish the chart to be.** Charts can be resized later.

— or —

4. **Select the New Chart command from the Chart menu.**

5. **Works creates a chart in the default type. Works gives default chart names such as "Chart 1," "Chart 2," and so on.**

   You can change the default chart type from within the Preferences dialog box within the spreadsheet module. Click and drag on the pop-up chart menu to select one of Works' other five chart types. The bar chart is the original default chart type.

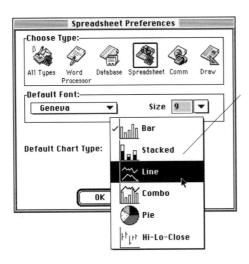

Accessing the Chart Type pop-up menu from the Spreadsheet Preferences dialog box allows you to select the chart type desired

6. **Make any modifications you desire to the chart.**

7. **With the new chart window active, choose the Save or Save As command.**

8. **Enter a name in the Save Document As text box.**

9. **To show the chart, choose its name from the Chart menu.**

You can also save changes to the chart once it has been named and use the Save As command to create copies of that chart to modify under a new name. Any time you save a spreadsheet, all of its associated charts are saved as well. Works enables you to define up to 16 charts for each spreadsheet. Your charts are not saved until the spreadsheet that created them is saved to disk.

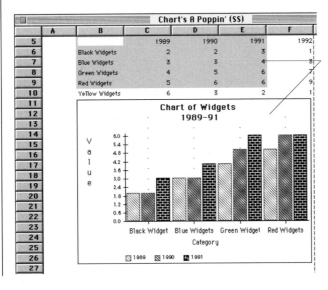

A selected range of data and the corresponding chart they generate

To switch back to the spreadsheet from a chart, click on the Spreadsheet tool (the thick cross cursor in the top left) in the Tool palette. You can then simply click anywhere in the spreadsheet, leaving the chart in the spreadsheet, or move the chart to a blank area of the spreadsheet so that it isn't in your way.

Defining a chart

Not all the data you select will be appropriate for the current chart type, so you will need to change the chart so that it suits your purpose. You modify a chart using the Define Chart dialog box found on the Chart menu. In this dialog box, you can choose a new chart type, respecify what cells are to be used and which cells the labels are to be found in, and set up how the graph will look.

The Define Chart dialog box for the default bar graph

Elements of the Define Chart dialog box include the following:

◆ *Chart Name.* Type in the name that the chart will be saved under.

◆ *Chart Type pop-up menu.* Click and drag to select the desired chart type.

◆ *Labels check box.* Click to put any selected text as labels for values on either the ordinate (Y axis) or abscissa (X axis).

◆ *Grid check box.* When checked, your chart displays and prints a dotted-line grid that lets you see how your data matches to the vertical scale. Grids are used in bar, stack, line, combination, and hi-lo-close charts, and are not used in pie charts.

◆ *Semi-Log check box.* A semi-log plot has an exponential scale on the ordinate and a linear scale on the abscissa. Semi-log plots are useful in making data with large differences in values meaningful.

♦ *Data by.* You can graph data in rows or columns. A bar chart would be either horizontal or vertical.

♦ *Labels in.* Enter the row containing the text you want to use for labels in the graph. Labels are explanations for your data. You do not need to define a label to create a chart.

♦ *Legend in.* Enter the column in the text box containing the legends in the spreadsheet. A *legend* is text that explains the data on the chart. You do not need to add a legend to create a chart.

♦ *Values in.* Type the cells that contain the data you want to graph. Works can chart up to four rows — each can come separately from anywhere in the worksheet.

♦ *From* and *Through.* Define the columns used for row values.

♦ *Vertical Axis.* Enter the minimum and maximum values. Works creates a relative scale, either numerical or semi-logarithmic, based on those minimum and maximum numbers.

Note that when you select another chart type, the Define Chart dialog box changes to reflect the different requirements of that charting type.

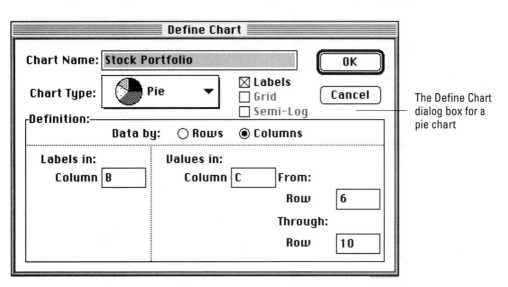

The Define Chart dialog box for a pie chart

Modifying a chart

Just like any other graphic, you can change a chart to suit your purpose. In addition to changing properties like names, you can also change most of the elements of a chart that were mentioned in the preceding list. Charts can be resized almost infinitely, and if you used scaleable fonts like TrueType or PostScript with the Adobe Type Manager, then your text will look smooth at any size. You can assign text attributes (styles, color, patterns, line width, typefaces, and so on) and move it to the position of your choice. Generally, if you can select an element in a chart, you can modify it to suit your purpose.

Not all elements can be moved, and some elements can be moved only in specific ways so that the overall purpose of the chart isn't changed. Therefore, you can't move the bars in a bar chart, but you can move pie slices away from the pie. You can, however, select those graphic elements to assign color, different fills, line widths, and other attributes. Works has default colors and patterns, but you are in no way confined to using them. Using color and patterns is a great way to emphasize the elements of the chart you create, and you should enjoy the results. The sections that follow include instructions for changing different aspects of a chart. By all means, experiment until you get the results you want. Work on a copy of the chart, and because it is so easy to create a new chart, don't worry about not getting it right the first time.

Changing a chart name:

1. **Select the desired chart type from the Chart menu.**

Chart
New Chart...
Define Chart...
Touch Up
✓Long Bar
House of Pies
Lift Lines
Record Stacks
Hamburger Combo
Hi-Lo-Close-Stock

2. **Choose the Define Chart command from the Chart menu, or double-click on the chart background.** Works opens the Define Chart dialog box.

3. **Type the new name in the Chart Name text box.**

4. **Click the OK button, or press the Return or Enter key.**

Changing values in a chart:

1. **If the Define Chart dialog box is not open on your screen, repeat steps 1 and 2 under "Changing a chart name."**

2. **Click on either the Data by Rows or Columns radio button.**

3. **Type the rows or columns in the Values in text boxes that contain the new numbers.**

4. **Enter the row in which the labels appear and the columns in which the legend appears in those text boxes.**

5. **Click the OK button, or press the Return or Enter key.**

Changing a chart type:

1. If the Define Chart dialog box is not open on your screen, repeat steps 1 and 2 under "Changing a chart name."

2. Click and drag a selection on the Chart Type pop-up menu.

3. Click the OK button, or press the Return or Enter key.

Changing labels and legends:

1. **Create or change any spreadsheet cells that will become labels or legends in your chart.** If the chart already exists and if the labels and legends were already defined for those cells, then your labels will update automatically because spreadsheet values and charts are dynamically linked. For undefined legends and labels, go to the next step.

2. **If the Define Chart dialog box is not open on your screen, repeat steps 1 and 2 in the "Changing a chart name" procedure.**

3. **Enter in the Labels in text box the row or column that the legends appear in.**

4. **Labels appear only when the Labels check box is on, so click on that check box if it is not selected.**

5. **Enter in the Legend in text box the column or row that the legends appear in.**

6. **Click the OK button, or press the Return or Enter key.**

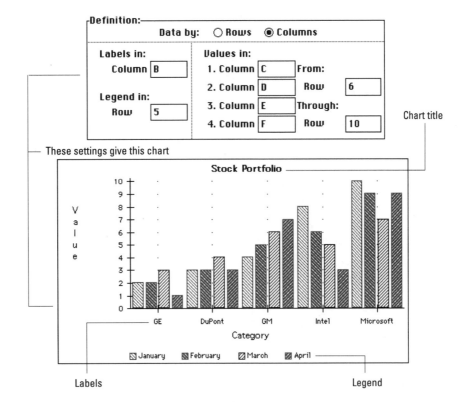

Changing vertical scales:

1. Open the Define Chart dialog box. A numeric vertical scale is the default.

2. Click on the Semi-Log check box if you want a semi-logarithmic scale, or turn off the Semi-Log option to return to a numeric scale. The Semi-Log option will not be available if you have the Grid check box turned off, so turn it back on.

3. Type values into the Minimum Value and Maximum Value text boxes. You can use both positive and negative numbers.

Works places labels and lines on the vertical axis at every ¹⁄₁₀ interval. Use rounded numbers like 0 to 100 to make the scale read in simple numbers.

4. Click the OK button, or press the Return or Enter key.

Charts are drawn objects that can be modified with good results. To modify a chart's elements, you use the Touch Up command; to add drawn objects, you activate the draw layer. When in the draw layer, you will not be able to modify chart elements. You can resize or move a chart and add drawn annotations like text and arrows to a chart for clarification.

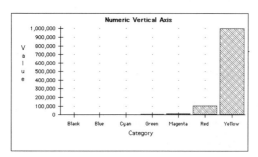

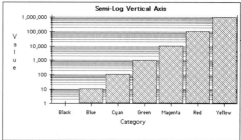

Resizing a chart:

1. Open the chart you want to resize by selecting its name from the Chart menu.

When the chart is selected, resize handles appear at each corner and in the midpoint of each border line.

2. Click on a midpoint handle and drag either left, right, up, or down to resize the chart in one direction.

3. Click on a corner handle to drag in two directions at the same time. All text and drawn objects are resized to scale.

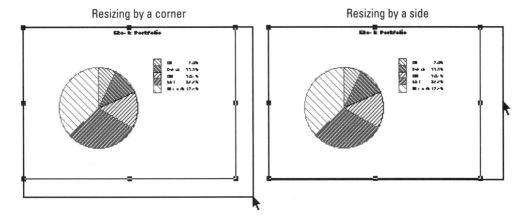

Resizing by a corner   Resizing by a side

Sometimes charts are too small to display properly on the screen but will output properly at the higher resolution of a printer. Try to print the chart before changing it.

To move a chart, click on the background of the chart, but not on a handle, and then drag the chart to a new location.

Charts print where you place them in the spreadsheet. You will not be able to either print or preview your chart while draw is on — only when the spreadsheet is active. To print a chart alone, move the chart to a blank area of the worksheet; then switch to the spreadsheet and select all cells surrounding the chart. When you choose Print from the File menu, only your chart appears.

Charts and the data that they represent are linked to one another. If you change a number used in a graph in your spreadsheet, the graph will change to reflect the new value. This feature makes the necessary adjustments to your data without your worrying about how thoses changes will affect the chart.

Sometimes you want to have a graph saved with the values plotted at the time of creation only. You want a snapshot of that data. For example, you might want to save a graph of sales at year end, or use a pie chart showing market share for different products at a particular time. To do this, you need to unlink the chart from the worksheet. Unlinked spreadsheets are a set of drawn objects.

Unlinking a chart:
1. **Open the chart you want to unlink by selecting its name from the Chart menu.**

2. **Choose the Ungroup command from the Arrange menu.**

Keep in mind that once you unlink a chart from a spreadsheet, you will not be able to reestablish that link. Therefore, you may want to unlink a copy of a chart to work on. Works offers you an option to duplicate that chart by using the Duplicate command from the Edit menu (or the Command-D keystroke). You may also want to create a copy of a graph to work on to make small changes, without having to re-create all of the work and settings used to create the graph in the first place.

Placing a chart in other documents

Charts are printed with their associated spreadsheet. You can use Print Preview in the File menu to see what the chart will look like when it prints. Charts are also very useful as graphics in other documents. You can also use a chart within a word processor, database, draw, or communications document by copying and pasting that chart through the Clipboard. Use a pasted chart to spruce up a report, newsletter, advertisement, or anything else you create in Works.

Copying a chart:

1. **Open the chart you want to copy by selecting its name from the Chart menu.**

2. **Give the Copy command from the Edit menu, or press the Command-C keystroke.** The chart replaces any other information that was previously on the Clipboard.

3. **Open another Works document by using the Open command from the File menu, or by pressing the Command-O keystroke.**

4. **Navigate the file system and double-click on the filename, or single-click and press the Open button.**

5. **Place the insertion point where you want the chart to go.** If you don't place an insertion point, Works copies the chart to the center of your screen.

6. **Choose the Paste command from the Edit menu, or press the Command-V keystroke.**

When you copy a chart to another tool, the chart becomes unlinked from the spreadsheet data that created it. That is, it will not be updated if you change the data in the spreadsheet. This unlinking is an unfortunate deficiency in Works because many other programs on the Macintosh enable you to link data between other applications and automatically update that information. Macintosh System 7 offers a Publish and Subscribe feature specifically meant for linking applications. If you need this feature, you may want to look at another application, such as Microsoft Excel, that supports Publish and Subscribe.

Deleting a chart

Works limits you to 16 charts per spreadsheet. If you need to create more charts, you may need to delete a chart. Deleting a chart in Works is only slightly easier than creating the chart in the first place. Simply open and select that chart, and choose the Cut or Clear commands from the Edit menu. You can also use the Backspace or Delete keys, or the Clear key on the numeric keypad if you have an extended keyboard.

Works posts an alert box to warn you before you delete a chart

Quick Tips

The following tips show you how to pick the right chart type to use with different kinds of data, effectively use charts for presentations, customize your charts, and tell you what to look for in a high-end charting program.

Picking the right chart type

Every Works chart is best suited for a specific, specialized purpose. Use the following guidelines for selecting the chart that is right for what you are working on at the moment:

+ *Bar chart.* Shows one series of values plotted against a single variable; for example, sales figures vs. year figures.

+ *Stack chart.* Shows a series of values and their components plotted against a single variable. Stack charts work best when each value in the series has two to five components.

+ *Line chart.* Shows trends of several series against the same variable.

+ *Combination chart.* Shows one series plotted against a single variable, while comparing that series to other series' performance against the same variable. You can use a combination chart to show sales for a regional sales area (that you wish to emphasize) vs. months, while plotting other regions or the total sales for a company.

+ *Pie chart.* Shows one series of values compared to one another. A pie chart is useful when showing market share.

+ *Hi-low-close chart.* Emphasizes the range of values that a series has vs. a variable, showing a final value in that series. It is the classic chart for stock performance.

+ *Numeric vertical scale.* Uses numeric values when the series values are similar to one another.

+ *Semi-log vertical scale.* Compares series values with large differences in a way that makes trends obvious and meaningful.

Customizing charts

Because a chart is a drawn graphic, you can select and change each individual element of a chart. Changes can be made to the following:

+ *Bars and Pie Wedges.* Add colors, shades, and patterns to each one individually.

+ *Labels and Legends.* Change their position.

+ *Text.* Select font, font size, style, and color.

+ *Lines.* Change width, pattern, and color.

Activating the draw mode for a chart:

1. **Select the chart by opening its window.**

2. **Click on the chart.**

3. **In the Chart menu, make sure that the Touch Up command is selected and has a check mark next to it.**

— or —

4. **Press the Option key and click on the chart.** This step has the same effect as selecting the chart and activating the Touch Up command.

5. **Select the element you want to alter.**

You can now apply different patterns, colors, fills, lines, and so on using the Tool palette. You can make particularly good use of the Overlay tool to change text from either matte, paint, invert, or erase.

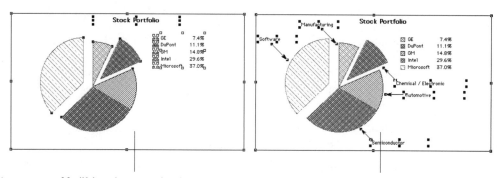

Modifying elements of a chart
with the Touch Up command

Modifying elements of a chart in the draw
layer with the Touch Up command turned off

Topic 5, "Using the Draw Module," explained how to change patterns, shades, colors, lines, fonts, and so on using the Tool palette. These same techniques work in the charting mode. Changing the colors or patterns of elements is a good way to make the elements noticeable. Works offers default colors and default patterns if you are working with a monochrome black-and-white Macintosh. These colors may not be your favorites and may not emphasize what is important to you in your graph — so you might want to change them to suit your purposes. You can even hide an element of a graph by making that element's foreground and background pattern the same.

To select a chart element, click on it to see its resize handles. To move a selected object, click and drag it to a new position. By moving a pie wedge or slice out of a pie chart, you can make that component of the pie stand out. Exploded pie charts emphasize that one element of importance.

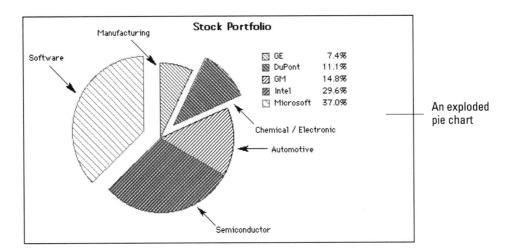

An exploded pie chart

Not every element of a chart is an object that you can move. When you select a chart element that cannot be moved, hollow handles appear instead of filled ones. If you want to completely change all elements of a chart, unlink the chart from the spreadsheet. An unlinked spreadsheet turns the chart into a completely drawn object where all elements can be selected. Note that once a chart is unlinked, you cannot link it back to the spreadsheet that generated it.

Using charts for presentations

Works' charts make great graphics for presentations. To make overhead graphics that you can show others, consider buying specially formulated transparency film that your printer can accept. In good office supply stores you will find packages of transparencies specially made for either impact (dot-matrix), inkjet, or laser printers. Dot-matrix and inkjet film will accept color ink, giving very effective presentation materials.

Many manufacturers make film transparencies; 3M makes perhaps some of the best. A package of laser transparencies (100 to a box) will cost about $20 to $25. You can also buy frames to put the transparencies in for better handling.

Looking beyond Works' charting module

Works' charting module is weak compared to other powerful spreadsheets. Wingz, which is noted for graphing, can offer over 50 different graph types, including some visually stunning 3-D graphics. Even Excel is endowed with strong capabilities. It is common to be able to change perspective around the three axes to any degree you want, preview the result, and then print it when you are satisfied. Nearly every major spreadsheet offered on the Mac is highly functional in this manner; you would be well satisfied with both Lotus 1-2-3 Mac and Claris Resolve.

If you want a package specifically meant for graphing, you can't do better than DeltaGraph Professional. This is a premier graphing package on the Macintosh for business graphics, and it has some scientific capabilities. For a more scientifically capable, but less visually appealing, graphing package, you may want to look at KaleidaGraph. If you are creating visuals for use in magazines, you may want to use a product like Pict-O-Graph that lets you graph data using symbols, figures, and drawings.

When you move up to a better spreadsheet or graphing package, you get the following:

♦ *More charts and graphs.* The range includes 2-D, bullet, organization, bar and stacked bars, line, area, pie and stacked pie, step, time line, X-Y line, scatter, double-X and -Y, contour fill and contour line, 3-D column, 3-D ribbon, 3-D area, wireframe, surface and X-Y-Z surface line, and X-Y-Z scatter or scatterline to name but a few.

♦ *Full drawing tools.* Every element that is selectable and scalable.

♦ *Professional output.* You can print to slides and to color devices as separated output for commercial printing, and so on.

♦ *Template Libraries.* Stored graphs are available for your easy use.

♦ *Slide show presentation.* You can display graphics on-screen successively in a timed sequence.

Summary

✔ A chart is a graphical representation of data found in a spreadsheet.

✔ Graphs make numbers more meaningful and understandable.

✔ Works has six different chart types: bar (the default), stacked bar, line, combination, pie, and hi-lo-close charts.

✔ Create a chart by selecting data in a spreadsheet and then choosing the New Chart command. Use the Define Chart dialog box to make any necessary changes. You can have 16 charts per spreadsheet.

✔ Use numeric vertical scale for series with similar values and the semi-log scale for series with large differences.

✔ Charts are linked to the data that creates them and change when that data changes.

✔ Charts are drawn objects: use the Touch Up command to select and modify chart elements. With the Touch Up command off and Draw on, add any objects you need to clarify the chart.

✔ Unlink a chart to turn it into a drawn object or graphic. You can also copy and paste a chart to another Works module.

✔ Use the right chart type for the job.

Topic 9
Using Works' Communications

Overview

Using the Communications module and a modem, you can go on-line to "talk" with people worldwide, browse an electronic library, research a topic, shop at home, send and receive files from your company's main office while on the road, use electronic mail, and do hundreds of thxings that make your life easier and richer. People have met and fallen in love on-line; found jobs, homes, and cars; bought airline tickets; checked the weather, sports, and the news. It seems that as time goes by, even more ingenious uses for electronic communication appear. With Works, you too can live in cyberspace, tuning into the pulses of the world.

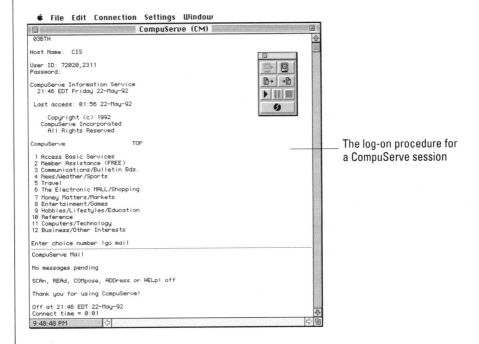

The log-on procedure for a CompuServe session

The Communications module in Works is basic yet highly functional. It allows you to connect to on-line services, bulletin board services (BBSs), other small computers, and even large mainframes. Once you set up a communications document and record a sequence to start up a session, then the next time you want to go on-line, that service, BBS, or computer is just a menu command away.

Understanding communications

Computers are digital data devices. That is, to store and process information in a computer, only binary information can be used. Transmission of data must either be all digital or must be converted to digital signals at the sending and receiving end. Most computer communications (below 19200 baud) are usually asynchronous — that is, data is sent in a bit stream with no clock synchronization. A start and stop bit marks the end of each computer character or block of characters in the bitstream. Computer communication requires that both devices use the same frequency.

The frequency of transmission is specified in *bits per second,* or bps. A more commonly used unit called the *baud rate* is used; it is a measure of the number of times per second that the electrical circuit can switch. Thus, while 300 bps is sent with one change in state, higher rates like 1200 bps are usually sent at 600 baud, with two bits of information per change in state. The higher the baud rate, the more information that can be transferred. At 2400 baud, approximately 800K can be transferred. At 9600 baud, that number rises to 3.2MB.

In a communications session, you must follow several steps:

1. **Open or create a communications document and provide any settings needed.**

   Important settings include the transmission connection used (Apple Modem Tool, Hayes Modem Tool, Serial Tool, or AppleTalk Tool); baud rate, frequency of data transfer (most often 1200, 2400, or 9600 baud); parity, an error-checking bit (even, odd, or none); data bits, the number of bits used to represent a character (seven or eight); stop bits, the number of bits between two characters (1, 1.5, or 2); terminal emulation (normally TTY or dumb terminal); and of course, the phone number you are calling. Terminal emulation (defined in the section "Communications settings") allows your Mac to behave like a simple display screen, echoing the characters sent and received by the computer hosting the communications session. The most popular terminal emulation is TTY, short for *teletype,* which harkens back to the day when teletype machines were used as communication devices. Mismatching settings will lead to no connection, unreliable connections (random or no characters), or other unexpected results.

2. **Make sure that your modem is attached properly and is on.**

Connection	
Open Connection	⌘D
Close Connection	⌘K
Listen For Connection	
Send File...	⌘U
Receive File	⌘L
Status Bar	▶
Start Timer	⌘G
Reset Timer	
Show Info...	⌘I
Start Capture...	
Resume Capture	
Reset Terminal	

3. **Choose the Open Connection command on the Connection menu to clear and initialize your modem.**

4. **The modem then dials a phone number.**

5. **Your modem then waits for and receives a handshaking tone that your modem acknowledges.**

   Handshaking is a series of messages that are exchanged between two computers in a communications session. The messages are recognized by the squeals your modem makes as the signals are sent and received. During handshaking the two computers determine whether different speeds and protocols are possible and agree to the best (most efficient) method that both modems and computers support for the communication session.

6. **You're connected. Then if you are on a service, you enter any required passwords or log-on information.**

   What you enter is specific to the service you're communicating with. For simple computer-to-computer communications, you might simply acknowledge your connection by typing a message to the individual on the other side.

7. **Exchange information: either in the form of simple text characters or as binary files.**

   Sending a file is called *uploading,* while receiving a file is called *downloading.*

8. **End the session by giving the log-off command.**

   Usually you type the word Quit, Exit, Off, or Bye for a service to end a session, called a log-off. For a direct connection to another computer, you might type a goodbye and then disconnect using the Close Connection command.

9. **A Close Connection command is then issued, which hangs up your modem, breaking the phone connection and reinitializing the modem once again.**

10. **The communications document is closed.**

Every communication session follows this pattern. Although data communication is a discipline loaded with jargon like baud rate, parity, XON/XOFF, upload, and so on, once you set up your communications document, you can largely ignore most of these terms and get on with the joys of expanding your world. In this Topic, I explain the details of many of these terms and their importance. Don't be intimidated by them, because generally you need to set things up only once.

The preceding sequence looks complicated. But keep in mind that while some of these steps are manual, many of them can be part of the automated sequence that you create in Works. So you don't really have to remember them.

What do you need to communicate?

In order to telecommunicate with others, you need Works properly installed on your Macintosh and a modem. You can also communicate through simple serial cable connections and over AppleTalk networks. Works' installation is covered in Appendix A. If you choose the Easy Install option, then the installer will place the Macintosh Communications toolbox into your System Folder. System 6 requires a toolbox installation, while System 7 has these programming tools already included in the system software.

When you connect two computers together directly using a serial cable and their two serial ports, data is transmitted digitally. This is an easy connection to set up, provided the two computers are in close proximity and have the same serial port standard. There is also a short length limit of about 24 feet before transmission becomes garbled and unreliable. Such a connection is called a null modem (no modem) connection and uses a null modem cable. Using the Serial Tool in the Communications toolbox, you can use this kind of setup to do data communications. You can use either the modem or printer port on a Mac for this purpose — they are identical. You only need specify which port is being used for communications. Data transfer speeds can be at the rated speed of the serial port. On Macs using the RS422 protocols, that speed can be up to 920000 bps. (The IBM PC uses the RS232C standard.)

Network connections are also digital systems and require only appropriate software once computers (or network nodes) are connected. An AppleTalk Tool supports network transmission. Network connections can be hundreds of feet between computers with signal boosters called *repeaters* that raise the distance to 1500 feet between nodes. Works is not a program that has its own network support: It can't be used simultaneously by several users, but it can be used on a network.

Telephones are analog devices supporting a variety of signal amplitudes. Telephone networks support very long-range transmissions, as you well know. In order for two computers to talk to one another, digital signals need to be converted to analog signals (digital to analog conversion, or DAC) for transmission through phone lines by the sending computer. The receiving computer must then reconvert analog signals back to digital

signals. Devices that do DAC are called modems (for *mo*dulator-*dem*odulator). Modems turn digital electrical signals into tones (modulation), and reconvert the tones at the other end to electric signals (demodulation) once again.

You can buy both internal modems (mostly as NuBus cards with extended network or fax capabilities) or external modems. Hayes, one of the first successful modem manufacturers, created what is called the "smart" modem — a term they copyrighted. A smart modem contains a microprocessor that can manage much of the necessary command set in a data communication session. The Hayes command set is an industry standard. Most modern modems are now smart; many now ship with chip sets for conversion of data into the fax compression routines. Most modems are also direct-connect devices; they plug directly into a phone line. Some older modems are acoustically coupled modems. You place the phone handset into a rubber cup for the phone connection. Acoustic systems are not as reliable as direct connections, and they are largely relics, not often found now. See "Buying a modem: What do you need?" and "Fax modems," toward the end of this Topic.

Because the process of setting up a communication service involves embedding settings into a document, using stationery is a very convenient method for encapsulating start-up information, while leaving your permanent settings unchanged. Stationery, if you recall, will open a copy of itself as an "Untitled" document. Works comes with a number of sample stationery documents for use with some of the more popular on-line services. You can have all of your communication documents in one folder; or, when in the Finder, highlight that document and create an alias using the Make Alias command from the File menu. That alias can serve as the launching icon for your service, and you can put it anywhere in your file structure, even your desktop.

Unfortunately, Works 3 has capabilities and uses services through the Macintosh Communications toolbox that were not available in prior versions of Works. You will not be able to open a previously created communications document in version 3 and have it convert successfully. Any documents that you used to communicate with in versions 2.0 or 1.0 will have to be re-created.

Introducing the Communications window

A communications document opens to a Communications window that contains a few features that are unique in Works. In the following figure, a window with a typical session in progress is displayed. As you type text, and by the other computer you're connected to returns text, the text area of the window fills up and scrolls up automatically. You can resize the window using the zoom or resize boxes to show more text, but soon the text area will fill.

Works creates an *overflow area;* other programs call it a *text buffer.* This buffer fills up with the text that disappears at the top of the screen. Shown in the following figure is the overflow boundary and the bottom of the text in the overflow area. The prompt "-Press Any Key-" was followed by a key being pressed, and the next line appearing was "BCS*Mac Multiline BBS — MAIN MENU." You can use the window scroll bars to view the contents of the text buffer or the previous contents of your text area.

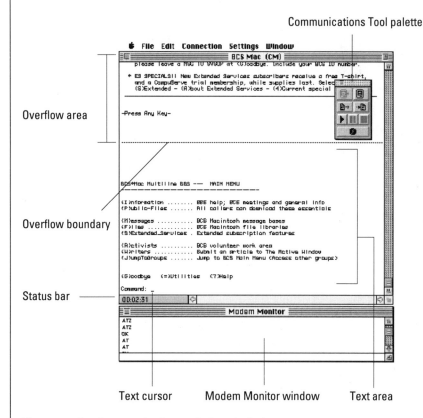

Communications Tool palette

Overflow area

Overflow boundary

Status bar

Text cursor   Modem Monitor window   Text area

Elements of a Communications window include:

◆ *Text area.* Text you enter and text that is returned appears here. As more text appears, old text scrolls up. You can control the behavior of the text in the window: its size, number of characters per line, and whether it jumps a few lines at a time or flows smoothly one line after another within the Terminal dialog box. Open this dialog box by choosing the Terminal command from the Settings menu or by pressing the Command-2 keystroke. Terminal settings are described in full in the section "Communications settings."

✦ *Overflow area.* Text overflow, or the text buffer, is an area of memory where text that doesn't fit into the Communications window goes. Use the window scroll bars to view the overflow area. To clear the overflow area of old text, choose the Clear Buffer command from the Edit menu.

You can adjust the text buffer size and, which follows a last-in, first-out principle. When the buffer fills, the oldest information is deleted first. You can control the size of the buffer by clicking the appropriate radio button in the Overflow Area Size box of the Communications Preferences dialog box (see the following figure). Settings include None, Small, Medium, and Large. A large overflow area will hold more text but leaves less memory (RAM) for Works to use. In a low-memory situation, for example, with Macs with 2MB RAM, you may want to use a small setting. To save all text that was displayed, capture that text in a text file (see "Capturing text" later in this Topic).

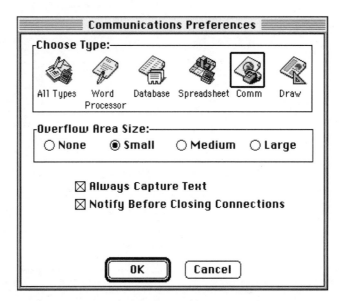

Other settings you can specify as a default are Always Capture Text and Notify Before Closing Connections. Captured text saves all of the text entered in the communications window to a disk file. The file is saved as ASCII text (without formatting) and can be opened within any word processor. The notification setting will always post an alert box before a connection is broken.

✦ *Overflow boundary.* This is a dotted horizontal line marking the boundary between the text and overflow areas. Depending on where you scroll vertically in the communications window, you may or may not see this boundary line.

◆ *Status Bar.* This bar shows the current time, the time duration of each session, the approximate amount of money spent in each session, or the current date. Current time and date are system settings you change in the General Controls panel or in the Alarm Clock desk accessory. To choose between these four modes, select the appropriate command from the Status Bar submenu on the Connection menu (see the following figure). For information about using the status bar, see "Keeping track of time and costs" toward the end of this Topic.

◆ *Modem Monitor window.* You will see this window only when you check the Display Modem Monitor Window check box in the Apple Modem Tool settings. The Modem Monitor window shows the commands being sent or received from your modem to another computer. This is useful for debugging communication sessions.

◆ *Text cursor.* This object shows where text will be entered to the left of the cursor. You can choose to show an underline cursor or a block cursor by changing the setting in the Terminal dialog box.

◆ *Communications Tool palette.* Icons in the Tool palette duplicate menu commands from the Connection menu. When you click on a tool that has options, a pop-up menu is displayed. Drag to the choice you want.

The Communications Tool palette contains only communication commands and does not open the Draw module in the main window. Draw is available in the header or footer of a communications document, or in captured text files, as it would be in any word processor file.

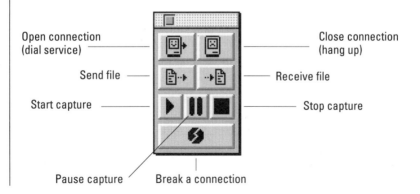

Open connection (dial service) — Close connection (hang up)

Send file — Receive file

Start capture — Stop capture

Pause capture — Break a connection

Use the Show Tools or Hide Tools command from the Window menu, or press the Command-T keystroke to display the palette or remove it from view. Using this command will affect the appearance of the Tool palette in all of Works' modes.

Starting an on-line session

The time you spend on an information service or BBS is called a *session*. Sessions begin when you log on and end when you log off. Logging onto a service generally involves giving a name or address and a password. Logging off most often requires you to type a command like Quit, End, or Off. Each service has different requirements. When you connect to another computer directly, there is no log-on or log-off; you simply dial the computer (Open Connection) and hang up (Close Connection) when you are done.

Depending on the kind of data communications session you are going to establish, you use a different connection tool — either the Apple Modem, AppleTalk, or Serial tools. When you use a modem to establish telephone communication with another computer, use the Apple Modem tool. Most modems use the Hayes modem command set (a standard in the computer industry); the Apple Modem tool includes these settings. The AppleTalk tool lets you exchange files with other computers on an AppleTalk network. The Serial tool is used to connect directly from your computer to another using a serial cable through your modem or printer port. The settings allowed in these connections tools are discussed in detail in "Communication settings" later in this Topic.

Every service requires different communication settings to establish successful sessions. Works ships with some sample communication stationery documents that you can use to work with large on-line services like CompuServe, GEnie, BIX, and others. To use these documents, you need to supply only the local telephone access number for that service, set your data transfer or baud rate for your modem in the Connection Settings dialog box (Connection menu), and record your log-on procedure, if desired.

Connecting to other services, like your local user group BBS, requires that you know and set several communication parameters, such as baud rate, data bits (bits per byte — word length), parity, stop bits, and handshaking. You will find a detailed explanation of these terms (and others) in the "Communication settings" section a little later in this Topic. Normally you can find this information in the documentation that an on-line service provides. If it isn't there, you must talk to a human being (if you can locate one) at the service directly to find out what is required. For BBSs, you may want to ask for the system administrator or operator. Humans do not require handshaking signals, but most respond to a friendly "Hello!"

Setting up a session:

1. **Select the New command on the File menu, or press the Command-N keystroke.**

2. **In the Save dialog box, enter a name for your new communications document and then press the Save button.**

3. **Select the Connection command from the Setting menu, or press the Command-1 keystroke.** The Connection Settings dialog box allows you to control the way data is exchanged between computers.

4. **Choose from the Method pop-up menu either the Apple Modem or Hayes Modem Tools for telephone sessions, the AppleTalk ADSP Tool for network communications, or the Serial Tool for direct computer-to-computer serial port connections.** Select the serial port and the options you want for that service. See the section "Communications settings" for more detailed information about these dialog boxes.

5. **In the Connection Settings dialog box, select the port and enter the telephone number and type (tone or pulse). Set the baud rate, data bits, stop bits, and parity settings needed for your session.**

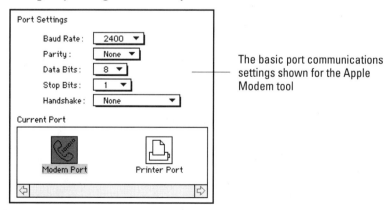

The basic port communications settings shown for the Apple Modem tool

6. **Close the Connections dialog box by clicking the OK button.**

Part II
Using Works' Tools

7. **Select the Terminal command on the Settings menu, or press the Command-2 keystroke.**

8. **Select the Terminal Emulation mode required for your session from the pop-up menu.** Use TTY for a "dumb terminal" setting required by most on-line services. When communicating with a Digital Equipment VAX computer, use the VT102 (for video terminal) or VT320 emulation.

9. **Also, use the settings in the Terminal Settings dialog box to control the appearance of your communication.** These settings are explained in detail in the section "Communications settings."

10. **Save your communications document and settings by choosing the Save or Save As command from the File menu.** You may wish to save the document as stationery to prevent changes being made to the original document.

11. **Enter the filename in the Save Document As text box and click the OK button.**

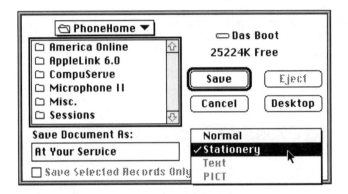

Connecting to other computers

At this point, your communications document is ready to use to start a session with a service or other computer.

Logging on to a service:

1. **Open the Communications document for the service or session you wish to start, using the Open command from the File menu. Or press the Command-O keystroke.**

2. **Choose the Open Connection command from the Connection menu, or press the Command-D keystroke.**

— or —

2. **Click the Open Connection tool on the Tool palette.** Works posts a dialog box asking for a phone number, if the Communications document doesn't have one already entered in the Connection Settings dialog box.

3. **Enter the number, including commas, in the sequence where you want Works to pause in the dialing sequence.**

4. **Click the Dial button.**

If you select the Open Connection Automatically check box in the Options dialog box by choosing the Options command from the Settings menu, then Works will automatically dial up the number when you open the Communications document. You can also choose to have Works log on automatically by clicking the Play Sign-On Script Automatically check box in the Options dialog box. You must first record a log-on sequence (see "Automating log-on" toward the end of this Topic) for this option to be enabled.

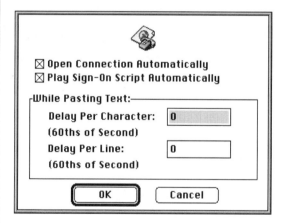

As part of the dial-up sequence, Works displays several alert boxes to tell you what it is doing. First, Works "clears its throat" by making a "Hmmmmm" sound. Then an alert box is posted telling you that the modem is being initialized and the number dialed. Following the dial-up sequence, Works tells you that the connection is established and at what data transfer rate.

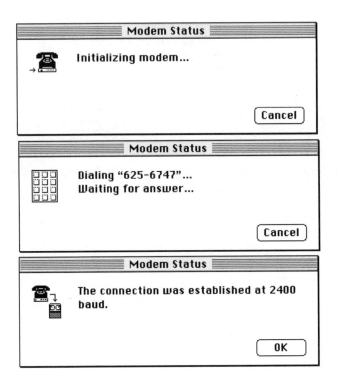

What you see after this point in the dial-up sequence depends on the service you are calling. The log-on sequence includes the following:

5. **The word "Connect" appears on your screen to indicate that your session has begun.**

— or —

5. **You will see some computer code followed by a greeting.** The other computer may wait for you to enter a Return character or two before proceeding to the log-on sequence.

6. **Enter your name or address, as required by the service you're connecting to, followed normally by a Return or Enter character.**

7. **Enter your password, as required by the service, followed by a Return or Enter character.** Most services put symbols like bullets (•) or asterisks (*) in place of what you enter for a password for security purposes. If you enter an incorrect password three times, most services invite you to sleep it off.

You can automate the log-on sequence as discussed in "Automating log-on" later in this Topic.

Many times you will need to dial a service more than once before you can connect. To free you from the drudgery of having to dial a busy BBS or on-line service repeatedly, Works lets you perform automated redialing.

Redialing automatically:

1. Choose the Connection command from the Settings menu, or press the Command-1 keystroke.

2. In the Connection Settings dialog box, check the Redial Times check box.

3. Enter the number of times you want Works to redial the service before giving up in the Redial text box.

4. Enter the number of seconds between redials in the Every Seconds text box.

5. Click the OK button, or press the Return or Enter key to dismiss the Connection Settings dialog box.

Logging off from a session:

1. Enter the command for the log-off required by your service: Quit, Exit, Bye, Off, or whatever.

2. Choose the Close Connection command from the Connection menu, or press the Command-K keystroke.

— or —

2. Click the Close Connection tool on the Tool palette. Works disconnects from the service, hangs up the telephone, reinitializes the modem, and posts an alert box.

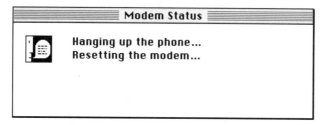

3. You can also click the close box in the title bar, or select the Close command (Command-W) or the Quit command (Command-Q) — both from the File menu — to break a connection.

All services mark a disconnect as if you logged off, shutting off additional charges. If you set the option Notify Before Closing Connections by clicking on its check box in the Preference dialog box, then Works will post an alert box. Setting this option is a good idea because it allows you to cancel the command in case you made a mistake.

Sometimes you want to set up your Mac to accept or answer telephone calls from other computers. After you agree on all of the settings required to match communications and protocols, use the following instructions to have your Mac accept or answer calls from other computers.

Setting up your Mac to answer telephone calls:

1. **Open a Communications document and choose the Open Connections command from the Connections menu, or press the Command-D keystroke.**

2. **Select the Connection command in the Settings menu and set the option Answer Phone After Rings. Enter the number of rings desired in the text box.**

3. **Select the Listen For Connection command from the Connection menu.** When the telephone rings, Works will instruct your modem to answer it. You cannot wait for an incoming call and place an outgoing call at the same time.

4. **Once the connection is established, continue to establish your communications session.**

If the computer is close by, it is often better to establish a serial or null modem connection between them.

Creating a serial communications session:

1. **Install the serial cables into the correct Macintosh port — either the Printer or Modem ports — as desired.**

2. **Open a Communications document.**

3. **Select the Connection command from the Settings menu and choose the Serial Tool from the Method pop-up menu.**

4. **Check that the correct port is chosen in the Port Settings section.**

5. **Click the OK button.**

6. **Select the Open Connection command from the Connection menu, press the Command-D keystroke, or click the Open Connection tool from the Tool palette.**

   You can also set your Macintosh to wait for an incoming signal from another serial computer here by choosing the Listen For Connection command from the Connection menu.

7. **Send and receive files using the Send File (Command-U) and Receive File (Command-U) commands on the Connection menu.**

   Serial connections are generally unreliable, so if you are having problems, check your cables. Also, make sure the correct ports have been chosen on both machines.

8. **When done, close the connection by using the Close Connection command on the Connection menu, pressing the Command-K keystroke, or clicking the Close Connection tool on the Tool palette.**

   If you wish to close the document and keep the connection open, there is a setting in the Connection dialog box, accessed from the Setting menu, for this purpose. Check the Hold Connection check box in the Under When Closing Document section. You may also want Works to alert you when closing the document to disconnect; this setting is the Remind To Disconnect check box found in the Connection Settings dialog box.

To use the Communications module to talk with other AppleTalk computers on a network and exchange text and files, follow the instructions below (assuming that the network is established).

Connecting to computers on AppleTalk:

1. **Open a Communications document.**

2. **Select the Connection command from the Settings menu.**

3. **In the Connections Settings dialog box, choose AppleTalk ADSP (AppleTalk device serial port) in the Method pop-up menu.**

4. **In the Name box, choose the name of the computer you want to talk with. Or you can find the computer you want to talk with from other network zones by selecting those zones and examining the nodes.**

5. **Click the OK button.**

   At this point, you can set up your Mac to answer other computers by choosing the Listen For Connection command from the Connection menu. Or proceed to step 6 to call another computer.

6. **Choose the Open Connection command from the Connection menu, press the Command-D keystroke, or click the Open Connection tool in the Tool palette.**

7. **Send and receive files, making sure that the file transfer protocols are matched.**

8. **When done, close the connection by clicking the Close Connection tool on the Tool palette, by selecting the Close Connection command on the Connection menu, or by pressing the Command-K keystroke.**

Communications settings

This section contains information to help you control and set communication options. The information is detailed and specific, so unless you have a specific problem you are trying to solve, you may want to skip to the next section, "Receiving and sending text."

Data communication requires that both computers participating in a session observe the same certain communication methods which are called protocols. A *protocol* is a widely agreed upon method for data exchange. There are both hardware and software protocols. Perhaps the most widely known protocol is the seven-layer International Standards Organization ISO/OSI model. Lower levels in this model are hardware protocols, middle levels are network protocols, and the upper levels are software protocols. The Macintosh system software and hardware takes care of the lower five protocol levels. Works allows you to change software protocols and make selections that switch data transmission to a network or other current carrying media. (For a complete discussion of communications protocols, see IDG's *Macworld Networking Handbook,* by Dave Kosiur and Nancy E. H. Jones.)

You need three classes of settings to establish an orderly communications session. The connection settings are used to determine the way your Mac communicates with another computer. There are four connection tools in the current Communication toolbox: the Apple Modem, Hayes Modem, AppleTalk ADSP, and Serial Tools. The first two are used for telephone connection using a Hayes-compatible or Apple modem, the third for AppleTalk network communication, and the fourth for direct serial line connection. The second class of settings is the terminal type you wish to have your computer emulate. The third class of settings is the file transfer method used to transmit data files. You can access the three classes of settings from the Connection (Command-1), Terminal (Command-2), and File Transfer (Command-3) commands from the Settings menu. In this section we look in detail at the options these settings allow.

The Connection dialog box contains the most basic settings for a communication setting. Use it to change the nature of the data transfer, how the data is handled, and what kind of transmission is used. Depending on which connection tool you use, you will see very different dialog boxes. Choose the connection tool from the Method pop-up menu.

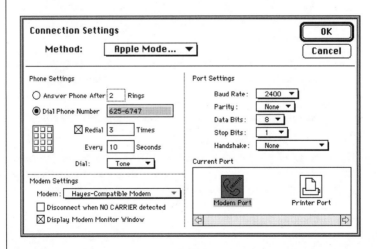

The Apple Modem tool lets your Macintosh provide the control signals to your modem, bypassing any microprocessor that the modem may have. Generally, you use this tool for a modem that is not a Hayes-compatible SmartModem, and use the Hayes Modem tool for one that is. The Apple Modem tool contains the following settings:

- *Phone Settings*. You can choose to either phone a number or have the modem answer an incoming call after a number of rings that you specify. When phoning a number, remember that you can use hyphens or parentheses, which are ignored, or use commas to pause the dialing sequence.

- *Redial*. Enter the number of times and the interval between them.

- *Dial*. Choose tone or pulse phone; you can't mix them in the Apple Modem tool.

- *Modem Settings*. Choose one of over 35 modem drivers from the pop-up menu by model or manufacturer. If you are unsure, try the Hayes-Compatible Modem driver (if it is one) or the Generic driver. You can also create a Custom driver using your manufacturer's information. Select the Disconnect when you need to leave your session unattended and you want to disconnect after a file transfer. Select the Display Modem Monitor Window check box when you want to view the commands issued by your modem in a window.

- *Port Settings*. Baud rate is the frequency of data transfer, parity is an error detection method, data bits is the number of bits in a character, stop bits is the number of bits between characters, and handshaking is a method used to indicate that a computer is ready to either send or receive data. Choose either the Modem or Printer Port, whichever one the modem is using — they are functionally identical. These parameters were discussed in the Overview section.

Telephone transmission is inherently troublesome, and computers use several methods to detect errors. One method called *parity* adds together the values of bits in a byte or block of bytes to check the value of the sum as a result that can be either 0 or 1. When the parity bit of a byte or block doesn't match the transmitted parity bit, the computer issues an error message, and retransmission of the block occurs. None indicates that parity is not used. Odd parity sets the parity bit to 1 when there is an odd number of 1-value bits in a byte. Even parity sets the parity bit to 1 if there is an even number of 1-value bits in a byte. Parity checking is a very basic error-correction scheme; there are more advanced schemes used now.

In order for two computers to communicate, they must use the same transmission rates and protocols. Handshaking is used by computers to tell each other what speeds and protocols are being used, when they are ready to send, and when they are ready to receive data. None means that handshaking is off. An XON/XOFF handshake is used to coordinate two computers so that one doesn't send data faster than the other can receive it. XON/XOFF is incompatible with Xmodem or Kermit file transfers (discussed later in this section). Other handshaking methods — DTR and CTS, DTR only, and CTS only — are more commonly used with the serial Tool. Use these three options when you have a serial connection between your Macintosh and another computer that uses these hardware handshakings.

The Hayes Modem tool lets you take advantage of that modem's built-in microprocessor for greater communication speed and accuracy. If you have this kind of modem, by all means use this tool — it offers several additional features. Not many new features appear in the Hayes Modem Connection dialog box shown in the figure below.

The Hayes Modem tool

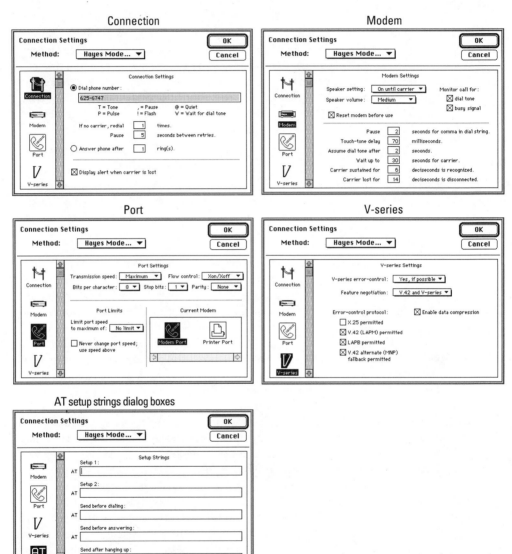

Connection

Modem

Port

V-series

AT setup strings dialog boxes

✦ *Connection settings.* Notably, Hayes modems allow you to mix both tone and rotary pulse dial tones for systems that use both. Other options include comma for pause; ! for flash or hang-up signal; @ for a quiet period; and W for a pause that waits for a dial tone. Use the Display alert as a default to remind you of the loss of your communication signal.

✦ *Modem settings.* Most of the settings here are technical settings for the Hayes series and don't need to be changed. Most useful of the settings are the Speaker volume, which you can use for changing the volume of the tones emitted. You can also listen to the modem until the carrier tone is established (the default), have the speaker always on or always off, or off when the carrier is on. Unless you're debugging a communication system, just listen to the tones until the connection is successfully established.

✦ *Port settings.* Most of these are similar to the settings found in the Apple Modem tool port settings. You can set transmission speed manually, or you can let the modem determine the transmission speed by setting it to Maximum. Flow control is the same as handshaking. In addition to modem speeds, you can also set Port Limit speeds.

✦ *V-Series settings.* Hayes V-Series SmartModems are a newer modem series that provide advanced error correction, data compression, and fallback. Consult your modem's user manual to change these settings, as needed.

✦ *AT setup strings.* Use these settings if you have a Hayes AT modem. Check your modem manual for the necessary character strings. ATs are older modems.

Normally, you set the speed of a modem to match the speed of the modem or service (which uses a modem) you are connecting to. One of the nice features that smart modems offer is the capability to switch to speeds below their maximum rated transmission rate, called *fallback*. Thus, if a 9600-baud modem calls up a computer with a 2400-baud smart modem, the handshaking signal will tell the two computers to use 2400 baud as their mutual rate. Also, if a telephone line gets noisy (and what telephone line doesn't) and signals get garbled, modems will detect a series of transmission errors and drop down to a lower speed. Many modems will drop down automatically, but if you are having problems with a communication session, reestablish the communication at a lower rate manually. That is often a cure for bad transmission lines.

The Serial Tool has no settings that were not previously explained in this Topic. There are fewer settings — only the basic Port Settings — and the Current Port selector appears. You can set as two options the capability to keep the connection open (Hold Connection check box) and to post a reminder to disconnect (Remind to Disconnect check box) when a document is closed. It's a good idea to set both options on at the same time.

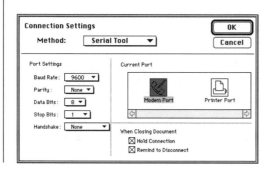

The AppleTalk ADSP is even simpler. Because the network specification provides all transmission protocols, you need only to provide the address of the node you wish to communicate to. Select the zone and the name of the node you want from the two scrolling text boxes. The users name appears in the Chooser desk accessory.

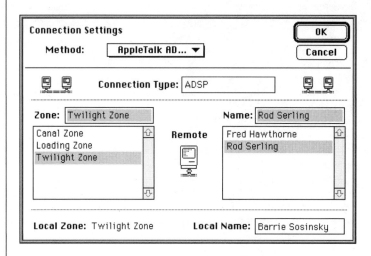

The second major class of settings is the terminal settings. These settings control the appearance of characters displayed on your screen, the nature of control codes for creating lines and pages, and word wrapping. Terminal emulation allows your computer to behave like a simple teletype or as a video terminal attached to a larger computer. Graphics terminal emulation is not currently supported by Works. Usually, you simply accept the default settings for these emulations; they do provide some customization features you will want to know about. You have the option of selecting any of the following tools — TTY, VT102, or VT320 — from the Emulation pop-up menu.

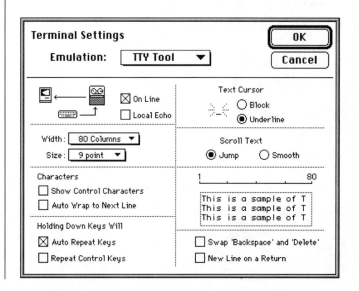

The so-called "dumb terminal," or TTY tool, is used for most modem communications to on-line services; it sends and receives only ASCII characters. Important features of the TTY tool include the following:

◆ *Local Echo.* Some connections require that each character be echoed back to the other computer. If you don't see any characters on your screen, turn this option on. If you see double characters, such as: "IIff yyoouu sseeee ddoouu...," then turn the echo off.

◆ *Width and Size.* These options control text appearance. Width can be 80 or 132 characters wide; size can be either 9 or 12 points.

◆ *Characters.* Show Control Characters is useful to determine anomalous print or display behavior by showing these codes as text equivalents. Control codes are specific to the Macintosh and to applications.

You can find control characters and their ASCII equivalents listed in technical manuals; these characters are mostly of interest to programmers. Some communications services require that you enter Control codes — for example, Control-X to stop a file transfer. To enter a Control-X, control code, simply type that keystroke. Auto Wrap to Next Line moves the cursor to the beginning of the next line when the end of a row has been reached.

◆ *Hold Down Keys.* These options are self-explanatory. Control keys like Command, Option, Shift, and Tab won't repeat, and only repeat as part of a combination keystroke (for example, Control-Z).

◆ *Text Cursor.* Use Block or Underline as you wish. Your choice is indicated in the graphic to the left of the radio buttons. Block cursors are useful in dense text or low-light situations.

◆ *Scroll Text.* Jump moves several lines at once; Smooth appears line after line. This is your preference, but most people prefer the jump option.

◆ *Swap 'Backspace' and 'Delete'.* For all Macs (except a Mac Plus), Backspace sends the delete ASCII 127 character, and Option-Delete sends the backspace ASCII 08 character. For a Mac Plus, the Backspace key sends the delete ASCII character, while Option-Backspace sends the backspace ASCII 08 character. This setting swaps the settings, letting you use Backspace instead of Option-Backspace.

◆ *New Line on a Return.* Set this option if text doesn't move to the beginning of the next line at the end of a row. Normally, Works takes line-feed control characters or the Return key and translates them into a line-feed followed by a character return.

Two smart video terminals are offered — the VT102 and the newer VT320 emulation. These command sets are a Digital Equipment Corp. (DEC) specification, and they are used extensively for communications to mini- and mainframe computers. VT emulation can display, send, and print special characters for word processing, escape codes, function keys, ringing terminal bells, and so on. Switch between these two emulations by selecting them from the Emulation pop-up menu. In order to use VT terminal emulation, use the following table:

Table 9-1:	VT Terminal emulation	
Appl. requirement (terminal)	Emulation tool	Select
DEC VT52	VT102 or VT32	VT52
DEC VT100 & VT102	VT102	ANSI/VT100
VT100 & VT102	VT320	ANSI/VT100
DEC VT220 (7-bit)	VT320	VT300 (7-bit)
DEC VT220 (8-bit)	VT320	VT300 (8-bit)

Separate settings exist for general, screen, keyboard, and character set functions. (Because there were fewer of them in the TTY Tool, they were condensed into a single dialog box for that tool.) To see each type, click on the scrolling box in the left-hand side of the Terminal Settings dialog box (see the following figures).

There isn't space here to fully document these terminal emulations, so you may wish to contact the system administrator for the computer you are communicating with for further information. Differences you will find with true VT102 or VT320 specifications include dark characters on a white background, cursor keys and keypad modes are not related (VT102), printer sequences to a local printer are ignored, Delete and Backspace keys can be swapped (VT102), DTR is not reset during a break (VT102), hardware sequences are not recognized (VT102), only 9- or 12-point characters are shown (VT320), and escape sequences for testing, local printing, and screen alignment are not supported (VT320).

The VT 102 tool

General   Screen

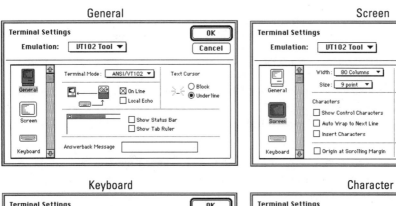

Keyboard   Character

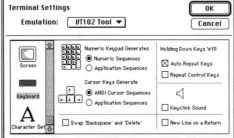
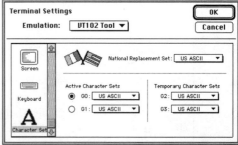

Following are some of the features you might want to use in your work. Unless otherwise noted, options that were discussed earlier in this section are identical.

◆ *Terminal Mode*. This can change between the ANSI/VT102 or the even earlier VT52 standard. ANSI is an international standards organization.

◆ *On Line*. Normally on, turning this setting off will halt data exchange while keeping the connection open.

◆ *Show Status Bar*. When on, a status bar appears at the top of your screen just below the title bar.

◆ *Show Tab Ruler*. When on, a ruler with tab settings appears below the title bar and status bar (if selected).

◆ *Answerback Message*. Some systems require a text string of up to 20 characters before they respond. Your system administrator can tell you what this message is.

◆ *Terminal ID*. (VT320 Tool only) This setting provides an ID code specifying terminal attributes to a remote computer. Ask your system administrator for requirements.

◆ *Lock Changes to*. (VT320 Tool only) When User Features is set on, the remote computer cannot change your Macintosh video display or keyboard settings. Defined Keys will lock your Mac from changes to any defined keys.

New options not found in the TTY tool include the following:

◆ *Characters*. The only new option here is the Insert Characters function. When set, this function inserts characters at the cursor location and does not delete characters that have already been entered. This function is supported by IBM PC, but not normally by Macintosh computers.

◆ *Origin at Scrolling Margin*. This keeps the insertion point within your scrolling region so that it cannot go off screen.

◆ *Inverse Video*. Creates white text on a black background.

◆ *Status Display*. (VT320 only) Invisible removes the status line, Visible makes it appear at the bottom of the screen, and Host Writable allows messages from the remote computer to appear.

Keyboard functions for the VT102 and VT320 Tools are identical (see the previous figure). New functions to be found in the Keyboard settings include:

◆ *Numeric Keypad Generates*. Numeric Sequences will make the numeric keypad enter numbers; Application Sequences enters escape sequences specified by DEC for that application (check documentation).

♦ *Cursor Keys Generate.* ANSI Cursor Sequences sends cursor control characters when you press arrow keys, while Application Sequences sends cursor control functions (defined by DEC) to the remote computer when you press arrow keys (check documentation).

♦ *Keyclick Sound.* When marked, this option provides a small click sound for each key typed, providing tactile response.

Most users find the key-click sound annoying. If you like it, however, you may want to install the shareware program Tappy Type on your Macintosh for more complete implementation of this function, or work on a real teletype machine. The sound should drive everyone around you nuts.

The TTY tool does not support character sets, nor does the DEC VT52 terminal mode. Other higher DEC VT emulations support numerous character sets for many languages — three for the VT102 tool, and 17 for the VT320 tool. Normally, in the U.S. you want the U.S. ASCII set; other countries set their character set as appropriate to that language or country, with only the U.K. using a slightly different version of ASCII. Once set, character sets are not changed unless the host application changes the set in the course of a communication with a multilingual host computer.

The following are character sets that are supported by the VT102 and VT320 terminal emulations. Normally, you choose one of the following sets just once to create your settings. If you are using your computer in a multilingual project, then you may have to switch among them. These character sets are provided by Microsoft and by DEC. In the standard Works package, choose one of the following:

♦ *National Replacement Set.* Specify the character set. The VT102 cannot produce some of the more specialized Macintosh characters (like accented characters, ligatures, and so on) and will beep to let you know when that happens.

♦ *Active Character Sets.* Select from either G0 or G1 with the VT102 tool, and from G0 to G3 in the VT320 tool for active characters sets.

♦ *Temporary Character Sets.* Temporary sets are used for character generation before switching to the active character set.

♦ *User Preferred Set.* (VT320) Provides either a DEC or ISO Latin character set.

The VT320 tool

General

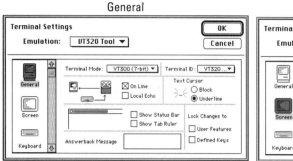

Screen

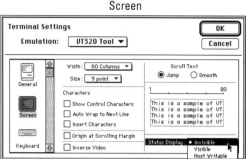

Character Setting

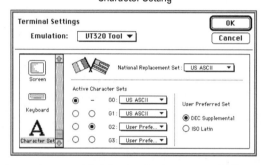

The last major setting provided in the Settings menu is for sending and receiving text or files using the File Transfer command. This setting controls the protocol used by both computers for text or binary file exchange. Three protocols are offered: the Text tool, the Xmodem tool, and the Kermit tool. Text applies to ASCII character transmission only without formatting or error-checking; while Xmodem and Kermit are protocols that specify formatting, error checking, and error correction. Text files can be sent but not received. Xmodem is the most commonly used file transfer protocol; it's very popular because it has built-in error correction. That is, as blocks of data are transferred, the Xmodem protocol checks the integrity of the data to make sure that the transmission was received correctly. Xmodem is relatively fast (although others like Ymodem and Zmodem are faster), which is another reason that it is popular. Kermit is used on a wide variety of computer types, especially larger computer systems that use the Unix operating system.

Information on the procedure for sending and receiving text and files may be found in the sections "Sending and receiving text as a character stream" and "Transferring files" later in this Topic.

The Text tool offers the following:

◆ *Timing Delays.* Enter numbers if the receiving computer is having difficulty keeping up with your transmission. This is rarely the case.

◆ *Line Endings.* Choose the options of ending a line with a carriage return, a linefeed, or both. Macs interpret a Return as both a linefeed and a return. Specify the requirements of the receiving system here. This is fairly easy to determine by looking at the output of the receiving system.

File Transfer Settings   OK
    Protocol: Text Tool ▼   Cancel

              When Sending Text ...

        Timing   Line Endings

        Delay Per Character: [0   ]   End Lines With: [CR   ▼]
        (60ths of Second)

        Delay Per Line: [0   ]   ☐ Wrap Lines at Column: [80]
        (60ths of Second)

Use the Xmodem tool for most file transfers. Features provided by this tool (see the following figure) include the following:

✦ *Method.* From this pop-up menu choose either MacBinary, MacTerminal 1.1, Straight Xmodem, or Xmodem text. Your choice is explained in the information box (question mark) below the menu.

Use MacBinary to transfer Macintosh files between two Macintosh computers. This setting retains the binary file structure (data and resource forks), Finder information like creator and application ID codes, and other Macintosh attributes. MacTerminal 1.1 is an older protocol that transfers binary files in three pieces; it is rarely used today. Straight Xmodem transfer is used to exchange text files with a non-Macintosh computer. For Straight Xmodem transfer, make sure that both computers are matched for their end-of-line control characters; otherwise, line endings and page breaks will not transfer properly. Xmodem Text will preserve the line and paragraph spacings.

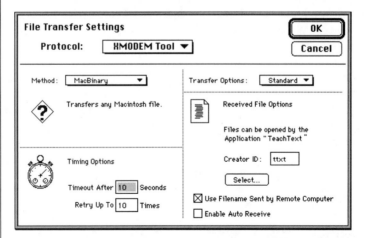

File Transfer Settings   OK
    Protocol: XMODEM Tool ▼   Cancel

    Method: [MacBinary   ▼]   Transfer Options: [Standard ▼]

    ?   Transfers any Macintosh file.   Received File Options

                                          Files can be opened by the
                                          Application "TeachText"

         Timing Options   Creator ID: [ttxt]

         Timeout After [10] Seconds   [Select...]

         Retry Up To [10] Times   ☒ Use Filename Sent by Remote Computer
                                       ☐ Enable Auto Receive

✦ *Timing Options.* Timeout After Seconds will slow your Macintosh to match a sending computer's slower speed — 10 seconds is the default. Your Mac assumes that no response in 10 seconds indicates a broken connection. Use delays when characters and lines are missing in received text. Retry Up to Times is the number of times that Works retransmits blocks of data that were received with errors or not acknowledged without breaking the connection. Normally, these settings are satisfactory.

✦ *Transfer Options*. You can select four options: Standard, CRC-16, 1K blocks, and CleanLink. Standard uses 128-bit blocks and simple error correction, while CRC-16 uses a more advanced form of error correction. The 1K block option is faster than either Standard or CRC-16 because it transfers larger blocks (1024 bit or 1K), but it uses the same error checking as the Standard option. CleanLink is a 1K option that is much faster than 1K blocks; use with an error-free link. Your connecting service will tell you what is supported.

✦ *Received File Options*. What you see in this section depends on what is selected in the Method pop-up menu. The Creator ID is a file attribute that determines which application will open the received file. This attribute appears only for the Xmodem settings. Click the Select button to change the creator application. Use MSWK to open a file in Microsoft Works, (text is opened in TeachText).

✦ *Use FileName Sent by Remote Computer*. This setting is best used with the MacBinary or MacTerminal 1.1 method. Xmodem transfers normally transfer with the filename intact. On is the default.

✦ *Enable Auto Receive*. Use this option for the MacBinary method; the option works provided that the sending computer supports it.

Kermit offers few settings that you haven't seen before. New options include the following:

✦ *Transfer Options:* The Classic, Long Packet, and Sliding Windows describe the size and structure of the data transmission. The service or remote computer application will tell you which options are supported and which Packet size can be used. Use the Classic option unless you know specifically that Long Packet or Sliding Windows is supported. Long Packet is the fastest Kermit option. Long Packet and Sliding Windows require exact data block size matching.

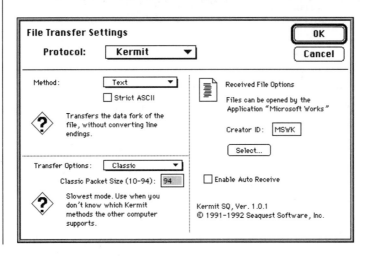

Phheww! If you read the last section through, you probably feel that all the mysteries of life have been revealed to you. Remember, changes that you make to all of these settings are saved only when you save your file. So be certain to save any time you have the settings the way you want them. Also, save the document under different names when you want to save different sets of settings.

Receiving and sending text

The text you see on your screen — text you enter and text returned by the remote computer can be captured to a disk file for review later at your leisure. It's normally a good idea to do this, and even to do it automatically by setting the option Always Capture Text in the Preference dialog box. You can always delete the capture file later after reviewing it; by doing that, you will not miss any important information that may come your way. Some communication programs allow you to print text as it appears on your screen and even save it simultaneously to a disk file. Works does not allow a real-time printing option, but you can review previous text by scrolling up through the Overflow area (see "Introducing the Communications window" earlier in this Topic).

Capturing text:

1. **Open a document, and select the Open Connection command from the Connection menu, or press the Command-D keystroke.** If you selected the Always Capture Text check box in the Preference dialog box, from the Preference command on the Edit menu, then capture is automatic.

2. **Otherwise, select the Start Capture command from the Connection menu.** Works posts a standard file input box.

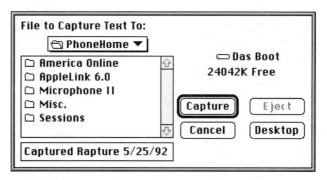

3. **Place the file where you want it in the file structure, changing folders or disks as desired.**

4. **Name the file or accept the default ("Capture short date").**

5. **Press the Capture button, or press the Return or Enter key.**

Once text capture is in progress, you have the following options:

✦ Pause capture by choosing the Pause Capture command from the Connection menu.

◆ Pause capture by clicking the Pause tool on the Communications Tool palette. This tool has a double line on it.

◆ Resume capture by choosing the Resume Capture command on the Connection menu.

◆ Resume capture by clicking the Resume tool on the Tool palette. This tool is a couple of white lines in a black background — the inverted Resume tool.

◆ Stop capture by choosing the Stop Capture command on the Connection menu.

A captured file is saved as a Works word processor file. All text that scrolls into the overflow area is saved to disk. When you pause or stop a capture in progress, text that appeared in the text area of the Communications window will not be saved, nor will any new text that appears, until you resume the capture.

Text can be sent as a file using the Text tool or as you type it to your screen. You can also paste text from the Clipboard into your Communications document and send that to a remote computer. Text sent as a file appears as a text file on the remote computer; text sent as a character stream appears in a window of the receiving person's communication software program.

Sending and receiving text as a character stream:

1. **Open a Communications document, and select the Open Connection command from the Connection menu, or press the Command-D keystroke.**

2. **Select the Transfer File command on the Settings menu, and change to the Text Tool, if needed.** Use Xmodem or Kermit for transferring files.

3. **A log-on signal, like the word Connect, or some computer code, will appear indicating that you are on-line.**

4. **If connected directly to an individual on the remote computer, simply type your message. Or, paste any text you want to send from the Clipboard into your Communications document.** Pasted text loses its formatting. It's that simple. When you are done typing, you will see the other person's reply typed to your Text area.

5. **Or if on-line with a communications service, navigate that service (check their documentation, if needed), and go to the area for messaging.**

6. **Address your message, or connect to the person you want to talk with.**

7. **Type your message or paste any text you want to send from the Clipboard into your Communications document.**

If you find that pasted text is sent faster than the remote computer can process it, slow down the transmission using delays. Enter some delays into the Options command dialog box, accessed from the Settings menu.

8. **When done, log off or terminate your session.**

To transfer a text file, make sure you use the Text Tool in the File Transfer Settings dialog box, and then use the procedure detailed below for uploading and downloading files. Text files can be opened by the Works word processor.

Transferring files

Once connected to another computer, transferring files requires setting the file transfer protocol, naming the file to be transferred, its placement on your disk if it is received, and issuing a command to either Send File or Receive File from the Connection menu. Works takes care of the rest. The procedure is simple and straightforward, and takes just a few seconds to perform. It's almost harder to explain than it is to do.

When sending and receiving text or files, Works can do background processing allowing you to work in other Works modules while data is transferred using the communications tool. If you are in System 7, or in MultiFinder in System 6, you can be working in another application in the foreground, while doing data transfer in Works in the background. Your computer allots a small amount of processor time to the background task, while giving most of its focus to the foreground application.

Downloading a file:

1. **Open a Communications document, and select the Open Connection command from the Connection menu, or press the Command-D keystroke.**

2. **Choose the Select Receive Folder from the Settings menu, or press its Command-F keystroke equivalent.** Works opens a standard file box.

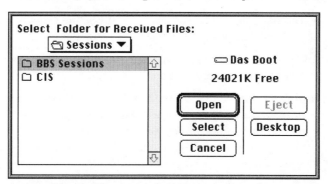

3. **Locate the folder in the file structure you wish to place the received file in.**

4. **Click the Select button.**

   If you don't select a folder (steps 2-4) to receive your downloaded file, it will be placed in whatever the current folder is at the time.

   If you can't find the file, either check the Works folder, or use the Find command on the File menu in the Finder to search for it by name.

5. **Check and change, if needed, the Transfer Files setting. Make sure that the correct transfer protocol (Text, Xmodem, or Kermit tools) is selected.**

6. **Give the download command in whatever service you are logged onto, specify the file to be downloaded.**

7. **If you are communicating with another computer directly without being on an on-line service, the other computer will message you that it is sending the file.** You do not need to perform Step 6.

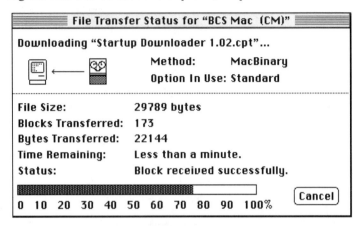

8. **Give the Receive File command from the Connection menu, or press the Command-L keystroke.** Works posts the File Transfer Status dialog box.

9. **Or, instead of Step 8, you can click the Receive File tool on the Tool palette.** Remember, you can switch to another application or Works module to continue working while Works transfers the file.

10. **When the file transfer is complete, Works beeps twice.**

When Downloading (receiving) and Uploading (sending), the File Transfer Status dialog boxes have the following features:

✦ *Name of File.* In the first line, the name of the file downloading is placed.

   Or, if uploading, the name of the file you selected from the Finder is found.

✦ *Method.* The Method depends on the protocol chosen and what you selected in the File Transfer settings. See "Communications settings" for more details.

✦ *Option In Use.* The same as described for Method.

✦ *File Size.* Size in bytes.

✦ *Blocks Transferred.* Blocks are determined by the transfer protocol. They are most often 128K or 1024K.

✦ *Bytes Transferred.* Shows successfully transferred bytes.

✦ *Time Remaining.* Approximate time in minutes.

✦ *Status.* Whether the block is being sent or received and whether the error checking indicates if it was successful. When successful, the block is written to disk.

◆ *Status Line.* Indicates the fraction of bytes transferred to bytes in the file.

◆ *Cancel button.* Click the Cancel button, or press the Command-period keystroke to terminate a transfer and not create the file.

You can also stop a file transfer in progress by selecting the Close Connection command from the File menu or by pressing the Command-K keystroke. Works then disconnects your computer, taking it off-line and canceling the file exchange. Also, you can use the Close command on the File menu, press the Command-W keystroke, or click in the close box of the Communications document window to perform the same function as the Close Connection command. Any file not completely transferred successfully is not recorded as a file in the file structure, even if parts of it were written to disk. Before disconnecting you, Works will post an alert box to allow you a graceful exit from the disconnect, in case you made a mistake.

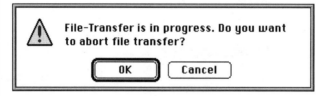

File-Transfer is in progress. Do you want to abort file transfer?

OK   Cancel

Uploading a file:

1. **Open a Communications document, and select the Open Connection command from the Connection menu, or press the Command-D keystroke.**

2. **Check and change, if needed, the Transfer Files setting.** Make sure that the correct transfer protocol (Xmodem, or Kermit tools) is selected.

3. **Give the upload command in whatever service you are logged onto, and specify the file to be uploaded in the resulting standard file box.**

4. **If you are communicating directly with another computer or person, then simply type a message that you are sending the file now.**

5. **Select the Send File command from the Connection menu, or press the Command-U keystroke.** Works awaits a signal from the other computer that it is ready to accept the incoming file; then it posts the File Transfer Status dialog box. Remember, you can switch to another application or Works module to continue working while Works transfers the file.

6. **When the transfer is complete, an alert box is posted.**

Printing your session

Printing a session is the same process as printing any other Works document. Both the text area and the overflow area are printed. Use headers and footers to add information that will make your document more understandable — adding pages, date, times, logos, or other graphics. Header and footer windows support the Draw layer. (Headers and footers are described in Topic 4.) You may want to Print Preview your document before printing it. For information about setting up page size, orientation, and margins, see Topic 3.

Quick Tips

The following tips show you more about various communications equipment and services.

Buying a modem: What do you need?

There are many fine modems on the market. The reliability of solid state electronics being what it is today, you can hardly go wrong buying a modem from nearly any vendor. Warranties run from one to ten years. Name brands like Hayes SmartModems are desirable, but products from Apple, Microcom, Practical Peripherals, Prometheus, PSI, Telebit, US Robotic, Shiva, Supra, and Zoom are equally worry free and much cheaper. All these modems are currently supported by the Apple Modem Tool, which means that you don't have to create your own device driver.

Because accompanying software is not an issue, if you are using Works to telecommunicate, other features are more important. Speed is the basic cost factor. You shouldn't really buy a modem at less than 2400 baud (about $100 to $150), which is the current standard today. If you are using your modem a lot, buy a 9600-baud modem — their prices are dropping, so that they now cost between $300 and $650. A 9600-baud modem will pay for itself quickly over a year or two with lower transmission times and connect charges. Services may charge you more to use 9600-baud lines, but when you work the arithmetic, you still come out ahead.

Getting a modem that supports the Hayes command set is a distinct advantage, because most of the industry supports it. Some modems put blinking lights on their front panel, showing you the condition of the modem sending and receiving data. Other modems' software puts simulated lights on your Mac's menu bar. I prefer the hardware solution. Just in case you're interested, the lights on a Hayes compatible modem mean the following: HS, high speed; AA, autoanswer; CD, carrier detect; OH, off hook; RD, receive data; SD, send data; TR, terminal ready; and MR, modem ready.

More advanced modems come with features like advanced error checking and file compression. These increase reliability and throughput. It's not uncommon to find 9600-baud modems with these features with throughputs in the 14400-baud range. Also, at 9600 baud and above, many of these modems offer data fax. Faxing uses a standard inexpensive chip set (like the Rockwell fax chip set) that can be added to lower priced modems for very little money. You can also find 2400-baud data modems that send and receive faxes at either 4800 or 9600 baud. Most modems sold are small external boxes; some are NuBus cards. Internal modems like the Shiva NetModem can support many users on a network.

Fax modems

A fax is a page that has been turned into a bit map and compressed for telephone transmission using the run length encoded (RLE) compression algorithm. The current standard widely used is the Group 3 CCITT standard; a higher resolution Group 4 standard is on the way. It is then decompressed back to a bit map for display by the receiving device. In place of fax machines, which are small copiers/digitizers/

printers/phones, you can use a fax modem for this purpose. Because graphics data can be produced at a higher resolution in a computer, there is less quality loss in using two computers to fax to one another. You can use a scanner for the purpose of turning hard copy into a graphic image, and print a received fax out to your printer. For best results, use strong sans serif fonts like Adobe's Lucida Sans or the Stone Sans font family. Avant Garde and Helvetica also work acceptably.

The major consideration in buying a fax modem is the quality of the software that comes with it. Without good software, a fax modem is a useless annoyance. I tried one brand of fax modem that I was unable to make work under any circumstance (bad software). When the software works well, like it does with the Dove Fax Modem, then faxing is just as simple as choosing a printer (in this case a fax) from the Chooser. You fax a document just like printing to a printer. Two other fax modems to consider are Orchid Technology's OrchidFAX and the Abaton's InterFAX 24/96.

Fax modems have become very popular lately; they account for nearly half of the current modem sales. In two or three years, faxing will be in the vast majority of modems sold, because the technology is so inexpensive to build into modems. Unlike the IBM PC, which is blessed with several good low-priced fax modems (like Intel's SatisFAXtion board), the Macintosh fax modem market is immature. We are just on the cusp of the introduction of a large number of sophisticated fax products, so you may want to watch the coming issues of consumer publications like *Macworld* magazine for reviews on the topic. A fax modem is an attractive purchase at this stage of the market development. There are PostScript fax devices that should appear in late 1993 that may make the quality of faxes and speed of transmission comparable to what you see on your laser printer.

Automating log-on

You could define a keystroke macro to open a file, dial up a computer, give the log-on, and even navigate within a service to the part of it you normally go to first (like the electronic or e-mail area). Macros are the subject of the next Topic. To make it even more convenient, Works incorporates a sign-on keystroke macro within the Settings menu. It's simple to set up and simple to use.

Creating a sign-on macro:

1. **Open the appropriate Communications document.**

2. **Give the Record Sign On command from the Settings menu, or press the Command-R keystroke.** This command turns on a keystroke macro recorder. Everything you type — commands and text — is recorded.

3. **Go through the connect and log-on procedure you use for the computer or service you're calling.** This procedure was detailed in the section "Connecting to other computers."

4. **At the end of your sign-on sequence, select the Stop Recording command on the Settings menu, or press the Command-E keystroke.** If you have previously recorded a sign-on sequence, Works will ask you if you want to replace it.

> ⚠ **Replace existing sign-on script?**
>
> [OK   ]   [Cancel]

5. **Click the Replace button to save your new sign-on sequence.**

6. **Save your document to save your sign-on sequence.**

It's a good idea to test your sign-on sequence right away, to see if it was recorded properly.

Playing back a macro:

1. **Open the Communications document, and create a connection by using the Open Connection command from the Setting menu.**

2. **Select the Play Sign-On command from the Settings menu, or press the Command-E keystroke.** You can halt a sign-on in progress by pressing the Command-period (cancel) keystroke.

Works looks for a set of characters from the other computer (a lead string) that signifies that the computer is looking for a particular text string. For example, the line "Name:" seeks a response, or "Password:" triggers the return of the appropriate text. If the lead string does not appear, Works will halt the sequence and, after a pause, post an alert box that lets you quit the sequence by clicking the Quit Script button. To continue with the sequence, click the Keep Trying button.

If your sign-on sequence works properly, you may want to consider making it part of the automated process of opening a document. Set the Play Sign-On Script text box within the Option dialog box from the Settings menu to automate this feature, along with the automatic dial-up sequence that precedes it. You may also want to record a macro that logs you off of your session.

Be careful with any document that has a sign-on recorded with it. Anyone who copies that document can log onto that service and sign on to your account, running up bills for you. They will not be able to view your password, however. Most services allow you to change your password whenever you want; once a month is a good practice. Also, choose a password that isn't a simple word. Hackers typically find passwords by dialing up and testing passwords from a data dictionary of words and names. Replacing letters with numbers that look similar to them is one good way of accomplishing this. Thus, "Barrie" might turn into "3arr1e."

Keeping track of time and costs

Using the Start Timer (Command-G) or Stop Timer commands on the Connection menu, you can control both the timer and the meter that tracks costs. The Reset Timer command allows you to change the current connection's tracking. The time of a session is determined by the time you start a connection and break it — unless you use the Reset Timer command to change that time.

To figure session costs, you must open the Show Info dialog box (when there is no connection open) by giving the Show Info command from the Connection menu or pressing its Command-I keystroke equivalent. Enter the cost per minute, hour, or by connection into the Estimated Cost text box. Works figures your cost based on this information and displays it in the Show Info box. If you open the Show Info dialog box (see the following figure) when a session is in progress, you will only be able to review the information contained therein. You will not be able to change rate data.

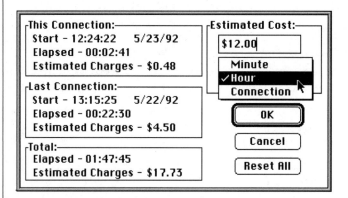

Costs and times for the current and previous connections are shown, as are the cumulative totals for this communications document. The Reset All button zeros out information and data for all sessions. Using one document for each service you dial up makes the Show Info data more meaningful. Show Info data is saved to the Communications document when you save the file.

Most services charge for their use, some charge a blanket fee per month; others charge by the minute. Companies purchase space on an on-line service to sell products, sell information, communicate with their customers, or to give some service. (See "The on-line services" at the end of this Topic for more details on what each service offers.) So logging onto different parts of a service may also generate an additional fee that will not show up in a simple Time * Rate calculation. Works allows you to track the time you use and the money you spend in the Status Bar to get a rough idea of your on-line bill, but these extra charges are difficult to track.

The on-line services

The on-line services are a boon to anyone working at home, working remotely, seeking information of any kind, and communicating with anyone anywhere in the world. The range of services available are extraordinary. You can find forums or conferences on hundreds of subjects: business, graphics, publishing, and others. Vendors support their product in forums. There's banking, weather, interactive multiperson games, libraries, and many other services available. About a year ago, *Macworld* magazine commissioned a contributing editor to spend a week living in his apartment using only the on-line services to satisfy his needs.

Some services require specialized software in their use, like America On-line. They give you the software when you sign up for their service. Others use a text based approach that lets you use whatever telecommunications software you have available. You will be able to use Microsoft Works for the latter class of service, but not the former. So Works can be successfully used with BIX, CompuServe, Delphi, and GEnie, and not with America Online, Connect, or Prodigy. The following table shows you your selections.

Table 9-2:	The On-Line Services						
Statistics	*AOL*	*BIX*	*CS*	*Connect*	*Delphi*	*GEnie*	*Prodigy*
Phone (800)	227-6364	227-2983	848-8199	456-0553	544-4005	638-9636	776-3449
Access Network	N	Tymnet	Prop.	Tymnet Acunet	Tymnet Acunet	Prop.	Prop.A
Start/Month	0 / 5.95	0 / 13.33	39.95 / 1.50	99.95 / 6	49.95 B/0	29.95 / 0	49.95 / 9.95
Hourly Cost $ P/OP	10 / 5	6 / 2C	12.80 / 12.80	10 / 5	17.40 / 7.20D	18 / 10	0 / 0
Interface	graphic	text	text	graphic	text	text	graphic
Proprietary software	Y	N	NF	Y	N	N	Y
Features							
Airline reservations	Y	N	Y	N	Y	Y	Y
Banking	N	N	N	N	N	N	YD
Bulletin boards	Y	Y	Y	Y	Y	Y	Y
Company forums	N	Y	Y	Y	N	Y	N
Conferencing (chats)	Y	Y	Y	Y	Y	Y	N
E-mail / file transfer	Y / Y	Y / Y	Y / Y	Y / YE	Y / N	Y / Y	Y / N
Encyclopedia	Y	N	Y	N	Y	Y	N
Fax (cost $)	1	N	0.75	0.80	1.25	N	N

(continued)

Table 9-2 :				The On-Line Services (continued)			
Statistics	**AOL**	**BIX**	**CS**	**Connect**	**Delphi**	**GEnie**	**Prodigy**
Games (interactive)	Y	Y	Y	N	Y	Y	Y
Movie reviews	Y	N	Y	N	Y	Y	Y
News/ weather	Y / Y	Y / N	Y / Y	Y / YE	Y / Y	Y / Y	Y / Y
Real time seminars	Y	Y	Y	N	Y	Y	N
Shopping	Y	N	Y	N	Y	Y	Y
Software libraries	Y	Y	Y	YE	Y	Y	N
Stocks (B/Q)	N / Y	N / N	Y / Y	N / Y	N / Y	Y / Y	Y / Y
U.S. Mail (cost in $)	2	N	1.50	2	N	1	N
# of Members	50,000	35,000	1,000,000+	17,000	100,000	195,000	400,000
Ratings							
Cost factors	Good	Ex	Good	Fair	Ex	Ex	Ex
Downloading files	Ex	Good	Fair	Ex	Good	Fair	N/A
Getting connected	Good	Fair	Ex	Fair	Ex	Ex	Good
Navigating	Ex	Good	Poor	Ex	Good	Good	Good
User interface	Ex	Good	Fair	Ex	Good	Good	Poor

Key: AOL = America Online; BIX = Byte Information Exchange; CS = CompuServe; GEnie = GE Network for Information Exchange; P/OP = Peak / Off-peak hours; Y = Yes; N = No; A = Not available in all areas; B = Includes two non-prime hours; C = Tymnet charges; D = $160 yearly plus Tymnet charges (A flat fee Tymnet program is $20/mo.); E = Extra Cost; F = Graphics Software (extra price): CompuServe Information Manager and the Navigator; Stock B/Q = Stock Brokerage Services/Stock Quotes; N/A = Not available; Ex = Excellent. Ratings are based on how new users will find the system. Experienced users will not have difficulty.

Source: Adapted from *Macworld* magazine September 1990, p. 198.

There are probably over 10,000 BBSs that you can log onto in the United States. Many are free, and undoubtedly some are wherever you are. BBSs come and go, as do the people that run them. Some BBSs that are run by user groups are stable and long lasting. You can obtain a list of BBSs from the better and larger user groups. The largest of the user groups are: the Boston Computer Society Macintosh User Group, Berkeley (CA) Macintosh User Group (BMUG), Washington Pi, New York Macintosh User Group, and the Chicago user group. Apple keeps a listing of user groups; call the toll-free number, 800-538-9696, for the closest one.

Looking beyond Works' Communications module

There are several products that you may want to consider if you want to upgrade your communication package. Unfortunately, none of these products are available from Microsoft. The best of the Macintosh programs are Software Ventures' Microphone II v. 4.0, White Knight, DynaComm, MacBLAST (for mainframe access), VersaTerm, and the shareware program ZTerm. Of the group, White Knight and Microphone are notable for their features; White Knight is inexpensive and features rich, and Microphone is pricier and smoother in operation. Good software lets you automate nearly every feature in a session and grow into the more advanced features over time. These programs eventually save you money by streamlining your on-line work and saving you time.

The more advanced features you will find are:

◆ *Automation.* Improved scripting or macro capabilities to automate any procedure in the program including autolog-in, log-offs, navigation, and constructing "front-end" systems to bulletin boards and services.

◆ *Buffered keyboard.* Use a buffer to work off-line, and then send the text of that buffer to another computer.

◆ *Filters.* Numerous file translation filters to remove garbage characters, do character replacement, and clean up files.

◆ *Wide Protocol Support.* In addition to Text, Binary, Xmodem, and Kermit, the protocols Ymodem, Zmodem, IRMA, and others are highly desirable.

Summary

✔ Works's communications tool allows you to send and receive text and files, connect to bulletin boards, and on-line services — putting a world of information at your fingertips.

✔ Computers exchange digital information as a bitstream, the speed of which is measured in bps, or more commonly as a baud rate.

✔ Communication over a phone line requires a modem; Works can also communicate over serial cables and using AppleTalk networks.

✔ A communication session requires that a Communications document be created and appropriate settings be made so that the communicating computers observe the same rules or protocols.

✔ To create a session: Open a document, connect to the other computer, log in, exchange data, log off, and disconnect.

✔ Text that appears in your document is scrolled upward into an overflow area. Text can be captured or saved to a disk file.

✔ Works can transfer files using the Xmodem or Kermit protocols, or as Text.

✔ Works can emulate a simple dumb TTY terminal, or as a VT102 or VT320 DEC terminal for main-frame communication.

✔ Buy at least a 2400-baud modem; 9600-baud is preferable, particularly if you do a lot of telecommunicating.

✔ Communications documents can automatically dial up a service or BBS and can have a log-on script that also initiates when the document opens.

✔ Using the status bar and the Show Info dialog box, you can track charges for a service.

Part III:

Integrating Works' Tools

Topic 10
The Macro Recorder

Overview

Works provides a utility in all of its modules to automate many of the steps you commonly use. This utility, called the Macro Recorder, allows you to record as a set of small programs called macros. These macros, which some programs call scripts, are recorded based on the keystrokes you type. You can record text you type, keystrokes, menu commands, mouse actions that you take, and save it all to a file. You assign a name and a keystroke to a macro for later playback at a time of your choosing. A macro in a file will run whenever that file is open and you press the appropriate keystroke. This kind of macro program is called a keystroke recorder because only your actions can be saved to a macro.

If you run System 6, you might have installed the Macintosh system software program MacroMaker. MacroMaker is another keystroke recorder, very similar to the one that is included with Works. MacroMaker disappeared in System 7, primarily because the programmable scripting language, AppleScript, will replace it soon.

Macro programs with graphical interfaces or with programmed scripting languages represent another, more powerful kind of macro recorder. Whereas with Works you can record macros that can run only inside of Works and are thus *local* macros (to Works), other programs such as QuicKeys, Tempo, Frontier, and AppleScript let you create *global* macros — macros that will run in any program.

In this chapter I cover the macro recorder in Works in detail. In addition to instructions on its use, this chapter is rich in sample macros you might want to create. Suggestions for macro files or sets of macros will help streamline your work. Macros let you concentrate on the business at hand instead of the mechanics of getting it done. They make repetitive tasks almost fun, while you watch your Mac work for you. Other third-party macro programs are also discussed in "Looking beyond Works' macro recorder."

Introducing the macro

A macro is a program recorded to disk. Macros can be simple, or they can be complex, but they are generally limited in scope. Macros can only achieve what the underlying programming allows. Macro recorders let you save a set of steps with very limited editing. Once recorded, a Works macro cannot be edited — only re-recorded. That makes Works' macro recorder simple to learn, but very incomplete.

You can't even change a keystroke equivalent for a macro once you assign it. The Works macro recorder is extremely limited in what you can achieve, although you can automate many tasks with it.

Macros were introduced in Works version 2.0 and have not undergone significant change in version 3.0. Unfortunately, most macros previously recorded will probably need to be redone in 3.0 to get them to function properly.

Some macro programs allow a much wider range of actions, including editing a sequence. In my opinion the best macro recorders are graphical in nature, like the Mac itself. CE Software's QuicKeys2 is an example of this type of macro recorder. Another approach involves scripting a program, of which the highly regarded Tempo II is an example. At their most complex, some macro languages are programming languages that allow almost entire access to the Macintosh toolbox. The best programmed macro recorders are written in a high-level natural language script.

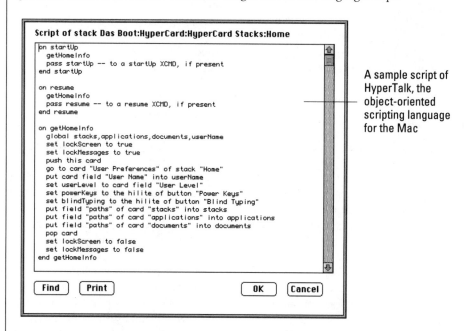

A sample script of HyperTalk, the object-oriented scripting language for the Mac

There is no reason why you can't run a third-party macro program behind Works in place of the facility that Works provides. In fact, I highly recommend it to you. QuicKeys2 or Tempo II will save you countless hours of mousing around. Simply leave Works' Macros Off command enabled when running these programs. Say goodbye to the countless limitations that Works' macro recorder saddles you with.

Common macro uses

Just about any task you will repeat is a candidate for a macro. In the section "Making the most of macros," a number of likely candidates are discussed. You don't have to record a macro for permanent use in a macro file. Sometimes, macros can serve for a single use. If you are recording in a spreadsheet a sequence of numbers that are incremented by some value, say by the value 1, you can record a sequence that copies a value to the next cell, adds 1 to that value, and then enters the incremented value into that cell. A single keystroke does the work of three. If you continue to record incremented steps, your macro can encapsulate any number of steps.

Obviously, the most useful macros are the ones that you will use over and over in your work. You can make Macros emulate some of the advanced features of more capable programs than Works. Microsoft Word, for example, allows you to store common text and formatting in a glossary table. Entries in that glossary can then be entered into your word processor. Using Works' macro facility, you can easily create a file of glossary macros. Although the use of the Word glossary is much faster than a running macro in Works, a Works macro glossary file will perform exactly the same function. Another example of this approach is the Word style sheets. A style sheet is a named set of paragraph formats. When you want to change a paragraph style in Word, you simply put the insertion point anywhere in that paragraph and give the Style command. In Works, a style sheet macro file will perform all of the formatting steps, albeit with less automation. You will have to select the entire paragraph before running a style macro, and each and every paragraph when changing the style. For more ideas on valuable macros to define, look at each section in this book that describes more advanced programs in that category.

Macros are saved in macro files so you can group macros in useful sets. You could have a word processor macro that served as a glossary, typing a letterhead address, boilerplate paragraphs, or your favorite sign-off phrase. Other word processor macros could format and create your headers and footers, set up your page, and so on — actions that could be part of a global macro file for use in any Works module. Every kind of Works document, and the draw layers of documents, can have specialized macros recorded for them.

Recording and playback

Recording a macro in Works is very similar to recording a program on your VCR, but the process is a lot simpler. There are no silly clocks to set or channels to remember. The essence of recording a macro is to turn on the recorder using the Start Recording command, perform all of the tasks that are part of the macro, and turn off the recorder using the Stop Recording command. To have a macro run, you put Works into the condition in which the macro was designed for, give the Playback And command, and select the macro by name. Alternatively, you can run a macro by invoking the keystroke — Option plus a key that you assigned to the macro. Every command used by Works macros is found on the Macro submenu of the Window menu in each of Works' modules.

You can record four actions in a macro:

♦ *Text you type.* Most ASCII characters can be recorded. This includes alphanumeric characters and some special symbols.

♦ *Keystrokes.* Any key combination that initiates a menu command can be recorded. Works will invoke that command in the macro sequence.

♦ *Menu commands.* The action of opening a menu and selecting a command can be part of a macro. A menu command does not require a keystroke equivalent to be selected, but it must be enabled at the time of recording (not dimmed) to be recorded.

Works macros can select only menu commands specific to Works. You cannot select items off the Apple or Application menus in System 7, nor can you select items off the Apple menu in System 6 using MultiFinder. You can select Apple menu items in System 6 using the Finder. To switch between MultiFinder and Finder in System 6, use the Set Startup command in the Special menu and reboot.

♦ *Clicks and drags.* Mouse actions are recorded as locations on your screen relative to the upper-left corner pixel. When you drag the mouse, the recorder registers the position of the Mouse Down event (click) and the Mouse Up event (release). Use clicks and drags to scroll about in a window, move a window by its title bar, or move objects about in a window.

A click's position may be recorded as a pixel location on the screen, but it is only meaningful in terms of the action it accomplishes in the window it's recorded in. If text is to be typed at a certain clicked location and the window moves, then that text may be incorrectly placed or not placed at all. Because the contents of a window can affect the relative size of scroll bars, it is not a good idea to record macros that take you to a position in a window using the scroll bars. Similarly, macros that go to a specific location in a document will also be volatile. Also, resizing a window can affect its successful operation. When recording and playing back macros, ensure that windows are in the same condition in both instances.

Because only two positions in a drag can be recorded in a macro, some drawn graphics cannot be accomplished using a macro. Any tool in which intermediate steps in a drag are important will not perform properly. An example would be the Freehand tool for drawing lines of any shape.

Recording a macro:

1. **Select the Macros On command from the Macro submenu of the Window menu.**

   Works check-marks the command when active; otherwise, the Macros Off command is check-marked.

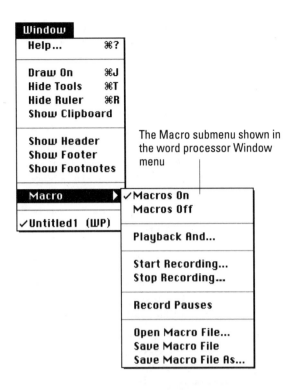

The Macro submenu shown in the word processor Window menu

2. **Create the condition in Works that you wish to record.** Depending on whether you check the Record Pauses command or not, Works will play back your macro at the same rate you recorded it or as fast as it can. In most circumstances you want the macro to be as fast as possible. Use Pauses whenever you want to slow a macro because it doesn't perform properly otherwise, to wait for a condition to occur, or to view all of the steps in a macro like dialog boxes opening and being filled in.

3. **To record pauses and create a timed macro, select the Record Pauses command from the Macro submenu.** Works check-marks the command when active.

4. **Select the Start Recording command on the Macro submenu of the Window menu.** The Start Recording dialog box appears.

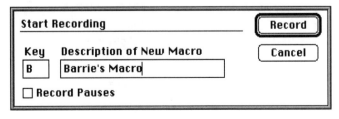

5. **Enter the key part of the keystroke desired into the Key text box.** That key combined with the Option key forms the keystroke that initiates the macro when that macro file is open. In the example shown in the previous figure, the keystroke for Barrie's macro is Option-B, for which you can use either the upper- or lowercase letter *B*.

You can use alphanumeric characters or the Tab key for the macro key. If you have an extended keyboard, the function keys F1 to F15, Home, End, PgUp, and PgDn are also available. There are some letters you can't use, ones that when combined with the Option key generate special accented Macintosh symbols — they are the letters *E, I, N,* and *U.* The Option-keystroke for these letters gives: ´, Option-E (+ Space or any other character); ˆ, Option-I; ˜, Option-N; and ¨, Option-U. For example, to type Ê, you would type Option-I followed by a Shift-E. You cannot use keystroke combinations of modifier keys like Shift, Option, Command, Control, and Caps Lock in combination, nor can you used reserved keys like the Backspace (Delete), +, =, -, and _ keys.

Works displays a message box if you try to use a forbidden key.

6. **Enter the name of the macro in the Description of New Macro text box on the Start Recording dialog box.** Try to use a descriptive name that will help you remember the purpose of that macro.

7. **Press the Record button to begin registering the macro.**

8. **Do the steps that will be part of the macro in sequence.**

9. **End the macro recording by selecting the Stop Recording command from the Macros dialog box.** Works posts the Currently Recording dialog box.

If you make a mistake while recording a macro, either by entering the wrong sequence or by pausing more than you would like, you can cancel a macro in progress.

10. **To cancel a macro at any time in the sequence, choose the Stop Recording command and press the Cancel button in the Currently Recording dialog box.**

You can record macros at any time in Works, even when no document is open on your screen. This allows you to define a macro that will either open a document, macro file, or Workspace you have previously saved, or even create new documents automatically.

Should you wish to have a macro run sometimes at its fastest speed and sometimes as a timed (paused) sequence, you can do so.

Mixing pauses into a macro:

1. **Record the macro up to the point you want a pause.**

2. **Select the Stop Recording command from the Macro submenu to open the Currently Recording dialog box.**

3. **Select the Record Previous Delay check box to insert pauses before the Stop Recording command was selected in the sequence.**

4. **Select the Record Future Delays check box to record the pauses and timing of the macro after the Currently Recording dialog box is dismissed.**

5. **Select both the Record Previous Delay and the Record Future Delays check boxes to record a pause previous to the Stop Recording command and to have a timed macro after the Currently Recording command is dismissed.**

6. **To continue recording a macro, click the Continue button.**

7. **To end a recording, press the Stop button.** Recording mixed sequences of fast-running and timed macros greatly increases your flexibility in the kinds of situations you can apply macros to. It also improves the chances that a macro will perform successfully more often.

Whenever you are done recording a macro, you should always test it to see if it operates properly before saving it to a macro file.

Playing a macro:

1. **Create the condition in Works that the macro requires to run in.** Macros are either global and will run in any opened Works document or without a document open, or they are local and require a specific document type open. For example, a macro that opens a Works file is global and may be played at any time, while a macro that runs the spell checker will not work in a spreadsheet. Also, some macros are recorded to be specific to a single Works document, generating a database report, spreadsheet chart, navigating an on-line service, or whatever.

2. **Select the Macros On command from the Macro submenu.** Works check-marks the command when the feature is active.

3. **If necessary, select the Open Macro File command on the Macro submenu.**

4. **In the Open Macro File dialog box, navigate through the file structure and select the macro filename; then click the Open button. Or double-click on the filename.** You can have only one macro file open in Works at a time.

5. **If you remember the keystroke, press it to run the macro.** If you press the Option-key keystroke and the macro doesn't run, you probably forgot to turn the Macros On command to enabled. If this is the case, you may type a character into your file that you may need to delete from your document.

— or —

5. **Select the Playback And command to open the Playback And dialog box. Double-click on the macro name, or press the keystroke and then the Return key, or select the name and click the Play button to run the macro.**

6. **To stop a macro sequence in progress, press the Macintosh's universal halt keystroke, Command-period.**

7. **To turn the macro feature off, select the Macros Off command from the Macro submenu.** If you can't turn the macros off, a dialog box may be open on your screen. Close the dialog box, and repeat step 7.

Using the Playback And dialog box is an easy way to accomplish several macro file management tasks. Elements of the Playback And dialog box include:

✦ *Playback Macro file.* Shows the name of the open macro file.

✦ *Macro description.* The names of the macros defined for this file. Select a macro and click the Play button to run the macro.

✦ *Keys.* Shows the keys assigned to the macro. Press the Option key to run the macro.

✦ *Record button.* Click this button or press the Return or Enter key to initiate a macro recording. This button is an alternative to selecting the Start Recording command from the Macro submenu.

✦ *Delete button.* Select a macro name in the Macro Description scroll box, and click this button to remove it from your file. You can also delete macro files by dragging their icon to the Trash in the Finder.

✦ *Cancel button.* Click or press the Command-period keystroke to dismiss the Playback And dialog box.

♦ *New button.* Click this button to create a new macro file. Works will prompt you to save changes to the current file before closing that file and then will open a new file.

♦ *Open button.* Click to Open another macro file. Works prompts you to save your changes before opening the new file.

♦ *Save button.* Click to save changes to a macro file. If the macro file is new, Works prompts you for a filename. This button is identical to selecting the Save Macro File command from the Macro submenu.

♦ *Save As button.* Click to create a new macro file under a name you choose. This button re-creates the Save Macro File As command from the Macro submenu.

Remember, any changes you make to a macro file are not recorded until you save that macro file.

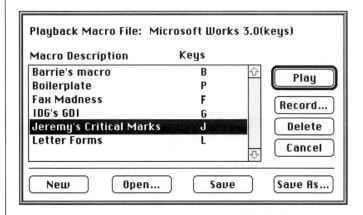

Understanding macro files

Macros are saved as Works files. Unlike other Works files, macro files are not displayed in document windows but are open in the background for use. You can have either no files or a single file open at any one time. Any time you record a macro, Works opens a macro file so that you can save that macro to a file. A file can contain any number of recorded macros.

If you have not previously saved a macro file, then Works opens the file as "Microsoft Works 3.0 (keys)," prompting you to save it under that filename or another name that you enter. You can also open a previously created macro file and save your macro to that file. Should you try to open a file with another macro file open, Works prompts you to save the changes made to that file before closing it.

Macro files are a great convenience in organizing your macros into sets. Record sets of local macros for specific documents or purposes, or global macros for use in all Works modules. Because each macro file can have all available keystroke combinations, you can create macros with duplicate keystrokes in different files.

Starting a macro file:

1. **Select the Macros On command from the Macro submenu to enable the feature.**

2. **Choose the Open Macro File command on the Macro submenu to display the Open Macro File dialog box.**

If a macro file is opened already, Works posts the alert box shown in the figure above requesting you to save changes before that file is closed. Click the Cancel button to abort closing the open file and opening a new file, click the No button to close the file without changes, or click the Yes button to save changes to the old file. Clicking the Yes button posts a standard Save dialog box.

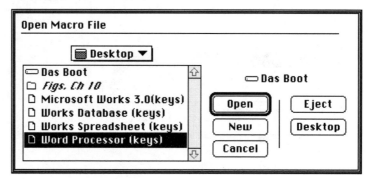

3. **Click the New button.**

4. **Record any macros to be placed in the file, if desired.** You can always record macros at any time that the file is opened or in another Works session.

— or —

4. **Create a new file from within the Playback And dialog box by clicking the New button.**

Opening a macro file:

1. **Select the Macros On command from the Macro submenu to enable the feature.**

2. **Choose the Open Macro File command on the Macro submenu to display the Open Macro File dialog box.**

3. **Navigate the hierarchical file structure to find the file you wish to open.**

4. **Select that file by highlighting its filename and clicking the Open button.**

— or —

4. **Double-click on that filename.**

Only one macro file can be opened at a time. Should you forget which file is opened, choose the Playback And command to view the filename at the top of the dialog box. Macro files have their own distinct icons so that you can find them easily.

Microsoft Works 3.0(keys)

Saving a macro file:

1. **Record the macros you wish to include in a file, or delete any macros from the Playback And dialog box.**

2. **Select the Save Macro File command from the Macro submenu.** If the macro file has been previously saved, Works saves your changes to disk. If the file is new, a standard Save Macro File dialog box appears so you can name the file.

3. **In the Save Macro File dialog box, enter the filename desired into the Save Macro File As text box.**

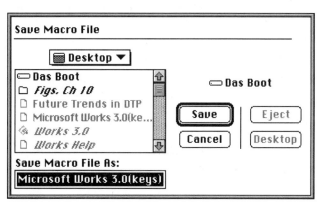

— or —

3. **Select the Save Macro File As command from the Macro submenu.** For a previously unsaved macro file, this command is identical to the Save Macro File command. For a previously saved macro file, this command lets you create a new macro file under a new name.

Quick Tips

The following tips show you how to organize your macro files, use macros most efficiently, and know what features to look for in a high-end macro program.

Organizing macro files

The best way to organize Works' macro files is by functional sets. At the minimum, you might want to define six macro files: a universal Works macro set, word processor, draw, database, spreadsheet, and communication macro files. Because you can have only one macro file open at any one time, this defeats the purpose of recording a universal macro file. You are better off recording commonly used macros into individual module files.

If you record many macros in a file, you will see increasingly slower performance. Works must search the macro file to find the recorded keystrokes. It makes sense to record specialized macro files for document types that fulfill a narrow need. Thus, if you were assembling a long document or a weekly newsletter, you could define all of the macros you needed regardless of the module being used. Because that file would contain only a few macros, it wouldn't matter if you mixed macros meant for different document types.

If you organize your macros into a single folder or place a macro with a template file in a folder, it will always be convenient to find the macro in the file structure. Opening and closing macro files takes only a few seconds, at most.

Making the most of macros

As global macros, consider:

+ Macros that open files or Workspaces.

+ Keystrokes to commands that have none. When an icon and menu command exists, it's a better idea to assign the macro to the menu command.

+ Combining commands with dialog box selections to give automated sequences.

+ Windows manipulations like Zoom, PgUp or PgDn, Home, End, and so on.

+ Easy Windows Help access, Balloon Help, or the Works Shortcut keys.

+ Page Setup and Document Setup sequences.

Good word processor macros are:

+ A glossary of commonly used phrases and boilerplate text. Any text string you commonly type can be included in this glossary.

+ A style sheet of formatted paragraphs.

+ Automated finds or replaces.

+ Header and footer creation.

Some recommended database and spreadsheet macros include the following:

♦ Repetitive data entry steps.

♦ Internal field data type settings.

♦ Externally applied formats to a field's display.

♦ Repetitive matches and finds.

♦ Macros that navigate a spreadsheet or database, taking you to a specific record or section of the worksheet.

♦ Automated report generation for databases.

♦ Automated charting for spreadsheets.

Because the draw toolbox tools are inaccessible to Works' macro recorder, it is difficult to record important draw macros. If you are willing to position the toolbox in an area of your monitor and leave it there, then you can use click macro steps to automate the Draw module.

Remember that in the Communications module, you can automate the log-on from within a menu command. That way, you never have to open a file to do this first important automated step. Other communication macros you might want to consider include the following:

♦ Navigating to a special section of an on-line service.

♦ Automating file transfer so that protocols and commands are given in a sequence.

Don't record sets of communication settings in a macro; use different communication documents for that purpose.

Looking beyond Works' macro recorder

The best macro program for beginner and intermediate Macintosh users is QuicKeys2 from CE Software. This program has gone through several versions and is highly functional. What separates QuicKeys2 from other products is its graphical programming interface. You don't have to know a programming language — all macros are recorded in sequences via dialog box selections. There is also a Record Real Time macro recorder. QuicKeys2 macros can be edited and saved as program sets or files that can be swapped in and out.

QuicKeys2 is slick, with a very capable toolbox. You can install a QuicKeys2 submenu into the Apple menu to launch your macros or bring up a screen listing with all of your macros activated by clicking on their names. Recent versions of the program are System 7-savvy, with an advanced interapplication programming capability. CE Software continues to add extensions to the program that improve its programmability.

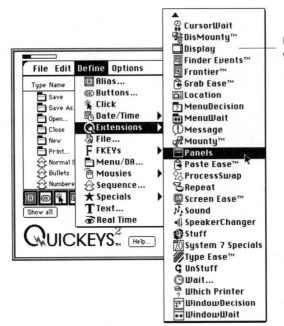

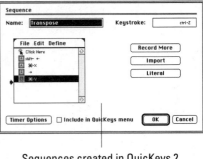

Using Extensions in QuicKeys 2 allows
you to perform many system functions

Sequences created in QuicKeys 2
can be edited in this dialog box

CE Software also publishes Tiles, which can serve as an extension to QuicKeys2 or can stand alone. With Tiles, many actions that you take on the Macintosh are preserved to a square icon called a tile. Windows of tiles collect automatically for an application or for your desktop. If you launch a file, a tile appears for that file. If you click on that tile in another session, the file would launch. You don't have to think about creating the macro, and if you don't use the tile (or launch the file) for a time interval you set, the tile is automatically deleted. QuicKeys2 macros can be tiles, allowing you to encapsulate sequences into an icon. Using tiles, in my opinion, is the approach Apple should have taken in AppleScript, but didn't. Tiles' only defect is its high memory allotment and slow performance. It's so easy to learn, though, you might want to check it out.

Infinity Microsystems' Tempo II macro program is also very highly regarded and preferred by users who are familiar with a programming language approach. It is somewhat more capable than QuicKeys2, but takes a little longer to learn.

UserLand's Frontier is the most complete and sophisticated scripting language available on the Macintosh today. The language, which is similar in feel to HyperTalk, has almost 350 verbs in 30 categories controlling files, windows, dialog boxes, text, outline processing, program management, string handling, and data or program resources. It can manage AppleEvents and create scripts that automate both local and global actions, letting you do multiprogram macros. Unfortunately, the current version of Frontier does not support run-time scripts where you double-click an icon to launch the macro.

Scripts in Frontier can be run in the background, serving as agents to perform automated tasks. Agents take the concept of macros one generation further; they are like adding intelligence to your Mac. Timed backups would be a simple agent, but more complex agents can be created that do data retrieval, analysis, and manipulation. If you used your Mac to examine pork bellies on the Chicago Mercantile Exchange every day, for example, you could have an agent open a communication document, log on, go to the pork bellies listing, download the information, log off, find yesterday's belly action, copy it, close the communications document, open a spreadsheet, paste in the data, chart it, and then print a report. Of course, then you could sleep in late.

Frontier is industrial strength. It's really for developers or highly motivated Mac users only. Its complexity and programmed approach (as opposed to the graphical scripting capability found in QuicKeys2) make Frontier hard to learn and work with. However, it rewards you with superb system controls. It is an advanced system that presages what is to come in system software in the next few years.

Coming soon to Macintosh system software near you is the long (long, long) awaited AppleScript macro programming language. AppleScript will be a programmed high-level language similar to HyperTalk (HyperCard's programming language), with wide capabilities. AppleScript should provide the underlying capability that IBM PC computers have had for a long time to create batch programs to perform complex tasks in system software. Expect AppleScript in late 1992. Because it will be part of Macintosh system software, it will likely be widely used.

Advanced macro programs should have the following features:

+ *Keystroke recording.* A "real time" or "watch me" mode that records actions.

+ *Editable sequences.* Every step in a macro should be capable of being modified.

+ *Wide access.* The capability to use many program and system software features.

+ *Logic.* Branching, loops, conditional statements, repeats, and other logical constructs greatly aid macro utility.

+ *Program language.* An easy-to-understand high-level programming language or a graphical programming (object-oriented) approach that creates the underlying code that makes macros powerful.

+ *System 7 support.* Macro programs should support AppleEvents, Interapplication Communications (IAC), and other advanced features that make System 7-savvy applications.

Summary

- A macro is a program saved to disk to be replayed later. It automates repetitive tasks you perform on the Mac.
- Works' macro facility is a macro recorder that saves text, menu commands, and mouse clicks and drags that you type to a macro.
- Macros are saved to files that are managed like any other Works file.
- Only one macro file can be open at a time from within another Works module.
- All commands for macros are found on the Macro submenu of each module's Window menu.
- Macros can run at the fastest possible speed, the speed you used to create the macro, or as combinations of both.

Topic 11
Spreadsheet and Database Functions

Overview

Functions are predefined equations that are included with and available for your use in Microsoft Works 3. Some functions calculate a result using arguments you define, other functions change data from one form to another, and some functions express relationships between data. Functions may be a complete equation in a formula by itself if that function is the only calculation in a particular cell or field. Equations or formulas can contain one or more functions as components, and each function can serve as an argument to the next function in the equation hierarchy.

All of Works' functions are available in the Spreadsheet module, and all but a few are also available for use in the Database module. Microsoft Works 3 provides 64 functions — the same functions that were used in version 2.0. These functions are arithmetic, mathematical, statistical, trigonometric, and logical. There are other date and time and "special-purpose" functions. Any or all of these may be used to automate a database or worksheet and ensure the accuracy of tasks you perform with Works.

You don't need to remember these functions or their syntax; you merely paste them into an equation. The following section, "Selecting and pasting a function," tells you how. You need only paste rather than remember, invent, and test complex calculations for common numeric and other relationships that you are likely to use in a spreadsheet or database.

You can use functions for simple tasks, such as adding a column of numbers, or for much more complicated tasks, such as figuring out a budget and payroll for a business. The quality of a spreadsheet and database is largely determined by both the way the document looks graphically and the overall logic of the calculations used. There is always a better way to calculate results, and you can always improve a worksheet and database with experience.

Getting into arguments

Functions describe relationships. You use a function to operate on a value or vari-able — called an *argument* — and Works returns a result as another value. Arguments can be a single cell, a range of cells, a function, a field name, or a combination of these. The resulting value can serve as the value that another function operates on.

A function is written in a precise syntax or form that you must use exactly to make the function operate correctly. Arguments of a function are contained in a parenthetical statement, and the function or equation expression always results in a number. An argument can be text, but its result cannot. Sometimes it is not obvious that functions always work with numbers. Date and time functions always return dates and times. Underlying these functions are mathematical systems that convert dates and times to numbers so that they can be manipulated. Any date and time is therefore only dis-played as a date and time; the Macintosh handles them internally as numbers — serial dates and times.

Let's look at some functions and their syntax:

1. =Sum(A2 + D1:D3 − 5)

2. =Count(1,2,3,4,5,6)

3. =Exp(Sin(A8) + Cos(B3))

Equations always begin with an equal sign. In the first equation, the function Sum operates on a single argument inside the parentheses. This argument contains a cell reference, a range of cell references, and a value. Calculations within parentheses are performed right to left (depending on the calculations required); arguments within nested parentheses are always evaluated first. In the third equation, the Sin and Cos functions are evaluated first, and the value they return is raised to an exponential.

Functions may be grouped into sets or categories based on the type and way they handle data. Every function uses the same basic "language" of argument notation. Essentially every argument is a "value" of some kind, but each type of value has a different name for clarity. The basic argument notation is:

+ *value(s).* An argument that must be a number, cell reference, formula, or data-base field name. This is the standard argument type. To distinguish among multiple values in one function, they are named "values-1," "values-2," and so on.

+ *number.* Same as value(s).

+ *range.* A range reference in a spreadsheet refers to a contiguous collection of cells. In a database, a range is a field name. Like values, multiple ranges are named "range-1," "range-2," and so on.

+ *lookup value.* The value in a function that looks up values from another location.

◆ *compare-range.* The value a function returns after comparing ranges.

◆ *cell-reference.* The value in date and time functions.

◆ *rate.* A value used in financial functions, for example, tax rate, interest rate.

There are more specific argument types for certain functions, and they are found in the explanations that follow each function's definition. An ellipsis (…) indicates an argument or set of arguments that can continue logically in a pattern or series, for example, rate-1, rate-2, rate-3… . An ellipsis is used to indicate that you can enter as many of these arguments, separated by a comma and no spaces, as your applications require.

Different functions serve different purposes, and each one serves one purpose alone. Used in tandem, Works' functions can be applied to many complex calculations. Some functions are mathematical, some statistical, and so on, but these are convenient distinctions for organizational purposes. You shouldn't hesitate to combine different types of functions into single formulas — that's exactly what they're there for. All of Works' functions are listed alphabetically by categories in the upcoming "Functions by Type" section. Examples are given for each function to help you understand their applications.

Selecting and pasting a function

You could manually enter any formula you choose into a cell by typing the formula into the entry bar. To do so often introduces errors. Sometimes Works will alert you that the syntax of your formula doesn't make sense, but often it won't. That is, you could have a perfectly valid expression that is simply wrong. Also, manual entry takes time. It's much easier, more efficient, and less error prone to build expressions automatically by using the Works Paste Function facility.

When you select a function within the Paste Function dialog box, Works puts that function into your equation at the insertion point, and highlights the values or the arguments that you have to replace. You always know where and how many values or variables you need to enter. This lets you build formulas without worrying about getting the syntax right. For information about functions and the required values and variables, see the extended list plus examples later in this Topic.

Automatically entering a function:

1. **Select the cell or field you wish to perform the calculation in by clicking on it.**

2. **Format that cell or field so that the data type is consistent with its purpose.**

3. **Optionally, format the cell or field so the display is as desired. You can perform this step any time after the equation is established.** For information on data types, see "Understanding Fields" in Topic 6. See also "Formatting a cell" in Topic 7.

4. **Pull down the Edit menu and select the Paste Function command, as in the following figure.** Works posts the Paste Function dialog box. Functions are available from the Edit menu in the Works spreadsheet and database.

5. **Select the kind of function by clicking the appropriate radio button.** Choose mathematical, statistical, logical, financial, date and time, or special functions. A brief explanation of the highlighted function appears in the Description box at the bottom of the Paste Function dialog box.

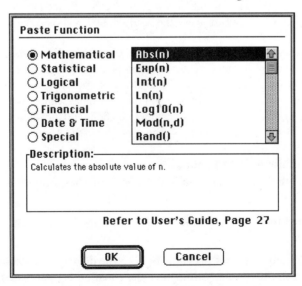

6. **Select the function you want from the scroll box on the right by double-clicking on its name. Or single-click to highlight your selection and press the OK button.** Works enters an equation symbol followed by the function, if there is no equation in the entry bar, as shown in the figure below.

🍎 File Edit Format Options Chart Window

| A1 | ✗✓ | =StDev(v1,v2,...) |

7. **Enter the values for the arguments into the equations.**

8. **Click the Entry box (check Check box in the Entry bar), or press the Return or Enter key.**

For example, when you enter the function MOD (for modulus), Works enters =MOD(n,d) into the menu bar. The arguments "n" and "d" are highlighted, prompting you to put in their real values. If an equation exists for that cell or field, the Paste Function command is dimmed and unavailable. Many times you want to have nested equations: To create those equations you may have to enter the equation manually.

Manually entering an equation:

1. **Select the cell or field you wish to perform the calculation in, by clicking on it.**

2. **Click an insertion point in the Entry bar.**

3. **Type an equal sign followed by the compound expression you wish to use.** Always type that equal sign; it's the way Works recognizes an equation. Pay special attention to the syntax of the expression — parentheses, commas, and spaces are very important to make Works correctly evaluate the equation.

4. **Enter the values for the arguments of functions as you enter the equation.**

5. **Click the Entry box (check Check box in the Entry bar), or press the Return or Enter key.** You can, of course, use the Paste Function command to place the first function in the Entry box and proceed by manually adding additional functions.

Once you enter the equation into the cell or field, Works checks to see if the expression is valid. It looks at the placement of parentheses, commas, spaces, and arguments to see if the syntax of a function was violated. If it finds an invalid expression, it displays the Incorrect Formula dialog box shown in the following figure. Keep in mind that even if Works does not display this error message box, your expression can still be wrong; when this error box does not appear, it simply means that Works can evaluate the expression and return a result.

> **There is an inappropriate use of a comma.**
>
> =ABS(567)*4,6
>
> [Cancel]   [Treat As Text]   [OK]

You can either correct your formula right in the Incorrect Formula box and then click the OK button, or, if you wish for whatever reason to retain the incorrect formula in the cell or field, click the Treat As Text button. Sometimes the expression serves as a label for the spreadsheet or database and doesn't need to be evaluated. A formula treated as text is not evaluated further and doesn't display as a value.

A few pointers about entering functions:

◆ The most efficient way to use functions is to paste them.

◆ When you type functions yourself, be careful to exactly duplicate the function. Do not type any extra spaces into your functions or formulas, and always include an equal sign at the beginning of each complete equation or formula.

◆ Spelling function names correctly is essential, but Works is *not* case sensitive. AVERAGE, Average, aVeraGe, and variants are all treated the same and will yield correct results.

◆ The spreadsheet-only functions are HLookup, Index, IRR, Lookup, Match, MIRR, and VLookup.

◆ Arguments entered incorrectly may or may not calculate, but your results will be wrong. Be certain that each argument *is correct*. You can't count on Works to display an error value (*Error* or N/A) because you may get what looks like — but isn't — a valid result.

◆ Always test your worksheet or database with simple values that you can check for accuracy.

◆ Some functions have "optional" arguments, particularly Financial functions. You may elect to enter the argument or not, depending on what parameters you are looking for in your output. Every optional argument has a default value that will either not interfere with the rest of your arguments or will affect the formula in exactly one way. Under each explanation that follows, these options and their default values are discussed fully.

- ✦ When entering cell references in a spreadsheet, click on each one. Works will insert an addition sign if there is no other operator or function entered to the left. When you click to drag a range of cell references, Works enters that range (A1:A6, for example).

- ✦ When you see a series of pound signs (#######) Works is indicating that the full value can't be seen. Widen the column to see the value in the cell or field.

- ✦ When *Error* is displayed, the value is too large to be displayed. For example, 1/0 gives infinity, and an *Error* is shown.

- ✦ An N/A message appears in a cell when the result of the expression is not a number. For example, the square root of a negative number yields an imaginary number and displays an N/A error message.

The following sections look at the specifics of all the functions that Works offers.

Functions by Type

Functions are like canned equations that you can use to evaluate data. Works has several types of functions that you can use: mathematical, statistical, logical, trigonometric, financial, date and time, and special purpose (mostly comparison) functions. Many of these functions will, no doubt, be familiar to you and won't require explanation. Others you may never have seen before. Each of these functions is explained, as are its requirements. Keep in mind that each function has its own syntax that you need to follow rigidly. Don't count on Works always alerting you to an error in construction and usage.

Following each function is an example of its usage. For most purposes, these examples will be evident and self-explanatory. They should get you started, and you can try the functions in your own work to experiment and figure out how they operate. Some of the functions, particularly the financial and special purpose/comparison functions are complex and are not obvious. If you are having a problem understanding one of the more difficult functions, you might want to look at a book on Microsoft Excel, from which many of the functions were taken. If you do, keep in mind that there may be small differences in construction and function between Works functions and Excel functions.

Mathematical functions

You can enter arithmetic operators like +, −, /, *, and ∧ directly into an equation. They are the most commonly used functions. Mathematical functions are the next most commonly used class.

- ✦ ABS(*number*). This provides an absolute value of a number, which is a number without a positive or negative sign. You can use arguments that are numbers, formulas, or cell references.

The absolute value of –5 and +5, for example, is 5, whether that is five lost or five gained. Use ABS to find the difference between two positive numbers if you don't know which is larger. In this example, if the numbers were 6 and 3, the two equations ABS(3–6) and ABS(6–3) both equal 3.

✦ EXP(*number*). This gives e (2.7182818) raised to the power of the argument, e^n, which is a *number*. EXP is also the opposite, or inverse, of the function LN, which gives the natural logarithm of a *number*.

For example, to one decimal place LN(9) returns 2.2, and EXP(2.2) returns 9. EXP uses the natural base e. You can use other bases if you wish by using the exponentiation operator (^) to designate a new one, x^y. See Topic 6, or the Log10 function, below.

✦ INT(*number*). This function gives the largest integer less than or equal to *number*, which is to say it functions only to round numbers down. You can use a number, formula, or cell reference for the argument.

For example, INT(10.9) equals 10; INT(–10.9) equals –11. If B2 contains the value 35.5, then INT(B2) returns 35 as a result.

✦ LN(*number*). This function gives the natural logarithm of a positive *number*, in base e. The logarithm is the power to which the base is raised to provide *number*.

For example, LN(EXP(6)) equals 6, and LN(6) equals 1.8.

✦ Log10(*number*). This function gives the base 10 logarithm of a positive *number*. Natural logarithms or base e exponents are the inverse of base 10 exponentiation.

For example, Log10(10) equals 1, Log10(1E7) equals 7, Log10(10^7) equals 7, and so on.

✦ MOD(*number, divisor-number*). The MOD function returns the modulus or remainder of the divisor (*number*) and dividend (*divisor-number*). The result can be positive or negative, but not zero. You can use either numbers, cell references, or formulas that return numbers in the MOD function.

For example, MOD(13,3) equals 1, as 3 goes into 13 four times, leaving a remainder, or modulus, of 1. Use the MOD function to calculate the remaining inventory or overages.

✦ RAND(). This function returns a random positive number between 0 and 1. The parentheses do not contain any arguments, but they are required by the function to note where in the formula this random number is placed. RAND returns a new random number each time its environment — the spreadsheet or database where it is placed — recalculates. RAND is primarily useful in certain types of mathematical model-making in which a certain quantity is unknown but must be between 0 and 1.

To mathematically simulate rolling two six-sided dice with Works, use =(INT(RAND()*6) + 1) + (INT(RAND() * 6 + 1). Every time you recalculate this expression, you are "throwing your dice" again.

◆ ROUND(*number,number-of-digits*). This function rounds *number* to *number-of-digits* (sometimes called the precision). This means that you can specify a positive number of digits, a negative number, or zero. If positive, ROUND will round to that many decimal places. If negative, it will round to the left of the decimal point. If zero, it will round to the nearest integer.

For example, ROUND(5.75,1) equals 5.7; ROUND(575,–2) equals 600; ROUND(5.7599,0) equals 6. Round is commonly used when handling currency because a result in dollars and cents only is useful to two decimal places. With a precision of 2, cents are returned; for 0, only whole dollars are calculated; and for –2, only hundreds would appear.

It is important to note that unlike formatting a cell or field to a certain number of decimal places, ROUND permanently truncates the resulting number to that precision, losing all other decimal places in memory.

◆ SIGN(*number*). This returns information on whether a *number* is positive, negative, or zero. If positive, the SIGN function returns the result 1. If negative, it returns –1. If zero, it returns 0.

For example, SIGN(10+2) equals 1; SIGN(2–10) equals –1; SIGN(2–2) equals 0.

You can use the SIGN function to perform simple mathematical logic. SIGN can determine what the rest of a formula should do based on the positivity or negativity of a particular argument or *number*. Thus, the equation =B1 + B2 * (SIGN(B3)) is an expression that will add, subtract, or ignore cell B2 based on the sign of B3.

◆ SQRT(*number*). This returns the square root of a non-negative *number*. If the *number* entered in a SQRT function is negative, you will get the *Error* message as a result.

For example, SQRT(64) equals 8, SQRT(8^2) equals 8, and SQRT(–64) equals *Error*.

If you need to determine the *n*th root, you must use the exponentiation function. For example, to find the fourth root of 16, put 4 into cell A1 (or wherever) and 16 into cell B1. Then the formula B1^(1/A1) returns the fourth root, or the number 2.

◆ SSUM(*values-1,values-2,...*). This function returns the sum of the numbers in the arguments as they appear on the screen (SSUM means "screensum"). As with other functions, arguments containing (or designated as) text, or which are blank, are ignored in the calculation.

For example, if cells B1:B4 contained the numbers 5.5, 6.5, 13, and 25.02134, and you were displaying out to only two decimals, SSUM would calculate SSUM(B1:B4) as 50.02. By contrast, SUM would calculate the complete "hidden" (non-displayed) value of the same range, which would of course be 50.02134. SSUM calculates the "display value" of *values*. The SSUM function is often helpful when using the results of other functions in cells, like logic functions, to build formulas.

♦ SUM(*values-1,values-2,...*). The SUM functions perform simple addition on its variables, calculating actual internally held values instead of displayed values that SSUM uses. Here too, text, designated text, and blanks are ignored. You are not limited to one value-set in either SSUM or SUM. You could use the formula =A1 + A2 + A3... instead of a SUM, but SUM is much more convenient.

For example, if B1:B4 contains the numbers 5, 6, 13, and 25 and if C1:C4 contains the numbers 2, 4, 6, and 8, then SUM(B1:B4) equals 49; SUM(B1:B4,3) equals 52; SUM(B1:C4) equals 69.

	A	B	C	D
1		Internal Values	Displayed Values	
2		1.52	1.5	
3		1.52	1.5	
4		1.52	1.5	
5	SUM ===>	4.56	4.5	<=== SSUM

Keep in mind that the SSUM function is different from the SUM function. SUM is the true calculated value based on the internally held numbers, whereas the SSUM function calculates based on what is displayed on the screen. The previous figure shows this difference in a worksheet. This can be confusing, as many times SUM and SSUM will calculate and display the same results; they often operate on the same values. You can use them interchangeably, test them, and only sometimes will they result in a different value. So pay attention to that difference, and use the function that is appropriate to your needs.

Mathematical functions essentially help you find values. Statistical functions, more-over, allow you to manipulate found values to find other, more complex and often informative values.

Statistical functions

Statistics is a way of finding, combining, assembling, classifying, tabulating, or pre-senting numerical data. For a crude example, how many cars (a *number*) pass a certain place on the highway (a *control* used to find that *number*) in a given period of time (another *control* used to find the number) is a statistical inquiry. Statistics are used to quantify, qualify, elucidate, or predict events involving numbers of things.

Works is not a statistical application. Full-function statistics applications can cost thou-sands of dollars and some require more power than most Macintosh computers can provide. What Works 3 does provide is a set of the six most important statistical functions for your convenience. You can use these functions to find important informa-tion about the data in your databases and spreadsheets.

The statistical functions Works provides are:

◆ AVERAGE(*values-1, values-2,...*). This adds the values designated and divides the sum by the number of values added. A reference argument containing text, designated text, or blanks will be ignored. Reference arguments should be numbers in cell references or formulas that return numbers.

For example, if B1:B5 contains the numbers 4, 6, 8, 10, and 12, then AVERAGE(B1:B5) equals 8 and AVERAGE(B1:B5,3) equals 7.166. Or, if you bought three items at $1.50, $2.00, and $2.25, the average cost of your purchases would be found by AVERAGE(1.5, 2, 2.25), which equals 1.5. On average, your purchases cost $1.50; cell or field formatting would show the number as a dollar figure.

◆ COUNT(*values-1, values-2,...*). This function counts the number of *numbers* in the designated *values*, not their value.

For example, if B1:B4 contains the numbers 4, 6, 8, and 10, then COUNT(B1:B4) equals 4. If cell B3 were blank or contained text, then COUNT(B1:B4) equals 3. Another example combines more than one *value*. If B1:B4 contains 4, 6, 8, and 10, and C1 contains 12, then COUNT(B1:B4,C1) equals 5.

◆ MAX(*values-1, values-2,...*). Returns the largest number available in the arguments designated. Text or blank references, as usual, are ignored. Should there be no maximum number, 0 is returned.

For example, if B1:B4 contains 4, 6, 8, and 10, then MAX(B1:B4) equals 10 and MAX(B1:B4,36) equals 36.

◆ MIN(*values-1, values-2,...*). The opposite of MAX, this function finds the lowest number among those designated.

For example, using the same B range as above, MIN(B1:B4) equals 4; MIN(B1:B4,36) equals 4; MIN(B1:B4,2) equals 2.

◆ STDEV(*values-1, values-2,...*). This function returns sample standard deviation of the designated values (numbers, cells, references). The underlying formula used to calculate a standard deviation is *SQRT(VAR(values-1, values-2,...))*.

For example, if B1:B5 contains the numbers 10, 7, 9, 27, and 2, then STDEV(B1:B5) equals 9.46.

◆ VAR(*values-1, values-2,...*). The VAR function returns the sample variance of the numbers designated. Values can be numbers, references, or formulas that return a number. Blank values and text are ignored. Works uses this formula to calculate variance: $(n(\sum(x^2) - (\sum x)^2)/ n(n-1)$.

For example, if B1:B5 contains the numbers 10, 7, 9, 27, and 2, then VAR(B1:B5) equals 89.5. Sample variance estimates a population based on a sample. Should you wish to calculate the true population variance, use the formula: VAR(*Population,Average(Population)*).

Logical functions

Logical functions test arguments and provide only two possible answers: Yes or No, 1 or 0. Arguments for logical functions must be values, not text. A value is normally an evaluated equation or expression. This type of logic, which allows only two answers, is called Boolean logic. Conceptually, logical conditionals (as formulas involving logical functions are sometimes called) answer only Yes or No. Technically speaking, the value 1 means TRUE and the value 0 means FALSE. So, if you formatted a cell or field as a number, you would see 1 when you typed Yes as the value or, for a text field, No when you typed in a 0.

Incidentally, Boolean logic is at the heart of all computer calculations. Computer logic must be translated to 1s and 0s because digital computers at their physical core operate on electric pulses of high and low voltages across circuits. When high charge flows, that is On, 1, or True. Ebb, or low-charge, the flow indicates a state of Off, 0, or False. That explains why a computer's main component, the motherboard, is also referred to as a logic board.

Works' logical functions include:

+ AND(*values-1,values-2,...*). This function returns the value 1 or TRUE, when all the values in the list of arguments are true. If one or more values is false, it returns 0 or FALSE.

  For example, using correct and incorrect simple addition: AND(1 + 1 = 2, 4 + 4=8) returns 1 or TRUE, while AND(1 + 1=3, 4 + 4=8) returns 0 or FALSE.

+ False(). This function returns the value 0 or FALSE at all times. It takes no arguments. This function is usually used as an argument to test the setup of a formula.

  You could use the formula IF(A1=A5,TRUE(),FALSE()) to return the values 1 (if A1=A5) or 0 (if not). By using the formula IF(A1=A5,"TRUE","FALSE"), the text strings "TRUE" and "FALSE" are returned in the same circumstance.

+ IF(*number, value-if-true, value-if-false*). The IF function is probably one of the most useful functions that Works offers. The IF function allows for conditional branching because it tests for a condition and, based on the result, can return either of two answers.

  Numbers can be values, cell references, or formulas that return numbers. IF is an if-then value. When the *number* is true, the result is the designated *value-if-true*, and when the *number* is false, the result is the designated *value-if-false*. The *v-i-t* and *v-i-f* arguments must be numbers.

  For example, consider cell B25, which contains the number 35. Then, IF((B25 > 33),5,10) equals 1 or TRUE.

  IF numbers generally examine a condition using a comparison operator like <, >, ≤, ≥, <= (less than or equal to), >= (greater than or equal to), <> (not equal to), or =. These operators were described in Topic 6. You can also use the simple values 1 or 0 to return the v-i-t or v-i-f arguments, respectively, but this defeats the purpose of the function.

For even greater utility, use nested IF statements to evaluate an expression with three conditions. For the equation IF(IF*(value-1,value-2)*,v-i-t,v-i-f,v-i-t,v-i-f), Works evaluates the inner IF statement first to provide a first branch, then evaluates the outer IF statement to provide another branch. Nested IFs are the cat's meow.

✦ IsBlank(*values-1,values-2,...*). Another if-then proposition. A completely blank or noncalculable (text) cell reference or set of cell references results in a 1 or TRUE, resulting from IsBlank. Any filled cells referenced in the argument will return a 0 or FALSE. The arguments in IsBlank must be cell references.

For example, if cells B1:B4 are empty, but B5 contains the number 50, then IsBlank(B1:B4) returns 1 or TRUE, while IsBlank(B1:B5) returns 0 or FALSE.

✦ IsError(*value*). This function returns 1 or TRUE when the *value* is the error message *Error*. Otherwise, it returns 0 or FALSE. This function uses only the specific error message *Error*. When the error message N/A is to be used, use the IsNA function.

✦ IsNA(*value*). This function returns 1 or TRUE when the *value* is the error message N/A. Otherwise, it returns 0 or FALSE. This works based only on the specific error message (or error value) N/A.

✦ NOT(*number*). This function returns the opposite result from the *number* it is acting upon. If *number* is 0 or FALSE, then NOT returns 1 or TRUE; and if *number* is 0 or FALSE, then NOT returns 1 or TRUE. NOT can also evaluate an expression for its validity.

For example, NOT(2+2=4) returns 0 or FALSE, while NOT(2+2=5) returns 1 or TRUE.

✦ OR(*values-1,values-2,...*). This function returns the value 1 or TRUE, if *any* of the values in the list of arguments is non-zero. If all values are zero, OR returns 0 or FALSE. Text and blanks are ignored in OR, and a zero means "0," not literally "nothing." The OR function means "and/or" because either or both values must be true for the function to return a true value.

For example, if range A10:A20 contained all zeros, OR(A10:A20) would provide 0 or FALSE. If cell E15 contained the number 3, then OR(A10:A20,E15) would provide 1 or TRUE.

You can combine the IF function with the AND and OR functions to build multiple conditions. For example, when using the AND function, AND(*value-1,value-2,value-3*), all values must be true to return a true. Adding the AND statement to an IF statement like IF(AND(*value-1,value-2,value-3*),v-i-t,v-i-f) provides more logic than evaluating a single expression because multiple conditions (values) have been tested.

- ✦ True(). Like False(), this function returns only one value. In this case, that value is 1 or TRUE. Also like False(), the True() function is mainly used for testing formulas by providing a known value (or *control,* as it is called in statistics). True(), also like False(), takes no arguments. It is normally used *as* an argument.

  For an example of how to use the True function, see the False function earlier in this section.

Trigonometric functions

Trigonometric functions are more valuable than high schoolers would have you believe. Fields such as engineering, navigation, surveying, and architecture rely on trigonometry to find relationships of angles. Most trigonometric functions are found in good pocket calculators.

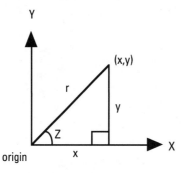

In the above figure, the basic trigonometric functions are illustrated; refer to this figure for the discussion of functions that follows.

The trigonometric functions are:

- ✦ ACos(*number*). Returns the arccosine of a *number.* The arccosine is the radian measure of the angle whose cosine is *number. Number* must be some value between –1 and 1 because that is the interval for the cosine. The angle, necessarily, will be in the range from 0 radians (at zero degrees) to π radians (at 180 degrees).

  For example, ACos(–0.5) equals 2.094 ($2\pi/3$ radians), which is turned into the formula ACos(–0.5)*180/Pi(). This equals 120 degrees, and you can use the Degrees function in the formula Degrees(ACos(–0.5)) to find the same answer, 120 degrees. See the Degrees function.

  For a real-world example of ACos, consider a bird that travels 40 mph south to north, with a perpendicular crosswind of 5 mph west. ACos lets you figure out the deviation of the bird from true north. In this case, it is Degrees(ACos(5/40) or 82.82 degrees. So the bird is flying 7.12 degrees west of true north.

♦ ASin(*number*). Returns the arcsine of a *number*. The arcsine is the measure of the angle whose sine is *number*, expressed in radians. *Number* must again be in the range −1 to 1, and here the angle will be between −π/2 and π/2. In the same way (and for the same reason) as the ACos function, you can use the Degrees function acting upon a formula containing this function's result as an argument for faster results.

For example, ASin(−0.5) equals −0.524 (−π/6 radians), and ASin(−0.5)*180/Pi() equals −30 degrees. To find the same result, you could use Degrees. Then, Degrees(ASin(−0.5)) returns the answer −30 degrees in one step. In the example of the bird used in the ACos function, you could have used the ASin function; the expression would have been Degrees(ASin(40,5)).

♦ ATan(*number*). Returns the arctangent of a *number*. As you probably suspect, ATan is a lot like ACos and ASin. The arctangent of *number* is the angle in radians of which *number* is the tangent. The angle will be in the same range as for ASin, which is −π/2 to π/2. Here again, the Degrees function simplifies the process of finding the angle in degrees.

For example, ATan(1) equals 0.785 (π/4 radians), and ATan(1)*180/Pi() returns 45 degrees. The simplified Degrees(ATan(1)) also equals 45 degrees.

♦ ATan2(*x-number,y-number*). Returns the arctangent of a point whose coordinates are (*x-number,y-number*). Here the arctangent is the angle, in radians, determined by the point with these coordinates. The angle must be in the range from −π to π, excluding negative π itself. You can use the Degrees function to find the result in degrees as with all the other arc- functions.

For example, ATan2(1,1) equals 0.785 (π/4 radians), and ATan2(−1,−1) equals −2.356(−3π/4 radians).

♦ Cos(*number*). Returns the cosine of *number*. *Number* must be an angle in radians. In the previous figure, Cos Z = x/r, where x/r is the number evaluated.

For example, Cos(23.401) equals 0.917.

♦ Degrees(*number*). This function very simply converts angles expressed in radians to degrees. To work, *number* must be an angle in radians. The formula used for this computation is Degrees=Radians*180/π.

For example, Degrees(2*Pi()) equals 360 degrees. For other examples, see the arc functions (ACos, ASin, ATan, and ATan2) above.

♦ Pi(). Returns the mathematical constant π, up to 17 decimal places. It takes no arguments, but the function must be written Pi() for formulas to work. Pi is commonly expressed to six places, as 3.14159.

♦ Radians(*number*). This function is the opposite of the Degrees function. It converts angles expressed in degrees to radians. In this case, the *number* can be a value, formula, or cell or range address (reference).

♦ Sin(*number*). Returns the sine of *number* when that *number* is an angle expressed in radians. In the previous figure, the sine is Sin Z = y/r, where y/r is the number evaluated.

For example, Sin(45) equals 0.851.

♦ Tan(*number*). Returns the tangent of a *number* when *number* is an angle expressed in radians. A tangent is the ratio of the x- to the y-coordinate on a circle, or the ratio of cosine/sine. In the previous figure, Tan Z = y/z; or, Tan Z = Sin Z/Cos Z, where y/z and Sin Z/Cos Z (both equivalent expressions) is the number evaluated.

For example, Tan(45) equals 1.619.

Financial functions

Whereas logical functions combined with mathematical functions can calculate financial problems (i.e., IF there's enough money in account A, THEN you can afford item x), the eight financial functions in Works provide directed, dedicated formulas for figuring out common issues of finances such as interest and market value. Using the financial functions is like having a personal digital accountant and investment banker.

Some financial functions require, or assume, certain things to work correctly. The functions PV, FV, NPer, Pmt, and Rate require constant payments. If the payment amount, timing, or rate of return varies, they will not calculate correctly. Some financial functions are available only in the Spreadsheet module of Works and are so noted in their descriptions that follow.

The arguments *pv, fv, nper, pmt,* and *rate* are the five standard parameters that apply to a series of constant cash payments made over time. These series of payments are known as "annuities." The *functions* that express the same values as these arguments, for example, PV, FV, NPer, Pmt, and Rate, provide one value given to the others.

The financial functions are:

♦ FV(*rate,nper,pmt,pv,type*). This function returns the future value of an investment. It calculates the value after you have made your last payment over a particular time and rate. The arguments it requires are *rate*, which is the interest rate in percentage points (monthly or annual); *nper*, which is the total number of payment periods, referring to the same period as *rate;* and *pmt*, which is the amount of payment (received or paid) each period.

Positive cash (income) is represented by a positive number; negative cash (outlay), by a negative number.

An optional argument is *pv*, the lump-sum value that a series of payments to be made later is worth today. You may leave *pv* out, and Works will calculate it as zero.

The argument *type* is also not required and can be used to designate whether payment is made at the beginning (enter 0) or end (enter 1) of each period. The default value is 0.

```
 r    ´  File  Edit  Format  Options  Chart
    B6              =FV(B1,B2,B3,B4,0)
```

	A	B
		Boat
1	Interest Rate	0.0066666666667
2	Number of Periods	240
3	Payment Amount	-100
4	Investment (PV)	-1000
5	Type	1
6	Future Value (FV)	$63828.84
7		

For example, you want to buy a boat that costs $75,000. You start your boat fund with $1,000 in a savings account, to which you will add $100 monthly for 20 years. Twenty years is 240 months. Suppose an interest rate of 8 percent annually; then your monthly interest is 8%/12. Your formula would be FV(8%/12, 240,–100,–1000,1), which equals $64,221.52 You're almost there.

✦ IRR(*range,guess*). This function returns the internal rate of return based on a series of cash flows. An internal rate of return is the interest rate you receive from (or pay to) an investment. IRR uses the payments and/or income you get, which is represented by the *range* of values usually found in a cell or field reference. The rate of return calculated by the IRR function in Works is the interest rate that gives the cash flow a net present value of zero.

IRR is only available in the spreadsheet — not the database.

In IRR, the *range* argument must be expressed in numbers. The numbers represent payments or income. The *guess* refers to your guess as to what the IRR might be. Begin with a number between 0 and 1, and continue to change your guess if IRR fails. IRR may fail in the end anyway, but some failures can be corrected by more accurate guesses. Twenty attempts are made by Works to figure the IRR, a technique called the "iterative" method, because the calculation is tried more than once before the failure message *Error* results.

```
 r    ´  File  Edit  Format  Options  Chart  Window
    B6              =IRR(B5:E5,25)
```

	A	B	C	D	E
		Office Building (SS)			
1		Year 1	Year 2	Year 3	Year 4
2	Cost	-100000	0	0	0
3	Income	35000	35000	35000	35000
4					
5	Total	-65000	35000	35000	35000
6	IRR	28.42%			
7					

As an example of the IRR function, say you buy an office building for $100,000, and your net income on the property for four years was $35,000 each year, and you estimate a rate of return of 25 percent. When you set up the function in the manner shown in the preceding figure, Works will return the true rate of return, which is 28.42 percent.

◆ MIRR(*range, safe, risk*). This function returns the modified internal rate of return when positive cash (income) and negative cash (outlay) flows are financed at different rates. The *safe* argument is the money you are paying out, an absolute quantity. The *risk* is the money you get back in interest. The MIRR function combines two IRR functions into one — payments made to the investment are negative values and income received is a positive value. You can think of the *safe* argument as being a finance rate and the *risk* argument as a reinvestment rate.

MIRR is not available in the Database module — only the spreadsheet.

 File   Edit   Format   Options   Chart   Window

B7		=MIRR(B2:E5,B8,12%)			

Office Building (SS)

	A	B	C	D	E
1		Year 1	Year 2	Year 3	Year 4
2	Cost	-100000	0	0	0
3	Income	35000	35000	35000	35000
4					
5	Total	-65000	35000	35000	35000
6	IRR	28.42%			
7	MIRR	7.91%			
8					

For the example of rental property described in the IRR function, you can apply the MIRR function. The investment is paying off a positive cash flow of 28.42 percent, as just shown (not too shabby!). If you borrowed all the money and had to pay back the note at the rate of 12 percent, then that would be your risk? The MIRR function returns a value of 7.91 percent, which is your true rate of return.

◆ NPer(*rate,pmt,pv,fv,type*). This function returns the number of payments at a specific interest rate for an investment to pay itself off. NPer lets you figure out the effect of an interest rate on the term of an investment.

The arguments for the NPer function are *rate* is the interest rate (in points) per month or year period; *pmt* is the amount of payment received or paid out per period; *pv* is the present value that a series of future payments is worth now (also called "lumpsum" value); *fv* is the future value you want to attain after the last payment is made. The fv argument is optional, and the default is 0. The argument *type* is also optional, so you can include when in each period payments are made. Enter 0 for beginning or 1 for end. The default is 0.

```
 r   ▲  File  Edit  Format  Options  Chart
  B7              │        │=NPer(B1,B2,B3,B4,B5)
```

	A	B
1	Interest Rate	1.00%
2	Payment Amount	-250
3	Present Value (capital)	$5000.00
4	Future Value	$20000.00
5	Type	1
6		
7	No. of Payment	80.81
8		

(Window title: Car Pay)

As an example of the use of the NPer function, you wish to pay off a car loan. At 12 percent interest (1 percent/month), a $250 monthly payment with $5,000 down on a $20,000 Nissan Pathfinder, paid at the beginning of every month would take 80.81 months to pay off. The above figure shows you how the formula NPer(1%,–250,$5,000,$20,000,1) was set up.

✦ NPV(*rate, values-1,values-2,...*). The NPV function returns the net present value of a series of future cash flows based on a (discount) interest rate. The argument *rate* is the interest rate in points. *Values* are cash flows, positive and negative, occurring at regular intervals.

As an example of the NPV, consider a $2,000 loan you make to a friend. He pays it back with 24 loan payments of $100 made at a 12 percent interest rate compounded monthly. The function NPV(1%,A1:A25), where A1=–$2,000, and A2 through A25 all equal $100, returns the money you make on the loan, $200.31.

✦ Pmt(*rate,nper,pv,fv,type*). This function returns the periodic payment of an investment provided there are constant cash flows. Arguments are the same as for NPer above.

As an example of Pmt, a lease on a $25,000 Toyota 4Runner, with a loan of 12 percent paid off in 60 months at the beginning of every month, with $10,000 to remain after the loan is paid off, results in the formula Pmt(.01,60,$25000,$0,1), which returns a monthly payment of $429.37. Buy the Pathfinder instead.

✦ PV(*rate,nper,pmt,fv,type*). This function returns the present value of an investment. Arguments are the same as for Pmt, plus Pmt itself, payments.

For example, the present value of a $50,000 Whole Life insurance policy will pay $1,000 every month on the last day of the month for 20 years at 12 percent interest when you turn 60. The formula to evaluate this policy is PV(12%,10,$500,$30000,0), which returns the amount $90,819.41. This is a profit of $40,819.41.

◆ Rate(*nper,pmt,pv,fv,type,guess*). This function returns the growth of an invest-ment. The arguments are the same as above. *Guess* refers to a starting point for solving the problem. At your option, you can enter a percentage amount or leave it out. The default is 10 percent. This function is calculated using the "iterative" method discussed earlier, which means that it tries to solve the equation 20 times and then, if it fails, returns *Error*.

In the preceding example, the insurance policy was a loan in which you lent $50,000 to the insurance company, and they paid you $90,819.41 over 45 years. To assess the rate, the formula Rate(45,($90819.41/45),–50000,0,0) is used, returning 2.94 percent. That's a very poor return; try putting your money into utility companies instead.

Date and time functions

Using date and time functions you can include event-specific information in your formulas. You can use date and time functions to calculate the number of days in a project or period, or to figure the time intervals between events. You can manipu-late the information using any combination of day, month, year, and time (in hours, minutes, and seconds).

For example, you could create a formula using date and time functions to figure out billable hours. You could enter the start date and time in one cell and later enter the completed date and time. A formula would calculate the elapsed time in hours (and fractions of hours) as well as calculate the total bill by multiplying the hours by a pay rate to return a dollar amount.

Works does not store dates and times for its own calculations the way you would write them. Instead, it has a serial number system for dates (from 0 to 49710, 0 being January 1, 1904, and 49710 being February 6, 2040). Works understands and can translate between a variety of normal date formats and its serial coding system. For example, 1/1/04 and Jan 4, 1904, are both understood by Works as 0. (Date and time formats were explained in Topic 6.)

Times are stored as decimal fractions of whole-date integers. For example, 32300.5 is the serial-decimal code for 12:00 p.m. on September 15, 1992. The 32300 is the date, and the (.5) is one-half of a 24-hour cycle, or noon. Time by itself, for example, might be 0.75 — which is decimal code for 6:00 p.m., or 18.00 hours (18 is 0.75 of the full 24-hour day). You can enter dates and times "normally," or you can enter the serial number yourself — although you probably wouldn't want to. See below.

The arguments for date and time functions are:

◆ *year*. Any year from 1904 to 2040 is valid.

◆ *month*. Any month from 1 to 12, or January through December is valid. Works can recognize months written in the styles of August or Aug and convert them to the serial month value 8.

◆ *day.* Any day between 1 and 31 is valid. For serial dates, Works recognizes the correct number of days in a specific month.

◆ *hour.* Hours can be from 1 to 23, with serial hours being equal fractions of ¼ or 0.04166667 of a day. Thus, 12 hours is 0.5 days.

◆ *minute.* Minutes can take a value of 1 to 59. Serial minutes are fractions of an hour, ⅟₆₀, which is converted to fractions of a day, ⅟₁₄₆₀ or 0.00069444 of a day.

◆ *second.* Seconds can take the value of 1 to 59. Serial seconds are converted to fractions of a day, ⅟₈₆₄₀₀ or 0.00001157. You need not remember the serial conversion factors; Works calculates them for you.

◆ *cell references.* That is, a cell address containing dates or times.

Many date and time functions "extract" one element of a date or time expression, for example, using only the minutes from 12:43:02 for a particular calculation. What the referenced cell must contain varies according to each function's purpose. There is also one date and time function, Now(), which takes no arguments. Now() returns the serial code for the current date and time. A number of functions provide only serial numbered dates and times.

Works uses a variety of methods for computing dates and times. Depending on the use of the value, Works converts between a number of serial formats — most of the date and time functions that are used change these formats to the most appropriate type or displayed format. To apply date and time functions, dates must be internally formatted either as dates or as numbers. The number format is available as an option under the Format menu and returns the serial number of a date and/or time. For more information on formatting, refer back to Topic 7.

Works' date and time functions translate values into a variety of forms to serve every computational need. Works treats the dates and times as serial numbers to standardize them on a scale that allows their easy internal conversion. Serial dates allow mathematical operations to be performed on dates and times. So although subtracting the value "March 1, 1990" from the value "May 25, 1993" has no real meaning, Works interprets it as finding the period between the two dates. These dates are held internally as the serial date values 31471 and 32652; subtracting them yields the elapsed number of days, displayed as 1181. Because serial dates are numbers, you can use them freely in formulas to find other quantities. The amount of money paid to a writer is $8/hour, when multiplied by the time (9 a.m. – 5 p.m.) yields $64. The times are converted to serial numbers, yielding 8.0 hours.

Most of the functions of date and time in Works use only cell references as arguments. This means that all date and time functions do is convert selected elements of dates and times into the serial dates for various uses.

The date and time functions are:

♦ Date(*year,month,day*). Returns the serial number to the date you specify.

Using the Date function, January 1, 1993, is evaluated as Date(1993,1,1), returning the number 32508. The Date function is normally the one you use when doing serial arithmetic.

♦ Day(*cell-reference*). Extracts the day of the month from an existing, entered date.

For example, if A1 contains 11/16/88, Day(A1) returns 16. Works uses a 1 to 31 scale for days in a month.

♦ Hour(*cell-reference*). Extracts the hour from an existing, entered time value. Hours are valued 0 to 23 (a one-day scale).

For a time entered into a cell of 5:34:22 p.m., the function Hour(8:34:22) returns 20 into a field that is formatted as a number. Internally, this serial time is the fraction 0.7322 of a day and is rounded up to the next whole hour's serial number.

♦ Minute(*cell-reference*). Extracts the minutes from an existing, entered time value. Minute values are expressed here on a 0 to 59 scale (per hour scale).

In the example above, Min(8:34:22 PM) returns the value 34, provided that you have selected the number display format for that cell or field.

♦ Month(*cell-reference*). Extracts the month from an existing, entered date. Months are valued on a 1 to 12 (annual) scale.

For example, Month(B2), when B2 contains August 27, 1952, will return the number 8, provided that you have selected the number format for display of that cell or field.

♦ Now(). Returns the current date and time in serial code. The Now function is controlled by your Macintosh's internal clock setting. Use the Alarm Clock DA or General Control Panel to change the current date and time.

Note that having many Now functions in a worksheet or database will slow down the operation as the function calculates. If what you want is a single date and time, and not the instant update that Now provides, consider copying and pasting the result of the Now function into the cell or field.

♦ Second(*cell-reference*). Extracts the seconds from an existing, entered time value. Seconds are valued 0 to 59 (a one-minute scale).

The Second function returns the numerical value of 22 when the time 8:34:22 p.m. is used as an argument.

♦ Time(*hour,minutes,seconds*). Returns the serial number for a time you specify.

♦ Weekday(*cell-reference*). Extracts the day-of-the-week from an entered date. Weekdays are valued 1 to 7: 1 is Sunday, 2 is Monday, ..., 7 is Saturday.

The Weekday function can be valuable in determining a number of logical functions. You can specify that someone only be paid if a day of the week is in the range 2 to 6 (Monday to Friday), or that a value like the number of weeks employed increment on a weekday of 6.

♦ Year(*cell-reference*). Extracts the year from an entered date. Years can be in the range of 1904 to 2040. If you enter only a two-digit number, Works assumes that the prefix is 19 and that you meant this century for the date.

The Mac has "one up" on mainframes, where only a two-digit year code was used in many older cases. Chaos results when the new century begins — some very sophisticated software will have to be rewritten at great price.

Special-purpose functions

Works provides nine miscellaneous functions that fall into several categories. One category of functions provides a comparison based on cells in different locations and values you specify: The Lookup, Match, and Choose functions are examples. These comparison functions look at data in one cell, and provide a value based on that data. Still other functions look for various error messages.

Special purpose functions are:

♦ Choose(*index,value-1,value-2,...*). The Choose function returns a value from the list of *values* based on the *index* reference. An *index* is an integer that Works uses to count off cell places. An *index* of 3 will return the value in the third cell or a range of cells. An *index* number of less than one, a non-integer number, or an integer that is larger than the number of values in the argument list returns the *Error* value.

⬛ File Edit Format Options Chart Window

A16		=Choose(5,A15:E15)

Choose Function (SS)

	A	B	C	D	E
15	5	10	15	20	25
16	25				
17					

For example, if cell A15 contains the number 5 and cell E15 contains the number 25, then Choose(5,A15:E15) returns the number in A16, or 25. If cell A16 is blank, then *Error* would be returned; but for a cell containing the value 0, 0 would be returned.

♦ Error(). The Error function returns the value *Error*. Use this function to test formulas. Like the NA, True, and False functions, the Error function returns a known value to test formulas.

Lookup functions search a table and return a value in that table. An index number is used to determine where in the table to look to find the value to be returned. There are three lookups: the lookup function, Lookup; the horizontal lookup, HLookup; and the vertical lookup function, VLookup. They are functionally identical, except for the direction in which they search a table based on that index number.

◆ Lookup(*lookup-value,compare-range,result-range*). Lookup locates the cell in *compare-range* that contains the largest value less than or equal to (≤) *lookup-value* and returns the value in *result-range* that is in the same relative location.

The values in *compare-range* must be in ascending order — 1,2,3,... going from bottom to top or left to right — for this function to operate properly. The *lookup-value* should not be smaller than the smallest value in that range. If it is, you'll get the *Error* message because no cell may be selected in the compare range. The two argument ranges should be:

1. **The same length.** They must contain the same number of cells.

2. **One-dimensional.** Each range can only be rows or columns.

3. **Either dimension.** You can mix a column range for one argument with a row range with the other argument.

Because the Lookup function uses two ranges, once the compare-range is queried, this function can search a spreadsheet in any location for the value corresponding to the compare-range value. The example shown in the following figure should clarify the Lookup function.

	A	B	C	D
1	300			
2	20	25	30	35
3				
4	100	200	300	400
5				

In the above figure, the Lookup function checks the lookup-range A2:D2 for a match of the index value 30. That match is found in C2, the third cell in the range. Then Lookup searches the result-range for the third value, returning the result 300.

The HLookup and VLookup functions are really just a special case of the Lookup function with more limited functionality. Here, instead of a second result-range being used, an index number points a number of rows in either the vertical or horizontal direction, respectively. These two lookup functions are the ones most classically associated with finding values in simple tables.

◆ HLookup(*lookup-value,compare-range,index-number*). HLookup locates the cell in the first row of *compare-range* with the largest value less than or equal to *lookup-value*. The lookup-value is the value being matched to a table of values. HLookup moves up or down in a table by the value of the cell specified by *index-number*.

In HLookup, *index-number* can be a positive number, a negative number, or 0. A number 1 tells HLookup to provide the value from the first (or top) row of the specified range; 2 uses the second row; 0 uses the row immediately above; –1, the value two rows above; –3, the value three rows above the range; and so on.

◆ VLookup(*lookup-value,compare-range,index-number*). VLookup locates the cell in the first column of *compare-range* with the largest value less than or equal to *lookup-value*, and then moves right or left to provide the value of the cell specified by *index-number*. The values in the first column of the range must be in ascending order. The arguments are the same as for HLookup and Lookup.

Here *index-number* is the number of cells VLookup is instructed to move right or left. For the *index-number* of 1, the *compare-range* column is used; 2 uses the value in the second column to the right of the range; 0 uses the value in the column immediately to the right; and –3, the value four columns to the left of the range.

⚫ File	Edit	Format	Options	Chart	Window
A1		=VLookup(0.3,A2:A6,4)			

VLookup (SS)

	A	B	C	D
1	300			
2	0.1	1	10	100
3	0.2	2	20	200
4	0.3	3	30	300
5	0.4	4	40	400
6	0.5	5	50	500
7				

The example shown above should help to clarify the use of the VLookup function. In this example, the VLookup function searches the compare-range A2:A6 for the lookup-value 0.3. It finds it in cell A4, and then moves three columns to the right to D4 because the index number is 4.

All three lookup functions — Lookup, HLookup, and VLookup — are only available in the spreadsheet and not in the Database module.

◆ Index(*range,row,column*). The Index function returns the value of the cell with a relative location in *range* specified by the arguments. You can think of the row and column values as specifying a vector of a length and direction pointing from the top-left corner of the range to the cell that is used to return the resulting value.

For example, Index(B1:D1,1,2) returns the value of cell reference C1. If B1 contains the number 10, and B2 contains the number 4, Index(B1:B2,1,1) returns the value of B2, which is 4. **Note:** Row and column references of 0,0 will always provide the value of cell A1.

Index is used in the spreadsheet only and not in the Database module.

✦ Match(*lookup-value,compare-range,match-type*). The Match function returns the number of the comparison in the *compare-range* that matches the *lookup-value*. When the *lookup-value* matches the first comparison number, the function returns 1, a match of the second value returns a 2, and so on. The Match function is the complement or opposite of the Choose function. Match finds a value in a list and returns its placement in that list; Choose takes the placement in a list and returns its value.

The argument *match-type* either counts the number of values greather than or equal to or less than or equal to the *lookup-value*. Match returns the location number relative to the *compare-range* of the cell that contains the value that matches *lookup-value*. Relative to the range means that in range C2:C5, the location value 3 would refer to cell C4.

Match-type is based on the choices shown in the following table:

Table 11-1:	Match values	
match-type	**Match returns**	**compare-range**
1	The largest value in a series less than or equal to the lookup-value	In ascending order: ...0, 1, 2, 3...
0	The first value in a series that is equal to the lookup-value	In any order
-1	The smallest value in a series greater than or equal to the lookup-value	In descending order: ...3, 2, 1, 0...
2	Text or blank value	A single value
8	Error value N/A	A single value
16	Error value *Error*	A single value

For a series from A1:E1, of 2, 4, 6, 8, and 10, the expression Match(5,A1:E1,1) yields 2 because the second value (4) is the largest value greater than or equal to 5; Match(5,A1:E1,0) returns *Error* because there is no matching value; and Match(5,A1:E1,-1) also returns *Error* because the series is in ascending order. With the same series, Match(6,A1:E1,1) returns 3, Match(6,A1:E1,0) returns 2, and Match(6,A1:E1,-1) returns *Error*.

The Match function can only be used in spreadsheets and not in databases.

✦ NA(). This function returns the value N/A. Again, this is mainly useful for returning a known value to test a formula.

The formula If(IsNA(B2)1,0) returns a 1 or TRUE if B2 contains a N/A value, or 0 otherwise.

♦ Type(*value*). This function returns the type of *value*. Type gives 1 when the value is a number, 2 for text or blank values in a cell, and 16 when there is an *Error* message in the cell.

For example, Type(B2) returns 2 when the cell B2 contains "Barrie," 1 when B2 contains the number 10, and 16 when B2 shows an *Error* message.

Next, we'll briefly consider some ways to use functions, the limits of functions, and the differences between the spreadsheet in Works and Microsoft's full-blown spreadsheet, the best-selling Excel.

Using functions

Every function serves an important purpose and will make using your spreadsheet and database *easier*. Of the 64 functions, you may discover you only use 10 to 15 regularly. Works contains a solid sampler of the functions most commonly used in larger spreadsheet and database applications. The logic of integrated software is to provide you with a cost-effective way to get the best and most important elements of the most important Macintosh software in a friendly, fast, affordable package.

Excel, by comparison, has about 170 functions, although you will still find yourself using the same 10 to 15 functions in your projects. What you pay for in these larger packages is the availability of that one special function for the times when you need it.

You can be as adventurous as you like with functions. Although each function performs one very specific search, translation, or calculation, these functions provide a very powerful formula construction-set to meet the most demanding single-user data management needs. Remember, Microsoft could have used any of the 170 Excel functions in Works; it chose the best based on considerable user input.

Quick Tips

The following tips show you how to decide on which function to use in a given situation and tell you what general limitations exist in functions.

Deciding which function to use

Some functions are easier to figure out than others, and there is nearly always an alternative way of constructing a spreadsheet to attain a result. In general, the most useful functions are Date, If, Round, the Lookup functions, ISNA, Average, SUM, MAX, MIN, Count, and Choose. Concentrate on learning to use these functions well as a first step in mastering database and spreadsheet construction.

You might want to refer back to the Topics on databases (Topic 6) and spreadsheets (Topic 7); these topics contain advice on logical construction. Keep in mind these following old saws:

♦ Start with what you're trying to solve. Spreadsheets and databases "figure" problems. The result you need is the first filter in determining which function you can use. The next consideration is the availability and nature of the data, which limits you even further. Often the function is obvious at this point. If it isn't, you will need to either use a combination of functions or a data conversion.

♦ Make the calculation a modular problem. Isolate the *elements* of the problems you're trying to solve. Break big problems into a series of little ones and combine them to make larger formulas.

To figure a budget of a department, break the project into its component parts and work up from there. If you're trying to create a spreadsheet to calculate the hours, pay, tax withholdings, overtime, and pay-due-dates for five employees, all of whom started on different days, what elements can be isolated? You're dealing with:

♦ Time in hours

♦ Time (hours) as a dollar amount

♦ Taxes as a percentage (rate) of that dollar amount

♦ Time in hours relative to other hours

♦ A dollar amount relative to that number

♦ Dates relative to other dates

♦ All five sets of the above

Two things are apparent. First, Works has functions to directly handle all or most of these calculations instantly. Works also returns "manual entry" formula choices that easily dispense with the rest. Looking back through the tables in this Topic, you will easily find the functions you need — and the ways in which to combine them can be obvious or more complicated depending on how complex you want your formulas to be.

Second, a number of formula possibilities exist. You need to add up hours and turn those hours into a dollar amount, from which a certain percentage is then removed. That presents one fairly easy formula. You could create another formula — a logical function-based formula — to figure overtime (for example, IF a worker works over 40 hours THEN his pay increases to 1.5x for each subsequent hour). And so on.

Using the Copy and Paste commands, you can create a separate spreadsheet for each employee (so you only write each formula or formula-set once) or, feeling brave, you can create a more complex spreadsheet or database file that accounts for and separates all five, or 50, employees. Remember, you can use spreadsheet blocks for this purpose, creating value tables to make changing the spreadsheet calculations a one-step process. Always ask yourself this question: What will happen to my work if this value changes? If the construction doesn't allow this flexibility, then it's time to consider a different approach.

Function limitations

Functions are really only limited in the sense that they do one thing and one thing only. This is like having a Swiss Army knife with 64 blades, but unlike the knife, you can't open a box with the ruler or scale a fish with the screwdriver. Each "blade" (function) is limited only to the purpose for which it was designed. So, you're stuck with a rigid and potentially frustrating limited set of choices. On the other hand, you have a large set of task-specific, reliable, and dedicated tools.

The limitations of a function are determined by the data it evaluates, the range or comparison it provides, and the type of data the function returns. When you think in those terms, each function's limitations become pretty obvious. The process of determining a function's limitations is exactly the reverse process of determining that function's suitability for a task.

Functions are "limited" in another, more ephemeral way — you might want to do something that none of the functions was designed to do, or even that some crazy combination of Works' functions *still can't do*. The 64 functions are a lot, but they aren't always enough. The 64 Microsoft chose for you might not be the 64 you would've chosen for yourself. Ask yourself: Do you really need to carry around the baggage of a large specific application just to get an extra function or two, once in a while? If not, use that larger program to massage the data into a form Works can use. If the answer is often yes, perhaps it's a good time to have that first breathing number-crunching monster on your desktop machine. But, leave it home, and put Works on your PowerBook. Empty RAM is happy RAM.

Summary

✔ Functions are preformatted equations that you can select and paste into your spreadsheet and database documents.

✔ You can use functions alone or in larger formulas.

✔ Every function performs only one calculation.

✔ You enter variables or constants (the argument list) in parentheses into functions.

✔ Arguments can be cell references, numbers, dates, times, interest rates, or other data.

✔ Works has 64 functions — all are available in the Spreadsheet modules.

✔ Functions not available in the Database module include Lookup, HLookup, VLookup, Index, IRR, MIRR, and Match.

✔ The functions are arranged by category. Works has arithmetic, mathematical, statistical, logical, financial, trigonometric, date-and-time, and some special-purpose functions.

✔ To select and paste a function into the active cell, pull down the Edit menu and select the Paste Function command. In the Paste Function dialog box, select from the category list Radio buttons and the function from the scroll box on the right.

✔ You can combine functions to create formulas for your specific project applications.

Topic 12
Exchanging Information

Overview

In order to achieve the full benefit of using an integrated package, you must be able to transfer data between Works modules easily. In this day and age, importing and exporting data to and from other applications, and using data from other computers is a necessity. In this Topic you will learn how to accomplish these tasks easily. The facilities in Works 3 represent a major upgrade compared to the previous version of the program and reflect the changing nature of the Macintosh's world.

Works makes transferring information almost transparent. Using the Macintosh Clipboard, you can transfer information between Works modules and other Macintosh applications. Some of these details were covered in Topic 2, in the section "Using the Macintosh Clipboard and Scrapbook," but this Topic looks at the subject in more depth. For importing and exporting files, Works uses a set of translation filters to convert from one type of data to another.

It's important to understand different data types so that you can select the correct filter or save a file in the correct format. Most of the times this simply requires that you know the source or destination of the information by program name and select that program in a pop-up menu. However, understanding the nature and the intended use of the data will make it easier to make the right selections, even when you aren't sure exactly in what programs it will be used. Sometimes you need to save files in a standard, non-program specific format. This Topic tells you how and which ones are best.

Understanding data basics

Data is the information your computer reads and writes, specified in the binary code of 1s and 0s. Computers can handle many different forms of information:

+ *Text*. The simplest kind of information. Your Macintosh uses the ASCII code to handle alphanumeric characters, special symbols, and control codes. This was discussed in Topic 9, "Using Works' Communications."

+ *Specialized text*. Databases and spreadsheets use characters to represent a jump to the next column or field, and to the next row or record. For example, a tab or comma character can mean "go to the next row or column," and a carriage return means "go to the next record or row." This is the basis for the TSV and CSV formats. Other kinds of text can describe formatting information in a text-only file. These are useful for moving information between disparate applications. For example, in a word processor, a symbol in the ASCII code that is not used as part of the basic character set can be used for bolding, another for italics, and so on. Different word processors assign symbols in the ASCII code in different ways.

✦ *Images*. Pictures, as discussed in Topic 5, "Using the Draw Module," can be stored either as bit maps (paint graphics) or mathematical relationships called *vectors* (drawn images). These two different image types are stored in different data representations.

✦ *Sound*. Digitized sound or voice is also stored in a computer file and contains information on which notes are played (their frequency) and for how long (their duration).

✦ *Video*. Moving pictures are a specialized kind of image and use special data descriptions. Apple's QuickTime is an example of a video specification.

Works makes heavy use of text, specialized text, drawn images, and imported paint images. At the present time, Works doesn't use sound or video internally; any capabilities present are those due to Macintosh system software. Undoubtedly, future versions of Works will incorporate the advanced capabilities of sight and sound being developed on the Macintosh.

Learning about file formats

Data, as you learned in the section "Filing with your Macintosh" in Topic 2, is stored in files. A file is marked in the file system, and can be stored anywhere on a disk. Files can be placed in contiguous sectors on a disk, or in various pieces scattered about the disk, depending on the disk's current usage. Data in files is stored in a special way or form called a *file format*. There are different formats depending on what computer is being used, what program is using it, the version of the program, and what kinds of data are included.

For example, Macintosh files are saved in two separate sections within the same file: a data section called the Data Fork and a resource section called the Resource Fork. Data is anything written to the file; resources are pictures, sounds, and other objects that can be used by an application. Files saved in the MS-DOS format have only a single section, so translation back and forth requires that file information be transformed into a single part for DOS. The hardware and software requirements to transfer data between Works on the Macintosh, and programs on the IBM PC (including Works or Works for Windows) is described in the section "Exchanging data between the IBM PC and Works."

Programs also save files in a special form called a *native file format* that is dependent both on the program and on the program version. Thus, you will find three versions of Works (Mac) files for 1.0, 2.0, and 3.0. Similarly, MS Word (Mac) has five versions from 1.0 to 5.0. Each one is slightly different from the next. Most people use either the current version, or the next to the most current version of the program, which simplifies the task of translation somewhat. Also, not every version requires a different file format, although most do.

Native applications cannot be used by other applications without translation. If a file is launched and the creator application is not found, then your Macintosh will post an alert box stating: "The Application is Either Busy or Missing." You can often open that file using the Open command within another application. Therefore, if you attempt to open a MacWrite file and MacWrite is not on your hard drive, then the file will not launch. You can use the Works Open command to translate the file first and then have it open within Works. Even if it appears that a program can use another's files, some kind of translation is occurring automatically in the background. Should you want to have your Works files open within MacWrite, you can save a Works file in the MacWrite format.

Some file formats are application-independent; they are agreed to by convention as being standard. The simple text or ASCII format is one such example. Another is the Microsoft's Rich Text Format, or RTF, a text description of formatted word processing files that can be opened by various applications. SYLK, the Microsoft spreadsheet format, or CSV, the database format, are other examples of standards that can be used in various applications. ASCII, RTF, SYLK, and CSV are examples of files in what's called an *interchange* format. An example of a graphics interchange file format is CompuServe's Graphics Interchange Format, or GIF. Interchange formats offer very good translation with few errors because they are true standards. Usually, an interchange format is specified by one, two, or three large software developers. It's counterintuitive, but the more developers, the less standard formats generally are.

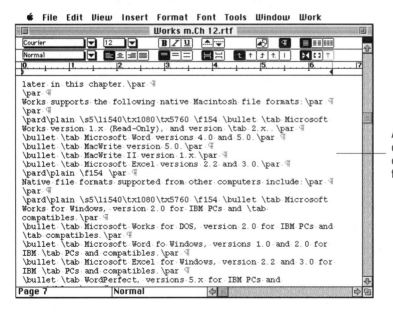

A Microsoft Word document in RTF format displays perfectly formatted in Works

Numerous graphics file formats are in use, including the four most important for Macintosh users: PICT, MacPaint (or simply Paint) format, Tagged Image File Format (TIFF or .TIF on the PC), and Encapsulated PostScript (EPS). Apple's PICT format is the general graphics format supported by the Clipboard; it can accommodate both object and bitmapped graphics. There are two versions: PICT and the newer color standard PICT2. Works supports them both equally well. PICT is for all intents and purposes a standard, and it serves the function of an interchange format in many cases. MacPaint is also supported by the Clipboard, but is limited in resolution to 72 dpi, and only supports bitmaps. MacPaint is fairly crude by today's standards, but is used for libraries of artwork (clip art) and is ubiquitous.

There are two forms or EPS and six versions of TIFF, making for translation errors in a few cases. Errors are rare and limited to older programs. However, TIFF and EPS are the two best supported cross-platform (between computers) graphic file format standards. PICT is the favored format for graphics on the Macintosh, TIFF is the recommended format for bitmapped images, and EPS is your best choice for drawn images. File translation programs generally do a good job with any of these three formats. Works opens and saves graphics only in PICT, so you need to translate graphics files to PICT to use them in Works.

Many, many other formats exist, particularly on the IBM PC for graphics. Some of the formats you may encounter there include ZSoft's .PCX, Windows' Bitmap (.BMP), Computer Graphics' Metafile (.CGM), Autograph's Data Exchange Format (.DFX), and Windows' Metafile (.WFM) to name but a few. Your task of moving data about is eased when you can convert to one of the more commonly used file formats mentioned above. Numerous file translation utilities exist to supplement the capabilities of Works. They are discussed in "Using file translation utilities," later in this Topic.

Works supports the following native Macintosh file formats:

♦ Microsoft Works versions 1.x (Read-Only), and versions 2.x.

♦ Microsoft Word versions 4.0 and 5.0.

♦ MacWrite version 5.0.

♦ MacWrite II version 1.x.

♦ Microsoft Excel versions 2.2 and 3.0.

Native file formats supported from other computers include the following:

♦ Microsoft Works for Windows, version 2.0 for IBM PCs and compatibles.

♦ Microsoft Works for DOS, version 2.0 for IBM PCs and compatibles.

♦ Microsoft Word for Windows, versions 1.0 and 2.0 for IBM PCs and compatibles.

♦ Microsoft Excel for Windows, versions 2.2 and 3.0 for IBM PCs and compatibles.

- WordPerfect, versions 5.x for IBM PCs and compatibles.

- Lotus 1-2-3, versions 2.x for IBM PCs and compatibles in the .WKS and .WK1 formats.

- AppleWorks, versions 2.0 and 3.0 for the Apple II series computers.

- AppleWorks GS (word processor only) for the Apple IIGS computer.

To use native file formats from another computer on a Macintosh, you must have a 1.4MB SuperDrive floppy disk drive and special software. Details are given for the mounting of MS-DOS or ProDOS (Apple II) disks in the section "Exchanging data between the IBM PC and Works."

Works also supports some standard file formats and some interchange formats that are application-independent. They are

- *Text*. Text is in ASCII, although RTF files are a specialized text format.

- *Rich Text Format, or RTF*. This format is an interchange format in the form of a text file that describes both text and formatting.

- *Symbolic Link, or SYLK*. This is the Microsoft spreadsheet interchange format used in Excel and some other database programs. SYLK can contain not only data, but formulas, too.

- *.WKS or .WK1 or Lotus 1-2-3*. This is the native file format.

- *Comma Separated Values, or CSV*. This is a standard database or spreadsheet format. In CSV, values are separated by commas and sets of values are separabed by paragraphs.

- *PICT2 (and PICT)*. This is the standard Macintosh graphics format.

Both CSV and SYLK are in a format that is commonly referred to as *delimited data*. Each value is separated by a character. CSV, the most common interchange format for databases and spreadsheets, derives from the BASIC language data structure. A delimiter is any character used to separate data. Here, the comma character separates value, while the Return character marks the ends of paragraphs, lines, rows, or records depending on the context. Both are delimiters.

It's fairly easy to convert files saved with delimiters. Utilities make the conversion automatic. You can also open those files in a text editor or word processor (as text), and do a search-and-replace operation to change the format structure. Besides CSV, there is also a Tab Separated Values, or TSV, format that is used in the STYL format of the Clipboard to transfer data between Works modules. Here tabs are used in place of commas, and the structure is described as tab-delimited files.

Works installs all of the filters for these conversions when you use the Easy Install option. Should you choose the Customize option, you may need to install the translation filters manually. These filters appear as documents inside the Conversions folder, which is inside the Tools folder in Works.

Works 2.had a very awkward utility called the Works-Works Transporter that disappeared in this current version. Works 3, uses translation filters from DataViz (Trumbull, CT) found in the more complete MacLink Plus/PC package that is discussed in more detail in the "Using file transfer utilities" section later in this Topic.

Cutting and pasting

Data used internally in Works modules is in one of the Macintosh standard file formats. You can use both the Clipboard and the Scrapbook as intermediaries for cutting and pasting data. If there isn't enough RAM to accomplish a cut and paste, try using smaller pieces of data to move, and repeating the process. This was described in Topic 2 in the section "Using the Macintosh Clipboard and Scrapbook." Using the Clipboard with Works is described in this section. The Scrapbook is a file that appears in the Apple menu, provided that it is on the startup disk you used. Information in any format can be stored in a Scrapbook, and copied and pasted into a document. You can buy utilities that allow you to create and work with multiple Clipboards (MultiClip) and Scrapbooks (SmartScrap and the Clipper). Solutions International, the publisher of SmartScrap and the Clipper, is no longer in business, so you might have to search around for a copy of this useful utility.

Both text and graphics is accommodated by the Clipboard using the STYLE or PICT formats, respectively. Text with or without formatting is saved in the internal STYL format of the Clipboard. Text in a word processor is copied with all formatting intact from one Works word processor document to another.

Database and spreadsheet data are copied in a similar manner. Database data is copied with field names followed by the selected records. Only the names of the fields with data that were selected are copied to the Clipboard. If you hold down the Option key while using the Paste command with database data, then the field name line is not copied to the word processor. Spreadsheet data is copied to the Clipboard with both row and column headers showing. If you open the Show Clipboard window, you can see the copied spreadsheet and database data with formatting.

However, if you try to copy spreadsheet or database data to a word processor, only text will be copied. The data from either of these modules is stored internally in the TSV, or Tab Separated Values, format; fields or cells separated by tabs, and records or rows separated by Returns. You can't see the tab or paragraph marks in Works' word processor, but you can see them in Microsoft Word or another word processor that has a Show Paragraph or Show Invisibles command. You can see how data from a database is copied to the Clipboard and then appears in MS Word from the Clipboard. Data inside a communication document is essentially the same as data inside a word processor.

Copying data from a Works database using the Clipboard

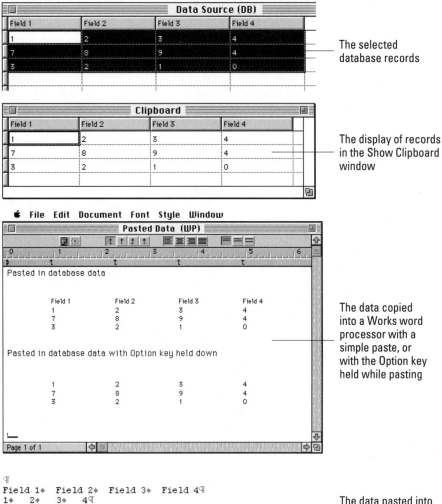

The selected database records

The display of records in the Show Clipboard window

The data copied into a Works word processor with a simple paste, or with the Option key held while pasting

The data pasted into Microsoft Word. Note the tabs and returns.

When copying data from one spreadsheet to another spreadsheet, or from one database to another database, Works places the data into the cells and rows or fields and records following the insertion point. Incoming data will overwrite any existing data, if needed. If Works can match the field names in a database to the incoming field names in the first record of the copied database records, then only the record data is copied — the field name header record is not copied. Data can be successfully transferred from a database to a spreadsheet or vice versa, provided that the data types of the recipient cells or fields are correct to accept the incoming data. For example, when you copy database data to a spreadsheet, one row of that spreadsheet will have cells containing the field names from the database. Going the other way, spreadsheet data will replace the appropriate number of fields and records by the incoming number of cells and fields.

The Draw module and draw layer creates graphics in the PICT format. The Clipboard can support both PICT data and STYL data, and it is smart enough to know which is the correct data to paste into a location. When copying drawn graphics, those graphics are pasted into the draw layer of any other module that supports draw. When copying both drawn and textual data, Works pastes those different data types into each of the two layers of a Works module. Remember, the word processor, spreadsheet, and database have draw layers; the Communications modules support drawn objects in the headers and footers only.

PICT is a rich format because it can support both object (vector or drawn) and bit-mapped (raster or paint) graphics. Unlike the MacPaint format, which is limited to bitmaps at 72 dpi, PICT2 can support much higher resolution. PICT serves not only as the internal data format for Works graphics, but you can also save files (as discussed previously) in the PICT file format. PICT2, used by the more recent Macintosh system software, supports full 24-bit color, color patterns, halftones, and many other graphic data. PICT, an older format, only supported eight colors and had much more limited capabilities. You are unlikely to use recent software that uses the older PICT, but the two formats are backwardly compatible. That is, PICT2 can open and use PICT data.

Using data inside Works

Works has its own format, and each version of Works has a somewhat different version of a file format. Generally, a later version of a program can open the file of an earlier version and translate it. Almost always that process is not complementary: You can't open a new file version in an older version of the application. Also, opening a file in the newer version converts the file and prevents you from opening that file again in the earlier version.

In Works 3 when you try to convert documents from Works 2, you will be able to successfully translate word processor and spreadsheet documents. The database documents from version 2.0 do not translate correctly and may require some reworking for version 3.0. Because so many of the communication settings and capabilities are new, communication documents need to be re-created from scratch. Draw documents are entirely new, and should you wish to place drawn objects from previous Works documents into a version 3.0 draw document, you will have to do so by copying and pasting the data. You should also not expect macro files to convert successfully.

The following table should help you in determining how to use information between Works modules:

Table 12-1:	Moving Data in Works	
Source	*Target*	*Results*
Word processor	Word processor	Formatted text is moved.
Word processor	Database	Text is copied to current field. If values are in TSV format, then field values are copied. Note that each field type must be correct.
Word processor	Spreadsheet	Text is copied to the current cell. If values are in SYLK, then cells and rows are copied.
Word processor	Draw	Text is copied and pasted into text objects.
Database	Word processor	Records become lines, values are separated by tabs. The first record contains values with the field names, unless you hold down the Option key while pasting.
Database	Database	If field names match, data is copied from field to field and record to record. If field names don't match, the first record contains field names, and all subsequent records are copied into fields. Data types must match for the copied values to transfer in the latter case.
Database	Spreadsheet	The first row contains field names, all records are turned into additional rows, and fields into cells.
Database	Communication	Same as word processor to word processor.
Report	Word processor	Only totals and subtotals are copied.
Spreadsheet	Word processors	Values are pasted as text if Show Formulas is not active. Text is in TSV format. If Show Formulas is active, then formula values are shown.
Spreadsheet	Database	Rows become records, cells become fields. Only values are moved.
Spreadsheet	Spreadsheet	Cell references, values, and equations are converted to the new appropriate location.
Chart	Other modules	Becomes a drawn graphic, no longer linked to data.
Draw	Other modules	Puts objects in draw layer. In Communications document, objects can appear in only headers or footers.
Draw layer	Draw	All objects all transfer correctly.
Communications	Other modules	Same as word processor.

Importing and Exporting

Importing and exporting data is the process of converting data to a file format that can be opened (read) or saved (written) by another application. Importing means to bring data into a program; exporting means to send data out of a program. When that application is on the same computer, then no further conversion is required. When you are transferring a file to another application on a different computer, you must also do the conversion required by that computer's file system. Works can write the data into another computer file format, but the disk must also be properly formatted in that other computer's formatting.

The terms importing and exporting are rather loosely applied. Because the Clipboard is used so often, occasionally people refer to moving data through the Clipboard as importing or exporting when another application is involved. This is not correct usage. Importing and exporting involves a permanent change in file format, and not the use of an intermediary format like Text, STYL, or PICT.

Understanding filters

A filter is a conversion routine that translates all of the information from one file format to another. To give you a general idea of how filters work, consider how text is used in a word processor. Text can be saved in ASCII format. ASCII has 256 characters (8-bit bytes), and only the first 128 characters need be assigned to alphanumeric characters, symbols, and important control characters like spaces, tabs, returns, and so on. The remaining 128 characters, called *upper*ASCII, are used to specify formatting within a word processor. How formatting is accomplished is some of the art and proprietary know-how of a good word processor. A translation from one word processor to another converts all of these formatting characters correctly.

Works uses the word *filter* to describe the stored criteria used in a database search, as you saw in Topic 6. A file translation filter is a conversion routine, and different in nature from the search routine used in a database. The translation utility doesn't search for part of the data set; it simply transposes the data into another form. Don't be confused by the use of the same word in both instances.

Graphics files are more complicated, but work on more or less the same principle. A graphics file may have a description of the data type and structure in an area of the file called the *header,* and the actual data follows that header. The data ends at an end-of-file mark. This construction is actually found for all file structures. In a bit map file, the data structure describes both the position (location) of a picture element in the bit map, and the color or gray scale value of the pixel. Conversion of one bit map file format to another changes the nature of the header, the way the bit map is described, and also the end-of-file marker.

Do yourself a favor — don't worry about how file formats are translated; programmers are paid to do that. Concentrate on what kind of data the file represents, how best to convert it, and what conversions should be most successful. Works has provided you with a good set of the most important translations, and they should suffice. Only TIFF and EPS graphics formats are missing from that basic set, as is the XTND system developed by Claris. The section "Using file translation utilities" discusses programs that translate hundreds of formats.

Importing a file means opening a file created in another application. When Works can't open a file, it appears dimmed in the Open standard file dialog box.

Importing a file:

1. **Select the Open command from the File menu, or press the Command-O keystroke.** The Open dialog box appears.

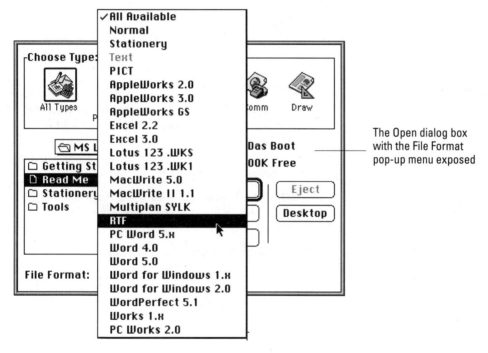

The Open dialog box with the File Format pop-up menu exposed

2. **To create a new document as a specific type, click on the document type icon in the Open dialog box to highlight it.**

3. **Select the All Available format if you wish to see all possible files that Works can convert.** The All Available filter is the default choice and is normally the one selected.

4. **To see files of a specific file format, select that format by name from the File Format pop-up list.**

To see a disk formatted in another computer's file structure in the Open or Save dialog boxes, you need to mount that disk on the Macintosh desktop. This requires SuperDrive, and either the Apple File Exchange or better yet the DOS

Mounter or Argosy Software's Mount PC utility. Other options for mounting non-Macintosh disks are discussed in "Exchanging data between the IBM PC and Works" later in this Topic.

5. **Select the name of the file you wish to open in the scrolling file list to highlight it and then click the Open button or press the Return or Enter key.**

— or —

5. **Double-click on the filename of the file you want to open.**

6. **Works converts the file to the type of document you selected and opens it in an untitled window.**

Exporting data involves saving that data in a form that another application can read.

Exporting a file:

1. **Select the Save As command from the File menu.**

2. **Choose the File Format type you wish to save in by clicking on the pop-up menu and selecting it by name.** For example, to save a file for use in MacWrite II, choose that format, or for use in Lotus 1-2-3, choose the Lotus 1-2-3 format. When the application format doesn't exist, use an interchange format. For example, use CSV to transfer a file into dBASE.

3. **Enter the filename in the Save As text box.** It's a good idea to name a file in a fashion that reminds you of the format. For RTF, consider adding .rtf to the filename, and so on.

4. **Click the Save button, or press the Return or Enter key.**

To save files for programs available on another disk, you will need to mount a disk formatted in that system software's format. See "Exchanging data between the IBM PC and Works" later in this Topic.

More about working with tables

Although Works doesn't offer a special format for constructing and working with tables, here are some guidelines that you may want to consider. You can create tables in word processor documents using the TSV format. Here, columns in table entries are separated using tabs, and rows in tables are separated using Returns or paragraph marks. To format the paragraph, apply tab and margin settings to each row (paragraph) and adjust interline spacing as required. All other formatting, character formatting, and paragraph formatting will move successfully between word processor documents, and tables will copy correctly without some formatting into the spreadsheet and the database.

When cutting and pasting a table formatted in a word processor to another application on the Macintosh, often the formatting will disappear. You will be left with unformatted text, but at least it will be in the TSV format. It shouldn't take you too long to reformat that table. Microsoft Word 5 has a very nice text-to-table conversion feature that will work successfully on TSV data. A MS Word table is a special construct that enables you to isolate table entries as individual paragraphs within the table. You can also save that table in CSV format for use in other applications like dBASE.

Should you wish to preserve formatting information in tables, use data from a spreadsheet or database. I find that the spreadsheet is the most convenient module for large table construction. Data transferred from those sources is in the TSV format, which is already a table format. CSV will work equally as well. You can also save data in file formats that will preserve character and paragraph formatting information.

SYLK allows you to save formatting information from your file for export. If you open SYLK data in another word processor, you may find that you will still have to create tab settings but that character settings are intact. Creating a table from imported SYLK text will only require that the table columns and rows be sized, which may be a fraction of the work. SYLK will also preserve the underlying logic of the table, although that won't be useful in this situation. It is useful when you use SYLK to transfer data from one spreadsheet to another spreadsheet.

Introducing Workspaces

There will be times when you have exactly the right set of documents open on your desktop for a project. Moving information between those open documents using the Clipboard is very convenient. Sometimes you require more than one document for an operation — a mail merge is a good example — because it requires that a database and word processor be open at the same time. To automate getting to that condition, Works provides a feature called a Workspace. In version 2.0 this feature was called a Desktop. A Workspace is a file that you can create from within any of Works' modules.

Creating a Workspace:

1. Open or create all documents that you wish to be part of your Workspace.

2. If necessary, save any untitled document under an appropriate filename.

3. Select the Save Workspace command from the File menu.

4. Enter the name of the Workspace in the Save Workspace As text box.
A Workspace is a file that is saved in the file structure.

5. Click the Save button, or press the Return or Enter key.

6. To open a Workspace, double-click on its icon in the Finder.

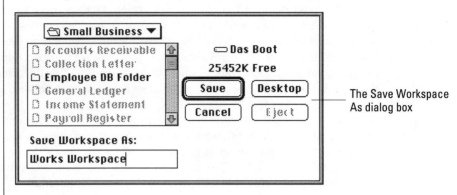

The Save Workspace As dialog box

— or —

**A Work-
space icon**

**7. From within the Works Open standard file dialog box with the All Types
icon selected, double-click on the Workspace filename.**

System 7's alias feature provides very convenient access to all your Workspaces in
whatever folder you choose. If you place a Workspace alias in the Apple Menu
folder within the System 7 System Folder, then those Workspaces will always be
available from the Apple menu.

Quick Tips

The following tips show you how to choose the best file format when importing or
exporting data, how to exchange information between Works and other applications,
how to exchange data between Works and an IBM PC computer, and how to use file
translation utilities.

Choosing the best file format to export and import

The best file format to transfer data with Works is the one that preserves the most
formatting possible and minimizes the amount of effort necessary to re-create the data.
Just what format is used depends on the situation.

The ideal is to use the same format to save in, as to open with. This allows an application to use its own translators to evaluate a file's contents. Obviously, that's impossible
for importing and exporting data. One would hope that the programs by the same
developer, in this case Microsoft, would be most successful in opening each other's
files. This is often the case. Because SYLK and RTF are Microsoft interchange file formats, you should also have very good luck using those formats.

Once you move beyond formats that Microsoft controls, you start to depend more
heavily on alternative means of file translation. The translators in Works, derived
from DataViz's MacLink Plus/PC, have been long tested for their efficacy. They are
your last resort, but they are also reliable.

When importing and exporting data to and from less secure formats, consider trying several different formats at the same time. It takes little time to save several different files in the source application or file. Also try to open them in the target application or file. You may get a good result that you can apply again, and you will certainly learn more about your data and application.

Exchanging information between Works and other applications

There are pitfalls to exchanging information between Works and other applications that can affect the success of the files that are opened. These pitfalls occur regardless of the success of the file translation. Although data can be exchanged with alacrity, underlying functionality is another story.

For example, some differences are noted in the Works manual between the Spreadsheet module in Works and files created by Microsoft Excel and Microsoft Multiplan. Multiplan is not widely used, but Excel is, so you may want to consider these. They are:

+ *Linked worksheets.* Excel and Multiplan have external references to other worksheets where cells, rows, columns, or selections can be referenced.

    When you copy and paste information between those spreadsheets and Works, those references are lost. This may cause a spreadsheet to malfunction or to give error values, so pay special attention to this difference.

+ *Unsupported character formatting.* Works doesn't support multiple fonts within a cell, shaded cells, and some other formatting information.

+ *Additional charts.* Excel and Multiplan have chart types that Works does not. These are lost in translation.

+ *Formula operators.* Database functions in Excel and Multiplan like intersection, union, and concatenation operators will not translate in Works.

+ *Formula error values are different in Works and Excel.*

+ *Arithmetic results may be different.* Excel and Works may display some small differences in calculations involving very large and very small numbers due to different internal calculating methods.

+ *The implementation of functions.* Some Excel functions like HLookup, Index, Match, Type, and VLookup are slightly different in Works. The IsError function gives a 0 if the argument is N/A in Works, whereas the IsError function gives a TRUE in Excel or Multiplan if the argument is #N/A.

+ *Logical functions.* Some logical functions like And, Or, Not, True, and False give a TRUE or FALSE value in Excel or Multiplan, when that same logical condition generates a 1 or 0 in Works.

With the exception of the linked spreadsheet construction in Excel, none of these differences are major, but they can affect minor aspects of spreadsheet operations or alter important calculations.

Every file translation involving data structure is bound to have some translational differences, unless the data structure is in a standard file format. Consider that databases suffer from the same constructional difficulties. Field definitions in other databases may perform logic, do autoentry, or be of a data type that will not transfer successfully. About all that you can be certain of when moving information from one spreadsheet or database to another spreadsheet or database is that the data will move correctly. You cannot expect the logic or underlying functionality to operate. If it does, and it will in some circumstances, then that is a plus. The aforementioned functional differences do not apply to graphic file formats. They are data-only structures, and when they transform correctly, there is no further need to check them out.

There are far too many combinations of programs available to discuss their differences with Works. Be aware of just what it is that you are translating and try to pinpoint the differences in functionality. These differences may help you determine what kind of translation is possible.

Exchanging data between the IBM PC and Works

You can exchange data between Macs and PCs in several ways, and the process gets easier with every passing year. Every solution requires both a hardware and software component.

Using the 1.4MB SuperDrive that comes with all recent Macintosh computers including the Mac Classic, Classic II, SX/30, LC, LC II, II series (with the exclusion of the Mac II), Quadra, and PowerBook series on, you can use 3½-inch MS-DOS floppy disks. Another solution is the Dyna Communications DynaFile, an external floppy disk drive that is a SCSI device. The DynaFile can be purchased as either a 3½-inch or 5¼-inch disk drive, or with two of either of those possibilities. Each of these drives accepts MS-DOS disks, and using software like Dyna's DOS Mounter, MS-DOS disks appear on your desktop just as any other Macintosh disk would. DOS Mounter software is included in MacLink Plus/PC. You can also buy from Apple an external drive that lets you mount Apple II 5½-inch ProDOS disks on a Macintosh. The disadvantage of using a floppy disk drive is that transferring files is a slow process, but this is the cheapest solution if you already own SuperDrive.

Some vendors sell file transfer software/hardware solutions. Traveling Software's LapLink Mac Pro, DataViz's MacLink Plus PC, and Argosy Software's RunPC products fit into this category. Here a serial cable is connected between machines, and software is launched on both computers to make transferring files a snap. Serial cable connection allows for rapid data transfer at the rate of about 65MB/hour when transferred at 19,200K/second. Should you choose to connect an IBM-compatible with a Mac by modem, these programs also allow that. These programs also come with translators for file conversion.

File transfer software became very popular with people who bought IBM-compatible laptops before the PowerBooks arrived, but they can be equally well applied to file transfers between two desktop machines. Their advantages include flexibility and speed of operation, log-ins and password protection, and excellent file translation. Many developers include their filters in their applications, just as Works has. The disadvantages are that you are limited in the serial connection to the length of the cable connections and that you have to learn the software. You really should have one of these products in your arsenal. All are good choices.

Another solution to transferring files between Macs and PCs involves setting up a heterogeneous network containing both types of machines. IBM PCs require a special network adapter card in order to be networkable. Sitka's TOPS network is one example; here TOPS contains file translators. You can also use AppleShare or electronic mail like Microsoft Mail, Sitka's InBox, 3Com's 3+Mail, CE Software's QuickMail, or Lotus' cc:Mail for the purpose of setting up a file server. Of the lot of e-mail software, CE QuickMail and Microsoft Mail are the best of the bunch. See Topic 14 for information on Microsoft Mail. Using network connections you can transfer large amounts of data, but they are relatively expensive and require setup and maintenance. You can also use the on-line services to transfer files and data.

Another alternative for file transfer is using communications software and connecting a Mac to a PC. The details on this process were described in Topic 9, "Using Works' Communications." You can use modems or null modem connections for this task. This method is slow (but not as slow as floppies), involves telecommunication charges (when using a modem), and requires specialized setup.

In order to exchange a Mac file to a PC, and vice versa, you need to associate that file with the application that it belongs to. The Mac uses a set of file signatures — the four-character (developer) file. For the Microsoft Works program, the type is APPL (for application), and the creator is MSWK. Any file with the MSWK creator type, when double-clicked, will launch in Works. PC applications have only a three-character extension associated with their files. So in order to correctly match a program to be translated on the PC to one on the Mac, that three-letter extension must be mapped to a four-letter one. This is called *extension mapping*. DOS Mounter allows very convenient extension mapping; you can also use ResEdit, CE Software's DiskTop, or Fifth Generation Systems' DiskTools for that purpose.

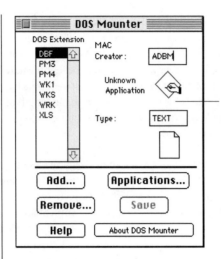

DOS Mounter is a Control Panel device that lets you mount MS-DOS disks on a Macintosh desktop, and do extension mapping of files

Using file translation utilities

Apple supplies the Apple File Exchange (AFE) as part of the Apple System Software package. With AFE open, you can mount or format MS-DOS disks or ProDOS disks on your desktop. There are a few translation filters that come with AFE, but you can use the DataViz MacLink Plus/PC translators to add over 150 extra translations to the AFE. These translators make conversions from Mac to Mac, Mac to PC, Mac to Wang, Mac to NeXT, and Mac to Sun computers, and vice versa. AFE is a weak product that is scheduled for a major upgrade. Apple is shipping a stand-alone package called File Exchange.

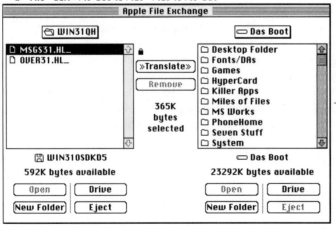

The Apple File Exchange is Macintosh system software that lets you mount MS DOS disks and do limited file translation. You can add DataViz translators to substantially improve the number of file translation capabilities.

Because AFE is so limited, if you are going to add the translators, it makes more sense to own the entire MacLink Plus/PC product. Claris MacWrite II can also use these translators to directly read other word processors (including MS-DOS ones like Word-Perfect, MultiMate, WordStar, XYWrite, Word, and others). Using Claris' new XTND technology, which is a set of external commands, you can install the translators by copying them and a driver using the MacLink Plus/Bridge utility. Works can read files from MacWrite II, but unfortunately, Works cannot use the XTND capability.

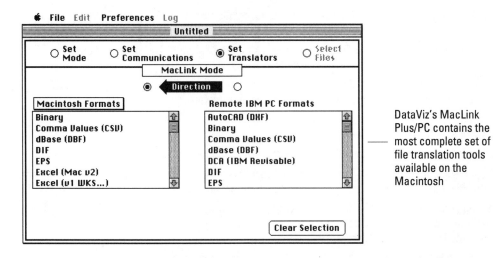

DataViz's MacLink Plus/PC contains the most complete set of file translation tools available on the Macintosh

LapLink Pro for the Mac is a better choice if you have less extensive needs for translation, and your intent is to do file transfers (with some translation) for a MS-DOS computer (or laptop) to a Macintosh.

Another approach to using MS-DOS disks on a Macintosh computer is to set up and run the SoftPC program from Insignia Solutions (Sunnyvale, CA). This program turns your Mac into a PC and provides the necessary utility to save DOS files in a partition on your hard drive. Insignia also sells a product called Access PC that is a System extension which treats MS-DOS disks as if they were Mac disks. PC files show up on the desktop, where you can copy, delete, and rename them, or you can format MS-DOS disks.

If you need to mount Mac disks on a PC, then consider using either Mac-to-DOS from Peripheral Land, Inc. (PLI, Mountain View, CA) or Mac-in-DOS from Pacific Microelectronics. The former product is the more highly recommended of the two. Your PC will need a 3 ½-inch 1.44MB floppy disk drive for the transfer. Mac-to-DOS will only read and write to the 1.44MB Mac format. To work with 800 or 400K Mac disks, the Copy II PC Deluxe Option Board from Central Point Software does the trick, although it doesn't work with the 1.44MB format.

Summary

✔ Data of various types can be digitized and stored in files.

✔ The manner in which data is stored in files is called a file format.

✔ Programs save files in their own format, called a native format. There are also standard formats used to move files between programs called interchange formats. Many other standard file formats exist, particularly for graphics.

✔ Works can read (open) and write to (save) 23 different file formats using a set of file translation filters.

✔ You can transfer data between Works modules using the Clipboard. The Clipboard uses the STYL format for textural data, and PICT2 for graphics.

✔ Just how successful you are in transferring information from one Works module to the next depends on the direction and nature of the data being transferred.

✔ Importing and exporting data is the process of converting data to a file format that can be opened (read) or saved (written) by another application.

✔ A filter is a conversion or translation routine that changes one file format into another.

✔ To open a set of documents quickly, create a Workspace file with the Save Workspace command on the File menu. This is useful for projects, mail merges, and other compound tasks.

✔ Although data can be successfully transferred, many times the underlying logic of a spreadsheet or database cannot. Make sure you understand the features missing in Works that will prevent some data from being transferred.

✔ Transferring information between Macintosh and other computers involves both a transfer step and a conversion step. There are both hardware and software solutions.

✔ A file translation utility like MacLink Plus/PC is nearly invaluable for cross-platform computing.

Part IV:

Advanced Features

Topic 13
Using Works on Your Portable

Overview

Portable computing is the wave of the future. In the years to come, most people's first computer purchase will be the one that they can take to school, to home or to work, to the beach, or to a client's office. Portable computing provides these opportunities, but this generation of portables also provides restrictions. Works was meant for the kind of on-the-go computing that Apple PowerBooks provide. In this Topic we are going to explore how to get the most from Microsoft Works and your PowerBook.

Topic 1 gave you some of the reasons that Works should be your first piece of third-party software. Memory requirements, versatility, practical features, and a low price are some of the benefits that Works brings to the table. These are also good features to have with any basic Macintosh computer, like the Classic II. Although some of the principles and practices described are strictly useful for PowerBooks, many will be applicable to problems you may face on your own computer system.

Introducing Macintosh Portables

Apple's entry into the portable computing market was late but well thought out. The initial offering of the Macintosh Portable was heavy and expensive but innovative. It really was only a portable in the sense that it was luggable; it had a better form-factor than the Macintosh Classic computers. Many people passed up the Portable and bought Classics because of the price difference between the two, so the Portable was not a commercial success. The Portable's innovative features include an active matrix screen and an eight-hour battery life. The penalty you paid in price bought you a sharp, bright display, and the penalty you paid in weight bought you the great convenience of not having to recharge constantly. Today, you can buy Portables in the used computer market for under $1,400, and at that price they are good deals.

The public was telling Apple that they wanted smaller, lighter computers. In 1991, Apple delivered. The PowerBook series was launched, with the concurrent introduction of the 100, 140, and 170 PowerBooks. The 100 and 140 have an enhanced Motorola 68000 CPU, whereas the 170 has a 68030. The line has been a great success, overnight turning Apple from one of the smallest suppliers of portable computers to the third largest supplier worldwide. Most of the discussion that follows relates specifically to using PowerBooks.

The Apple PowerBook portable computer family

One of the really nice things about the PowerBook is the patented wrist rest on the front of the case. The trackball, although small and light, is usable, but some users complain about the clicking mechanism. The keyboard on a PowerBook lacks some features that might trouble you if you are used to an extended keyboard. You can have a Caps Lock symbol appear in the menu bar to the right of the Help menu, however, often that isn't enough feedback when you accidentally turn on the Caps Lock by brushing against it. Using Ed Ludwig's (Abbott Systems) shareware program Caps Lock, you can have a PowerBook alert you with a beep sound (and other ways) when the feature is turned on. Also, the keyboard lacks a numeric keypad, something that accountants and other people doing math will miss. You can, however, buy the Kensington Notebook Keypad ($139.95).

Opinion varies among experts about the necessity of carrying a PowerBook with or without a floppy. Floppy drives add weight and consume power. If you use a serial cable or a modem for file transfer, you can get away without one and live with the PowerBook 100. However, having a floppy disk drive lets you copy data, change your software, and start up in an emergency. I prefer to have a PowerBook with a floppy disk drive for those reasons.

The display on the PowerBooks can be difficult to read in bright conditions. This is especially true for the 100 and 140 models, which use reflective light LCD technology panels, less true for the more expensive 170 model, which uses an active matrix light emitting transistor display. (The extra cost of the display is the primary difference in the large price difference in the models.) It can be difficult to see the I-Beam cursor on a PowerBook screen, so you may want to consider installing the shareware extension Cursor Fixer by Dennis Brothers. This adds a thick I-Beam cursor to all applications.

Users familiar with ResEdit can also copy and paste special cursors to other applications. Within ResEdit, you can also use the painting tools to edit cursors. It's pretty straightforward, and ResEdit is fun to play with. Many a programmer started out life as a ResEdit "Resource Hacker." Cursors are modified within the CURS template. ResEdit was long undocumented, creating an underground culture of ResEdit devotees. Recently, some books have appeared that have demystified ResEdit for the average user. For more information on using ResEdit, and for examples of the interesting things you can do with it, the following books are helpful:

♦ *Zen and the Art of Resource Editing*, 3rd Ed., Derrick Schneider, 1992, Peachpit Press, Berkeley, CA. The BMUG guide to ResEdit.

♦ *ResEdit Complete*, by Peter Alley (Apple Computer), 1991, Addison-Wesley, Reading, MA.

♦ *ResEdit Reference 2.1*, by Apple Computer, 1991, Addison-Wesley, Reading, MA.

Packing up the Old Kit Bag

One of the most important things to take with you on the road is an emergency startup disk. For any number of reasons, you can corrupt your hard drive's system folder and not be able to start your machine. It isn't often easy to diagnose why that happens, but if you can't start up and get at your files, you will not be able to continue working. So taking along a startup disk can really come in handy.

In System 6 and earlier you could get a decent amount of system software onto a 1.4MB floppy disk — maybe even your entire system. System 7 came along, and suddenly you have to struggle to just get your machine up and running with the software that fits on a 1.4MB floppy disk. Using the System 7 installer, use the minimum system script to create a startup floppy disk. This will get you started. Then create a compressed version of your PowerBook's normal System folder and copy that file to another disk. You can use StuffIt, Compactor, DiskDoubler, or whatever compression program you want. Just be sure that the software lets you split the compressed file into floppy disk-sized pieces. Now, when disaster strikes, you insert your startup disk into your PowerBook, and then copy and decompress your System folder to replace the damaged system. At most, you will be carrying three additional floppies around with you.

If you are going on the road, it always seems that you are collecting things for your old kit bag. A two-prong to three-prong connector here, a phone wire there, an alligator clip, and an old tooth comb. Systematize your collection so that you cover all your needs, it will save you lots of time in critical situations. Farallon sells a kit called the Portable Pack ($495) for just this purpose. The Portable Pack includes two phone cables, two modular Y-splitters, two modular cable extenders, phone cable with a modular plug at one end and alligator clips at the other, two PhoneNet connectors, a Phone-Net to LocalTalk adapter, a 3-1 electrical tap, a screwdriver, a Swiss Army knife, copies of Timbuktu and Timbuktu Remote (see "Remote Access" later in the Topic), an excellent connection guide, and all in a nylon pouch. You can save money collecting all of the pieces in the Portable Pack if you don't need Timbuktu, but this kit sure is a convenience.

If you intend to use a PowerBook on an EtherNet network, there are several portable solutions that you might want to consider. The first are SCSI devices by Asanté and Nuvotech that allow a Macintosh to connect to any EtherNet cabling scheme. Another product called DynaPORT SCSI/Link from Dyna Communications is a small external SCSI connector that can allow you to connect to different EtherNet connections. SCSI provides much higher data transfer rates than a LocalTalk connection. Keep in mind that if you connect via AppleTalk remote access, using SCSI/Link won't speed up your data transfer — only a modem will do that.

Backing up is critical, no less so when your computer is small and mobile. Let's face it, a laptop computer is more susceptible to being dropped and damaged, stolen, or lost than the one sitting at home on your desk. You can employ several strategies to protect your investment in the data you carry around with you. One good strategy is to copy all of your PowerBook's software to a backup disk. On the road, copy to a floppy disk only those files that you work with regularly, as well as those that have changed. This reduces the problem of backups to a manageable one and increases the chance that you will back up often.

Some people also find that it makes sense to send important files they create on the road to themselves at their electronic mail address. This is another backup strategy. If disaster strikes, when you get home (or anywhere else), you can find your work in your mailbox.

The software you purchase is sold to you with a license to use that software on one computer only, in most cases. This means that, in theory, you should purchase a second copy for your PowerBook. Luckily, few vendors are enforcing this odious one-owner, one-CPU software policy. Most are content with your being the registered owner of the single copy you use on your own personal computers.

Many good carrying cases are available for the PowerBooks. You really shouldn't travel without one. New ones seem to appear every day. The Madsen Line (Corte Madera, CA, 800-851-1551) makes some of the handsomest carrying cases I have seen. Other good choices are the cases from West Ridge Designs (ca. $80, 800-548-0053), and the Targus Universal Case ($69) and Targus Premier Case ($179).

Considering Memory and Storage

Memory and disk space are the two largest constraints that a PowerBook places upon you. You can't have enough of both. You can get by with 2MB RAM — Works was built to work in that size environment. If you can afford to, an upgrade to 4 or 8MB is worthwhile — more for other tasks you might want to accomplish than for what Works requires. Having a large amount of memory in your PowerBook enables you to set up and work in a RAM disk, dramatically improving your battery's lifetime between charges (see "Improving battery life").

Keep in mind that you can buy two different kinds of memory for your PowerBook: dynamic, or DRAM, and pseudostatic, or pSRAM. DRAM is cheaper and more plentiful, but pSRAM is faster and requires less power consumption. You can also get pSRAM on flexboards that save you from using an extra RAM socket. These boards are a little hairy to install, but they save you space and money. You can get them from TechWorks (Austin, TX, 800-688-7466), PSI Integration (Cambell, CA, 800-622-1722), MicroTech (East Haven, CT, 800-626-4276), and LifeTime Memory, among others.

Anytime you open the PowerBook case to change its hardware, you are voiding the Apple warranty. This means that if you buy third-party memory and install it, an Apple dealer can refuse to make repairs to your hard drive if it turns out to be defective. Frankly, most problems appear in the first month of use, and the Apple warranty doesn't extend long enough to be truly valuable. Reach for the Torx T10 and T8 screwdrivers, install your own memory, and save the additional cost. Apple memory is too expensive for what it is. You can get cheaper memory modules from MacConnection (Marlow, NH, 800-MAC-LISA) and from TechWorks (800-688-7466). The former comes with an instruction video, and the latter comes with an excellent installation manual.

Pare down your software to the minimum needed to work successfully. At the current time, there are no color PowerBooks (this will change soon), so leave color tools behind. INITs, Extensions, and Control Panel Devices require a lot of additional memory, so take only the ones you need or the ones that are the most useful to you. The Adobe Type Manager is great software for on-the-road demos or for printing to laser printers, but you can certainly make do with TrueType and save the memory requirements. TrueType is every bit as good and is supported in system software. You probably don't need a screen saver for short sessions; those are most useful for burn-in on the phosphors of a CRT (cathode ray tube) display, although a PowerBook screen left on for extended periods of time (24 hours) can also be damaged. So leave those flying toasters or dancing clocks behind when you anticipate normal usage.

Hard drive size limitations are another matter completely. The original models of the PowerBooks were released with 20 and 40MB hard drives. These sizes (particularly the 20MB size) are inadequate for modern computing. More recent models are arriving on the scene with 80MB drives and larger. Examples are the MicroTech (East Haven, CT, 800-626-4276) RoadRunner and APS (Kansas City, MO, 800-235-2750) Quantum GO-80 drives at $599 and $675, respectively. Buying a larger hard drive is money well spent. A large hard drive not only has faster access, but will reduce power consumption slightly because software access is faster. If you bought a PowerBook with 40MB, you can move up to a third-party drive and sell the 40MB one to someone else for about $250–$300.

A number of companies offer background compression software for expanding your hard drive's capacity. They don't really change the capacity, but they fit more software into your drive. Salient Software's AutoDoubler is one example of this class of software. You might think that on-the-fly compression and decompression of software and data on your disk would really slow down your PowerBook, but this is not the case. Compression is taking place in the background when you are not using processing power; decompression is taking place only when you need those particular files. These products will increase disk access and lower your working time between recharges, but that might be a compromise that you can live with.

Remote Access

Chances are that you will be using your modem heavily while on the road. It just doesn't make long-term financial sense to try to save money buying a slow modem; 9600 bps is a good investment that will save you money on connect time. Most 9600 bps modems also come with send and receive fax capabilities. Having a 9600 bps modem can make a major difference in what you can achieve with AppleTalk Remote Access. At 2400 bps you can download about 800K worth of files in an hour; 9600 bps allows you to retrieve 3.2MB of files. Some 9600 bps modems come with data compression schemes. When they connect to another modem that has that same scheme, data transfers in the 14400 bps range and above can be achieved.

The PowerBook 170 has a built-in 2400 bps data modem with 9600 bps send fax, but you can do better with third-party solutions. The WorldPort fax modems from US Robotics are one alternative; they come in various speeds. Another alternative is the Global Village PowerPort V.32 ($795). The PowerPort plugs into the internal modem slot of a PowerBook, and sends and receives faxes and data at 9600 bps. Another good choice is PSI Integration's PowerModem ($299), a 2400 bps data/9600 bps fax send/4800 fax receive unit. The PowerModem ships with the STS fax software; it's the same excellent software that makes the Dove Fax/Modem so highly rated.

You can buy both internal and external modems; each has its own advantages. You will never lose an internal modem, and it is the most convenient to carry. You can use external modems on any machine, and they are now so small that carrying them as an additional piece presents little difficulty.

AppleTalk Remote Access Software comes with the PowerBooks, and it offers an easy solution for access to your desktop computer in another location. In essence, if you leave your desktop computer on and call into it, you can have it act like a server to your PowerBook. This way, you can back up your PowerBook files remotely, retrieve needed software and files, and do other data management tasks routinely. In order to call in to your desktop computer, that computer must be on. This presents you with the problem of either leaving your computer at home on all the time or setting up a system that allows you to turn on your computer remotely.

To have your computer turn on when you call in and turn off at an interval of your choosing, there are two products you can use. If you have a Mac II series computer, Farallon Computing's Remote WakeUp Cable for $50 will send a signal to your computer's keyboard for startup. This will happen with any incoming phone call. With the CDEV software included with the WakeUp Cable you can shut down the Mac after any time period. Mac Classics, or Mac SEs, and SE/30s don't have a power-on switch on their keyboards. Sophisticated Circuits' PowerKey ($99) hardware adds this functionality, and their PowerKey Remote ($50) software then lets you set the shutdown conditions, effectively duplicating the functionality of the WakeUp Cable.

When you use the Apple internal data/fax modem with the 140 or 170, use the Portable Control Panel setting to indicate whether you are using an external or internal modem. Whenever you use the Communication module in Works, it will know what port to activate. Another setting lets you have your PowerBook wake up automatically whenever there is an incoming phone call.

Remember to always turn off AppleTalk when you are not using it. As explained in the section "Improving battery life," this software draws a lot of power and lowers your working session time considerably.

Remote access is also possible using Microsoft Mail's Dial-In Utility. Works supports Microsoft Mail by including a Send Mail and Receive Mail command in the File menu. The details for using Microsoft Mail and for remote access with this method are found in Topic 14, "Using Works in Business."

Printing on the Road

Deciding whether to take your printer with you on the road is a difficult decision. Printers add more weight to your kit than any other item. Most weigh as much as your PowerBook itself. None of the current generation of printers are as light and as convenient as they could be, although some of these printers give good print quality. The best printers are inkjets that run on batteries giving about 25 to 100 pages a charge, and they are whisper quiet.

Of the current crop, the Canon BubbleJet BJ-10e ($350) offers about the best compromise of print quality and weight vs. price. The Apple StyleWriter is equally good but less portable. Other alternatives include the GCC WriteMove and Kodak Diconix 150, smaller printers with a lower print quality. The next generation of portable printers to come will, no doubt, be much better still. For example, to see how small printers can become, look at the Citizen PN48. This is a letter-quality dot-matrix printer that weighs under three pounds.

If you are going somewhere where there are LaserWriters to be found, then leave your printer behind. Pack only the serial or AppleTalk cable and a disk of printer drivers. You can always walk into a service bureau to print your work. If you are in a hotel, consider sending yourself a fax. You can do this from MCI Mail or through CompuServe or by using your fax modem. This seems silly, but it isn't much more expensive then going to a service bureau, and boy, is it convenient.

Another approach is to use a file translation utility like the ones discussed in Topic 12 to make a copy of your files in an MS-DOS format. My preference is to use DataViz's MacLink Plus PC, but Argosy Software's RunPC also works well. Then, if there are any IBM PC compatible machines around, you can use them to print your work. This approach is the most bothersome one, but it can get you by in a pinch. A Macintosh can also drive an IBM PC printer; you can carry along a printer cable like Orange Micro's Grappler with a disk of drivers. It's a funny thing that most computer users feel squeamish about letting you connect your computer to theirs, but they are entirely comfortable about letting you connect to their printer.

Knowing What To Take with You

Security software is even more valuable in a PowerBook than it is on your desktop. Access to an address or salary database can do a lot of damage in the wrong hands. You can limit who sees your data by installing password protection using programs like La Cie's great formatting software SilverLining, Magnum Empower series, or the shareware programs MacPassword or LockOUT. These programs will deny access to a disk or partition to anyone who doesn't know the password. Some other programs will allow people to get into your system by simply rebooting the PowerBook, but not these.

LockOUT provides protection for your PowerBook

There are even more sophisticated security programs on the market that encrypt your data so that it cannot be read without the password. No password, no access, no data — period. This is a crowded product category with many good software choices. Most of these, like Fifth Generation's DiskLock, Kent Marsh's MacSafe II or NightWatch programs, SuperMac Technology's Sentinel, and Crypt Master from Information Security Corp., use the National Bureau of Standards Data Encryption Standard (DES) system. Some systems like ASD Software's FileGuard allow individual file and folder password protection; these programs are more valuable in networking environments than on a PowerBook. Security software is a large product category with many levels of features to choose from.

If you are using your PowerBook with a floppy disk drive and you will be using other people's floppy disks, you may want to install virus protection software on your PowerBook. The best programs are commercial ones: Symantec's SAM, Microcom Inc.'s Virex, Fifth Generation's AntiToxin, or Microseed's Rival. These programs not only detect viruses; they also attempt to repair the damage. Several good shareware offerings are constantly updated: John Norstrad's Disinfectant, Chris Johnson's GateKeeper, and

Jeffrey Shulman's Virus Detective are the three best and are all widely distributed. Make sure that whatever program you choose, you get the most recent versions. Then, only the improbable occurrence of a new virus strain that has yet to be detected should get through your defenses.

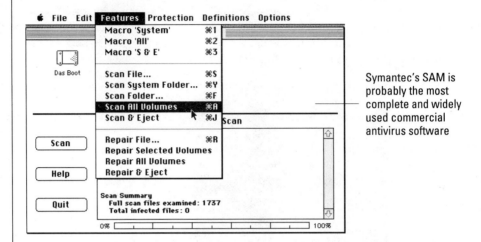

Symantec's SAM is probably the most complete and widely used commercial antivirus software

Whatever software you choose to install, make sure that it includes a system extension or INIT to intercept viruses on floppy disk drives at insertion; all of the aforementioned products do that. It is better to prevent a virus than to cure it. You should always try to replace software that is infected rather than to repair it. Backups are your ultimate line against virus infection. With a virus detection program properly installed, it will be difficult for you to get a virus. Just exercise caution when downloading software from a service in an area where the software has not been checked first.

Viruses have always gotten more attention than they deserve in the press; they make good reading. They sound romantic, like artificial life. Chances are that you will rarely see one.

One valuable piece of software to take with you on a PowerBook is JAM Software's Smart Alarms. This event-reminder program and appointment diary can really be useful for a person with a busy schedule. Although you can use Works to duplicate the appointment diary, the event reminder functionality is not yet a part of the Works program. Other programs in this category are CE Software's Alarming Events, Essential Software's Easy Alarms, Now Software's Up-To-Date, MacShack Enterprises' MyTimeManager, and some others. You can find demo editions of some of these programs on many of the on-line services.

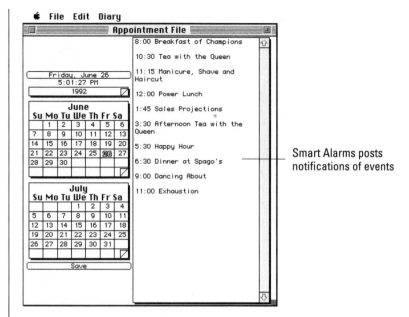

Smart Alarms posts
notifications of events

Programs that manage dates and times, calendars, and to-do lists are called *personal information managers,* or PIMs for short. PIMs are about the most useful general piece of software that you can carry on a PowerBook, and they complement Works well. Works has some elements of a PIM — you can duplicate an address database, to-do lists, and other features — but not all of the important ones. Hopefully, Microsoft will address this omission in a subsequent release. For a good look at fully developed PIMs, see Concentrix Software's Connections or Pastel Development's DayMaker. HyperCard has served as the program of choice on the Mac for PIMs. An earlier program called Focal Point (now unsupported) from HyperCard guru Danny Goodman has seen several years of service on my computer.

Transferring Files

There are several ways to transfer files from a PowerBook to another machine. The most simple is to use a floppy disk. You can also use a modem to create a null modem through a direct serial connection, or use telephones to connect two computers using communication software. Telecommunication is the subject of Topic 9, and you can refer to that Topic for further information.

If you are transferring files regularly, you can't beat the convenience of Traveling Software's LapLink Mac. LapLink provides the serial cables and software for both connected computers to let you transfer files easily. LapLink can also translate file formats, a feature that is not as important for a PowerBook as it is for IBM PC laptops-to-Mac connections.

Because the PowerBook 100 doesn't have a floppy drive, you might want to use a feature called "SCSI-docking." In the Portable Control Panel you can set up the 100 as a SCSI disk and choose the SCSI ID number so that it doesn't conflict with other devices on your SCSI chain. Then you can attach that special Apple SCSI connector (with a small square connector on one end and the normal D-shaped 50-pin connector on the other) between your PowerBook and desktop Macintosh. SCSI connections are high-speed data transfers with typical rates of 2 to 3MB/minute.

Quick Tips

The following tips show you how to improve the battery life of your portable computer, explain what you can buy to spruce up your portable computer, and list other resources to find out more about your portable computer.

Improving battery life

The battery life between charges is a major disappointment in PowerBooks, as it is in all portable computers. Under normal use, you can get about an hour and a half between recharges. That is simply not enough for an entire work session, and it's almost a good enough reason to wait until the next generation of laptop computers gets here in the next year or two. Getting a spare battery can help the situation. You can also get a five-pound $189.95 Lind Electronic Design (800-659-5956 or 612-927-6303) battery, but these will limit your portability. (Wasn't this why you bought a PowerBook in the first place?) Lind also sells a $99.95 car cigarette lighter adapter for on-the-road recharging.

Given that a recharge takes minimally three hours to make your battery last an hour and twelve hours to get the full charge, it behooves you to find ways to improve the amount of computing you can get done in a single charge. Your battery is not fully charged, even when all of the squares in the Battery DA are filled. The things that draw the most current are the mechanical elements of the PowerBook, floppy and hard drive I/O, disk spinning, and the display. Turn down the brightness of the display, and put your hard drive to sleep when not needed.

The Battery DA tells you when your PowerBook is charged or low. Don't take the charged indication too literally, as it can appear charged at lower states.

Putting a hard drive to sleep means stopping its spinning; usually the sleep mode is accompanied by a darkened screen. Because it takes much more energy to start up a hard drive (due to friction) than it does to keep it spinning, it only makes sense to send that hard drive off to the land of Nod when you will not require a read/write for at least a minute or so. You will also notice a lag in the operation of your PowerBook while the hard drive is spinning up. Keeping your hard drive off is the major key to battery life extension. Choose the Sleep command on the Special menu to both stop the hard drive spinning and turn off the screen display.

With Bill Steinberg's SpinD FKey installed, a simple keystroke sends your PowerBook hard drive to sleep. SpinD is part of a package called PBTools 1.2, which contains the SafeSleep extension. SafeSleep requires a password to prevent access to a waking PowerBook. Andrew Welch's Portable Siesta is a CDEV that puts both the hard drive and screen to sleep. Yet another FKey called PowerSleep from Urs Calibran will also send your PowerBook out for ZZZs. Use SpinD when you wish to keep working in memory on a PowerBook so that you can see the screen the other products; to conserve memory. Note also that when you send your PowerBook to sleep on a network, it can be disconnected.

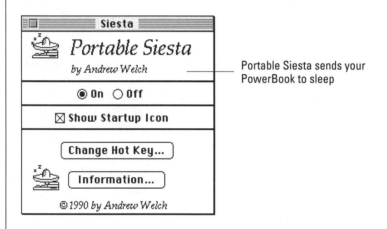

Portable Siesta sends your PowerBook to sleep

The Portable Control Panel also enables you to configure your PowerBook so that it sleeps after a certain number of minutes. The screen will stay on, however. The Stay Awake When Plugged In check box will keep your PowerBook awake and is useful for prolonged network sessions. Be aware that keeping a screen on for 24 hours or more can damage the screen, so when this option is chosen, an alert box is presented to indicate this fact. The best screen saver for a PowerBook is one like QuickTools' Sunset, which presents a white background. Another feature in the Portable Control Panel is the System Rest radio button. When a certain period of inactivity is detected, this feature slows down the PowerBook. This can be a problem for extended calculations or background processing like printing, so turn the Don't Rest radio button on in those cases.

```
This portable Macintosh slows down after a
period without user interaction or communication
with a peripheral device (a modem or disk drive,
example). This "Rest" feature is intended to save power
when the system is idle and waiting for user interaction.

Some applications may not be idle when the system slows;
to turn off this feature when using such applications,
choose "Don't Rest". To turn on the Rest feature again,
choose "Rest".

        ● Rest                    OK
        ○ Don't Rest
                              Cancel
```

The PowerBook's Don't Rest dialog box

RAM disks offer a considerable battery life improvement. A RAM disk, as you have learned, is a portion of RAM set aside as a storage device. You can place system software, applications, and data files into the RAM disk, and all access is then totally electronic and requires little current. RAM disks require, of course, a fair amount of RAM. RAM disks are different from RAM caches (which you create in the General Control Panel). A RAM cache saves the most recently used instructions in memory to be used in place of a disk access: They increase operational speed and are dynamic. RAM disks, on the other hand, are storage devices that contain what you copy to them. RAM disks are not dynamic, but they are volatile. That is, the data in RAM disks disappear when the current is removed.

Configure the RAM disk with a minimal System folder and a Startup Device CDEV, which should consume about 1.1MB RAM. A 3MB RAM disk gives minimal disk space, and if you install 8MB of RAM in your PowerBook, then this becomes a very practical solution. Using a RAM disk backed up as a file occasionally to a hard drive or as a compressed file to a floppy disk, you can get over five hours of computing out of a battery charge.

Setting up a RAM disk is the most important reason to stuff your PowerBook with memory. You can configure a RAM disk from within the Apple Memory Control Panel.

Two very good shareware products have appeared: Roger Bate's RamDisk+ and George Nelson's RAMStart. Both save the RAM disk as a file on your hard drive at various intervals, thus preserving your work if there is a power failure. Put your System folder and Microsoft Works into the RAM disk, and any documents that you are working with at the time. This will dramatically improve both your PowerBook's performance (no disk I/O) and its power consumption. Jim Heid's *Macworld Complete Mac Handbook* (IDG Books Worldwide, Inc.) contains a nice section on RAM disks and memory in general.

```
┌─────────────────────────────────────────────────────┐
│ RamDisk+                                        v2.31 │
│  ┌──────────┐    ┌──────────┐      ┌──────────────┐   │
│  │  Cancel  │    │  Help... │      │     OK       │   │
│  └──────────┘    └──────────┘      └──────────────┘   │
│                  ┌─────────┐ 9 K                       │
│                  │Selected:│                           │
│        Specify size of RAM disk:   ┌──────┐            │
│                                    │ 3000 │            │
│                                    └──────┘            │
│                ( between OK and OK )                   │
│           Note: Can't create a RAMdisk under MultiFinder│
│                                                        │
│  Volume Name?   ┌──────────────────┐   ┌────┐          │
│                 │ •RAMdisk•        │   │    │          │
│                 └──────────────────┘   │    │          │
│  Your Name?     ┌──────────────────┐   └────┘          │
│                 │ Barrie           │   ┌──────┐        │
│                 └──────────────────┘   │ Icon │        │
│                                        └──────┘        │
└─────────────────────────────────────────────────────┘
```

Another really significant battery draw is the use of the AppleTalk feature on a PowerBook. It's easy to turn AppleTalk on to print or for some other purpose like remote access and then forget that it's running. Get into the habit of checking the Chooser to see that AppleTalk is no longer on.

The road show

One of the most important reasons for carrying a PowerBook about is to demo things. The small screen size, lack of an on-board grayscale display, and no video-out port makes road shows impractical for a large group. You can install video-out capability to your PowerBook by using an Enviso NoteBook Display Adapter video board. The model for the PowerBook 100, capable of only 1-bit monochrome output, connects to the memory expansion connector and costs $695 with 1MB RAM or $895 with 2MB. The video-out plug then exits through the backup-battery door. The Notebook Display Adapter 030 for the PowerBook 140 and 170 models, with 0, 2, or 4MB ($795, $1,195, or $1,595), supports 8-bit color to 12-inch and 13-inch RGB and VGA monitors. The Enviso boards work well, and their software enables you to use the external monitor as either a two-monitor setup with different material on both or in a Presentation mode with a mirror of the PowerBook screen on the external monitor.

Radius has another external monitor solution called the PowerView SCSI. This box emulates a Radius video card, connects to the external SCSI connector of a Power-Book, and has its own power supply. This diminishes the portability of a PowerBook somewhat (more due to bulk than weight), but at $599 this solution is a reasonable compromise, much less expensive than the Enviso solution. PowerView supports a variety of monitors, like Apple's 13-inch RGB monitor, but is slower and less responsive than the Enviso boards. Because most projectors built for the Macintosh are meant to be compatible with video cards for the 13-inch RGB monitor, any of these solutions will work for presentations.

If you are willing to accept a little less portability, then the Macintosh LC II represents a nice road machine. You get color, good processor speed, a somewhat portable pizza box configuration, and all at a good price. Instead of taking a monitor with you, consider buying an overhead display adapter and projection panel. Some good choices include Apercom Corp.'s LimeLight-2 ($995) for grayscale, Proxima's MulitMode II ($2,199) or Ovation LCD ($8,495), NView Corp.'s ViewFrame II+2 ($1,995) or ViewFrame Spectra ($5,995) projection panels.

Finding other resources

There's a lot more to know about PowerBooks and portable computing in general. Because this is a book on Microsoft Works, there isn't the space here to fully describe all the features. We have touched on the high points.

By the way, if you ever run into problems with your PowerBook, give the Apple PowerBook Hotline a call at their SOS-APPL line, 800-505-2772. They are there to help you.

Summary

- Apple's PowerBook series of notebook computers are valuable machines for on-the-go computing.
- The PowerBook 100 is an economical choice with no internal floppy disk drive, a 68000, and an LCD display. The 140 adds a floppy disk drive. The 170 model has a 68030 CPU and a bright, active matrix display screen.
- Create a kit bag of useful items: an emergency startup disk, connectors, and so on, to help you work on the road.
- Put as much RAM into the PowerBook as you can afford, and get the largest hard drive. Works requires only 2MB RAM and limited disk space, but these additions will make your computing easier.
- Buy and use the fastest modem you can afford, preferably a fax modem.
- Use AppleTalk Remote Access software to call up your main desktop computer.
- Use security, virus detection, and backup software with your PowerBook. Also useful are personal information managers and event organizers.
- Use the Sleep mode to improve battery life.
- A RAM disk is the single best solution to improving battery life and performance.
- PowerBooks have some limitations for use as portable display and demo stations. Use external video devices to circumvent these restrictions.

Topic 14
Using Works in Business

Overview

In this last Topic you will find some examples of how to put Works to use for you. As you have seen, there are certainly a lot of tools in Works that you can apply to common problems. Hopefully this Topic will make you want to try out some of your own projects in Microsoft Works.

Works is so popular that some very useful templates have been developed to enhance your productivity with the program. Several are commercially available at a very reasonable price. A sample of some templates even come free with Works to get you started. Nothing can get your creative juices flowing faster than seeing what other people can do with Works. For example, although you can create a resume yourself in the Works word processor, all that formatting setup takes time. It's hard to get exactly that right look the first time around — you could instead buy a product like RésumExpert from Heizer Software that contains 40 different resumés to play with.

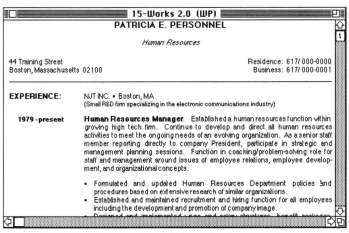

RésumExpert provides preformatted stationery resumes to simplify resume tasks

Courtesy of Heizer Software

Using Works in Business

A check book is one of the easiest and most satisfying first projects you might want to attempt in Works. You can create a check book in either the Database or Spreadsheet modules; each has its own advantages and disadvantages. Creating a check book in a database lets you manage and print forms, like checks, easily. However, in order to get summary information, you will need to create and run a report. Spreadsheets show you summary information at a glance, and all of the data is always accounted for. You can also see charts that will help you understand how your money was spent or where it came from. For the convenience of seeing the overall view of data that you get from working within a spreadsheet, however, you lose the natural, easy way that a database can manage forms.

Check Book (SS)

	A	B	C	D	E	F	G	H
1								
2				A C C O U N T	S U M M A R Y			
3	1st Entry			Starting Balance :	6985.23	No. of Transactions :		23
4	920101			Payments to Date :	-6667.80	No. of Payments :		18
5	Last Entry			Deposits to Date :	2064.05	No. of Deposits :		5
6	920115			**Current Balance :**	**2381.48**	Net Temp Sum :		0.00
7								
8	Date	√ No.	Cl	Payable to	Payments	Deposits	Type	Memo
9	920101	403		Dean Witter	2000.00		XI1	John's Acct
10	920101	404		Dean Witter	2000.00		XI2	Mary's Acct
11	920102	405	x	1st Fed Mortgage	694.57		DIM	
12	920102	405	x	1st Fed Mortgage	112.34		XM	
13	920103	406	x	PGE	67.38		EHE	
14	920103	406	x	PGE	56.78		EHH	
15	920104	407	x	Valley TV Cable	12.25		EHC	
16	920104					500.00	XS	Transfer
17	920105					1000.00	IS1	John
18	920105					500.00	IS2	Mary

The Check Book template from the Heizer catalog, implemented in a spreadsheet

Courtesy of Heizer Software

The decision to use a database vs. a spreadsheet is one that you face often in business. For a check book, the best bet is to use a spreadsheet so that you have the overall view. In a check book, you are primarily interested in your condition; graphical use of your data in forms is less important. Actually, there's no reason why you can't use both modules to help you with your task. Create and print a check using a database, and then import that data into a spreadsheet where it can be analyzed. This method is easy using cut and paste on the Clipboard, as discussed in Topic 12.

Spreadsheet and Database Publishing

Spreadsheet and database publishing are slang terms that are now applied to using data in those modules to print your work. Although the concepts are similar — both use a calculating engine to print — the kinds of output each module is capable of are very different. Database publishing generally applies to creating pages of repetitive data, whereas spreadsheet publishing refers to modifying a spreadsheet so that the output of the worksheet appears graphical. Printing a single database record as a form is not database publishing — repetitive data record output is.

Works' database offers you several different ways to do database publishing depending on the type of effect you are trying to achieve. If each record is to be placed in a repeating form, then use the database itself to print page after page of data. You might want to do this for a catalog of compact discs, a personnel telephone directory, or an inventory listing of parts for an automobile repair company. By placing headers and footers appropriately, your printed work will look very professional. This type of publishing enterprise works well when not much explanatory text needs to be placed in the document at any point. The data itself is the main ingredient, and any text needed is added as an accompanying label.

Often, you need a lot of explanatory text to make database-published work meaningful. It's cumbersome to try to do this within a database only, so your best bet is to use the mail merge feature of your word processor. (Strictly speaking, this is not database publishing since it involves a word processor, but the net result can be quite similar.) Text formatting in a word processor is much better, and using the text column feature of a word processor's Draw module creates newspaper-like output. When you use a word processor merge for database publishing, you can create title pages, tables of contents, and other book features that make your document seem more complete and professional.

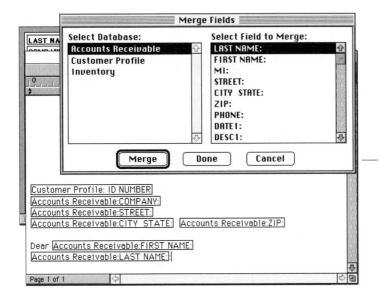

Using multiple databases in a mail merge can greatly improve your flexibility in printing data

Merging a database into your word processor can result not only in improved text handling and formatting, but also in the ability to use the data from more than one database in the same printed output. This new Works feature can really help you accomplish jobs quickly that once required that you create and manage new databases specifically constructed to provide a mail merge. Remember that when you use a mail merge, only the currently selected records in a database(s) are printed out.

The last useful method in database publishing is to create a report that displays data. This method is useful when the graphical nature of the report is limited and when you need totals and subtotals. Use drawn graphics, headers, and footers to make your report more meaningful.

The All-Purpose Mortgage spreadsheet from Heizer Software illustrates some elements of spreadsheet publishing: labels and underlining

Courtesy of Heizer Software

Spreadsheet publishing uses the cell matrix to create documents. If you recall Topic 7, you may remember that text used as labels can flow past the cell boundary into additional adjacent cells. Only a character typed into the adjacent cells will prevent the label from appearing. That feature, along with bounding cells with borders, can create the appearance of a form in a database. Additionally, you have all of the tools available in the Draw module for your use. The disadvantage in using draw tools to spruce up a spreadsheet for printed output is that drawn elements don't move as the underlying spreadsheet changes — for example, as you resize a column.

It doesn't make sense to create simple underlines with draw. However, you can create arrows, color, patterns, and other devices with draw that really make your spreadsheet shine. Given the right creative flair, you can make a spreadsheet appear as though it were created in a word processor. Text can be added in draw, placed into text columns, and complimented by the extensive and well-positioned tables of your spreadsheet. One additional feature of spreadsheet publishing is the ability of spreadsheets to contain charts. Charts are covered in Topic 8.

Using Works' Stationery Templates

In order to give you a taste of what Works is capable of, and to introduce you to some of the third party products available for the program, Works ships with some stationery (template) documents. They are there for your immediate use and cover three general categories of templates: small business, education, and personal productivity. These are English language templates, meant for use in the US, Canada, Great Britain, New Zealand, and Australia. If you are using a copy of Works in another country, your localized package may be somewhat different.

Small business templates shipping with the Works package include the following:

♦ *Accounts Receivable.* A company database for tracking current balance, last billing date, and account activity. Use this database along with the Collection Letter for billing overdue balances, and sending reminders to clients. This template is available from Microsoft.

♦ *Collection Letter.* This word processor file contains merged database fields from the Accounts Receivable database to produce a letter to bill clients. Merged fields include the customer's name, address, and current balance. This template is available from Microsoft.

Remember, in order for a merge to operate successfully, you must have both the word processor and database open at the same time.

♦ *Employee Database.* This database allows you to keep biographical data on employees including the current pay and last review. An instructional word processor file called *Employee DB Instructions* is also included. This file explains how to use the database. This template is available from Heizer Software.

♦ *General Ledger.* The general ledger provides a spreadsheet that manages debits and credits to provide current balances. This template is available from K-12 MicroMedia Publishing.

File   Edit   Format   Options   Chart   Window

General Ledger (SS)

			POST.				POST.
	GENERAL LEDGER						
	ACCT:	100 CASH					
			POST.				POST.
	DATE	ITEM	REF.	DEBIT	DATE	ITEM	REF
	Jan 1	BALANCE	G1	1,100.00	Jan 31		C2
	31		G2	1,979.00			
		DEBIT BALANCE		1,192.00		CREDIT BALANCE	

The General Ledger spreadsheet template in Works can get your business up and running quickly

♦ *Income Statement.* This spreadsheet lists income, assets, and debits for a business. It also allows you to analyze income by type. This template is available from Heizer Software.

 File Edit Format Options Chart Window

D22		213					

Income Statement (SS)

	A	B	C	D	E	F	G
1				INCOME STATEMENT			
2							
3							
4	Date:	6/29/92		1986	N/A	N/A	
5				----------	----------	----------	
6	1 SALES			23454			
7	2 Cost of Goods Sold			12,322	0		
8				----------	----------	----------	
9	3 GROSS PROFIT			$11,132	$0	$0	
10							
11		Operating Expenses		8234			
12							
13	4 Advertising			567			
14	5 Bad Debts			233			
15	6 Commissions			4623			
16	7 Depreciation/Amortization			592			
17	8 Dues & Subscriptions			95			
18	9 Employee Benefits			3591			
19	10 Equipment Lease Expense			454			
20	11 Insurance			987			
21	12 Legal & Accounting			500			

An Income Statement is one of the documents that a business uses to file its annual report

◆ *Payroll Register.* This spreadsheet tracks employees, pay rate, hours worked, and total wages overall. This template is available from K-12 MicroMedia Publishing.

◆ *Weekly Travel Expenses.* This spreadsheet provides a weekly expense report for employees to use. This template is available from Heizer Software.

Accounts receivable, general ledger, and the income statement are the three most important accounting modules that a small business can run. While these stationery templates are not as complex as some others you might see, they are entirely adequate for many businesses.

Education stationery templates shipping with Works include the following:

◆ *Bibliography.* Use this database to manage information used in a research project: an article, book, thesis, or research paper. This template is available from K-12 MicroMedia Publishing.

◆ *Character Sketch.* This word processor file, designed for students in grades 6-9, aids in learning descriptive writing. Students follow the step-by-step session in the file to create an essay. This template is available from Humanities Software.

◆ *Class Newsletter.* This sample newsletter includes headlines, graphics, and linked text columns. It is useful for learning how to work with the word processor and draw together. This template is available from TI&IE.

◆ *Gradebook.* This spreadsheet for teachers is useful for calculating student grades from component tests and exercises. It also calculates the class average for a grade category. This template is available from Microsoft.

- *Inventions.* A sample database of over 200 inventions, with the inventor name, and the date of the invention. Instructions to use this database are found in the file called *Invention Ideas*. This template is available from TI&IE.

- *Student Resume.* This file illustrates how to position and format text within a word processor document. It sets up a resume that students can use by simply typing in appropriate text. The file contains its own instructions. This template is available from Microsoft.

The following personal productivity stationery are included in Works:

- *Auto Finance Analyzer.* This spreadsheet lets you calculate the true cost of an automobile based on a schedule of payments at a certain interest rate. The spreadsheet contains instructions for use. By juggling interest rates, down payments, and loan terms, you can figure out costs and carrying charges. This template is available from Heizer Software.

- *Home Purchase Analysis.* This spreadsheet uses your income and debt ratio to assess the maximum affordable monthly mortgage payment. You can figure out whether a house is affordable based on your current means. This template is available from WorksWare.

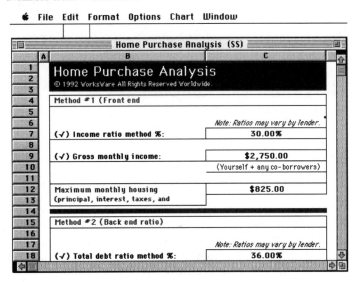

- *Mortgage Amortization.* This spreadsheet produces an amortization schedule for a house loan. Enter the amount of the loan, loan term, and interest rate, and the spreadsheet calculates your payments. This template is available from TI&IE.

- *Simple Interest.* This spreadsheet calculates a schedule of interest from an investment of a certain size at a certain interest rate. This template is from available TI&IE.

Stationery templates open up as untitled documents that you can save and rename for your use. This saves you from having to make a duplicate copy of a file for your use and protects the original document from change. Stationery was described in Topic 3. In Topic 14, the terms stationery and templates are used interchangeably.

Third-Party Templates

To obtain information on third party templates available for Microsoft Works, contact the following:

1. Heizer Software, 1941 Oak Park Blvd., Suite 30, P.O. Box 232019, Pleasant Hill, CA 94523, 800-888-7667 (orders), 510-943-7667, and Fax 510-943-6882.

2. Humanities Software, 408 Columbia, Suite 22, P.O. Box 950, Hood River, OR 97031, 800-245-6737.

3. K-12 MicroMedia Publishing, 6 Arrow Road, Ramsey, NJ 07446, 201-825-8888 or call 800-292-1997.

4. TI&IE (Teachers Idea and Information Exchange), P.O. Box 6229, Lincoln, NE 68506, 402-483-6987.

5. WorksWare, 8031 Broadleaf Avenue, Van Nuys, CA 91402, 818-989-2298.

Microsoft Corporation includes templates for Works when the product is shipped but is not a commercial source of additional stationery.

The Heizer WorksXChange

The Heizer Software catalog was started seven years ago by Ray Heizer to distribute useful software products created by unknown authors who don't have the wherewithal to support their own products. This well-regarded company pays authors a royalty and helps them market their work through direct catalog sales. As noted above, several of the stationery templates in the Works package are available from Heizer Software.

Heizer Software began by offering Microsoft Works (the WorksXChange) templates, and grew to include Microsoft Excel (Excellent Exchange) templates and Claris Hyper-Card (HyperCard Exchange) stacks when those programs became available. There are other eclectic products — some are developers' tools offered in the Heizer catalog — but luckily for Works users, much of the catalog is devoted to Works templates. More than 22 pages of the 48-page catalog is loaded with Works products that you can apply in your business and everyday life. There isn't room to talk about them all here, only to discuss the categories and highlight some of the best products. For a small taste of the WorksXChange, consider ordering the sample disk which costs $4 and has a dozen or so demonstrations.

Heizer's catalog includes templates for accounting, architecture and construction, business, calendars, education, engineering, entertainment, farming and ranching, finance, manufacturing, navigation, personal, publishing and advertising, real estate, science, and sports. Nearly all of the templates offered are either spreadsheets or databases; prices range from $10 to just under $100, with an average of about $20. Some of these products have developed over the course of three different versions of Microsoft Works.

Hit templates in the Heizer Software catalog for Works include the Schedule C Accounting System ($25); Construction Cost Estimator - Residential ($40); Commercial/Industrial Construction Estimator ($89); Complete Construction Cost Estimator ($79); Business Plans for Retail, Manufacturing and Professional Services ($15 each); Income Statement, Balance Sheet, and Financial Ratios for Corporate, Partnership, and Proprietorship ($15 each); Inventory Tracker ($20); Project Scheduler ($15); Monthly Calendar ($8); Grading and Attendance Set ($30); Check Book ($15); Personal Budget ($19); Home Inventory ($9); Personal Financial Planning Set ($96); Retirement Analyzer ($25); Business Valuation ($19); Stock Portfolio ($15); RésumExpert ($49); Historical Events Day-by-Day ($35); All-Purpose Mortgage Calculator ($20); Added Payment Mortgage ($19); Multi-Unit Property Management ($40); Real Estate Analysis ($30). And that's just a sample!

Some of the templates you will find perform very sophisticated functions indeed. They prove that you don't always need the most complex program to get complex projects done. Works has a lot of power, and any one of its modules would have been considered state-of-the-art just a few years ago. The Heizer catalog serves not only as an inspiration to what is possible in Microsoft Works, but the templates serve as a starting point for you to get your own version up and running quickly.

The Real Estate Analysis spreadsheet template from the Heizer catalog lets you determine the value of property and manage its rental and sale

Courtesy of Heizer Software

Humanities Software

Humanities Software is one of the largest suppliers of whole language reading and writing software products for school children. Their WRITE ON! series opens in Works' word processor to present a writing curriculum that students can use or adapt. There are over 100 titles with many diverse subjects.

WRITE ON! software lets students compose, edit, and publish poems, letters, reports, stories, journals, essays, and other literary works. Each piece has prompts, passages, and examples on disk and accompanying handouts that guide a student through the exercises. The reading and writing software products are for children in grades K-3 to 9-12, with some products for children with special needs.

The idea behind Humanities Software products is to have the student learn writing and reading by actually doing some writing and reading. WRITE ON! is process writing, incorporating strategies from whole language, literature-based instruction, cooperative learning, and writing. The curriculum is designed to encourage students to write more and integrate their writing into their learning. Like Works, WRITE ON! can be net-worked; the products are sold with a site license for use in the classroom. A typical title costs between $80 and $100, with packages of five related titles costing about $315 to $415.

K-12 MicroMedia Publishing

K-12 MicroMedia Publishing provides two distinct services for Microsoft Works users. It produces a free comprehensive catalog which details a myriad of teaching, reference, training, and support materials available for use with Microsoft products. The company also publishes several products that interface with Microsoft Works for the Mac, the most exciting product being its Fields of Learning multimedia programs.

Fields of Learning is a series of complete supplementary teaching packages for the science and social studies curriculums. It provides a dynamic approach to each subject by tapping into all the bells and whistles associated with interactive multimedia (color, sound animations, interactive glossaries, charts, graphs, scanned images, graphics, access to laser video discs, and an abundance of print materials for off-screen study). Optional laser video discs interact with several areas of the lessons and activities, in-cluding the extensive databases.

Each learning module offers innovative ways to integrate Microsoft Works into the curriculum through the software, books, and other print materials. Problem-solving activities leading to process thinking are designed around the spreadsheet, database, and word processor, and the program itself contains many documents from each of the applications for use with recommended activities. *Fields of Learning: Life Science* is available for a 45-day preview to educators. *Fields of Learning: U.S. History* (with multicultural overtones) will ship late 1992.

In addition to its multimedia packages, K-12 MicroMedia Publishing has developed the popular SchoolWorks series of preprogrammed applications for the teacher, student, librarian, coach, department head, and administrator. Using the power of Microsoft Works combined with the SchoolWorks enhancements, the harried educator will find quick and easy solutions to literally hundreds of tedious, mundane tasks.

All Fields of Learning software and SchoolWorks products include a site license. To preview any product or for more information, contact K-12 MicroMedia Publishing.

TI&IE

The Teachers' Idea & Information Exchange (TI&IE) was established to combat one of the occupational hazards of teaching — a sense of isolation. Teachers often lack the opportunity to compare notes and exchange ideas with other teachers in their community, and rarely do so with colleagues across the country. TI&IE is a nationwide network for computer-using educators. The exchange is meant to allow teachers to share ideas, information, templates, files, tips, techniques, software reviews, book reviews, questions and answers with each other.

Members of TI&IE receive four Microsoft Works data disks (quarterly) each school year. The annual subscription fee is $39.95; a Sampler Disk and Catalog are available for $4.95. Subscribers also receive a substantial discount on other products available through TI&IE. Data disks include files for lesson plans, grades, research and cooperative learning activities, a ready-to-use word processor, a database, and spreadsheet files (complete with teaching suggestions). Teachers and administrators at all levels benefit. Classroom teachers who are current TI&IE subscribers may make as many copies of the quarterly disks as needed for use in their classrooms and share the disks at the building level with other teachers. District licenses are also available.

TI&IE is a group of teachers from all fifty states and Canada who exchange information using Microsoft Works files. Subscribers add their templates to a collection that is culled every month for a set of disks to be sent out to other subscribers. A typical quarterly release contains a collection of work from gradebook spreadsheets, research calendars, files for lesson plans and schedules, physical fitness and sports spreadsheets, library applications, administrative files, special education files, and an extensive collection of database files.

The focus at TI&IE is on work that is teacher-created and teacher-tested. Lesson plans, cooperative learning research topics, activities involving higher level thinking skills, simulations, whole-language applications, classroom management ideas, and many other files are part of the collection that can be obtained from the TI&IE data disks. StoryWorks, part of the TI&IE collection, focuses on interactivity; teachers create their own on-screen tutorials, quizzes, interactive fiction, timelines and hypertext applications. The StoryWorks products use Microsoft Works word processor files to create custom-made stack software and can add sound effects and scoring to enhance situation specific learning tools. Microsoft Works is the text engine that drives the TI&IE learning process.

WorksWare

WorksWare publishes Realty Works, a set of Microsoft Works templates that let brokers and agents manage all aspects of residential and investment property sales. The features offered in Realty Works include modem access to the Multiple Listing Service (MLS); buyer qualification and multiple loan analysis; a system for tracking listings; creating and mailing letters; sorts for a database of buyers that organizes the buyers by price range; property type, and by motivation; a seller's net proceeds report; a home buyer's cost analysis report; and a property management system for homes, apartments, and condominiums. Realty Works also provides sample newsletters and flyers for advertising.

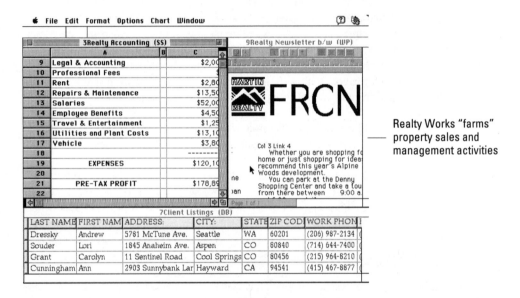

Realty Works "farms" property sales and management activities

Realty Works is a complete realtor office-management package that can be quite useful to individuals owning and managing property. For financial analysis, there are templates that prepare reports for loan amortization and summaries, investment analysis, income activity, commissions and expenses, and personal financial net works. You can also analyze both principal and interest in the monthly payments for each year in under two seconds.

In the jargon of the realty industry, Realty Works provides a complete "farming" system for all activities necessary to manage property. Realty Works is available for $149 retail, and there are DOS and Windows versions available for Works on those platforms.

Using Forms

All businesses use forms — some are the homemade variety; others are purchased from commercial sources. Most business use the database to print forms because the same data can be used in multiple forms (up to 16 per file). There's a lot of set up involved in placing fields or text in the exact position so that they will print to a form correctly. You could measure each place on the form with a ruler and then use the rulers in Works to line up your fields, but there is a better way. Here's a shortcut to set Works up quickly for your special form; this process works equally well for a spreadsheet or word processor file.

Setting up a form:

1. **Use a flatbed scanner to scan your form at 100% size.** It's important to use a flatbed scanner and not a handheld or sheetfed scanner as these types of scanners introduce inaccuracies into the scan. The resolution of the scan is not important, nor do you need to capture all of the color information.

2. **Run the scan as black-and-white (often this is called line art), and save it as a PICT file.** If you have an image processing program like Aldus Digital Darkroom, Adobe PhotoShop, Letraset ColorStudio, or the version of DeskPaint that ships with many scanners, lighten the resultant scanned image so that the lines appear gray. This will make it easier to see the results of your efforts in Works.

3. **Open the database that you are going to use to print the form.**

   You can also use this procedure for word processor and spreadsheet files.

4. **Open a new draw document.**

5. **Place the PICT file in the draw document.**

6. **Select the entire PICT object, and copy it to the Clipboard.** Some scanners let you scan directly into the Clipboard, allowing you to paste that form's graphic directly into the draw layer of your database. This allows you to skip Steps 4, 5, and 6.

7. **Switch to the forms mode in the database and begin placing your fields and text objects, as desired.**

Name

Company

Address

Address 1

City State Zip

Telephone Number

___ Using a template
to recreate a form

This concept of placing a template drawing in a layer to be used to create a duplicate drawing is the one that Adobe Illustrator uses. In Works, you use the template to place your printed output on the forms. Isn't that easier than trying to measure fields or text to fit?

You can also choose to duplicate the form in the draw layer by drawing lines, typing text objects to match the text of the form, creating patterned screens, and duplicating all elements of the form. When you are done, select PICT for the form and delete it. This approach works best when you have grayed the form so that you can see the objects you are placing. Having the drawn form frees you from ever having to buy that printed form again. Your printer prints it on demand. When information on that form changes, such as an address or telephone number, that information is easily changed.

Cut sheet forms work well with this approach because they always feed into the printer at the same position. Unless you require duplicate or triplicate forms, cut sheet is the way to go. You can always use a second page to print out copy information. Some companies will even sell you sheets with two or three different colors mixed one after the other.

If your business requires duplicate or triplicate forms, you may need to use carbon paper and an impact (dot matrix) printer. You can try using the sheet feeder that Apple sells for the ImageWriter, but most carbon paper forms are attached at the top of the page and are difficult to feed into a printer platen. The best results are obtained with pin-fed forms. When rolling pin fed paper into the platen, there will be one exact spot where the paper is correctly positioned. It can be difficult to place the first form into the correct position, even if you know exactly where that spot is. If your business uses a lot of the same multiple part forms, then consider dedicating a dot matrix printer to outputting that form only. Once you position the first form correctly, all other forms will be correct.

There are any number of places that you can find special computer forms. All of the major commercial forms printer have them, and chances are office supply superstores carry a nice selection. One place that sells over 1600 computer forms is NEBS (800-225-9550 or Fax 800-234-4324), ask for their Computer Forms & Software catalog. Although Works is not listed for its compatibility with any forms in the NEBS catalog (as are many other programs), many forms are applicable.

For special paper for laser and ink jet printers to give your printed output that special look, you might want to look at the papers offered by PaperDirect. PaperDirect (800-A-PAPERS) offers designer color paper to give your printed output a commercial printing look. Some of the designs are simply spectacular and can be used for brochures and mailers, letterhead, perfs and scores, reply cards, certificates, labels, envelopes, and more. PaperDirect offers the PaperKit, a sample of their premium papers, with three mailings for $14. A very extensive sample kit that shows hundreds of letter-sized papers is sent with your first order. Their products offer a great way to create business and personal high quality printing without going to a commercial printer.

Using Works on a Network

Works doesn't offer any special networking capabilities except for the appearance of Microsoft Mail's Send and Receive command in its file menu. You can't work on files with more than one user at the same time or communicate with more than another user with the Communications module. One person can open a Works file as a read/write document; other users can then open the document only as a read-only document. Any time you open a file within Works, any other person trying to open that file will get a message telling them that the file is busy or missing. With this exception, there's nothing stopping you from using Works on a network in the normal way.

Depending on the size of the data file you will be working with, that file can reside either on the server or on a client node. Small files that should be accessible to all are best placed on a server or centrally located computer on the network. Large files, like databases, should be kept on the computer on which they are used the most. You can, however, use a server for printing and communication services.

The server is often a powerful Macintosh computer, but in small networks a computer like a Mac SE/30 with a fast hard drive can be an adequate server. Servers serve the network as long as the computer isn't tied up with processing other data requests like running a program, calculating a spreadsheet, or complex graphics printing.

Installing Works on a server:

1. **Turn off any virus detection software; it can freeze the installer.**

2. **Insert *Works Disk 1 - Install* into your floppy disk drive.**

3. **Click the Customize Button in the Easy Install dialog box.**

4. **Select the Run Works From Server option from the list to install Works for use as a shared application.**

— or —

5. **Select the Install Works From Server option if you will install Works later on individual client nodes on the network.**

6. **Press the Install button, and insert disks as the Installer requires you.** The Installer then posts an Installation Complete dialog box.

7. **Click the Restart button to restart your Macintosh.** Don't forget to turn your virus detection software back on.

Most networks have a person called a network administrator. It's a good idea to have that person complete any installations to or from the server and to help you with any network issues with which you may be unfamiliar. For a comprehensive look at Macintosh networking, see the *Macworld Networking Handbook,* by Dave Kosiur and Nancy E. H. Jones, published by IDG Books Worldwide, 1992.

When you open a Works file, you copy that file into the memory (RAM) of your computer. Saving that file to disk writes that information back to the place of origin. Both steps use the network when other computers are involved, and the network can be a bottleneck. LocalTalk networks are fine for files in the 20 to 200K size, but slow down considerably for files over 500K. Files over 1MB will noticeably affect AppleTalk network performance. Even a faster EtherNet network will offer only about a 25 percent faster response time with large files. Careful placement of Works files for good network performance is therefore very important.

The best way to use Works in a network environment is to have the Works program installed on each node in the network. Indeed, if you set Works up this way, Microsoft requires that you have a separate licensed copy of Works for each machine the software is loaded on. You slow down the network significantly when you swap the code necessary to load Works from a server (a host computer) to a client (node). If you intend to use Works' communication services, you will need to have a communications toolbox loaded on each machine where those services are required. For Works to access communications tools, you must load them with the system software at startup.

Installing the Communication tool:

1. **If you are installing Works from another Macintosh on the network, make sure that the other Macintosh is turned on.**

2. **Turn off any virus detection software.**

3. **Select the Chooser from the Apple menu.**

4. **Click on the AppleShare icon to highlight it, or highlight whatever other network icon (such as Netware) you might be using.**

5. **Click on an AppleTalk Zone and the name of the server that contains the Works files.**

6. **If necessary, enter the name of the server item, and then click the OK button.**

7. **Close the Chooser.**

8. **Double-click on the network folder.**

9. **Open the Works files, and then double-click on the Communications Installer button.**

    You should have installed Works on a server to do the previous step.

10. **Click on the Install button in the Easy Install dialog box.**

11. **After the Installation Complete dialog box appears, restart your Macintosh.**

Remember to reinstall your virus detection software.

You can install Works on a client Macintosh from the Works installer disks, as described in Appendix A. You can also install Works on a server (see above), and use that server to install Works on client computers. Installing Works from a server to many other computers is much more efficient than installing on each machine individually. Of course, you need to be sure that the network software and connections are working properly before you begin.

Installing Works from a server:

1. **Check that the server is on and working properly.**

2. **Turn off any virus detection software.**

3. **Select the Chooser from the Apple menu.**

4. **Click on the AppleShare (or other network icon), an AppleTalk zone, and the server that contains the Works files.**

5. **Enter a name and password, if required, and then click the OK button.**

6. **Highlight the server item you need, and then click the OK button.** You should see a network folder icon on your desktop; this means that you are connected to the server.

7. **Close the Chooser.**

8. **Open the network folder by double-clicking on it.**

9. **Open the folder with the Works files, and then double-click on the Installer button.**

10. **Click the Install button in the Easy Install dialog box.**

11. **Enter your name and company when it is requested.**

12. **After the Installation Complete dialog box is posted, click the Restart button.**

13. **Reinstall your virus detection software.**

Unless you install additional software on your network, everyone will have access to the same Works files. There are some minor protection features in System 7, and some network software offers restricted access to folders and disks you specify, but not always and maybe not in as sophisticated a manner as you might require. Security software is covered in Topic 13, so you may want to read the section on securing a PowerBook for product information.

You can use Works as a shared application with a copy running on the server. Each person uses that copy on their client machine. This slows a network considerably, as noted earlier, but this situation is fine for small networking environments, like a three- or four-Macintosh office. Only one Works license is required in this type of situation. You can also place a copy on each Macintosh. That copy should be a personal copy that no one else uses.

Using Works as a shared application:

1. **Select the Chooser from the Apple menu.**

2. **Click on the AppleShare icon (or other network icon), the AppleTalk zone, and the server name that contains the Works program, and then click the OK button.**

3. **Enter a name and password if required, and then click the OK button.**

4. **Close the Chooser.**

5. **Double-click on the Microsoft Works Folder icon, and then click on the Microsoft Works 3 program icon.**

If you want to open a Works document on a network as a shared document (open by two or more users), then place that file on the server, or grant access to the part of your hard drive that has that file in it. Macintosh System 7 has a networking capability that allows users to share or restrict access to individual files or folders. You can only open a Works file as a read/write access file if no one else currently has that file open as a read/write file. This feature prevents the data from one person conflicting with the data from another. Imagine the chaos if one user opened up the same database record or field as another and tried to enter data into it. Works will alert you if you try to open a read/write file that can only be opened as a read only file. If you intend to just look at a file, and not change it, then open it as read only so that other workers can continue with their work without waiting for you to close the file.

Opening a shared file:

1. **Select the Chooser from the Apple menu.**

2. **Select the AppleShare icon (or other network icon), an AppleTalk zone, and the file server with the file you want to open. Click the OK button.**

3. **Choose the Guest or Registered User option button.** A Guest has read-only privileges; a Registered User has read/write privileges. For a Registered User, enter your name and password when prompted.

4. **Click the OK button.**

5. **Click on the server item you want to open; then click the OK button.** A network folder appears on your desktop indicating that you are connected a the server.

6. **Close the Chooser.**

7. **Launch Microsoft Works 3, if needed.**

8. **Choose the Open command on the File menu, or press the Command-O keystroke.**

9. **Open the network folder; then open the document and click the OK button**.

Remember, if you have read-only privileges you can still make changes to a file by creating a copy of that file for your own use using the Save As command on the File menu. To restrict access to a file, you need to place that file in a folder that is protected from unauthorized entry. Clearly, read-only access will not suffice for sensitive documents. Consult the Macintosh System 7 file-sharing and protection section of the System 7 documentation, or your own network's documentation for further information.

Using electronic mail

Works has some built-in features to support Microsoft Mail version 2.0 or later. Microsoft Mail enables you to send and receive messages over a network. You can also attach a file to a message. Any other file sent to you from another application can be opened in Microsoft Works, provided that Works contains an appropriate translation filter for the task. These filters are described in Topic 12. Since Works now has many filters in it, a considerable range of document types can be opened. This includes all data types — word processor, graphics, database, and spreadsheet files. Once opened, you can use the data from various applications as you would use data from any other Works file.

Microsoft Mail can also support a dial-in modem communication session. When you dial in from Works (great on a PowerBook on the road), you can use the Microsoft Mail Dial-In Utility to connect to your mail account. Information on this process is contained in the *Microsoft Mail Dial-In User's Guide*. You may also want to refer back to the Microsoft Mail manual for instructions to use the mail feature in Works.

Assuming that you have Microsoft Mail operating on a server, and that you have a mailbox, you can send and receive mail from Works. The procedure is straightforward.

Sending a mail message from Works:

1. **Open or create a Works document.** Mail is available from any of the Works modules.

2. **Save the file to your disk using the filename of your choice before sending it. It's a good idea to retain a copy of your work.**

3. **Select the Send Mail command on the File menu.** Works displays a list of all possible Microsoft Mail mailboxes in a scrolling list.

4. **Select the name(s) of your correspondents and then select the Add button.**

5. **Type the title of your mail message in the RE text box.** Use a descriptive phrase, or leave the RE text box blank, as you desire. What you type in the RE text box is displayed by Microsoft Mail in the Summary window.

6. **To add a note (for example, a routing slip) to the mail message, click an insertion point in the Message window, then type your note, if desired.**

7. **Click the Send button to send the message.**

Your message is then sent to all of the recipients that you specified and appears in their Summary windows for them to open.

Receiving a message in Works:

1. **Choose the Open Mail command in the File menu.** Microsoft Mail opens the Summary window that contains a list of all messages that have been sent to you.

2. **Select the message(s) you wish to display by clicking on it, or by holding the Shift key and clicking and dragging to extend the range of messages.**

3. **Click on the Open button to display the message.**

— or —

3. **Double-click on a message name to open that message.**

Once a mail message is opened, it is displayed in its own separate window. Mail messages stay in your mailbox until you delete them.

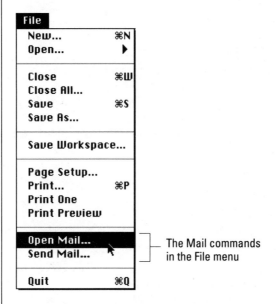

The Mail commands in the File menu

Deleting a Microsoft Mail message in Works:

1. **Choose the Open Mail command from the File menu.**

2. **Select and highlight the message(s) in the Summary window that you want to delete.**

3. **Click on the Delete button.** Be certain that you want to delete the message before you click the Delete button because you will not be able to retrieve that message once it's deleted. If you haven't opened a file, and you try to delete it, Works will post an alert box asking if you wish to delete a message you haven't seen.

Summary

- ✔ Spreadsheet publishing involves using a spreadsheet to produce formatted documents from a single form. Database publishing, which refers to printing repetitive data, is used to produce catalogs, address books, and other types of directories.

- ✔ Database publishing can be done either within the Database module in a form or as a mail merge with an associated word processing document.

- ✔ Stationery templates, documents that are prebuilt and preformatted, can save you a lot of time and effort.

- ✔ Works ships with a set of 17 templates from five different companies for your use.

- ✔ The Heizer Software catalog is the largest independent source of Works templates. Other companies offering templates include Humanities Software, K-12 MicroMedia Publishing, TI&IE, and WorksWare.

- ✔ You can scan in a picture template of a form to create and reproduce forms within Works.

- ✔ Microsoft Mail is supported directly through the Works File menu.

- ✔ Although Works doesn't have any special network capabilities, you can open and use Works' files on a network.

Appendixes

Appendix A
Installing Works

Works' Requirements

Works will operate on all Macintosh computers that have the following characteristics:

✦ *Macintosh Plus or later computer.* You can successfully operate Works on Classic, Classic II, Mac SE, Mac SE/30, Mac LC, Mac LC II, Mac II series, Portable, and PowerBook computers. You will not be able to operate Works 3 on either a Mac 128, Mac 512, or Mac 512 KE. Earlier versions of Works (2) will operate on a Mac 512 or Mac 512 KE.

✦ *RAM of 2MB or more.* Works 3 requires a Macintosh with 2MB RAM installed. The program itself requires a memory partition of 1024K or 1MB in addition to the system requirement of 1MB. Works 2 could run in a 512K partition.

✦ *Disk storage of 5MB.* Full installation of all Works files including all templates, help files, and tutorial files requires 4.5MB of free unused disk space. You can choose to install Works itself without tutorial or stationery templates, which requires only about 3MB of disk space.

✦ *HyperCard version 2.1.* This is required to run the Works tutorial stacks, an optional teaching tool.

Using the Installer

You installed earlier versions of Works by clicking and dragging the file icons from the program disks over to your hard drive. In version 3.0, you install Works on your system using the Installer, the Macintosh program installation utility. If you have used the Installer before to create a system on your hard drive, then you will be familiar with its operation. The Installer has been used beginning with System 6 and later versions.

Installing Works:

1. **Turn off any virus software that is currently running on your machine.** The INIT or Extension component detects mounted volumes (such as floppy disks) that can cause the Installer to hang. Programs such as Symantec's SAM, Mainstay's AntiToxin, Microcom's Virex, and the shareware programs Disinfectant, GateKeeper, Virus Detective, and others all have these components.

2. **Insert the *Works Disk 1 - Install* into your floppy disk drive.**

3. **Double-click on the disk icon to open the disk window, if necessary.**

4. Double-click on the Installer icon.

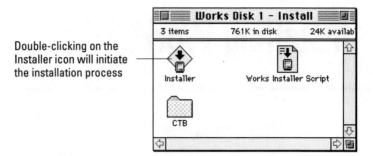

Double-clicking on the Installer icon will initiate the installation process

A start-up screen appears:

5. Click OK to dismiss the start-up screen, and the Installer will appear:

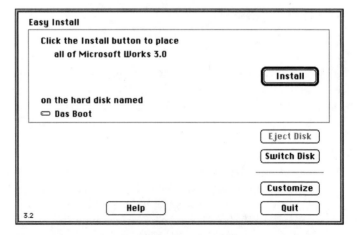

6. Click the Install button to install Microsoft Works using Easy Install option. Works will install all components of the package and use all five disks. If you want to install only certain elements of the package, see the following section to do a custom installation.

7. **If you have other applications running, Works posts the alert box shown in the following figure asking if the Installer can quit all open applications. Click the Continue button, or press the Return or Enter key to continue installation.**

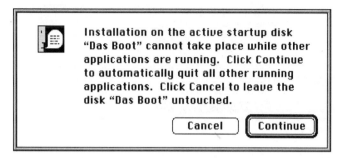

8. **When Works posts a dialog box requesting your name and company name, fill in the requested information.**

9. **Works then posts a progress dialog box first determining what disks are needed. Then it asks you to insert each required disk in turn.**

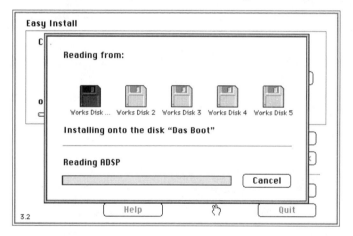

When the Installer has completed its installation, an alert box is posted asking you to restart your Macintosh.

10. **Click on the Restart button.** Once your Macintosh restarts, you can double-click on the Works icon to launch Works.

Deciding between Easy vs. Custom Install

The default Installer option is called the Easy Install mode. It places every possible Works file on your hard drive in the right places. Some files are unnecessary for the experienced user, like the large HyperCard tutorial stack. Others, like the Works Help system, although useful, take up a lot of disk space. You may not be able to, or want to, install all these files. That's where the Custom Installation option comes into play.

When you click the Customize button in the Installer screen, the Customize Install dialog box appears. This dialog box lets you choose each and every component of Works that you want the Installer to install. Click on a desired component, hold the Shift key and then click on any other desired component, or click and drag a range of desired components. This is standard dialog box selection technique. Don't worry about getting it right the first time; you can always run the Installer later to place additional files on your hard drive.

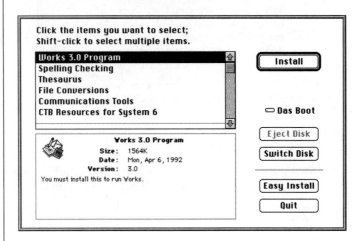

As you click on each component in the Customize dialog box, you will notice information about the filename that is being installed, what that file does, and the size of the file. The following table summarizes this information, and also tells you where the file is supposed to end up once the Installer has worked its magic.

Table A-1:	Installed Works files		
Filename	*What it does*	*Where it goes*	*Size*
Works 3.0 Program	Runs Works.	Works folder.	1564K
Spell Checking	Checks spelling in word processor.	Spelling folder inside Tools folder.	398K
Thesaurus	Gives synonyms in word processor. Installs with dictionary file.	Thesaurus folder inside Tools folder.	798K
File Conversions	Translate files to/from other formats.	Conversions folder inside Tools folder.	810K
Communications Tools	Allows use of the communications module.	Extension folder in System Folder (7), or in System Folder (6).	888K

(continued)

Table A-1: Installed Works files (continued)

Filename	What it does	Where it goes	Size
CTB Resources	Enables the Communications tools in System 6.	Extension folder in System Folder (7), or in System Folder (6).	77K
Learning Microsoft Works	HyperCard tutorial stack to demo program.	In Works folder.	906K
Getting Started	Folder of example files for use with the Getting Started manual.	Getting Started folder inside Works folder.	58K
Microsoft Works Help	On-line help system.	Help folder inside Tools folder.	1064K
Stationery	Sample templates folder.	Stationery folder inside Works folder.	176K
Run Works from Server	Sets up Works so that it can be run from a network server.*	Works folder.	4K
Install Works from a Server	Installs Works from a server onto a client Mac.*	Works folder.	4K
Read Me	Installed automatically — not a selectable option. Late-breaking instructions.	Works folder.	3K
TeachText	Opens Read Me file. Installed automatically.	Works folder.	21K

Note: *For more information, see *Guide to Using Microsoft Works for the Macintosh on a Network,* part of your Works' documentation.

In an installation, Works writes a preference file called MSWorks Prefs inside the System Folder (top level). If you delete the MSWorks Prefs file, when Works restarts, it creates a new file with the default preferences. A number of conversion files are placed into the Microsoft folder within your System Folder. The Microsoft folder also contains some settings in the Thesaurus, Spelling, and Help folders. The Help folder contains the MacHelp engine that runs the Microsoft Works Help file.

The Communications toolbox is a standard feature of System 7.0.1. You only need install it when you are using an earlier system. Installing the Communications toolbox places the following files into the Extension folder of your System Folder (in System 7): ADSP, Apple Modem tool, AppleTalk ADSP tool, Serial tool, Text tool, TTY tool, TTY font, VT102 Tool, VT102Font, VT320 Tool, VT320Font, and the Xmodem tool. In System 6, these files are placed at the top level of the System Folder, and installation of the CTB file puts a system file called CTB Resources into the System Folder as well.

Files on the Installer disk are in Aladdin's compressed StuffIt Deluxe format. You could copy those files to their intended location, and then use UnStuffIt Deluxe to decompress those files. UnStuffIt Deluxe is available on bulletin boards and on-line services.

Installing Works on a Portable

Installing Works on a Portable presents you with a special set of problems. These problems are discussed in Topic 13. Basically, you want to install only those components of Works that you actually use. This technique conserves both precious disk space and even more precious RAM. Chances are that the bare minimum files you will have to install include the Works 3.0 Program and the Communications tools. These two components install in 2.4MB of disk space. The following components of Works are optional: Spell Checker, Thesaurus, and File Conversions. These options depend on how heavily you use those parts of Works. The optional components add an additional 2MB worth of files.

To specify the components you want to add, use the Custom Install option discussed in the previous section.

Appendix B
Keyboard Shortcuts

Command	Key sequence	Menu	Usable in
Absolute Reference	Command-E	Edit	SS
Auto-Close Shape	N while drawing		DRAW
Bold	Command-B	Style	WP/DB/SS
Bring to Front	Command-F	Arrange	DRAW
Calculate Now	Command-equal	Options	SS
Cancel Printing	Command-period		ALL
Clear Object or Text	Delete/Backspace	Edit	DRAW
Click Default Button	Return	Dialog Boxes	ALL
Click Default Button	Enter	Dialog Boxes	ALL
Close	Command-W	File	ALL
Close Connection	Command-K	Connection	COMM
Copy	Command-C	Edit	ALL
Copy Ruler Settings	Command-K	Document	WP
Cut	Command-X	Edit	ALL
Decrease Font Size	Command-[	Style	WP
Define Filter	Command-K	Data	DB
Delete or Remove	Delete/Backspace		ALL
Draw On/Off	Command-J	Window	WP/DB/SS
Duplicate	Command-D	Edit	DRAW
Duplicate Previous	Command-E	Edit	DB
Fill Down	Command-D	Edit	SS
Fill Right	Command-R	Edit	SS
Find	Command-F	Edit	ALL
Go Down One Window	Page Down key	Ext Key	ALL
Go To Document End	End key	Ext Key	ALL
Go To Document Start	Home key	Ext Key	ALL
Go To Page...	Command-K	Page	DRAW
Go Up One Window	Page Up key	Ext Key	ALL
Group	Command-G	Arrange	DRAW
Help	Command-?	Window	ALL
Hide/Show Ruler	Command-R	Window	WP
Hide/Show Tools	Command-T	Window	ALL
Increase Font Size	Command-]	Style	WP
Insert Footnote	Command-E	Document	WP
Insert Page Break	Shift-Enter		WP
Insert Record	Command-I	Data	DB
Italic	Command-I	Style	WP

(continued)

(continued)

Command	Key sequence	Menu	Usable in
List View	Command-L	Form	DB
Match Records	Command-M	Data	DB
Merge Fields	Command-M	Document	WP
Move Down One Cell	Down arrow		SS
Move Down One Field	Down arrow		DB
Move Left One Cell	Left arrow		SS
Move Left One Field	Left arrow		DB
Move object one pixel down	Down arrow		DRAW
Move object one pixel left	Left arrow		DRAW
Move object one pixel right	Right arrow		DRAW
Move object one pixel up	Up arrow		DRAW
Move Right One Cell	Right arrow		SS
Move Right One Field	Right arrow		DB
Move Up One Field	Up arrow		DB
New	Command-N	File	ALL
Next Page	Command-equal	Page	DRAW
Next Record	Command-equal	Data	DB
Open	Command-O	File	ALL
Open Connection	Command-D	Connection	COMM
Paste	Command-V	Edit	ALL
Paste Ruler Set	Command-Y	Document	WP
Perfect Shape or Line	Shift while draw		DRAW
Previous Page	Command-hyphen	Page	DRAW
Previous Record	Command-hyphen	Data	DB
Print	Command-P	File	ALL
Quit	Command-Q	File	ALL
Receive File	Command-L	Connection	COMM
Save	Command-S	File	ALL
Select All	Command-A	Edit	ALL
Select Multi Objects	Shift-select		DRAW
Send File...	Command-U	Connection	COMM
Send To Back	Command-B	Arrange	DRAW
Show Info...	Command-I	Connection	COMM
Spelling...	Command-L	Document	WP
Start Timer	Command-G	Connection	COMM
Thesaurus	Command-D	Document	WP
Touch Up	Option-select	Chart	SS
Underline	Command-U	Style	WP
Undo	Command-Z	Edit	ALL
Ungroup	Command-U	Arrange	DRAW

Key:

WP = Word Processing module
DRAW = Draw module
DB = Database module
ALL = Available in all modules

SS = Spreadsheet module
COMM = Communications module
Ext Key = Extended Keyboard keys

Appendix C
Glossary

The following is a list of useful terms for the Macintosh interface and Microsoft Works 3. Cross-references within this listing are italicized, so that the Glossary is self-contained. References to Topics are also mentioned.

alignment. The way a paragraph is spaced against a margin.

application. 1. A computer program or set of programs intended for specific tasks, or 2. the specific use of some software itself. Works is one application but contains five modules. The Works program has only one *icon*, which means it is one Macintosh application, but because it handles a variety of independent tasks, it is also called *integrated software* or an integrated application. Works is one software application in sense 1 but has dozens of applications in sense 2.

ascending sort. The "sort" command orders listed information in one of two orders, and an ascending sort orders low to high (that is, 0 to 9, A to Z). See *descending sort*.

background. 1. A program working behind the scenes in memory, or 2. a color assigned to the fill behind objects. In sense 1, all kinds of computations take place without your normally being aware of them. Automatic spreadsheet recalculation can be a background activity; repagination (the method of expanding or shrinking pages in the word processor to fit the text you type) is a background activity; the "auto-save feature," is a background activity. "Background printing" allows you to continue working on one document while printing another.

Balloon Help. A help system that displays small windows of information describing features on your screen. Accessed in the Help menu. See Topic 2 for details.

baud. A telecommunications term referring imprecisely to bits per second. *Modems* are rated by their speed in baud, such as 300 baud, 2400 baud, 9600 baud. The current personal computer standard remains 2400 baud, but in the next few years (as prices drop on faster modems), 9600 baud will become the new standard.

bit. The basic unit of information in the binary system; how computers store and manipulate data.

bit map. A video representation of an image stored in a computer's memory. Pictures, including some *fonts*, are made of up of picture elements (dots called pixels). The bitmapped graphics consist of thousands of these dots — much like newspaper photographs — in a mosaic or tile pattern. Bitmapped graphics are often referred to as raster graphics. See also *draw, object-oriented graphic*.

button. An object you *click* in a *dialog box* to perform an action or to acknowledge having received information. Typical button messages are OK, Yes, No, Cancel, and so on. Double-outlined buttons are the default and can be activated by pressing the Return or Enter key.

byte. A set of contiguous bits used to group bits into computer words.

cdev. An acronym for control panel device. A cdev is a small utility program which, rather than accessing by double-*clicking* its *icon*, you either open the Control Panels folder (in System 7.x) or open the Control Panel *DA* under the Apple menu (in System 6.x) to activate, deactivate, or give the program instructions. Some cdevs are also *INITs*. An example of a Macintosh cdev is the mouse control panel.

cell. The compartments that make up the matrix grid you work on in all spreadsheets. Also the designated blocks in some tables (such as those in Microsoft Word). Each cell can contain any kind of information you enter, such as formulas and values. However, internal data formats (text, number, date, time, and so on) for cells, and external display and output formats (like font size) need to be specified.

cell reference. An address that defines the position of a cell in a spreadsheet. The cell C2 would be in the third column, second row. Absolute cell references refer to the cell address, no matter where that reference is copied to. Relative cell references point to a cell a certain distance and direction away. When a relative reference is copied, the cell it points to changes to the cell the appropriate distance and direction away. See Topic 7 for details.

chart. A graph that turns spreadsheet data into a visual display. Works supports line, pie, bar, stacks, combinations, and hi-lo-close graphs. See Topic 8 for more details.

Chooser. An Apple System *DA* which allows you to select which printer, which *modem*, and which serial *port* to use. The Chooser also allows you to *toggle* AppleTalk networks on and off.

click. The action of quickly pressing and releasing the mouse button. Double-clicking icons (two fast clicks together) is the way you can launch *applications*. Click speed can be set in the Keyboard *DA*, as can the repeat rate.

Clipboard. An area of memory where the most recent item cut or copied is stored. When you *paste*, whatever you're pasting is residing in the Clipboard. You can see what's in the clipboard by selecting the Show Clipboard command from the Window, View, or other menus in most applications.

close. This feature removes a file or document from memory but keeps the program loaded. You can *click* the *close box*, select the Close command from the File menu, or use the *command-key equivalent* each application provides.

close box. The small white box in the upper-left corner of each document *window*. To close a file, simply *click* the box. Windows are discussed in Topics 2 and 3.

column. 1. In spreadsheets, the name of each vertical division of *cells*, or 2. in word processing or desktop publishing, vertical divisions of text on a page.

command-key equivalent. See *keystroke equivalents*.

communications. The ability of two computers to share data in real-time. See Topic 9 for more information.

compatibility. Refers to whether or not two file types, two applications, two hardware *platforms*, or two other things can exchange information. For example, Works is compatible with most other Macintosh word processors and spreadsheets.

connection. A data link between two computers with an agreed protocol for transferring information.

copy. The command to use — available under the Edit menu in every Mac application — when you want to have something moved within or between documents without removing the original; or what you do when you make a complete duplicate of a file, folder, or disk.

cursor. A position of a movable icon or picture that lets you control an action at that point. Cursors are moved by the mouse.

Cut. The command to use — available under the Edit menu in every Mac application — when you want to move something within or between documents and want the original to disappear. For example, if you have a paragraph on page 5 of a document and feel it would be better on page 8, rather than deleting and retyping, you would simply cut it on page 5 and *paste* it on page 8.

DA (or Desk Accessory). DAs are programs available under the Apple menu that you can access when using another application. This was particularly useful under System 6.x with only the *Finder* — then DAs were "applets," or small applications that used another program as a host. With *MultiFinder* and System 7.x, their novelty is somewhat reduced as they can be any application, but they are still important elements of the Mac environment. Alarm Clock, Calculator, Chooser, Control Panel, DiskTools, Puzzle, and SuitCase II are examples of desk accessories.

data view. A mode of the database in which data is entered.

database. A file that organizes information in related groups called records, with each data entry in a *record* belonging to a data type called a *field*. See Topic 6 for more information.

delimiter. A standard which separates information into a table-like form from where it is easily accessed and manipulated. Tabs in a word processor or fields in a database are the most typical delimiters. Delimiters are important in setting up *file formats*.

descending sort. The opposite of an *ascending sort*, whereby listed information is reorganized in descending order (that is, Z to A, 9 to 0).

design view. A database mode in which you create fields and forms.

dialog box. The boxes with which you communicate with the *Finder* and many applications. Dialog boxes allow you to make extended choices after many commands are initiated, especially those that have an ellipsis (…) after their name in the menu.

document. An individual "project." Sometimes called files (correctly but imprecisely). Every document has its own name. Double-clicking a document file *icon* in the *Finder,* or its name in the file structure, will launch its parent *application* and open the document file.

drag. The action of holding the mouse button down, rolling the mouse, and releasing the mouse button. If an object is selected, a drag moves that object. Drags are also used to select a range of objects.

Draw. A module in Works that creates graphics that are represented by mathematical relationships such as vectors. Draw can create its own document or open as a layer above Works modules. What you see in a word processor window (or another type) is the combination of what is in the word processor layer and the draw layer above it. Drawn graphics are sometimes called *object-oriented graphics*. Draw is the subject of Topic 5.

entry. The contents of a cell or a field.

entry bar. An area of a spreadsheet or database that data in a *cell* or *field* (respectively) is entered. Topics 6 and 7 describe entry bars.

Excel. The best-selling Macintosh graphical spreadsheet. Currently in version 4.0, Excel is the big brother of the spreadsheet in Works 3.

export. The process of "sending" part of a file or document somewhere else, often including a translation of file-type for *compatibility* purposes. See *import*. Import and export capabilities of Works are the subject of Topic 12.

field. Each entry area in a database. A completed set of fields comprises a *record*.

file format. The way a file is constructed. Can refer to *platform* type (for exmple, IBM/PC format versus Mac format) or *compatibility* within one platform. For example, Excel and Works use the same file format for spreadsheets, but MacWrite II and Works' word processor use different formats, so to *export* from one to the other requires a translator.

filter. A set of criteria used to select database records.

find. An operation that searches for an occurrence of a character string. See *search*.

Finder. The standard file and memory management utility included as the shell in Macintosh *operating systems*. When you double-click an *icon*, the Finder is what "finds" and launches the application you have requested or require. See Topic 2 for more information about the Finder.

font. Characters or typefaces in a family or designed style. Examples of fonts are Helvetica, Times, and Bookman. Fonts can be styled using the Style menu; some fonts like Helvetica Bold have all of their characters in bold.

footer. The space set off, and usually accessible only in its own window, at the bottom of word-processed pages. Footers typically include page-number notation, date printed, or titles of some kind. All five main Works modules can open footers in their own windows. Footers are covered in Topic 4.

form. 1. The graphical display or another view of a database that can be printed. Up to 16 forms per file can be created. 2. a document set up to print in standard output.

form letter. A document with placeholders that lets you customize the document to create similar documents. See also *mail merge*.

format. 1. The process of preparing a floppy disk to be *compatible* with a particular *platform*, or 2. a *file format*, the way data is organized in a file. See Topic 12 for more information.

function. In spreadsheets or databases, functions are equations that take a value or argument and return a calculated value. Functions can be *pasted* directly into *cells* as complete formulas, or as elements of formulas that provide automation. Functions typically provide common equations to save you time and frustration. Works provides 64 functions, 56 of which are appropriate to the database. See Topic 11 for more details.

gray scale. A shade of black mixed with white.

group. A set of drawn objects that is manipulated as a single object (see Topic 5).

GUI. Graphical user interface. The part of the *operating system,* which includes *icons* and pull-down menus, that serves as an interactive environment for the user. The Apple Macintosh and Microsoft Windows include GUIs.

hardware. Any physical or mechanical element of a computer system. CPUs, mice, keyboards, monitors, hard disks, floppy disk drives, *modems*, and scanners are examples of hardware.

header. The set-off space, usually accessible in its own window, in word processing documents. The header is usually used to provide a letterhead, the date, or a notation such as "Memorandum." Headers typically include page-number notation, date printed, or titles of some kind. All five main Works modules can open headers in their own windows. Headers are described in Topic 4.

HFS. Hierarchical file system; the way the Macintosh organizes files. See Topic 3 for more information.

icon. A pictographic representation of files, folders, and other items on the Macintosh. Many icons can be double-clicked to *open* them, and many show you what the file is graphically. For example, Works provides a different icon for each type of document you can create.

indent. The distance between the margins and the beginning of a paragraph. See Topic 4.

insertion point. A flashing bar indicating where text will be typed. Text appears to the left of an insertion point.

import. The opposite of *export*. This is what you do when you bring an outside element into a document. Typically, graphics (created in a graphics program) are imported to spice up word processing documents. Topic 12 describes importing data into Works.

INIT. An initialization program, a program whose icon must be in the System Folder to work properly. These programs automatically load and run every time your Mac is turned on, thus adding extra functionality to the System file. Some are patches for system software defects. Typical INITs include virus-protection software and screen savers. In System 7, INITs are called extensions.

integrated software. This refers to one application (or application package) which actually contains a number of smaller programs linked together as one. Works is integrated software. Topic 1 describes integrated software, its advantages, and disadvantages.

keystroke equivalents. A combination of keys pressed at the same time. Usually a modifier key(s) is pressed and held, followed by any other key. Many keystrokes are used to perform menu commands.

label. An explanation typed into a spreadsheet *cell*.

list view. A database mode that puts *records* in rows and *fields* in columns. It looks similar to a spreadsheet worksheet.

logging on. Starting an on-line telecommunication session to a service by dialing, setting up a connection, and giving a password. Works lets you automate this process, as explained in Topic 9. Also called signing on.

macro. An automated sequence of keystrokes or commands — a small program, if you will. Macros are saved to a file for replay later. See Topic 10 for a description of the Works macro recorder.

mail merge. An operation where data in a *database* is used to print form letters in a word processor and to make multiple customized copies. See Topic 6.

menu. The lists at the top of the screen from which you select commands. They change based on what application you are using (or which module of integrated software you are using), and the contents of a menu can change based on the condition of the application at the moment. The horizontal list of the menu titles (for example, File, Edit, and Font) across the top is called the *menu bar*. Click on a menu to see its contents; drag to select a menu command.

modem. An acronym for modulate-demodulate. A modem is a box or NuBus card which translates information between computers and telephone lines. Two computers directly connected (via LAN or AppleTalk, for example) do not require modems, but any computers "talking" over phone lines do. Modems are rated by the speed at which they send and receive data. See *baud*.

MultiFinder. A semi-multitasking update of the *Finder* available on Macintosh Systems 5 and 6. MultiFinder allows you to *open* more than one *application* at a time. You can switch between programs loaded in memory (context switching) to make them run. Some processes such as background communication and printing, can occur while you work in the foreground. True multitasking programs like Unix let more than one application run at a time and protect each from actions of the other.

object-oriented graphic. A picture or piece of a picture which is defined as a mathematical object rather than random strokes on a page. Rather than "erasing" objects, you "edit" them. Object graphics are excellent for forms, charts, tables, and technical work, but you couldn't (well you could, but not on a regular Mac) render a picture of a person or some water lilies with this feature. Works provides object graphics with its draw tools. See *Draw*.

On-line Help. A help system available while using certain applications. This feature saves time by prompting you while you work. Works has On-line Help, as described in Topic 3.

Open. The command you use to display an object's contents and work within a given document, file, application, folder, or window.

operating system. The software, which mostly works in the *background*, which gives instructions to your computer's *hardware,* sets the *platform* and *compatibility* standards for your computer, and gives you a way to interact with your computer (in the Mac's case, a *GUI*). In order for any other software to work, system software must be loaded and running on a computer. See Topic 2 for further information.

overflow area. A part of a communication window in which text that can no longer fit scrolls up into.

page break. Where a page ends and a new page begins. Works calculates page breaks automatically (see Topic 4), or you can manually set your own.

Page Setup. The File menu command that allows you to set parameters for printing the document you are currently working on. Topic 4 fully describes the options available for page setup and printing.

paste. What you do when you put an item into a document. Graphics, text, and other items can be pasted. In spreadsheets and databases, *functions* are pasted also.

platform. A computer system standard like the Macintosh. Generally noted by the chip in the CPU and the system software being run. For instance, the IBM PCs (which are based on Intel chips and either MS-DOS or MS Windows system software) and Macintoshes (which are based around Motorola chips and run the Mac OS) are different platforms.

point. A measure of font size. Typical font sizes are 10, 12, 14, and 24 points, although hundreds of point-sized fonts are possible. A point is $\frac{1}{72}$ of an inch, the smallest detail that could be created by a typeface maker in lead type.

port 1. The computer term for "outlet," where things can be plugged in, or 2. a term used to refer to an *application* originally designed for one *platform* being subsequently rewritten, or ported to another. For number 1, look at the back of your Mac. All those holes are serial, SCSI, and other ports. In the case of number 2, consider Works as an application originally developed for a DOS *platform* that was ported to the Macintosh. Although it's unusual for ported software, the Mac version is vastly superior.

preferences. A Works Edit menu item that lets you create certain default settings to meet your needs. Graphics programs might offer you the preference of a number of different *file formats*, and a word processor might let you choose a default *font* preference (the default font in the Apple *ROMs* is Geneva 12-*point*). Once preferences are set, they never need to be set again. They will run properly until you change them.

Print Preview. A mode of Works that lets you see what will be printed. Use the Print Preview command on the File menu to activate this mode. Topic 3 describes this feature.

printer driver. A program that translates display or stored data to data that an output device can use. Accessible from the *Chooser*, printer drivers are small software programs which create a communication bridge between your computer and your printer(s). To use a given printer, your Mac needs to contain that printer's driver in the System Folder (System 6 and before) or as an extension (in the Extension folder in System 7). You need to select the current printer driver in the Chooser DA.

protocol. A generic name for any number of telecommunications standards. These are software driven; any *modem* can use any protocol. Typical protocols include Kermit and Zmodem. Topic 9 describes communication settings and protocols.

quit. Close all documents (or files) and leave the current *application* altogether removing all components from memory.

RAM. This stands for random-access memory. RAM is volatile memory; when you turn your Mac off, everything in RAM goes away, which is why it's a good idea to *save* frequently. RAM chips reside in slots on the logic board, and how much RAM you have determines how many files or applications you can have open on your computer at any given moment. The more RAM, the more work you can do. Typical Macintosh configurations have 1, 4, or 8MB of RAM. To see how much RAM you have, select "About the Finder" or "About This Macintosh" from the Apple *menu* on the desktop. Sometimes RAM becomes fragmented, so there are only scattered chunks rather than a large piece. If you can't start a program when there is enough memory, restart your Macintosh. See Topic 2 for more information about RAM and memory.

record. 1. In databases, each set of completed *fields* comprises a record, and 2. in *macro* writing, a method by which to write macros automatically while you work. Database records are the fundamental unit or group that is used to organize information. See Topic 6 for information about databases.

report. A printed table for database data organized in a specific way. *Databases* let you save reports by name for later use. See Topic 6.

resize box. A small box at the bottom right corner of a *window* that lets you change the size of a window by clicking and dragging on it.

ROM. This stands for read-only memory. This is the permanent memory in your Macintosh. Unlike RAM chips, which plug into the logic board, ROM chips are permanently soldered onto the board. ROM contains the basic instructions for the computer hardware. What the *operating system* addresses on the board is the ROM chips.

row. In spreadsheets, each horizontal separation of *cells*. Spreadsheets are the subject of Topic 7.

RTF. An *import/export* and *file format* standard used by Microsoft for its Word, Works, and Write programs, and across *platforms*. A Works file *saved as...* RTF can be *opened* by a DOS/Windows version of Word, for example. See Topic 12.

ruler. A bar across the top of word processing documents (above the document *window*) which allows you to set parameters such as spacing, tabs, and so on. The measurements on these rulers are in units that you can set in the Preference dialog box. Rulers are also found in *header* and *footer* windows. Settings on a ruler refer to the attributes of the current paragraph. See Topic 4 for information on the use of rulers. Also, rulers are found in *draw* documents, but they only display measurement, not paragraph attributes.

Save. An action (or the command you use) to store information in *RAM* to be more permanent storage like your hard disk or a floppy disk (or other media). Saving a file replaces that file with the changed contents. If you have never saved a file, Works prompts you to name the file first.

Save As.... A command which allows you to save the current document to a second location, under a different name, or in a different *file format*.

scroll bars. A window element along the right and bottom of a *window* that lets you move your view of the window's contents. See Topic 2 for information on how to use scroll bars.

search. A search is a variation of a find that normally finds all occurrences of a character string at one time. Searches in databases allow you to specify criteria or rules for a search; sets of rules are called *filters*. Using filters, you can organize your data into groups. See Topic 6 for more information.

selection. An item is selected to manipulate it in some way. *Icons* or filenames are highlighted to indicate their selection.

software. All the "stuff" (usually called programs) your computer uses to run and work that is not *hardware*.

spell checker. An automated feature that matches your typed words to words in a dictionary. It flags any character strings that don't match. Topic 4 describes the spell checker in the Works word processor.

stand-alone software. This refers to an *application* with one stated purpose, for which it is usually very well- (or over-) equipped. Word and Excel are examples of stand-alone software. See *integrated software.*

stationery. A document which opens as an untitled copy. Also known as a *template.*

style. A modification you can make to entered text. The standard Macintosh styles are italic, bold, underline, outline, shadow, condensed, and extended. Any number of styles can be combined for effects ranging from the stunning to the illegible, and many software packages offer numerous styles in addition to those always available.

tear-off palette. A palette is an independent tiny window where a set of *tools* are located. Palettes which can be "torn-off" may be *dragged* anywhere on the screen (for your convenience) off of the toolbox from which they pop up.

template. A document used to create another document. It usually contains many or most of the features you need to start the new document. See also *stationery.*

text. A data type which allows any ASCII character to be typed. Data types are described in Topic 6. Other data types include numbers, dates, times, pictures, sounds, and so on.

text object. Text displayed in a *draw* document or draw layer. Text objects are most commonly placed in text columns for positioning and linked autoflow. Topic 5 describes text objects.

text capture. The information in a communications session appears in the Communications window and can be saved as a text file to disk.

thesaurus. An automated dictionary of similar-meaning words. Look up a word in the thesaurus to find synonyms, antonyms (opposite meanings), and related words. See Topic 4 for more details.

toggle. Toggles are two-position switches — on or off. A menu command that is toggled on shows a check mark to indicate that the feature is active and no check mark when inactive. Choose a command once to toggle it on, again to toggle it off.

tool. A single-purpose cursor- (or mouse-) controlled item. In graphics, where tools are normally discussed, this might include a rectangle tool (which can only make rectangles), a pencil tool (which can only draw a very thin line), and other things in the *Tool palette.*

Tool palette. A floating toolbox that lets you change the mode of the document from word processor or spreadsheet to draw, or from spreadsheet to charting, for example. Depending on the mode, different *tools* are displayed. To show the Tool palette, use the Show Tools command (Command-T). Remove the Tool palette from your screen by using the Hide Tools command.

transpose. To change a spreadsheet selection's *rows* into *columns,* and columns into rows, as explained in Topic 7.

window. A view of part of a file's contents. Windows let you move the view about to see other contents of the file. Windows are described in Topic 2 for the Finder, and Topic 4 for word processors. Other specialized aspects of windows are discussed in each of the Topics on Works modules.

window panes. A split of a window into two scrolling horizontal and/or vertical sections. See Topic 6.

word processor. An automatic-typing and page-typesetting environment with special writing tools. See Topic 4.

workspace. Called a desktop in Works 2, this is the saved condition of your screen at any time. When you open a workspace, all files you were working with appear (see Topic 12).

zoom box. This box is located in the upper-right corner of most Macintosh file and document *windows.* The zoom box expands the current window to fill most of the screen (in System 6 and before) and will completely show the contents of the window to the limit of the screen size in System 7. *Clicking* the zoom box a second time returns the window to normal. Windows are described in Topic 2.

Appendix D
Task Index

Index

— X —

— Y —

— Z —

Macworld Authorized Editions

Macworld Guide To Microsoft Word 5
by Jim Heid, *Macworld* magazine's "Getting Started" Columnist

New from the bestselling author of *Macworld Complete Mac Handbook*.

Learn the new Word the easy way with this *Macworld* Authorized Edition.

Highlights:
- Up-to-date for Word 5 — covers all new features
- With step-by-step instructions for mastering everyday word processing tasks
- FREE Illustrated Quick Reference Card includes keyboard shortcuts and type tips

$22.95/$29.95 Canada   ■   ISBN: 1-878058-39-8
448 pages. Available now.

Macworld Guide To System 7
by Lon Poole, *Macworld* magazine's "Quick Tips" Columnist

This *Macworld* Authorized Edition is the most recommended guide to System 7.

"You'll find everything you need to know about System 7 in this book."
— Bob Levitus, author of *Dr. Macintosh*

Highlights:
- Optimize the new features of System 7
- Valuable hardware and software compatibility lists
- Scores of undocumented insider tips and secrets
- NEW! System 7.0.1 Update covers system enhancements and bug fixes

$24.95/$33.95 Canada   ■   ISBN: 1-878058-16-9
384 pages. Available now.

Macworld Networking Handbook
by Dave Kosiur, Ph.D., *Macworld* magazine Contributing Editor, and **Nancy E. H. Jones**

The *Macworld* Authorized Edition for anyone who manages Mac networks.

Highlights:
- The only practical, hands-on guide that explains Macintosh networking from the ground up
- Design, installation, and management of AppleTalk internets explained simply
- Expert advice on optimizing your network
- Covers Apple-to-IBM, Apple-to-DEC networking

$29.95/$39.95 Canada   ■   ISBN: 1-878058-31-2
600 pages. Available now.

Macworld Complete Mac Handbook
by Jim Heid, *Macworld* magazine's "Getting Started" Columnist

The most complete guide to getting started, mastering, and expanding your Mac.

Highlights:
- Loaded with tips and techniques for using the Mac and Mac software better
- For beginners or seasoned veterans
- FREE *Macworld* System 7 Reference Card

$26.95/$35.95 Canada   ■   ISBN: 1-878058-17-7
576 pages. Available now.

IDG BOOKS

Macworld Authorized Editions

Macworld Music & Sound Bible
by Christopher Yavelow

"Invaluable for anyone interested in music and sound on the Mac."
— Alan Kay, Mac Guru

Finally, the definitive guide to music, sound, and multimedia on the Mac.

Highlights:
- Covers the latest hardware, software, and techniques in music and sound
- With interviews and forewords written by industry notables including Herbie Hancock, Craig Anderton, Mark Lacas, Patrick Moraz, Morton Subotnick, and more
- Over 1400 pages crammed with everything you need to know about using music, MIDI, and digital audio in composition, performance, film, video, multimedia, and programming
- Over 500 illustrations and figures

$37.95/$47.95 Canada ■ ISBN: 1-878058-18-5
1456 pages. Available now.

Macworld Guide To Microsoft Excel
by David Maguiness

Build spreadsheets quickly with this *Macworld* Authorized Edition to Excel 4.

Highlights:
- Crunch numbers easily with this quick-start guide to Excel — task-by-task instructions make it simple
- Use the straightforward tutorials and start working right away
- FREE Illustrated Quick Reference Card
- Tabbed for easy look-ups

$22.95/$29.95 Canada ■ ISBN: 1-878058-40-1
448 pages. Available in November.

**IDG
BOOKS**

Order Form

Order Center: (800) 762-2974 (7 a.m.–5 p.m., PST, weekdays)
or   **(415) 312-0650**
Order Center FAX: (415) 358-1260

Quantity	Title & ISBN	Price	Total

Shipping & Handling Charges

Subtotal	U.S.	Canada & International	International Air Mail
Up to $20.00	Add $3.00	Add $4.00	Add $10.00
$20.01–40.00	$4.00	$5.00	$20.00
$40.01–60.00	$5.00	$6.00	$25.00
$60.01–80.00	$6.00	$8.00	$35.00
Over $80.00	$7.00	$10.00	$50.00

In U.S. and Canada, shipping is UPS ground or equivalent. For Rush shipping call (800) 762-2974.

Subtotal _____

CA residents add applicable sales tax _____

IN residents add 5% sales tax _____

Canadian residents add 7% GST tax _____

Shipping _____

TOTAL _____

Ship to:

Name _____

Company _____

Address _____

City/State/Zip _____

Daytime phone _____

Payment: ☐ Check to IDG Books   ☐ Visa   ☐ MasterCard   ☐ American Express

Card # _____   Expires_____

Please send this order form to: IDG Books, 155 Bovet Road, Suite. 610 San Mateo, CA 94402.
Allow up to 3 weeks for delivery. Thank you!

BK=BOBWKS

Fold Here

Place
stamp
here

IDG Books Worldwide, Inc.
155 Bovet Road
Suite 610
San Mateo, CA 94402

Attn: Order Center / Microsoft Works 3

IDG Books Worldwide Registration Card

Macworld Guide To Microsoft Works 3

Fill this out — and hear about updates to this book and other IDG Books Worldwide products!

Name _____

Company/Title _____

Address _____

City/State/Zip _____

What is the single most important reason you bought this book? _____

_____

Where did you buy this book?
- ❑ Bookstore (Name _____)
- ❑ Electronics/Software store (Name_____)
- ❑ Advertisement (If magazine, which? _____)
- ❑ Mail order (Name of catalog/mail order house _____)
- ❑ Other: _____

How did you hear about this book?
- ❑ Book review in: _____
- ❑ Advertisement in: _____
- ❑ Catalog
- ❑ Found in store
- ❑ Other: _____

How would you rate the overall content of this book?
- ❑ Very good   ❑ Satisfactory
- ❑ Good   ❑ Poor
- Why? _____

How many computer books do you purchase a year?
❑ 1   ❑ 6-10
❑ 2-5   ❑ More than 10

What are your primary software applications?
_____
_____
_____

What chapters did you find most valuable? _____

What chapters did you find least valuable? _____

What kind of chapter or topic would you add to future editions of this book? _____

_____

Please give us any additional comments. _____

_____

Thank you for your help!

❑ I liked this book! By checking this box, I give you permission to use my name and quote me in future IDG Books Worldwide promotional materials. Daytime phone number_____ .

❑ FREE! Send me a copy of your computer book and book/disk catalog.

Fold Here

Place
stamp
here

IDG Books Worldwide, Inc.
155 Bovet Road
Suite 610
San Mateo, CA 94402

Attn: Reader Response / Microsoft Works 3